The Newly Industrializing Countries of Asia

SECOND EDITION

Gerald Tan

TIMES ACADEMIC PRESS

© **1992, 1995 Times Academic Press**
An imprint of Federal Publications (S) Pte Ltd
(*A member of the Times Publishing Group*)
Times Centre
1 New Industrial Road
Singapore 536196

First published 1992
Reprinted 1993
Second Edition 1995
Reprinted 1997

ISBN 981 210 075 X

Printed by Press Ace Pte Ltd, Singapore

This book

is dedicated to

Ronald, Alan and Raymond

Contents

List of Figures   xi

List of Tables   xii

Preface to the Second Edition   xiv

Preface   xv

CHAPTER 1: INTRODUCTION   1
Definition of Newly Industrializing Countries (NICs)   1
The Role of the Asian NICs in International Trade   5
The Asian NICs in World Development   7
Structure of the Book   14

CHAPTER 2: THE GROWTH PERFORMANCE OF THE NICS   17
Introduction   17
Growth Performance Since the Mid-1960s   18
    Growth of Income   18
    Increase in Savings and Investment Ratios   21
    The Role of Foreign Capital   26
    Financial Development   39
    Role of Government   41
    Export Orientation   46
    Growth of Manufactured Exports   47
    Growth of Employment   51
    Growth of Productivity   52
Changes in Economic Structure   54
    Shift towards Manufacturing   54
From Import-Substitution to Export-Expansion   61
    Import-Substitution as a Development Strategy   61
    Import-Substitution as a Self-Terminating Strategy   64
    Export-Expansion as a Development Strategy   66
    Risks of Export-Oriented Industrialization   70

Changes in Income Distribution and Living Standards   72

The Kuznets' Hypothesis   72

Critiques of the Kuznets' Hypothesis   73

The Asian NICs as Exceptions to the Kuznets' Hypothesis   74

Changes in Population Growth   79

Economic Development and Population Growth   79

Declining Fertility in the Asian NICs   80

Improvements in Education   81

Educational Attainment in the Asian NICs   81

Education and Economic Growth   81

Conclusion   84

Appendix to Chapter 2: The Effective Rate of Protection   86

The "Standard" Case   86

The "Tariffs on Inputs" Case   88

The "Negative Value-Added" Case   91

CHAPTER 3: EXPLAINING THE EMERGENCE OF THE NICS   93

Introduction   93

The Mainstream View   93

The Technological Ladder Hypothesis   94

The Pursuit of Market-Oriented Policies   100

Export-Oriented Policies   102

The Role of Foreign Capital   105

Macroeconomic Stability   106

The Role of Government   109

The Success of the Asian NICs   111

The Radical View   113

Historical Factors   114

Japanese colonization   115

British colonization   116

Geographical Factors   117

Strategic location   117

Economic location   118

Political Factors   118

Seige mentality   119

Authoritarian but efficient governments   120

Cultural Factors   121
Luck   128
Conclusion   130
Appendix to Chapter 3: Singapore's Transition from
LDC to NIC   132
  Introduction   132
  Singapore as a Less Developed Country   132
    Colonial heritage   132
    A commercial and trading centre 133
    A relatively developed city-state 134
    Political uncertainty, 1959–1965 135
  The Growth Phase, 1965–1973   137
    Expulsion from Malaysia   137
    Withdrawal of British forces 138
    The import-substitution phase 138
    Export-oriented industrialization 139
  Emergence as an NIC, 1979–1984   141
    Factors explaining Singapore's emergence as an NIC 142

CHAPTER 4: THE ROLE OF JAPAN IN THE RISE
OF THE ASIAN NICS   144
Introduction   144
Economic Complementarity   144
Trade between Japan and the Asian NICs   149
The Role of Japanese Foreign Investment   152
The Upvaluation of the Yen   157
Conclusion   162

CHAPTER 5: THE RISKS OF EXPORT-ORIENTED
INDUSTRIALIZATION   164
Introduction   164
The First Oil Crisis   165
The Second Oil Crisis and the Recession of the Mid-1980s 166
The Depth of the Recession   167
Causes of the Recession   170
  External Causes   171
    The 1979 oil crisis   171

Slow-down of the US economy 172
Exchange rate appreciation 173
Changes in consumer demand 173
Decline in other markets 175
Internal Causes 176
End of the construction boom 176
Rising costs 178
Slow-down in tourism and other industries in Singapore 179
Large-scale firms in South Korea 181
Small-scale firms in Taiwan 183
Economic Recovery 184
Recovery of the US Economy 184
Slower Growth in the 1990s 184
Conclusion 185

CHAPTER 6: PROSPECTS FOR THE ASIAN NICS IN THE 1990S 187
Introduction 187
More Difficult Trading Conditions 188
Slow Down in World Trade 188
Recession in Major Trading Partners 189
Increasing Protectionism 190
Currency Re-alignments 193
Rising Trade Surpluses 193
Appreciation of Currencies 194
Changes in Technology 195
Robotization 195
Computer-Aided Manufacturing 195
Computer-Aided Inventory Control 196
Changes in Consumer Preferences 197
Rising Costs 198
Tightening Labour Markets 198
Loss of Competitiveness 200
Meeting the Challenges of the 1990s 201
Reduced Dependence on the USA and EU 202

Developing Domestic Markets 202
Moving Off-shore 203
   Transplanting production to developed countries 203
   Moving production to less developed countries 204
Moving up the Technological Ladder 205
Importing Labour 207
Setting up an Asia-Pacific Trading Bloc 208
Conclusion 210

CHAPTER 7: MORE NICS IN TIME? 213
Introduction 213
Optimistic Views 214
Pessimistic Views 218
Distinguishing Features of an NIC 221
Malaysia as the Next NIC of Asia 223
Thailand as the Next NIC of Asia 233
Indonesia as the Next NIC of Asia 239
Conclusion 246

CHAPTER 8: THE ASIAN NICS IN WORLD TRADE
AND DEVELOPMENT 248
Introduction 248
The NICs and the USA 248
   Trade Flows between the USA and the Asian NICs 248
   Capital Flows between the USA and the Asian NICs 251
   The North American Free Trade and the Asian NICs 252
The NICs and the EU 254
   Trade Flows between the EU and the Asian NICs 254
   Capital Flows between the EU and the Asian NICs 256
   The Unification of the EU Market and the Asian NICs 256
The NICs and Australia 257
   Trade Flows between Australia and the Asian NICs 257
   Capital Flows between Australia and the Asian NICs 269
   The Prospects for a Pacific Economic Community 272
   Australia and the Asian NICs: Challenges and
   Opportunities 282
The NICs and China 283
   Economic Links between China and the Asian NICs 283

The Relationship between China and Hong Kong   285
The Relationship between China and other Asian NICs   287
The NICs and Eastern Europe   288
The Decline of Communism in Eastern Europe
and the Asian NICs   288
Conclusion   290

CHAPTER 9: CONCLUSION   291
The Costs of Rapid Economic Growth   291
The Supression of Individual Freedoms   291
Working Conditions   293
The Poor and the Disadvantaged   294
Environmental Problems   296
Lessons from the Asian NICs   300
The Pursuit of Market-Oriented Policies   301
Capitalizing on Comparative Advantage   302
Macroeconomic Stability   302
High Rates of Saving and Investment   303
Export-Oriented Industrialization   303
The Role of Government   304
Quality of the Labour Force   306
Flexibility and Pragmatism in Economic Policies   307
Dealing with the Risks of Export-Orientation   307
The Costs of Becoming Too Successful   307
The Growth of World Trade   308

APPENDIX: COMPUTER-AIDED TEACHING   309
Introduction   309
Using the *Revise* Program   309
Setting up Revision Exercise with *Revise*   310
Suppressing Explanations Temporarily   319
Suppressing Questions   321
Setting up a File of Instructions   323
Computer-Aided Essay Marking   329
Programs Available from the Author   332

Bibliography   334
Author Index   367
Subject Index   00

List of Figures

Figure 1.1:   Share of World Trade, 1965–1992
Figure 1.2:   Per Capita GNP, 1990
Figure 1.3:   Living Standards, 1980 and 1990
               Real Per Capita GDP
Figure 1.4:   Per Capita GNP of Singapore, Hong Kong and
               Taiwan as a Percentage of Australia's Per Capita
               GNP, 1968–1990
Figure 2.1:   Growth of GDP (1980–1990) and Per Capita GDP
               (% of US Per Capita GDP) 1990
Figure 2.2:   GDP Growth and GDI/GDP Ratios (1981–1990)
Figure 2.3:   The Two-Gap Model
Figure 2.4:   Foreign Aid and Domestic Savings
Figure 2.5:   Foreign Investment and Capital Flows
Figure 2.6:   Financial Deepening and Economic Growth,
               1980–1990
Figure 2.7:   The Lewis Model
Figure 2.8:   Declining Average Agricultural Surplus
Figure 2.9:   The Welfare Effects of Import-Substitution
Figure 2.10:   Cross-Section Versus Time-Series Tests of the
               Kuznet's Hypothesis
Figure A2.1:   The Effective Rate of Protection
Figure A2.3:   The "Tariff on Inputs" Case
Figure A2.4:   The "Negative Value-Added" Case
Figure A2.2:   Nominal and Effective Rates of Protection
Figure 3.1:   The Technological Ladder Hypothesis
Figure 3.2:   Values and Economic Performance
Figure 4.1:   Yen-US$ Exchange Rate and NIC Exports
Figure 5.1:   Average Export Growth, 1984–1989
Figure 5.2:   Singapore: GNP Growth Rate and Unemployment
               Rate, 1979–1987
Figure 5.3:   Recession in the Mid-1980s
Figure 9.1:   Manufacturing Wages and Productivity

List of Tables

Table 2.1:   Growth Rates of Real GDP

Table 2.2:   Gross Domestic Savings and Gross Domestic Investment

Table 2.3:   Government Surplus

Table 2.4:   Savings-Investment Gap

Table 2.5:   Growth of Exports

Table 2.6:   Changes in Export Structure

Table 2.7:   Manufacturing Productivity Growth in Singapore

Table 2.8:   Structure of Employment

Table 2.9:   The Composition of Output

Table A2.1:   Value-Added in World and Domestic Prices

Table A2.2:   The "Tariff on Inputs" Case

Table A2.3:   The "Negative Value-Added" Case

Table 3.1:   Changes in Export Structure

Table A3.1:   Indicators of Development, 1967

Table 4.1:   South Korea's Trade with Japan, 1987

Table 4.2:   Japanese Foreign Investment in Asian NICs and Near-NICs

Table 5.1:   Growth Rates of GDP, 1983–1990

Table 5.2:   Growth Rates of Exports

Table 5.3:   Export Growth Rates, 1985

Table 5.4:   Singapore: Demand and Supply for Property

Table 7.1:   Structural Change in the Malaysian Economy

Table 7.2:   Malaysia's Major Exports and Export Markets

Table 7.3:   Malaysia's Manufactured Exports

Table 7.4:   Foreign Investment in Thailand

Table 7.5:   Thailand's Principal Exports

Table 7.6:   Thailand's Exports

Table 7.7:   Food Production Per Head in Indonesia

Table 7.8:   The Indonesian Economy

Table 7.9:   Indonesia's Manufactured Exports, 1991

Table 8.1:   Exports and Imports of Asian NICs to the
               USA 1992
Table 8.2:   Net Investment Committments in the Singapore
               Manufacturing Sector
Table 8.3:   Trade between the Asian NICs and the EU
Table 8.4:   Australian Exports
Table 8.5:   Australia: Principal Exports to Singapore
Table 8.6:   Australia: Principal Exports to Hong Kong
Table 8.7:   Australia: Principal Exports to South Korea
Table 8.8:   Australia: Principal Exports to Taiwan
Table 8.9:   Australian Manufactured Imports
Table 8.10:   Australia: Principal Imports to Singapore
Table 8.11:   Australia: Principal Imports to Hong Kong
Table 8.12:   Australia: Principal Imports South Korea
Table 8.13:   Australia: Principal Imports Taiwan
Table 8.14:   TCF In Australia's Imports from Northeast Asia
Table 8.15:   North East Asia's Share of Australian TCF Imports
Table 8.16:   Australian Trade Balance with Asian NICs
Table 8.17:   Australia: Stock of Foreign Private Investment
Table 8.18:   Australian Stock of Total Investment Abroad,
               1991–1992
Table 8.19:   APEC Trade Intensity Indexes, 1986 and 1992

Preface to the Second Edition

The second edition of this book has given me the opportunity to revise and expand most of the material contained in the first edition in the light of recent developments in the world economy and to utilize the most recently available statistical data.

Since the first edition was published, the Uruguay Round of the GATT has been successfully concluded, a unified market has been established in the European Union, and proposals to establish a regional trading group in the Asia-Pacific Region have taken a major step forward with the meeting of heads of state at the Seattle Summit. In addition, the World Bank has just put its imprimatur on the development of East Asian countries, declaring their economic success a miracle (World Bank 1993).

The comments which I have received from my students and colleagues who have used the first edition of this book in university courses, have been helpful in enabling me to make a number of improvements in the treatment of various topics. As a result, every chapter of this book has been revised and some have been considerably expanded to include new material.

I wish to record my gratitude to my students at Flinders University and at the Elton Mayo School of Management, University of South Australia, as well as to many colleagues at both universities, for their positive comments and helpful suggestions which have enabled me to improve many parts of this book. I hasten to add that the responsibility for any lingering errors in this edition rests entirely with me.

I also wish to record my gratitude and appreciation to my wife, Stella, who has borne the burdens of being married to an author with the support and understanding that are well beyond the call of duty.

G.T.
Adelaide

April 1995

Preface

The Newly Industrializing Countries (NICs) have been the fastest growing economies in the world since the 1960s. Within the space of 25 or 30 years, they have transformed themselves from poor, less developed countries to semi-industrial economies, on the verge of joining the ranks of the advanced industrial countries of the world. Since the 1960s, they have achieved rates of economic growth that are three or four times higher than any other country in the world, and registered rates of growth of manufactured exports which are unprecedented in world history.

Indeed, some NICs have already overtaken developed Western European economies in terms of per capita income and standard of living. Singapore and Hong Kong have been classified as high-income countries by the World Bank since 1991, and are now regarded as developed economies. In terms of the share of industry in total economic activity, many NICs are more industrialized than the advanced industrial countries of the world. They are now major centres of world manufacturing and important participants in world trade. They are the only countries in the world, since Japan, which have progressed from less developed country status and are well on their way to becoming developed economies. As such, their experience may hold important lessons for other countries in the Third World, who wish to emulate their success.

In view of this spectacular achievement, it is surprising that most text books on development economics give only passing attention to the NICs and some do not mention them at all. While there are many specialist monographs and papers in professional journals which deal with the development of the NICs, there has been no systematic comparative treatment of their development which is readily accessible to students of economic development.

This book was written to fill this gap. It is intended for third-year university students studying development economics, Asian economic development and related subjects. Some knowledge of economics is therefore assumed. Only the NICs of Asia (Hong Kong, Singapore, South Korea and Taiwan) are discussed in this book. Some attention is also given to the prospect of other less developed countries in Asia (particularly Malaysia and Thailand) joining the ranks of the NICs in the near future.

Whilst this book was written primarily as a textbook for university students, it will also be of interest to the general reader, particularly those in business and government, who are interested in forging or expanding their economic links with the Asian NICs.

In addition to a systematic treatment of the emergence, growth, development and future prospects of the NICs, an additional feature of this book is the availability of a computer-aided teaching program, called *Revise*, which can be used by students to test their understanding of the material covered. It can also be used by teachers to set up their own revision exercises and other teaching material for their courses. Teachers may also find a computer-aided essay-marking program, called *Essay*, useful. Appendix A describes the various ways in which these computer-aided teaching programs can be used, and how they can be obtained.

This book is based on a series of lectures that I have given to final year students, both at the Flinders University of South Australia and at the Elton Mayo School of Management, University of South Australia. I wish to record my gratitute to the large number of students who have been through these courses over the years and have provided me with useful comments on how the course and the computer-aided teaching program might be improved. I am grateful to a number of anonymous referees who made useful suggestions which have enabled me to improve various parts of this book. Leonie Hardcastle read an early draft of Chapter 8, and made some very useful suggestions, most of which have been incorporated in the chapter. Merry Ewing helped by giving me access to some South Korean data. The *Far Eastern Economic Review* kindly gave me permission to reproduce the material contained in Tables 4.2, 5.1 and 5.3.

I also wish to express my gratitude and appreciation to my

wife, Stella, for the support, understanding and encouragement that she has given me through the years. While thanking all the above for the help that they have given me, I hasten to add that final responsibility for the contents of this book rests with me alone.

G.T.
Adelaide

CHAPTER 1

Introduction

Definition of Newly Industrializing Countries

The Newly Industrializing Countries (NICs) are a group of countries which, in terms of world economic development, are in a transitional stage between the less developed countries (LDCs) of the Third World and the advanced industrial countries (AICs) of the West. They are sometimes referred to as Newly Industrializing Economies (NIEs), in order not to upset political sensitivities, since China does not recognize Hong Kong and Taiwan as countries in their own right (they are regarded as provinces of China). Other descriptions of these countries include the terms semi-industrial countries, middle-income major exporters of manufactures, transitional economies, or (when referring to the NICs of Asia) the "gang of four" (G4 countries). The NICs of Asia are also referred to, in the popular media, as the four dragons, or the four tigers of Asia.

In this book, the term Newly Industrializing Countries (NICs) will be used. The NICs are often regarded as the only countries in the world, since Japan, which have progressed successfully from the status of less developed countries and are well on their way toward developed country status. This feat is all the more impressive when it is realized that it was accomplished within a space of only 25 or 30 years. As such, they are the only examples of "successful" economic development since Japan and are often held up as models for other LDCs to emulate. In recognition of this achievement, recent issues of the World Bank's *World Development Report* now classify some NICs (Hong Kong and Singapore) as "high-income" economies and group them in the same category as the developed OECD countries (World Bank 1991:207).

There is no generally accepted definition of what criteria define a NIC. Indeed, the search for a definition which would embrace all the countries generally regarded as NICs is likely to be elusive (Holloway 1991a:58). None of the major textbooks on development economics gives an account of the characteristics a country should possess before it can be considered an NIC and all the major development economics textbooks give different lists of countries which are deemed to be NICs (Hagen 1986:120-121; Gillis et al. 1987:460; Todaro 1985:22–23; Colman and Nixson 1986:282).

In 1979, the OECD defined Newly Industrializing Countries as countries with per capita incomes of between US$1,100 and US$3,500 in 1978 and with manufacturing sectors which accounted for at least 20% of GDP. This group of countries included Argentina, Brazil, Chile, Mexico, Uruguay, Hong Kong, Singapore, South Korea, Taiwan, Greece, Israel, Spain, Portugal, Turkey, Bulgaria, Hungary, Romania and Yugoslavia (OECD 1979).

In 1986, Balassa and Michalopoulos echo this definition, but include a slightly different set of countries in the category of NICs:

> Although there are various definitions of NICs the newly-industrializing countries have been defined ... as having per capita incomes between $1,100 and $3,000 in 1978 and a manufacturing share of 20% or higher in 1977. They include Argentina, Brazil, Chile, Mexico and Uruguay in Latin America, Israel and Yugoslavia in the Europe-Middle East area, and Hong Kong, Korea and Singapore in the Far East (1986:8).

In the 1990s, such definitions are rare. A recent study states that:

> The countries that are normally classified as the NICs, those that now have manufacturing sectors of a similar relative size to those of the industrialized countries (more than a quarter of GDP), are in fact an extremely diverse group in terms of recent growth or

other conventional measures of performance, as well as in industrial structure and non-economic characteristics: Hong Kong, India, Singapore, South Korea, Taiwan, Argentina, Brazil and Mexico (Page 1990:4).

The lack of any clear, and generally accepted, definition of the characteristics which enable a country to be called an NIC has led one recent author to proclaim:

> NIEs are facing an identification problem. Which countries, for instance, do belong to the category? Economic theory has nothing satisfying to offer. The group has no legal definition either. In the end we have to confess that the country lists are open-ended and quite arbitrary (Lorenz 1989:222).

The author then includes amongst the NIEs, Spain, Portugal, Greece, Yugoslavia, Israel, Turkey, Poland, Hungary, Romania, Bulgaria, Morocco, Algeria, Tunisia, Libya, Egypt, Malta, Cyprus, Taiwan, South Korea, Hong Kong, Malaysia, Thailand, Singapore, Philippines, Indonesia, Argentina, Brazil and Mexico (Lorenz 1989:224).

A recent attempt to define an NIE (Chowdhury and Islam 1993:2–5), incorporates qualitative as well as quantitative criteria. These are specified as a savings ratio of 15% or more, a real per capita GDP of US$1,000 or more, a share of manufacturing in GDP and employment of at least 20%, and a score of 0.75 or more in the United Nations Human Development Index (to reflect qualitative improvements in well-being). This leads the authors to identify 22 countries as NIEs in 1988. These range from the four Asian NICs to such countries as Malaysia, Thailand, Colombia and Peru. What might be regarded as important economic characteristics of the NIEs are excluded from the criteria. These include a sustained period of rapid economic growth of both per capita GDP and manufactured exports, structural change towards industry and manufacturing, export-oriented industrialization and many others (which will be discussed in Chapter 7).

A recent study by the World Bank (1993:2–3) casts a slightly different net and focuses on eight high performing Asian economies

(HPAEs) in terms of their sustained rapid economic growth and declining inequality in income distribution. These include Hong Kong, Singapore, South Korea, Taiwan, Malaysia, Indonesia, Thailand and Japan.

The problem of definition does not arise for the purposes of this book. The Newly Industrializing Countries of Asia (Asian NICs) are generally agreed to include Hong Kong, Singapore, South Korea and Taiwan. At present, some countries in Southeast Asia (especially Malaysia and Thailand) are thought to be at the threshold of NIC status, but at the time of writing, have not been included in the ranks of the Asian NICs yet. The countries are sometimes referred to as "near-NICs" or "second-tier NICs".

The four Asian NICs which are discussed in this book are characterized by the following major economic features:

1. Rapid economic growth since the 1960s. Between 1960 and 1985, Asian NICs registered growth rates of real per capita GDP of about 6.5% per annum. This was a much higher rate of growth than other countries in the world (James et al. 1989:6).

2. Highly industrialized, with industry accounting for a large proportion of GDP. In 1985, the share of industry in GDP in the Asian NICs ranged from 30% (Hong Kong) to 50% (Taiwan). This is a higher share than that of many advanced industrial countries (James et al. 1989:11).

3. Highly export-oriented, with exports accounting for a large proportion of GDP. In 1985, the share of exports in GDP was over 100% in the small city-states (Hong Kong 106%, Singapore 125%). In South Korea, the share of exports in GDP was 36%, whilst in Taiwan, it was 55%. By contrast, Japan's share of exports in GDP in 1985 was 16% (James et al. 1989:23). It is interesting to note that, according to a recently published survey, the four Asian NICs are at the top of a list of emerging economies ranked according to competitiveness (FEER 1992a:51).

4. A high proportion of manufactured goods in total exports. With the exception of Singapore, the share of manufactured goods in total exports in the Asian NICs was over 90% in 1985. Singapore, which still acts as an entrepot for other Southeast Asian countries, had a 53% share of manufactured goods in total exports in 1985 (OECD 1988:15). By 1989, this had increased to 77% (World Bank 1991:234).

5. Rapid growth of manufactured exports since the 1960s. Between 1965 and 1973, the growth rate of manufactured exports of the Asian NICs ranged from 20.5% per annum for Hong Kong, to 49.8% for South Korea. Even in the more difficult trading conditions of 1973–1985, the growth rates of manufactured exports of the Asian NICs ranged from 13% per annum for Hong Kong, to 21% for South Korea (OECD 1988:14).

These features will be discussed in detail in the next section, and in the next chapter.

The Role of the Asian NICs in International Trade

The success of the Asian NICs in export-oriented industrialization since the 1960s has given them an important place in the international trading system. They are some of the most outward-looking countries in the world. In terms of the total trade (exports plus imports) as a percentage of GDP, Hong Kong's trade ratio in 1985 was 205%, Singapore's trade ratio was 270%, South Korea's trade ratio was 72%, while Taiwan's trade ratio was 99% (since GDP is defined as consumption plus investment plus government expenditure plus exports-imports, it is not surprising that total trade [exports *plus* imports] exceeds GDP). These are very high trade ratios, compared with Japan's trade ratio of 29%, or the trade ratio of the USA, which was 17% (James et al. 1989:23).

In 1965, the Asian NICs' share of world trade was 1.5%. Since then, this has grown steadily to reach 9.2% in 1992 (approximately the same as Japan's share of world trade in 1992). As Figure 1.1 shows, the Asian NICs have increased their share of world trade steadily since 1965. Hong Kong, alone, accounted for 3.2% of world trade in 1992, while the other Asian NICs each accounted for about 2% of world trade. This is a remarkable achievement by any standards. India, a much larger country than any of the Asian NICs, accounted for only 0.3% of world trade in 1992.

In terms of the total volume of trade, in 1992, Hong Kong was ranked tenth in the world (up from rank 23 in 1978). South Korea was ranked thirteenth (up from rank 20 in 1978), Taiwan was ranked twelfth (up from rank 25 in 1978) and Singapore was ranked sixteenth (up from rank 26 in 1978). In 1971, South Korea was the world's thirty-eighth largest exporter of goods. By 1988, it had become the world's eleventh largest exporter. Its current ranking (in 1992) is thirteenth. The importance of the Asian NICs in world trade is also reflected in the value of exports per head of population. The city-states of Singapore and Hong Kong had the highest value of exports per head in 1992 (US$23,188 and US$20,522 respectively), much higher than other countries with small populations (for example, Belgium/Luxembourg and Switzerland, whose exports per head were US$11,833 and US$9,717 respectively) South Korea now accounts for 2% of total world trade (Choi 1991:2). In 1983, the Asian NICs accounted for 8% of world manufactured exports. Hong Kong, through its production facilities in the free trade zones in China, is now the world's largest producer of toys and the world's largest producer of time pieces (watches and clocks). Singapore is the world's largest producer of computer peripherals (such as printers and hard disks), Taiwan is the world's largest producer of electronic mice, scanners and monitors for computers, while South Korea is the second largest producer of motor vehicles in Asia and one of the world's largest exporters of high quality shoes.

Figure 1.1
Share of World Trade, 1965–1992

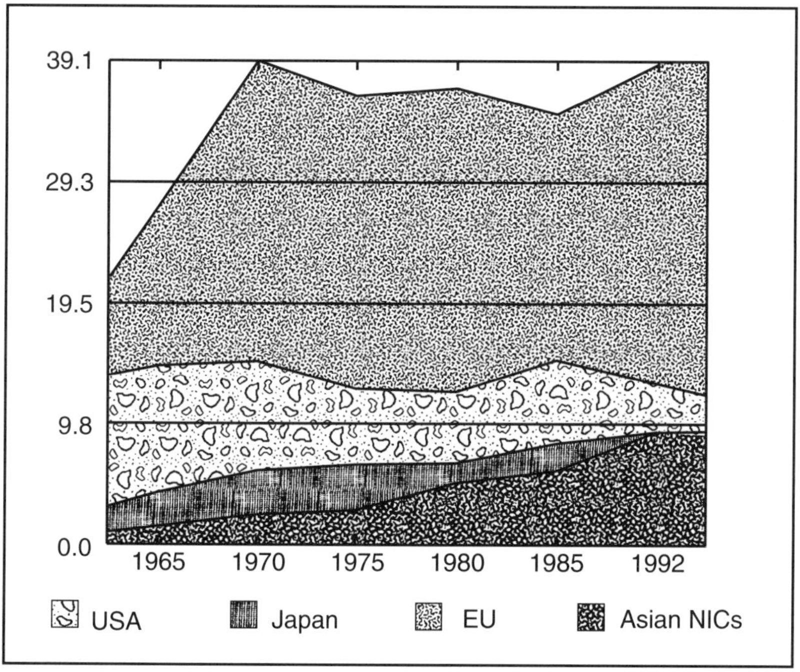

Source: International Monetary Fund, *Direction of Trade Yearbook*, (various issues); Council for Economic Planning and Development, *Taiwan Statistical Data Book*, (various issues).

The Asian NICs in World Development

The rapid economic growth of the Asian NICs since the 1960s has been accompanied by declining fertility, rising per capita incomes and improved standards of living. In 1962, South Korea was one of the poorest countries in the world with a per capita income of US$100. Between 1962 and 1985, South Korea's economy grew by an average of 8.5% per year, giving it a per capita income of US$2,800 in 1985 (Economist 1989a:83). By 1989, South Korean per capita income had grown to US$4,000 (Economist 1989b:25). All the other Asian NICs have undergone this transition.

As Figure 1.2 shows, by 1990, some Asian NICs had achieved per capita incomes that were higher than those of many Western European developed countries. In 1990, the per capita incomes of Hong Kong and Singapore were higher than those of Ireland, Spain, Portugal and Greece. In 1992, Taiwan's per capita income just exceeded the US$10,000 mark, putting it in the same league as the other Asian NICs. Of the 23 richest countries in the world (in terms of per capita GNP), Hong Kong and Singapore were ranked nineteenth and twentieth (World Bank 1992:219). At current growth rates, the per capita incomes of Hong Kong and Singapore are expected to exceed those of New Zealand, Australia and the United Kingdom by the mid-1990s.

Figure 1.2
Per Capita GNP, 1990

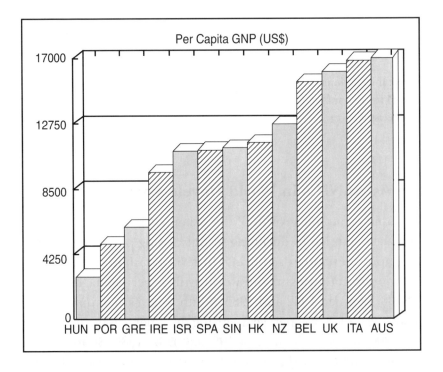

Source: World Bank 1992, *World Development Report 1992.*

In the Asia-Pacific region, most of the Asian NICs are rapidly catching up with the developed countries in the region. Singapore's real per capita income in 1980 was about half that of Australia. As Figure 1.3 shows, by 1990, Singapore's per capita income was about 95% of Australia's per capita income. The per capita incomes of Hong Kong and Taiwan were not far behind. Between 1980 and 1990, Australia's real per capita income declined by about 8% while Singapore's real per capita income increased by almost 100% (FEER 1991a:63). At current growth rates, Singapore's per capita income will exceed that of Australia by the mid-1990s. A 1992 survey of the affluent in Asia indicated that average *household* incomes in Hong Kong (US$146,000) and Singapore (US$106,000) were higher than in Australia (US$104,000). Average household investments in Hong Kong and Singapore were also significantly higher than in Australia (FEER 1992c:34).

The speed with which the per capita incomes of Singapore, Hong Kong and Taiwan have risen relative to Australia's per capita income is shown in Figure 1.4. This shows the per capita GNP of Singapore, Hong Kong and Taiwan (current values) as a percentage of Australia's per capita GNP.

In 1968, the per capita GNP of Hong Kong and Singapore was 28% of Australia's per capita GNP. By 1980, Hong Kong's per capita GNP was 49% of Australia's per capita GNP and Singapore's was 44%. In 1990, Hong Kong's per capita GNP had reached 82% of Australia's per capita GNP, while Singapore's per capita GNP had reached 89% of Australia's per capita GNP. Taiwan's per capita GNP, which was just over 10% of Australia's per capita GNP in 1968, rose to 58% of Australia's per capita GNP in 1990.

These impressive increases in per capita income have been accompanied by significant improvements in the standard of living in the Asian NICs. Singapore now boasts the highest standard of living (in terms of per capita income) in Asia, apart from Japan. In fact, if one takes into account such amenities as the provision of modern sanitation, the standard of medical services, public transport, the standard of private housing, the number of world-class hotels and restaurants, and access to golf courses (many of which

Figure 1.3
Living Standards, 1980 and 1990
Real Per Capita GDP (US$1,000)

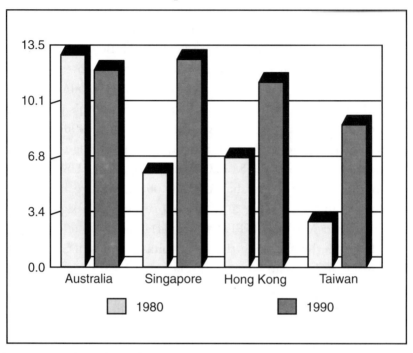

Source: World Bank, *World Development Report*, (various issues), Council for Economic Planning and Development, *Taiwan Statistical Data Book*, (various issues).

are flood-lit so that golf can be played at night), the standard of living in Singapore is higher than that of Japan! This is reflected in the fact that recent Purchasing Power Parity (PPP) estimates of real per capita GDP put Singapore's per capita GDP at US$15,110 in 1989. This was higher than that of Japan (US$14,310), the UK (US$13,730) and New Zealand (US$11,155) (FEER 1992b:65). This explains why Singapore is the favourite destination for expatriate Japanese businessmen (FEER 1991d:90). Between 1960 and 1989, the average South Korean calorie intake increased from 2000 to 3000 calories. Between 1965 and 1985, per capita rice consumption rose by 40%, the number of doctors per 10,000

South Koreans doubled, the number of dentists trebled, as did the number of hospital beds per 10,000 people. The increase in health care and nutrition has resulted in the average 14-year old South Korean in 1985 being 11 cm taller than his or her counterpart in 1965 (Economist 1989b:25–26).

Although the Asian NICs have had similar experiences of rapid economic growth and development since the 1960s, there are important differences of economic structure and policy between them.

The city states of Hong Kong and Singapore are characterized by very small agricultural sectors and vibrant manufacturing and services (mainly trade and financial services) sectors. In recent years, rising wages and tightening labour markets have caused Hong Kong to relocate much of its labour-intensive manufacturing industries to southern China and to concentrate on its services sector. As a result, the share of manufacturing in GDP in Hong Kong has declined over the last ten years, while that of services has increased. Singapore is in a similar situation, but without a southern China at its doorstep, has found it more difficult to shift its labour-intensive industries to neighbouring countries. Recent attempts to develop a "growth triangle" encompassing the Indonesian Riau group of islands south of Singapore, and the southern Malaysian state of Johor, are manifestations of Singapore's attempts to cope with its diminishing comparative advantage in labour-intensive manufacturing industry (Lee 1991). Singapore differs from Hong Kong in one other important respect. While much of Hong Kong's export-oriented manufacturing industry is domestically owned, Singapore's export-oriented manufacturing industry is dominated by foreign-owned companies. As much as 70% of the assets of Singapore's manufacturing sector are owned by foreigners. Local manufacturing caters mainly for the domestic market. In this respect, Singapore stands out amongst all the Asian NICs (Koh 1987). In Hong Kong, South Korea and Taiwan, foreign investment in the manufacturing sector does not account for more than 20% or 30% of total capital.

Figure 1.4

Per Capita GNP of Singapore, Hong Kong and Taiwan as a Percentage of Australia's Per Capita GNP, 1968–1990

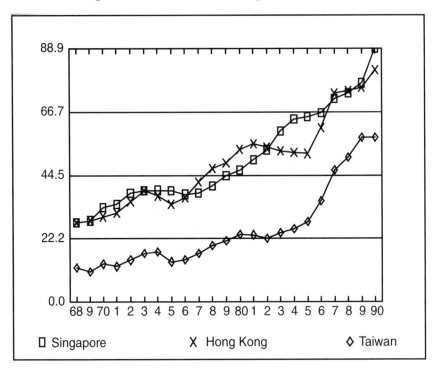

Source: World Bank, *World Development Report* (various issues), Council for Economic Planning and Development, *Taiwan Statistical Data Book 1992.*

South Korea and Taiwan have larger populations and land masses than Hong Kong and Singapore. However, like the two city states, they are resource poor compared to many other less developed countries. One major difference between South Korea the other Asian NICs, is the nature of industrial development. In South Korea, the Park government (which took over power in a *coup d'état* in the early 1960s), nurtured the development of large scale industrial groups (the *chaebol*) through its control of the availability of investment funds. The six largest *chaebol* in South Korea control about 75% of all industrial activity. The other Asian NICs, on the other hand, developed small to medium scale industry. The consequence of this difference is that South Korea enjoys some advantage of large firm size, such as financial resources, a concentration on heavy industry, etc., so that by the 1990s, South Korea was able to challenge Japanese industrial power and technology in many fields (for example, consumer electronics, steel-making, automobiles, etc.). Large scale firms, however, have some disadvantages, the most important of which have to do with inflexibility and bureaucratic inefficiency in the face of rapidly changing markets.

The other three Asian NICs, having opted for industrialization on the back of small to medium scale firms, enjoy certain advantages. Rapid reaction to changing markets, innovative entrepreneurship and a low profile which shields them from protectionist glares, are amongst these advantages. However, small size also means smaller financial muscle, an inability to develop heavy industry, a lack of funds to undertake research and development and continued dependence on other (mainly foreign) firms (Economist 1990a; Suh 1986).

The experience of the Asian NICs over the last decade has prompted some changes in industrial strategy. South Korea is trying to reduce the dominance of the *chaebol* by encouraging small to medium scale firms. The other Asian NICs are trying to move in the other direction, to develop larger firms and to enter into the manufacture of products of higher technology.

The economic success of the NICs of Asia makes them an important subject of study. An understanding of the factors which have enabled them to achieve such rapid strides in living standards may provide lessons for other countries in the developing world which want to emulate their experience. It may also provide important information for developed countries which trade with them.

Structure of the Book

This books attempts to provide a systematic analysis of the NICs of Asia as a group of countries which have achieved successful economic development since the 1960s. While there are several books on individual countries in this group, there are relatively few, if any, which offer a comparative analysis of the Asian NICs as a group. The principal focus of this book is to study the factors which explain the success of the NICs and to draw out lessons, if any, for other developing countries. While many of these factors are economic, some are political and social in nature. Throughout the analysis, the experience of the Asian NICs is related to important policy debates in the professional literature.

Chapter 2 presents a detailed account of the growth experience of the Asian NICs since the 1960s. The process of structural change, export-oriented industrialization and their socio-economic consequences on income distribution and standards of living are examined.

Chapter 3 discusses two major views about the emergence of the Asian NICs. On the one hand is the "mainstream", or "World Bank" view, which explains the emergence of the Asian NICs as the outcome of a natural process of development in the world trading system, emphasizing the importance of market-oriented reforms. On this view, the emergence of the Asian NICs is not an exceptional event, and more NICs can be expected to appear as other countries implement the appropriate policies (favourable international trading conditions permitting). On the other hand is the "radical" view, which interprets the emergence of the Asian NICs as a unique event, unlikely to be replicated by other less developed countries. A reconciliation of these apparently divergent views is suggested in this chapter.

Chapter 4 examines the role of Japan in the rise of the Asian NICs. The role of Japanese foreign investment in fostering economic complementarity with the Asian NICs is the focus of special attention. Recent developments associated with the upvaluation of the Yen and the impact this is likely to have on the Asian NICs are also discussed.

Chapter 5 deals with the risks of export-oriented industrialization and the recession of the mid-1980s which affected all the Asian NICs severely. The causes of the recession, and the lessons it taught the Asian NICs, will be of some importance to other developing countries which wish to embark on a strategy of export-oriented industrialization.

Chapter 6 discusses the problems which face the Asian NICs in the 1990s and beyond and examines the strategies which they are pursuing in order to deal with the challenges of the future. Tightening labour markets, rising costs, increasing protectionism and rapid technological change, are all making the maintenance of continued rapid economic growth more difficult for the Asian NICs.

Chapter 7 examines the question of whether there are likely to be more NICs emerging over time, following in the footsteps of the original four in Asia. Both theoretical and empirical evidence are examined to throw some light on this question. While some writers suggest that there are already several developing countries waiting in the wings and just about to enter NIC status, others argue that world trading conditions have deteriorated to such an extent as to make this very unlikely.

Chapter 8 deals with the relationship between the Asian NICs and their major trading partners. The USA and EU (European Union) are the most important of these (the relation between Japan and the Asian NICs is the subject of Chapter 4). Of particular concern, is the rising tide of protectionism, both in the USA and the EU, and the trend toward regional trading blocs. The relationship between Australia and the Asian NICs is also discussed in this chapter. Australia is the closest, geographically, of the developed economies to the Asian NICs, and yet has not been able to participate in, and benefit from, the very rapid economic growth of the countries to its north. Why this is so, and what might be done to redress this situation, are matters which are discussed in this section. The possibility of the establishment of a trading bloc in the Pacific is also examined. The chapter ends with a discussion of the relationship between the Asian NICs and China, and with some views of the possible impact of the decline of communism in Eastern Europe on the Asian NICs. China, with its large pool of cheap labour, presents both an opportunity and a challenge for the Asian NICs. Eastern Europe, on the other hand, has vast resources of skilled, but relatively cheap, labour close to the European Union. Once the dust of political upheaval has settled in Eastern Europe, countries in this region could become serious competitors in markets presently dominated by the Asian NICs.

Chapter 9 draws the lessons which the experience of the Asian NICs hold for other developing countries which want to embark on a strategy of export-oriented industrialization.

An Appendix at the end of the book describes a computer-aided teaching program called *Revise*, which can be used by teachers to set up revision exercises and other types of teaching material (for any course). The Appendix also describes a computer-aided essay-marking program called *Essay*. A set of revision exercises and examination questions covering the material in this book is available on disk from the author. These computer-aided teaching programs will be of interest to teachers in colleges and universities.

CHAPTER 2

The Growth Performance of the Asian NICs

Introduction

After the Second World War, all the countries which now make up the Asian NICs were amongst some of the poorest, less developed countries in the world. All the Asian NICs emerged from the war bereft of much of their social infrastructure as a result of Japanese bombing, which destroyed large parts of their industry, transport and communications facilities. Real per capita GNP in South Korea and Taiwan in 1950 was less than US$100, whilst Hong Kong's per capita GNP was about US$200 and Singapore's about US$400 (in 1950, Japan's real per capita GNP was US$251). Domestic savings ratios were relatively low, ranging from −0.8% of GNP in Singapore to 10.7% of GNP in Taiwan. With the exception of Hong Kong, the Asian NICs all depended on foreign capital inflows to sustain investment and economic growth in the 1950s (Papanek 1988:28,32).

In terms of economic structure, Singapore and Hong Kong were primarily entrepots, servicing their respective hinterlands. Industrial activity was limited to processing raw materials for export. South Korea and Taiwan were agricultural economies, with trade playing a small part in total economic activity. Yet, in the relatively short space of 25 or 30 years, all these countries have transformed themselves into dynamic economies, major centres of world manufacturing activity and important participants in world trade. In terms of level of development and standard of living, the Asian

NICs are now on the verge of graduating into developed country status. Hong Kong and Singapore have already attained levels of per capita GNP that are above those of several developed economies.

Growth Performance Since the Mid-1960s

During the 1950s, all the Asian NICs were re-building their economies after the devastation of the Second World War. In addition, they were also preoccupied with internal and external political problems.

Hong Kong was concerned with the large numbers of refugees fleeing Communist China. Singapore, although granted self-government by the British in 1957, was embroiled in internal political unrest and Indonesian "confrontation", until its expulsion from the Federation of Malaysia in 1965. South Korea and Taiwan were both concerned with the military threat from their respective Communist neighbours.

During the decade of the 1950s, however, South Korea and Taiwan developed their manufacturing sectors behind tariff walls, through a strategy of import-substitution and with help from the USA in the form of foreign aid. By the late 1950s, however, saturation of the domestic market, in addition to the announced intention of the USA to end foreign aid, led South Korea and Taiwan both to embark on an export-oriented industrialization strategy. Singapore had a brief flirtation with import-substitution in the early 1960s, but like Hong Kong, the small size of the domestic market soon made it apparent that export-oriented industrialization was the only path to economic prosperity.

Growth of Income

The era of rapid economic growth in the Asian NICs began in the early 1960s for South Korea, Taiwan and Hong Kong. In Singapore, it began in 1965, when it was forced to leave the Federation of Malaysia. Since then, all the Asian NICs have experienced consistently high growth rates of GDP.

In terms of nominal GDP growth rates, the Asian NICs recorded some of the highest rates of growth in the world during 1965–1989. Between 1966 and 1973, Singapore's rate of growth of GDP was above 10% every year and averaged 12.4% per annum over the eight-year period. Over the same period, South Korea's rate of growth of GDP was more variable, but averaged 10.1% per annum. After the first oil crisis in 1973, the growth rates of all Asian NICs slowed down, but still remained much higher than those of most other countries. The superior growth performance of the Asian NICs is shown in Figure 2.1. The average growth rates of GDP of Hong Kong (HK), Singapore (SI), South Korea (SK) and Taiwan (TA) were amongst the highest in the world for the period 1965–1989. By the end of the 1980s, some of the Asian NICs had already begun to slow down as the world economy slid into recession. The near-NICs, China (CH), Thailand (TH), Malaysia (MA) and Indonesia (IN), have also recorded very high rates of GDP growth over the 1965–1989 period, many of them only slightly below the growth rates of the Asian NICs.

The growth rates of GDP of the Asian NICs are between two and three times higher than those of the developed countries. This reflects the fact that the Asian NICs (and the near-NICs) are catching up with the developed countries. The per capita GDP levels of the Asian NICs are now just under 50% of USA per capita GDP. This is already higher than the per capita GDP of some developed countries (such as Spain, Portugal, Greece and Ireland). If current growth rates persist, the per capita GDP of the Asian NICs will soon surpass those of some of the richer developed countries (such as UK, whose per capita GDP in 1989 was 66% of US per capita GDP). The growth rates of their real GDP have been high for most of the post-war period. This is shown in Table 2.1.

For most of the sub-periods shown in Table 2.1, the Asian NICs achieved either double-digit, or close to double-digit growth rates of real GDP. The 1980s are an exception, as all the Asian NICs were hit by a severe recession in 1984–1985 and faced more difficult trading conditions throughout the decade. Nevertheless,

Table 2.1
Growth Rates of Real GDP (% per annum)

Country	1950–1960	1960–1970	1970–1980	1980–1990
Hong Kong	9.2	10.1	9.8	7.1
Singapore	5.4	9.2	9.3	7.3
South Korea	5.1	9.5	8.2	9.9
Taiwan	8.1	9.6	9.7	8.5

Sources: Asian Development Bank, *Key Indicators of Developing and Asian Countries,* (various issues); Asian Development Bank, *Asian Development Outlook,* (various issues); World Bank, *World Development Report,* (various issues); World Bank, *World Tables,* (various issues), Far Eastern Economic Review, *Asia Yearbook,* (various issues); Council for Economic Planning and Development, *Taiwan Statistical Data Book,* (various issues).

they still managed to maintain impressive rates of GDP growth. For the period 1960–1985, the Asian NICs recorded average growth rates of real per capita GDP of about 6.5% per annum. This means that they were able to double their real per capita GDP about once every 11 years! Britain took approximately 60 years to double real per capita income after 1780, the USA took about 50 years after 1840 and Japan took roughly 35 years after 1885 to do the same (Economist 1991a:73). Between 1950 and 1983, real per capita GNP increased by 27 times in Hong Kong, 15 times in Singapore, 25 times in South Korea and 28 times in Taiwan.

These growth rates are spectacular in three important senses. First, compared with the growth rates of real per capita GDP for other less developed countries over the same time period, the Asian NICs grew four times as fast as other LDCs. Second, compared with the advanced industrial (OECD) countries, only Japan was able to match the growth of the Asian NICs. Third, these growth rates are about three times higher than the growth rates achieved by the advanced industrial countries (for example, USA, USSR, Japan) during the time periods in which they began their rapid

Figure 2.1
Growth of GDP (1980–1990) and
Per Capita GDP (% of US Per Capita GDP) 1990

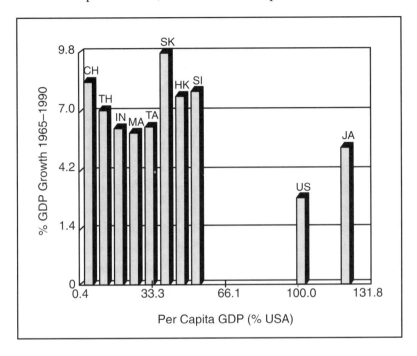

Source: World Bank 1992, *World Development Report 1992*; Council for Economic Planning and Development 1993, *Taiwan Statistical Data Book 1993*.

industrial development. Between 1885 and 1913, the average rate of growth of GDP in the USA was 4.4% per annum. In the USSR and Japan, it was 3.3% per annum (Gregory and Stuart 1986:327,329; Klein and Ohkawa 1968:10).

Increase in Savings and Investment Ratios

The rapid growth of the Asian NICs since the 1960s was achieved, amongst other factors, through increasing rates of investment, mainly in export-oriented manufacturing industry and social infrastructure. This was initially financed through foreign capital inflows as domestic savings rates were low relative to investment requirements. However, by the 1970s, the rise in per capita incomes, coupled with government policies which encouraged saving, enabled investment to be financed mainly through domestic sources. As Table 2.2 shows, by the 1980s, the Asian NICs had attained savings ratios that are some of the highest in the world.

The significant increases in the saving rates of the Asian NICs has been due to deregulation of financial markets which resulted in positive real rates of interest (Fry 1991a:16–19). This was aided by the development of a secure financial and banking system, subject to strict government monitoring in order to bolster consumer confidence. In Taiwan, a postal savings scheme was established to tap the savings of small savers. In the case of Singapore, forced savings were made through a national superannuation scheme, known as the Central Provident Fund, which exacted contributions both from employers and employees (by the 1990s, contributions to the Central Provident Fund accounted for 40% of employee incomes). In the late 1970s, savings in Singapore received another boost through the provision of tax-free interest earnings on deposits with the government-owned Post Office Savings Bank. By 1992, Singapore registered the highest savings rate in the world at 47.2% of GDP.

Another important feature of the savings performance of the Asian NICs is the fact that government budget surpluses (revenue

Table 2.2
Gross Domestic Savings and Gross Domestic Investment
(% GDP)

	1950–1960		1960–1970		1970–1980		1980–1990	
Country	GDI	GDS	GDI	GDS	GDI	GDS	GDI	GDS
Hong Kong	9.1	9.2	20.6	20.6	26.1	29.2	40.9	45.4
Singapore	11.4	–0.8	23.4	14.9	40.3	28.6	42.2	42.0
South Korea	11.4	3.2	23.2	13.7	29.6	22.0	30.9	32.0
Taiwan	18.1	10.7	21.4	18.4	29.9	31.4	22.7	31.3

Sources: Same as Table 2.1.

minus expenditure) contributed to higher rates of domestic savings (Fry 1991a:26–29). As shown in Table 2.3, from the 1970s, all the Asian NICs recorded positive government surpluses, even during the period 1985–1990, when the Asian NICs were caught in the throes of a severe recession. The prudent management of government finances in the Asian NICs stands in sharp contrast to that of other countries. In 1990, government deficits as a proportion of GDP were –16.4% in Mongolia, –10% in Sri Lanka and –11.4% in Nepal (Asian Development Bank 1993:279). In Australia, public savings during 1991 and 1992 ranged from –1% of GDP to –5% of GDP, whilst private savings ranged from 1.5% of GDP to 4% of GDP. As a result, national savings declined from 0.5% of GDP in 1991 to –1% of GDP in 1992 (Kaye and Wallace 1993:3).

In addition to the above, the rapid growth of incomes in the Asian NICs, coupled with declining fertility rates (which led to falling dependency ratios), also led to high savings ratios (Fry 1991a:20–23).

High savings and investment ratios are only one part of the story of the growth performance of the Asian NICs. Equally (if not more) important, is the fact that the Asian NICs were able to allocate their investment funds efficiently in high-yielding, export-oriented projects, rather than squander them in low-yielding projects, or projects which later turned out to be financial disasters (Fry 1991a:29–32). This was achieved through the efficient operation of markets and will be discussed in more detail below.

The growth of the Asian NICs has been propelled by a vibrant private sector. The share of investment accounted for by the private sector has been about 20% of GDP for the period 1969–1989. For other less developed countries, it has been about 11% of GDP. In addition, public sector investment in the Asian NICs has tended to complement private sector investment (in a counter-cyclical sense), exhibiting a rising share of GDP when the share of private sector investment is falling (World Bank 1993:42–44).

Prudent management of public sector finances in the Asian NICs also resulted in macroeconomic stability which was reflected in relatively low average rates of inflation and stable exchange

Table 2.3
Government Surplus (% GDP)

Country	1970–1975	1975–1980	1980–1985	1985–1990
Hong Kong	3.7	4.2	3.0	3.3
Singapore	7.1	7.3	11.0	1.2
South Korea	1.9	2.7	3.1	0.5
Taiwan	6.2	6.4	3.1	0.4

Sources: Same as Table 2.1.

rates (Fry 1991a:27; Fry 1991b:31–32). In addition, there was much less variability in the fluctuations in the rate of interest and in prices in the Asian NICs than in other less developed countries. During 1961–1991, the average rate of inflation in Hong Kong, Singapore and Taiwan ranged from 4% to 8% per annum. In South Korea it averaged 12% per annum. In contrast, the average rate of inflation in other less developed countries averaged 62% per annum over the same period, whilst in Latin America, it averaged 192% per annum. The maintenance of macroeconomic stability (in particular low rates of inflation) encouraged savings in the Asian NICs as the real value of savings was not dissipated by rapidly rising prices.

There is now considerable empirical evidence which supports the view that high savings and investment ratios are associated with high rates of economic growth. The direction of causation between savings ratios and income growth appears to be from high income growth to high savings ratios. When incomes are growing rapidly, there is more income available which can be diverted into savings. Granger causality tests appear to confirm this direction of causation (World Bank 1993:244). In the case of investment, both theory and evidence suggest that the direction of causation is from high investment ratios to high income growth. High investment ratios increase the capital stock, which then provides the capacity to increase output (Barro 1991:425–427; Levine and Renelt 1992).

Figure 2.2 shows that amongst the developing countries in the Asia-Pacific region, there is a broad positive correlation between high investment ratios and the growth of GDP. Countries with high investment ratios, such as China (CHI), Singapore (SIN), South Korea (SK) and Bhutan (BHU), have much higher rates of GDP growth than countries with low investment ratios, such as Fiji (FIJ), Burma (BUR), the Philippines (PHI) and Papua New Guinea (PNG). Econometric studies confirm the broad positive (and significant) correlation between investment ratios and rates of economic growth (Barro 1991:425–427; World Bank 1993:322). It is therefore not surprising that the Asian NICs have enjoyed higher growth rates of GDP than most other countries in the world. Their investment ratios have also been amongst the highest in the world.

Figure 2.2
GDP Growth and GDI/GDP Ratios (1981–1990)

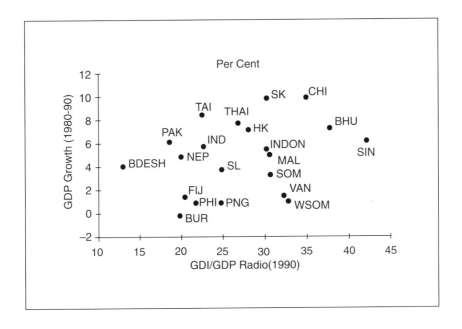

Source: World Bank 1992, *World Development Report 1992*; Council for Economic Planning and Development 1993, *Taiwan Statistical Data Book 1993*.

The Role of Foreign Capital

The role of foreign capital in economic development is a contentious issue in development economics. *Mainstream* economists argue that foreign capital (whether in the form of foreign aid or foreign investment) contributes to economic growth and development by increasing the capital stock and the level of technology (and thus, productivity) of less developed countries (Chenery and Strout 1966; Chenery and Carter 1973). *Radical* economists take the opposite view, arguing that the long-term effect of foreign capital inflows is to "de-capitalize" less developed countries because the repatriation of profits and repayments of loans and debts in any given year, more than outweigh the inflow of foreign capital (Bornschier 1980; Bornschier et al. 1978).

The rationale of the mainstream view is the "two-gap" model of Chenery and Strout (1966). According to this view, a less developed country which attempts to raise its rate of economic growth is likely, *ex ante*, to face two gaps in its national income accounts.

The first gap is the savings-investment gap, which is caused by the inability to generate a sufficient level of domestic savings to finance the level of investment required to achieve a higher growth rate. If domestic consumption is already at a minimum (and domestic savings at a maximum), attempting to raise the rate of economic growth may require a level of investment that cannot be financed by domestic savings. Hence, a savings-investment gap appears.

The second gap is the export-import gap (or foreign exchange gap). As a country attempts to increase its rate of economic growth, imports will rise as capital goods are required to achieve a higher growth rate. In addition, higher growth also induces the import of consumption goods as incomes rise. For many less developed countries, foreign exchange earnings from exports cannot be increased quickly. The reason for this is that agricultural and mineral exports usually require a long gestation period before large increases in output can be obtained. In addition, even if output can be increased, export markets may already be saturated so that prices fall. Thus there may be a ceiling to the foreign exchange earnings of less developed countries in the short- to medium-term. This gives rise to a foreign exchange, or export-import gap.

While these two gaps must be equal *ex post* (since an excess of investment over savings must be matched by an excess of imports over exports), this need not be so *ex ante*. If the *ex ante* savings-investment gap is larger than the *ex ante* export-import gap, the economy is said to be constrained by the shortage of domestic savings. In this case, the savings-investment gap is said to be binding. If the *ex ante* export-import gap is larger than the savings-investment gap, the export-import gap is said to be binding and the economy is said to be trade constrained (Chenery and Strout 1966:683).

In either of these circumstances, foreign capital (either in the form of foreign aid or investment) serves to augment the capital stock of the less developed country and enables it to attain a higher level of investment and growth than would have otherwise been possible. The mainstream view, therefore, sees the inflow of foreign capital as beneficial to less developed countries. Figure 2.3 illustrates the main features of the two-gap model.

In Figure 2.3, total output is measured on the horizontal axis to the right of the origin. The growth rate of the economy is measured on the horizontal axis to the left of the origin. Savings are measured on the vertical axis above the origin, while imports are measured on the vertical axis below the origin.

Suppose that a less developed economy has an output of 0Y. The economy may export some of this output in exchange for some imports. Given the terms of trade, the transformation of exports into imports is depicted by the slope of the line YM in the lower right-hand quadrant of the diagram. Suppose that there is a maximum amount that can be exported (shown by the vertical line E_{max}). This may be due to the difficulties of increasing production, or to the saturation of the export market. The maximum amount that can be exported is shown as YY' on the horizontal axis, and the maximum amount that can be imported is shown as $0M_{max}$. With this maximum level of imports, a maximum growth rate of $0g$ can be sustained.

The Harrod-Domar growth model can be expanded to include trade: $g = s/v + (m-x)/v$, where g = growth rate, s = marginal propensity to save, v = capital-output ratio, m = marginal propensity to import, x = marginal propensity to export). The lower left-hand quadrant of the diagram depicts the relationship between the growth rate and imports, while the upper left-hand quadrant depicts the relationship between the growth rate and savings.

In the upper left-hand quadrant, the relationship between growth and the level of savings is shown by the slope of the ray $0V$, which is equal to $v\dot{Y}$, since $S = vYg$. Given v and Y, and increase in g will require an increase in the level of savings.

In the lower left-hand quadrant, the relationship between growth and imports $g = (m-x)/v$ is shown by the slope of the ray $0T$, which is equal to $M/g = vY + E/g$, where M = total imports and E = total exports and the other variables are as previously defined. This can be rearranged to give the relationship between imports and the growth rate, $M = vYg + E$. Given v, Y and E, any increase in g will imply and increase in the level of imports M.

With YY' exported, the economy has $0Y'$ available, either for consumption or saving. Saving can only be increased if consumption is decreased. This is shown by the line Y'S (whose slope is 45°) in the upper right-hand quadrant of the diagram. Suppose that there is a minimum level of consumption below which it is not possible to achieve (the country may already be at subsistence level, or reducing consumption further may not be politically feasible). The minimum level of consumption is shown as the vertical line C_{min} in the diagram. With consumption at $0C_{min}$, the maximum level of savings is $0S_{max}$. Given this level of savings, and a constant capital-output ratio, the maximum level of growth that can be sustained by domestic savings and exports is $0g$.

Now, suppose the country wanted to raise its rate of growth to $0g'$. With a fixed capital-output ratio, this would imply that $0S'$

Figure 2.3
The Two-Gap Model

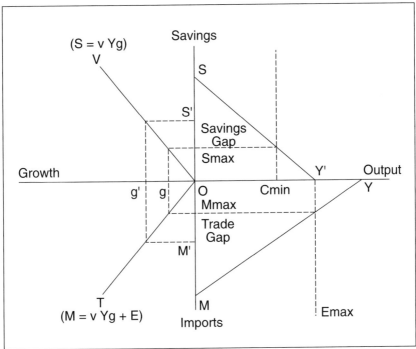

of savings would be required (in order to increase investment by the same amount). Since maximum domestic savings are $0S_{max}$, a savings gap of $S'S_{max}$ appears.

Similarly, a higher growth rate of $0g'$ would require imports of $0M'$. Since exports can only finance a maximum import level of M_{max}, an trade gap of $M'M_{max}$ appears. The role of foreign capital is to provide the resources which can be used to close the larger of these two gaps, and allow the country to achieve a rate of growth which would otherwise not have been possible. This can be illustrated in the following manner. Total output can be written as:

$$Y + F = C + I + (E - M)$$

where Y = output, F = foreign capital, C = consumption, I = investment, E = exports and M = imports. This can be transformed into:

$$S + F = I + (E - M)$$
$$I = S + F + (M - E)$$

Taking changes on both sides of the equation gives:

$$\Delta I = \Delta S + \Delta F + (\Delta M - \Delta E)$$
$$\Delta I = (\alpha' + f + \mu)\, \Delta y$$

where $\alpha' = \dfrac{\Delta S}{\Delta Y}$, $f = \dfrac{\Delta F}{\Delta Y}$, $\mu = \left(\dfrac{\Delta M}{\Delta Y} - \dfrac{\Delta E}{\Delta Y} \right)$, the marginal net import ratio.

Since the marginal capital-output ratio, $k = \dfrac{\Delta K}{\Delta Y} = \dfrac{I}{\Delta Y}$,

$$I = k\Delta Y = krY$$
$$\Delta I = kr\Delta Y$$

where r is the rate of growth of output. kr is therefore the rate of growth of investment that is required to sustain the rate of growth of output r. In equilibrium, this has to be financed by domestic savings, foreign capital or net imports:

$$kr = \alpha' + f + \mu$$
$$f = kr - (\alpha' + \mu)$$

Therefore, foreign capital inflow (measured as a percentage of income), is the difference between kr, the growth of investment required to sustain the growth rate r, and the sum of the domestic savings ratio α' and the marginal net import ratio, μ. If the growth of investment cannot be met by an increase in domestic savings and net imports, foreign capital is needed in order to fill the shortfall, so that the growth rate r can be attained.

Foreign capital can therefore be beneficial to a less developed country, as it can be used to close either the investment gap or the trade gap and enable the country to attain a growth rate that is higher than would otherwise have been possible.

The *radical* view denies this. Instead, radical economists argue that the effect of foreign capital inflows on less developed countries is detrimental. Foreign capital is used to substitute (rather than add to) domestic savings and thus release domestic resources for consumption. The net effect of this is to reduce the domestic savings rate. In addition, foreign capital inflows, particularly in the form of foreign aid, are often used to finance large-scale infrastructural projects which do not result in large increases in productivity in the short- to medium-term. This tends to increase the capital-output ratio. Viewed in terms of a Harrod-Domar growth framework, the decline in domestic savings, plus the rise in the capital-output ratio, it is argued, will tend to reduce the growth rate of the economy (Griffin and Enos 1970).

The impact of aid on domestic savings can be illustrated with the following diagram. In Figure 2.4, total income, which is measured on the horizontal axis, is 0A. Suppose that of this, 0a is consumed and aA is saved. Domestic savings, aA is also shown as 0b on the vertical axis, which measures total savings. The country is at point W on the line AA' (which has a slope of 45°). The savings ratio (total savings divided by income) is 0b/0A.

Suppose that aid equal to AB is received. If all of it is saved, consumption remains at 0a, domestic savings remains at aA, but total savings rise to aX (which is equal to 0e). The savings ratio rises to 0e/0B. This is the mainstream view. If all the aid is consumed, consumption rises to 0A=WZ. Domestic savings remains at 0b, and the savings ratio declines to 0b/0B.

Suppose, however, that only *part* of the aid is consumed while the rest is saved. This is depicted by the point Y on BB'. Consumption rises to 0c. Domestic savings fall to cA (which is less than aA). Total savings rise to 0d (which is greater than 0b). The savings ratio could rise, fall or remain unchanged, depending on the proportion of the aid that is saved compared to the proportion of income that is saved.

Suppose that saving out of income (domestic savings) is $\alpha = S_d/Y$, where S_d is domestic saving and Y is income. Suppose also that saving out of aid is $\beta = S_a/Y$, where S_a is saving out of aid. The savings ratio, after aid is received, is $\sigma = (S_d + S_a)/(Y + A)$. After aid is received, the difference between σ and α is:

$$(\sigma - \alpha) = \frac{(\beta - \alpha)}{\dfrac{Y}{A} + 1}$$

Note that the value of α will be lower after aid is received and some of it is consumed, since domestic savings will fall. If savings out of aid are greater than savings out of income ($\beta > \alpha$), then the savings ratio will rise after aid is received, even if some of the aid is consumed since ($\sigma - \alpha$) > 0. Only if savings out of aid are less than savings out of income will the savings ratio, σ, fall. If the capital-output ratio is unchanged, the receipt of foreign aid need not lead to a decline in the savings ratio, and need not lead to a decline in the growth rate, even if some of the aid is consumed.

Figure 2.4
Foreign Aid and Domestic Savings

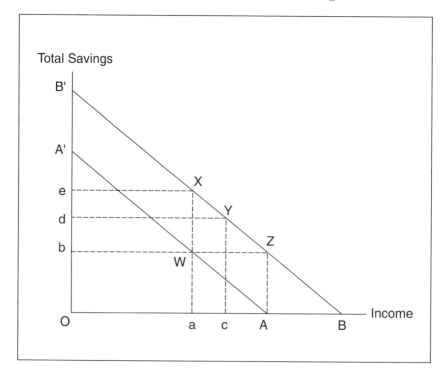

According to radical economists, foreign capital inflows, particularly in the form of foreign investment, have another detrimental effect on less developed countries. Since foreign investors repatriate their earnings in the form of profits, royalties and fees, radical economists argue that in most less developed countries, the outflow of capital in the form of profits, management fees and the like, often exceeds the inflow of capital in the form of foreign investment. Thus, instead of adding to the capital available to less developed countries, foreign investment leads to a decline in the capital available to less developed countries. This is known as the *de-capitalization* hypothesis. According to Frank (1969:162–163):

> It is widely believed that the United States and other developed capitalist countries contribute more capital to the underdeveloped countries than they receive from them. Nonetheless, all the available statistics ... show precisely the opposite.

An examination of the relevant data does indeed show that in any given year, the outflow of capital in the form of profits, management fees, etc., repatriated by foreigners does exceed the inflow of foreign investment (Weisskopf 1974; Davey 1975; Frank 1969:163; Griffin 1971:144–145). However, this argument is erroneous because it compares two financial flows which are related to each other in a way that ensures that one will eventually exceed the other. The inflow of foreign investment is determined by investment opportunities in a country. The outflow of capital in the form of profits, management fees, etc., repatriated by foreigners depends on the accumulated capital stock owned by foreigners and the rate of profit earned by foreigners (assume that there are no taxes on profits earned by foreign-owned firms because of the granting of a tax holiday). If foreigners repatriate a stream of income earned on a growing stock of capital, the simple arithmetic of investment will ensure that the outflow of capital will eventually exceed the inflow of foreign investment.

If the amount of foreign investment entering a country is I every year (let us assume that it is a constant amount), then the capital stock owned by foreigners over time will be *In*, where *n* is the number of years over which foreign investment has been entering the country. Suppose the rate of profit on capital earned by foreigners is π and that all profits earned by foreigners are repatriated. Then the outflow of capital in the form of repatriated profits will be πIn per year. Since the capital inflow is constant while the capital outflow is rising over time (because of a rising capital stock), a time will come when the capital outflow must exceed the capital inflow. In the above example, the time at which the capital inflow will be *exactly* the same as the capital outflow is given by:

$$\pi In = I$$

$$n = \frac{1}{\pi}$$

If $\pi = 0.10$, then in ten years' time, the outflow of capital repatriated by foreigners will be equal to the inflow of foreign investment. In the eleventh and subsequent years, the outflow of capital will greater then the inflow of foreign investment. If other variables remain unchanged, the higher the rate of profit, π, the sooner will the outflow of repatriated profits exceed the inflow of foreign investment.

To illustrate the argument, suppose that every year, $10 million of foreign investment, attracted by profitable investment opportunities, enters a less developed country. In ten years' time, the capital stock owned by foreigners will be $100 million. If the rate of profit earned by foreigners is 10%, and all profits are repatriated, then in ten years' time, the outflow of capital will be $10 million (equal to the inflow). In the eleventh year, the capital stock owned by foreigners will be $110 million and repatriated profits will be $11 million (greater than the inflow of $10 million). Thus, the simple arithmetic of investment will ensure that the outflow of capital as a result of foreign investment will eventually exceed the inflow because of a growing stock of capital owned by foreigners. The essentials of the argument will remain unchanged if we relax certain assumptions, such as a constant inflow of foreign investment, or a 100% repatriation of profits. For example, if the inflow of foreign investment is rising over time, this means that the capital stock owned by foreigners will be rising faster over time, and so will the amount of profits repatriated.

What is more relevant to the argument is how the foreign-owned capital stock is utilized. Suppose that the capital/output ratio is v. At any point in time, the foreign-owned capital stock will produce an output of In/v. Suppose further that part of this output is exported (foreign-owned firms are export-oriented) and the export/output ration is e. Foreign exchange earnings generated by foreign-owned firms will be $In\left(\frac{e}{v}\right)$. The net effect of foreign investment on capital flows will depend on:

$$In\left(\frac{e}{v}\right) - \pi In$$

As long as $\left(\frac{e}{v}\right)$ is greater than π, the foreign exchange earned by foreign-owned firms will be greater than the foreign exchange that is repatriated in the form of profits, management fees, etc. As an example, if the capital/output ratio (v) is 3, the export/output ratio (e) is 1 (foreign-owned firms export all their output), and the profit rate (π) is 0.10, then (e/v) will be 0.3333 and will exceed π. In this case, the foreign exchange earnings generated by foreign-owned firms will exceed the profits repatriated by them. Even though foreigners are repatriating profits, this is more than offset by the foreign exchange they generate through their export earnings. Obviously, the relative magnitudes of the productivity of foreign capital (v), the export intensity of foreign-owned firms (e), and the profit rate earned by foreign-owned firms (π), are critical in determining the impact of foreign investment on less developed countries.

Figure 2.5 presents a diagrammatic illustration of the argument. In Figure 2.5, time is measured on the horizontal axis. Foreign investment inflow is at a constant rate of I. The foreign-owned capital stock grows by In over time and is shown by the line $0K$ in the diagram. Profit repatriation by foreign-owned firms is

Figure 2.5
Foreign Investment and Capital Flows

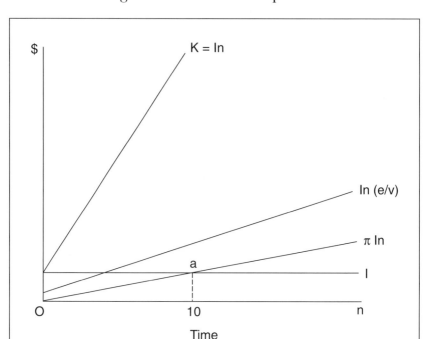

shown by the line $0\pi In$. If $\pi=0.10$, the outflow of repatriated profits will equal the inflow of foreign investment (point *a* in the diagram). After the tenth year, the outflow of repatriated profits will exceed the inflow of foreign investment.

If foreign-owned firms are export-oriented, and if $(e/v) > \pi$, the foreign-exchange earnings generated by them will be greater than the outflow of repatriated profits. This is shown in the diagram by the line $0In(e/v)$ having a steeper slope than $0\pi In$. Note that if the inflow of foreign investment is rising over time (the foreign investment curve will have a positive slope), this means that the slope of the capital stock curve $0K$ and the curve depicting repatriated profits πIn will be steeper. The time at which the outflow of capital is equal to the inflow will change, but the essentials of the argument will not be affected.

The radical view is also flawed from a theoretical point of view. Since capital inflow will reduce the rate of return on capital in the capital-importing country and raise the productivity of labour, the share of national income accruing to capital will fall relative to labour. Wages and per capita income will rise in the capital-importing country. Savings and investment will also rise, resulting in an increase (rather than a decrease) in the capital stock of the capital importing country (Ruffin 1993:8–11).

Empirical evidence on the effects of foreign capital in less developed countries is mixed. Although early studies (Griffin and Enos 1970; Weisskopf 1972) of the impact of foreign aid on domestic savings rates appeared to suggest an inverse relationship, recent studies using better data and more sophisticated statistical techniques tend to support a positive relationship (Papanek 1972,1973; Dowling and Heimenz 1983; Rana and Dowling 1988; Lee et al. 1986; Synder 1990; Morriset 1990). Similarly, initial attempts to test the *de-capitalization* thesis tended to show an inverse relationship between the stock (not the flow) of foreign investment and economic growth (Bornschier 1980). However, a number of methodological problems suggest that these results should be viewed with caution. For example, Bornschier's data set includes Japan, Greece, Ireland, Italy as "less developed countries", and excludes Singapore and Hong Kong in the sample (Bornschier 1980:208). Recent studies, correcting these anomalies and utilizing more recent data (Singh 1985), have not confirmed the radical view that foreign capital is detrimental to economic growth.

In the case of the Asian NICs, there is little doubt that foreign capital inflows have helped to close the savings-investment gap and to finance the levels of investment required for rapid economic growth (Chen 1993:52–56). As Table 2.4 shows, this was particularly true during the 1950s and 1960s. By the 1980s, higher domestic savings rates enabled most of the Asian NICs to reduce their dependence on foreign capital and some (for example, Taiwan, South Korea and Singapore) became net capital exporters (Economist 1990a:18).

In Taiwan, foreign capital inflows contributed 43.9% to

Table 2.4
Savings-Investment Gap (% GDP)

Country	1951–1960	1961–1970	1971–1980	1981–1990
Hong Kong	0.1	0.0	3.1	2.8
Singapore	–12.2	–8.5	–11.7	0.5
South Korea	–8.2	–9.5	–7.0	1.4
Taiwan	–7.4	–3.0	1.5	10.4

Sources: Same as Table 2.1.

economic growth in 1953–1955 and 35.3% in 1955–1960 (Liang and Lee 1975:294). In South Korea, foreign capital accounted for 41% of total investment in 1953 and 65% in 1961 (Byun et al. 1975:375). Although much of this was in the form of US military aid, US aid to South Korea and Taiwan did play an important part in the economic development of both countries (Jacoby 1966; Krueger 1979). In the 1970s and 1980s, Taiwan and South Korea reduced their dependence on foreign capital inflows (this time in the form of foreign investment). Singapore and Hong Kong, however, continued to accept large flows of foreign investment. In 1984, foreign-owned firms in Singapore comprised 21% of all establishments but accounted for 62% of capital expenditure and 63% of value-added of the manufacturing sector (Koh 1987:24). Between 1965 and 1973, some 35% of gross domestic capital formation in Singapore was financed by net borrowing abroad (Krause 1987:7). During 1986–1991, foreign investment accounted for about 30% of gross capital formation in Singapore and about 12% of gross capital formation in Hong Kong. By contrast, the ratios for Taiwan and South Korea were 4% and 2% respectively (FEER 1993a:67). Between 1962 and 1983, foreign investment accounted for only about 5% of total capital inflows into the South Korean economy (Amsden 1989:92).

During 1985–1990, the main sources of foreign investment in Hong Kong were Japan (25.9%), the USA (34.9%) and the EU

(12.9%). Whilst the share of total foreign investment in Hong Kong accounted for by the USA has been declining over time, that of Japan and the EU has been rising steadily. Most foreign investment in Hong Kong went into electronics and electrical products (43.2%). In Taiwan, the main sources of foreign investment during 1952–1991 were the USA (28.0%), Japan (29.0%) and the EU (15.0%). Most of this went into the production of electronic and electrical appliances (25%), as well as chemicals (16%). During 1982–1921, Japan (40.0%) accounted for the largest share of total foreign investment in South Korea. The USA (27.8%) and the EU (25.5%) were the next largest sources of foreign investment in South Korea. Most of the foreign investment in South Korea went into petroleum and chemicals (22%), hotels (20.2%), electronics and electrical appliances (14.2%) and transport equipment (9.3%) (Chen 1993:44–51). In Singapore, the three main sources of foreign investment during 1986–1990, were the USA (38.7%), Japan (37.3%) and the EU (22.6%). Much of this went into petroleum refining, electronic products, electrical machinery and transport equipment (Chia 1993:80,96).

Financial Development

All the Asian NICs experienced financial deepening as reflected in the growth of financial assets, the increasing role of financial intermediation in the economy and the development of specialist financial institutions. This is particularly true of Hong Kong and Singapore. Financial deepening can aid economic growth by mobilizing savings and by allocating investment through financial intermediaries in an efficient manner (Fry 1991a:29–30).

One commonly used measure of financial deepening is the ratio of "broad" money M2 (defined as currency, savings, demand and time deposits) to GDP. In 1965, the value of M2/GDP in Singapore and Hong Kong was about 55%. In South Korea it was 12% and in Taiwan, 29%. By the early 1980s, Singapore's M2/GDP ratio was 70%, Hong Kong's was 112%, South Korea's was 38% and Taiwan's was 80%. The ratios for Hong Kong and Singapore were higher than that of the USA (64%), reflecting their status as important world financial centres (Riedel 1988:14; James et al. 1989:70; Kohsaka 1987:325–346). By the 1980s, the degree of financial development in the Asian NICs was much higher than most developing countries in Asia (Arndt 1983:92). Figure 2.6 suggests a broad positive correlation between the growth of GDP and the M2/GDP ratio.

Although Figure 2.6 does suggest a broad positive relationship between financial deepening and economic growth, the relationship is not strong and there are important exceptions. While most of the Asian NICs (Hong Kong, Singapore and Taiwan) have high M2/GDP ratios and high rates of economic growth, this is not the case for South Korea or China. Both these countries have relatively underdeveloped financial sectors in which many transactions are still carried out in unofficial curb markets. In South Korea and Taiwan, government control over banks and other financial institutions has led to the allocation of finance by administrative means. However, in recent years, a number of measures have been undertaken to liberalize the financial sectors of these countries (Holloway and Clifford 1991:64–66).

While there is some evidence to support the view that financial deepening is related to economic growth, the exact nature of this relationship is subject to considerable debate (Dornbusch and Reynoso 1989:205–206). One suggestion is that financial deepening, which is usually accompanied by change from negative to positive real rates of interest, results in a more efficient use of capital and an increase in total factor productivity which then leads to higher rates of economic growth (Fry 1991a:15–39).

Since the latter part of the 1960s, both Singapore and Hong Kong have been encouraging the establishment of international banking and financial institutions, and are now regarded major world centres of international finance. By the 1980s, over 100 foreign banks and other financial institutions were operating in Singapore. In 1992, the average daily turnover in foreign exchange transactions in Singapore amounted to US$75 billion (higher than that of Zurich). In Hong Kong the average daily turnover in foreign

Figure 2.6
Financial Deepening and Economic Growth, 1980–1990

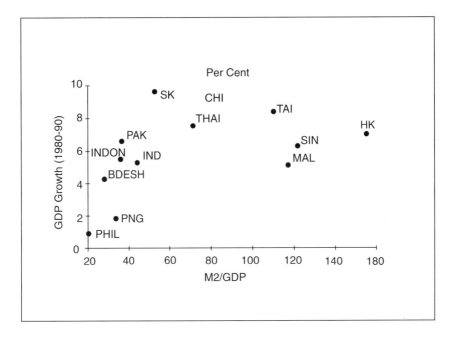

Source: World Bank 1992, *World Development Report.*

exchange transactions was US$71 billion (higher than that of Frankfurt). Current uncertainties with respect to the future of Hong Kong after it reverts to mainland China are likely to increase Singapore's role as an international financial centre (Krause 1987:73).

Role of Government

The role of government in economic affairs has been recognized to be an important determinant of the growth performance of developing countries (World Bank 1991:128–149; 1993:79–103). The *mainstream* view is that governments should play a minimal role in economic affairs. This is usually limited to intervening in order to correct for market failures which result in externalities.

Examples include public ownership of natural monopolies, intervening in the price mechanism in order to minimize environmental pollution and the subsidization of the training of the labour force. The main principle involved is that governments should intervene only in areas where the market is not working properly and where government intervention can improve matters (World Bank 1991:128–131; 1993:82–86). In addition, intervention should take the form of measures which alter market signals (such as prices), rather than measures which attempt to supplant markets. Apart from these, the principal role of government is to provide an environment within which private enterprise can flourish. This usually involves providing security against external attack and internal chaos (by the maintenance of armed forces, police and other security agencies), the provision of social infrastructure and the establishment of a legal framework (Friedman and Friedman 1980:49).

Proponents of the above view claim that the economic success of the Asian NICs is to a large measure due to the minimal role played by their governments in economic affairs (Friedman and Friedman 1980:54–55,80; Pennar 1993b:29). The growth performance of the Asian NICs has been characterized by a relatively small (compared to many other less developed countries) role played by the government in economic activity. (There is some evidence to suggest that the size of government is inversely related to economic growth (Landau 1983; Barro 1991:430–432).) This should not be construed to mean that the Asian NICs adopted a completely *laissez faire* approach to economic management, or that governments played a minimal role in economic activity. On the contrary, the governments of all the Asian NICs (even that of Hong Kong) played an important part in economic affairs. Governments frequently intervened in product and factor (mainly labour and capital) markets, participated directly in the ownership of enterprises in many sectors of the economy and influenced the pattern of investment in order to achieve their economic goals. In Hong Kong (as well as in Singapore), the government provided low cost public housing, education, transport and medical care.

This kept the cost of living down and pre-empted demands for wage increases in spite of the long hours of work which most workers had to endure (Castells 1992:49; Nolan 1990:56). According to this view, it is a myth to believe that governments in the Asian NICs took a "hands-off" approach in business and economic affairs (Lim 1983; Foster-Carter 1989; Wade 1990; Park 1990; Krause 1989; Ho 1987; Pang 1988:226–233; Bradford 1987; Goldstein 1988c; Riedel 1988:28–37; Fajnzylber 1981:120–126; Johnson 1985:63–89; Amsden 1990:5–31; Castells 1992:33–70; Henderson and Appelbaum 1992:1–26).

However, as a proportion of total economic activity, the size of the government sector in the Asian NICs (with the exception of Singapore which has, in recent years, been privatizing government-owned enterprises [Balakrishnan 1990]) has been relatively small. In 1989, central government expenditure as a proportion of GDP was 15% in Hong Kong, 17% in South Korea, 18% in Taiwan and 21% in Singapore. These are comparatively low shares compared with some other countries (Indonesia had a ratio of 25% and Malaysia, 29%) (Rowley 1990a:53). In some African and Latin American countries, this ratio goes up to 40% or more (in 1989, the ratio of government expenditure to GDP in Botswana was 50.1%, in Panama it was 38.4% [World Bank 1991:225–226]). Governments in the Asian NICs have not maintained large welfare programmes or propped up inefficient public enterprises. Governments in the Asian NICs have also not laid large claims on output. In 1989, government consumption ranged from 7% of GDP (Hong Kong) to 10% of GDP (Singapore and South Korea). In Taiwan, government consumption was 15% of GDP. In other less developed countries, the share of government consumption in GDP was much higher. For example, Saudi Arabia recorded a share of 32%, Israel 29%, Namibia 28% and Papua New Guinea recorded a share of 25% (World Bank 1991:222–223).

The governments of all the Asian NICs intervened in economic affairs by providing capital (often at subsidized rates) for (and sometimes participating directly in) investment projects, bearing the costs of activities which generated positive externalities (such as the training of labour and the development of export markets), intervening in product and factor markets in order to correct distortions created by past policies (for example, devaluing the exchange rate and providing subsidies in order to make exports competitive, and preventing wages from rising too fast in order to encourage employment).

There is some debate as to whether government allocation of capital funds to targeted industries (known as "directed credit") has played an important role in the industrial growth of the Asian NICs. The South Korean experience in using directed credit to stimulate the development of heavy industry in the 1970s is largely regarded as a failure. However, this may have been due to specific features of the South Korean experience, such as the large degree of subsidization involved in providing capital to targeted firms, the heavy reliance on central bank credit (which contributed to high rates of inflation) and foreign borrowing (which led to a build up of foreign debt), and the large number of losses incurred. Directed credit is more likely to be successful if it is limited in scale and duration, prudently financed so as to avoid macroeconomic instability, does not involve large subsidies and operates through financial institutions which are efficient and which have adequate resources to vet projects and monitor performance (Vittas and Cho 1994:11–12).

In all the Asian NICs (except Hong Kong), the government intervened by participating directly in business through the ownership of banks, hotels and manufacturing firms. In Singapore, for example, the number of firms wholly or partially controlled by the government (through a number of holding companies) increased from 13 in 1967 to 450 in 1983, and had a total capitalized value of S$2.4 billion in 1983 (Krause 1989:436–454).

The important point about government intervention in the Asian NICs is not that it did not occur, but that it occurred in order to correct distortions and weaknesses of the private enterprise system (Papanek 1988:38–39). Government intervention was implemented with the aim of working with, rather than against, the market (Hill 1986; Ariff and Hill 1985:154). The aim was to affect market outcomes through changes in relative prices, rather than through administrative controls. A recent issue of the World Bank's World Development Report describes this as a "market-friendly" approach to government intervention (World Bank 1991:6). According to this view, which has been expressed by other writers, government intervention in the Asian NICs was primarily "market-sustaining" rather than "market-repressing" (Lim 1981:4,8; Koo and Kim 1992:121). Even in Singapore, where government intervention in economic and social life is pervasive (in January 1992, the Singapore government banned the import and sale of chewing gum because vandals were putting gum in the doors of MRT trains and preventing their proper operation [Balakrishnan 1992a:20]), the role of government in the economy is thought not to result in a distortion of relative prices (Krause 1987:4).

This is not as tautologous as it might appear (Rodan 1989:26), since the implied definition of "market-sustaining" government intervention is in terms of the methods used, not its results (Johnson:1985:68). Government intervention which affected market signals was not always successful and policy mistakes were not always avoided. When they occurred, incorrect policy decisions became apparent very quickly and the market mechanism exacted its penalties, often with vengeance (Krueger 1990:110). This often resulted in a reversal of government policy. The attempt of the South Korean government to develop heavy industry through tariff protection in the 1970s and the decision of the Singapore government to raise wages substantially in the 1980s are examples of this (Fujita and James 1989; Economic Committee 1986). When it was clear that these market interventions had failed, they were quickly reversed.

The development of the Asian NICs was not characterized by the adoption of *laissez faire* policies or by government intervention alone, but by a judicious combination of the two (Ranis 1989; World Bank 1991:9–11). Government intervention in the NICs was aimed at strengthening the ability of the economy to take advantage of market forces in order to capitalize on comparative advantage. This is in stark contrast to government intervention in other less developed countries, which was often in contravention of market forces and which often resulted in the maintenance of inefficient industries by a host of government regulations and subsidies (Macomber 1987:474–481). The experience of the Asian NICs suggests that it is not so much whether governments intervene in economic affairs, as the *nature* of that intervention. Where governments have intervened to facilitate market forces or where they have not intervened and allowed markets to perform their functions, economic growth has usually been enhanced. The opposite has frequently resulted when government intervention has frustrated the workings of markets. In addition, government intervention in the Asian NICs has been formulated by strong governments and executed by relatively efficient and honest administrations which have been insulated from pressure groups. This has prevented the formulation and implementation of government policy from being captured by interest groups and used to their own advantage.

Another aspect of the role of government in the Asian NICs is that all the Asian NICs are characterized by a close relationship between government and business. There is close co-operation and consultation between government and business groups, and senior civil servants, on retirement, have little difficulty making the transition to the private sector. Government, on the other hand, has no problems with co-opting business leaders to serve in the administration. There is a two-way flow of talent between government and business. Government and business see themselves, not as adversaries, but as partners in the pursuit of common goals. In all the Asian NICs, governments provide a favourable and stable business environment, one that encourages, rather than obstructs the creation of wealth (Krause 1987:55).

Export Orientation

All the Asian NICs are highly export-oriented. For the city-states of Singapore and Hong Kong there was no alternative to export-orientation since their domestic market was small. However, even the larger Asian NICs (South Korea and Taiwan) are highly dependent on exports. In 1990, the share of merchandise exports in GDP was 152% in Singapore, 48.7% in Hong Kong, 45.7% in Taiwan and 26.1% in South Korea. For middle-income and lower-middle-income less developed countries, the ratio of exports to GDP was 19% in 1990. The high degree of dependence of the Asian NICs on trade is one of their distinguishing features (Page 1991).

Export-orientation and openness to foreign influences played an important part in increasing efficiency and productivity in the Asian NICs. The import of foreign technology and the increased competition from having to export to world markets, stimulated productivity and encouraged firms in the Asian NICs to adopt international best practice in their operations. In many Asian NICs, exports were promoted and subsidized by governments.

Growth of Manufactured Exports

The growth of manufactured exports is probably the most widely known feature of the growth performance of the Asian NICs. The shift towards manufactured exports in the Asian NICs can be seen in the rise in the exports to GDP ratio and in the rise in the ratio of manufactured exports to total exports. In 1960, exports as a proportion of GDP were 82% in Hong Kong, 163% in Singapore, 3% in South Korea and 11% in Taiwan. Hong Kong and Singapore have always been important centres of world trade. In 1988, Hong Kong's export/GDP ratio was 115%, Singapore's was 133%, South Korea's was 35% and Taiwan's was 47%.

This rapid increase in the export intensity of the Asian NICs was accompanied by an equally rapid increase in the share of manufactured exports in total exports. In 1960, this ratio stood at 91% in Hong Kong, 20% in Singapore, 14% in South Korea and 27% in Taiwan. By 1988, the share of manufactured exports in total exports was 91% in Hong Kong, 74% in Singapore, 93% in South Korea and 86% in Taiwan. Hong Kong, even in 1960, was already concentrating on the export of manufactured goods, but the other Asian NICs rapidly caught up with Hong Kong in this respect.

Table 2.5 shows the growth rate of exports (for the Asian NICs, most exports are manufactured exports), from the 1960s.

From the 1960s, all the Asian NICs (with the exception of Singapore) recorded double-digit growth rates of exports. By the late 1980s, over 90% of the exports of the Asian NICs (excluding Singapore) were made up of manufactured goods. Even in the more difficult trading conditions of the 1980s, most Asian NICs managed to maintain double-digit growth rates of exports. This achievement in export growth should be seen in perspective. During 1980–1990, world trade grew by only about 3% per annum. In spite of this, the exports of Asian NICs grew by between two and four times this rate of growth.

The growth of exports is significant, even in the entrepots such as Singapore and Hong Kong, which re-export much of their imports. In Singapore, for example, net domestic exports (exports net of import content) rose steadily from 10.4% of GDP in 1965 to 23.3% of GDP in 1985 (Krause 1987:67).

The initial export spurt in the Asian NICs in the 1960s took the form of the export of labour-intensive manufactured goods,

Table 2.5
Growth of Exports (% per annum)

Country	1960–1970	1970–1980	1980–1990
Hong Kong	14.5	22.4	12.3
South Korea	38.6	37.2	11.6
Singapore	3.3	28.2	7.3
Taiwan	18.1	14.1	12.1

Sources: Hong Kong Department of Statistics, *Exports*, and *Imports* (various issues); Ministry of Finance, Taipeh, *Monthly Statistics of Exports*, and *Monthly Statistics of Imports* (various issues); Singapore Trade Development Board, *Singapore Trade Statistics* (various issues), World Bank, *Yearbook of International Trade* (various issues).

since their comparative advantage lay in exploiting their cheap labour. Textiles, clothing and footwear were the main export items. As late as 1980, labour costs in garment manufacture in the Asian NICs (except Singapore) were one-fifth of what they were in the USA. Hourly wages of textile workers in South Korea were 16% of their counterparts in the USA, while productivity was 64% of US levels (Hoffman 1985:371–392). Another indication of cost differences is suggested by the fact that in 1981, the price of men's suits in Hong Kong and Taiwan was 17% of that of similar items in the EU. By the late 1980s, labour-intensive manufactured exports were becoming less important as the Asian NICs responded to increasing wage rates and appreciating exchange rates by moving into more technology and capital-intensive exports. Table 2.6 shows this transition.

Table 2.6 clearly shows that in 1970, textiles and clothing accounted for large shares of the total exports of Hong Kong, South Korea and Taiwan (wages in Singapore were much higher than those of the other Asian NICs, making Singapore relatively less competitive in the export of textiles). The share of exports accounted for by textiles and clothing declined significantly in South Korea and Taiwan between 1970 and 1989. Textile

Table 2.6

Changes in Export Structure

(% Total Exports)

Item	Textiles & Clothing			Machinery		
Year	1970	1980	1989	1970	1980	1989
Hong Kong	44.3	40.7	39.5	11.8	17.5	23.3
Singapore	5.6	4.3	5.0	11.0	26.8	47.0
South Korea	41.1	29.9	23.9	7.2	20.3	35.0
Taiwan	29.0	21.8	16.3	16.7	24.7	35.6

Source: ESCAP 1991, Management of external sector policy, *Economic and Social Survey of Asia and the Pacific*, p. 151.

manufacture is still important in Hong Kong, but here, the movement has been into higher value-added, up-market fashion clothing in order to support higher wages (Stillitoe 1985b).

In the case of footwear (another labour-intensive manufactured product) Taiwan and South Korea were important world exporters in the 1970s. In 1976, Taiwan accounted for 42% of all imports of non-rubber footwear into the USA. South Korea accounted for another 12%. By 1989, Taiwan's share declined to 30%, whilst South Korea's share increased to 20%. Much of the exports of footwear from Taiwan and South Korea are now in the form of high quality and high priced shoes made for well known brands (such as Nike) (Clifford 1992a:56–57). In 1990, South Korea was one of the largest producers of high quality shoes in the world, and exported 38 million pairs of shoes (Gittlesohn 1990:53). However, it was already losing its comparative advantage in this line of export and has been shifting its shoe production to lower cost countries such as Indonesia (Clifford 1992b:58–59).

The shift into skill-intensive, higher technology exports is shown in the table by the large increases in the share of machinery exports in the total exports for all the Asian NICs. These include a whole range of products, from electrical weighing machines that are used in most supermarket checkouts, to printers and disk drives for computers and to machine tools. The shift into these skill-intensive, higher technology exports reflects the fact that the Asian NICs have been gradually losing their comparative advantage in labour-intensive, manufactured exports as a result of increasing costs of production because of rising wages.

Most of the exports of the Asian NICs went to the USA. In 1986, 48% of Taiwan's exports went to the USA. For South Korea, the proportion was 40%, while for Hong Kong, it was 31%. Singapore was the least dependent on the US market. Only 23% of Singapore's exports went to the USA in 1986. The two other major markets for the exports of the Asian NICs were the EU (which took about 25% of NIC exports) and Japan (which accounted for about 15% of NIC exports).

Growth of Employment

The rapid growth of exports since the 1960s was based, initially, on the export of labour-intensive manufactured goods. In the early phase of the growth of the Asian NICs, wages were kept low and the power of trade unions was proscribed so as to encourage labour-intensive industries. As a result, employment in the manufacturing sector grew rapidly in all the Asian NICs (Fujita and James 1990:737–753).

The experience of the Singapore economy illustrates this point. Between 1957 and 1963, manufacturing employment grew by 3.5% per annum, barely keeping up with the rate of growth of the labour force (3.4% per annum). Between 1969 and 1992, manufacturing employment in Singapore grew by an average of 6.9% per annum while the labour force grew by 4.1% per annum. The number of workers employed in the manufacturing sector increased by more than 3.5 times, from 110,000 in 1969 to 412,000 in 1992. Total employment increased by about 4 times, from 399,000 in 1969 to 1,576,000 in 1992. During this period, an average of about 50,000 jobs a year were created in the economy as a whole. In the manufacturing sector, an average of 13,000 jobs were created every year. Apart from manufacturing, the growth of employment was concentrated in other labour-intensive sectors of the economy, such as construction, finance and banking, and the tourism and hospitality industries.

Singapore's unemployment rate, which was about 9% in 1965 declined steadily to reach 2.7% in 1984. Although it rose to 6.5% in 1986 (as a result of the 1985–1986 recession), by 1990 it had declined to 1.3%. By this time, Singapore had moved from a labour surplus economy to a labour shortage economy and had begun to import large numbers of foreign workers. By 1980, there were an estimated 120,000 foreign workers in Singapore, accounting for 7% of total employment (Lim and Pang 1986:23,59,61). In some sectors such as construction, they made up 20% of those employed. By 1990, there were an estimated 300,000 foreign workers in Singapore, accounting for 30% of total employment (Athukorala 1993).

Although manufacturing employment has increased significantly in the other Asian NICs (Riedel 1988:17), the import of foreign workers has been less overt. In the late 1980s, however, both Taiwan and Hong Kong had begun to import foreign workers in response to growing labour shortages (Economist 1991c; Baum 1991a; Salem 1989a).

Another feature of the growth of employment in the Asian NICs is the increase in the employment of women. Again, the experience of Singapore illustrates a pattern that is common to all the Asian NICs. In 1955, women made up only 18% of total manufacturing employment in Singapore. By 1980–1983, they made up 43% of manufacturing employment. In 1991, this figure reached 50%. This rapid rise in the participation rate of women in the labour force enabled Singapore to sustain high rates of economic growth as it counteracted the decline in fertility which took place through this period. One important factor which explains this trend is the increase in educational opportunities for women. By 1987, Singapore (as well as the other Asian NICs) had provided primary education for all girls. At the secondary school level the enrolment rates for girls were as high as, or higher than, the enrolment rates for boys (World Bank 1993:47). A similar pattern can be observed in the other Asian NICs (Papanek 1988:72; Cho and Koo 1983).

Growth of Productivity

The high savings and investment rates of the Asian NICs since the 1960s are reflected in high rates of growth of productivity in the manufacturing sector, in spite of a concentration in labour-intensive exports. Table 2.7, which shows data from the Singapore economy, illustrates this.

As the table shows, productivity growth in the manufacturing sector in Singapore grew at an average of 4.4% per annum between 1975 and 1990. In some years (1981 and 1983) productivity growth was between 8% and 9% (Economic Committee 1986:222). Between 1966 and 1974, productivity growth in manufacturing increased by 7% per annum (Lim and Pang 1986:63). Similar growth rates can be observed in other Asian NICs. Between 1963 and 1978, productivity growth in manufacturing in South Korea increased by an average of 5.1% per annum (Roberts 1985:10). Between 1980 and 1984, the average change in labour productivity in South Korea averaged 11.5% (Amsden 1989:201). Between 1977 and 1992, average labour productivity in manufacturing grew by 5.8% in Taiwan (Council for Economic Planning and Development 1993:22). These rates of productivity growth are at least double those of most other countries and underlie the rapid growth of output and income in the Asian NICs since the 1960s (Chenery 1988:46; World Bank 1993:56).

Table 2.7

Manufacturing Productivity Growth in Singapore

Year	Prod Growth
1975	5.3
1976	4.2
1977	4.2
1978	2.6
1979	4.3
1980	6.1
1981	9.7
1982	−2.9
1983	8.3
1984	5.9
1985	−1.5
1986	13.6
1987	3.7
1988	2.0
1989	3.8
1990	4.6

Source: Economic Committee 1986, *The Singapore Economy: New Directions*, (Singapore: Ministry of Trade and Industry), Report of the Economic Committee; Department of Statistics, *Singapore Yearbook of Statistics 1990*.

Changes in Economic Structure

The rapid growth of the Asian NICs since 1960 has been associated with a shift in economic structure towards the manufacturing sector. In South Korea and Taiwan, this shift was mainly from the agricultural sector. In Hong Kong and Singapore, it was mainly from low productivity activities in the services sector (such as those associated with entrepot trade and the informal urban sector). As the Asian NICs developed modern manufacturing sectors, some of them also developed modern financial sectors. Since the 1970s, Hong Kong and Singapore have developed into important world financial centres. This is reflected in their relatively large service sectors.

The shift to manufacturing has also been accompanied by a shift towards the export of labour-intensive manufactured (as opposed to primary product) exports.

Shift towards Manufacturing

The shift in economic structure towards the manufacturing sector is consistent with the Lewis model (Lewis 1954) of the development of a dual economy. Lewis argued that less developed countries could be viewed as being made up of two distinct sectors: a large, traditional, low-productivity, subsistence agricultural sector and a small, modern, high-productivity, industrial sector. In the agricultural sector, there is surplus labour, in the sense that the marginal product of agricultural labour is zero (this contentious assumption has been shown, in principle, not to be critical to Lewis's argument [Uppal 1969]). According to Lewis, the task of economic development is to raise the savings rate in the economy, stimulate the industrial sector by increasing investment in it and transferring surplus labour from the agricultural to the industrial sector. Figure 2.7 illustrates the main features of the Lewis model.

In Figure 2.7, the agricultural sector is depicted in the lowest panel by a production function OBA, which is characterized by surplus labour of the amount LaL". After OL$_a$", the marginal product of labour in agriculture is zero (depicted by the horizontal section

Figure 2.7
The Lewis Model

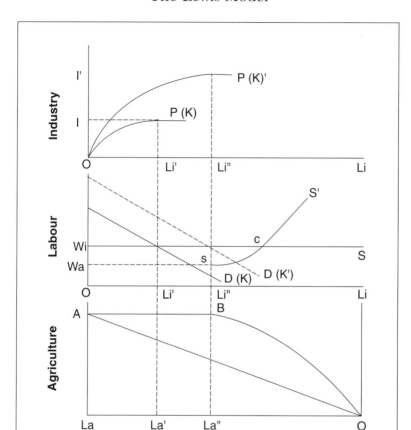

of the production function AB). All agricultural workers are, however, paid the average product of labour, depicted by the slope of the ray OA in the diagram. The vertical distance between the production function OBA and the ray OA represents the agricultural surplus (that is, the excess of production over consumption).

Economic development begins by an expansion of the industrial sector. This can be accomplished by the government offering businessmen financial incentives to invest in manufacturing industries. In order to expand the industrial sector, workers have to be persuaded to move from agriculture to industry in order to provide labour to industry. This, according to Lewis, could be achieved by entrepreneurs offering an industrial wage, W_i in the middle panel of Figure 2.7, that is only slightly higher (Lewis suggested a 30% margin) than the agricultural wage, W_a. This wage differential was to cover the higher cost of living in the urban centres (where industry would be developed) and the other (psychological and social) costs of moving away from home. At this industrial wage, there would be "unlimited" supplies of labour, depicted by the horizontal supply curve, W_iS, since the number of workers attracted to industry would be so large that a firm could expect to hire any number of workers at the industrial wage rate.

The process of economic development begins by increasing investment in industry and increasing the capital stock to K. This generates a demand for labour in the industrial sector (depicted by the curve D(K) in the middle panel of the diagram). Given the supply of labour, OL_i' of labour will be demanded. These would be drawn from the agricultural sector (L_aL_a' in the lowest panel of the diagram is the same as OL_i in the middle panel). When L_aL_a' of labour moves from agriculture to industry, agricultural output (L_aA in the lowest panel of the diagram) does not fall, because workers with zero marginal product were involved in the transfer of labour. With OL_i' of labour in the industrial sector, industrial output is OI in the top panel of the diagram (the production function in industry which corresponds to the capital stock K, is OP(K) in the top panel of the diagram).

As long as surplus labour is available, the average agricultural surplus (defined as the agricultural surplus, divided by the number of workers who leave the agricultural sector) remains constant. This is depicted in Figure 2.8 below as the angle a. As surplus labour leaves the agricultural sector, consumption of agricultural output will fall (along the ray 0A) but agricultural output remains constant at L_aA. This agricultural surplus is used to feed the workers who migrate to the cities to work in the industrial sector.

However, once all surplus labour is exhausted, any further movement of labour from agriculture to industry, will result in a fall in the average agricultural surplus (depicted by the angle b in

Figure 2.8). This is a reflection of the increasing inability of the agricultural sector to feed the population, as agricultural output falls when workers with positive marginal product leave the agricultural sector (Hall 1983:42).

Lewis assumed that all profits in industry would be reinvested, so that with a larger capital stock, K', the demand curve for labour shifts to D(K') in the middle panel of the diagram. More labour ($L_a'L_a''$ in the lowest panel of the diagram) will be drawn out of the agricultural sector. With the industrial labour force at OL_i'', industrial output will increase to OI'. This is shown in the top panel of the diagram.

Figure 2.8
Declining Average Agricultural Surplus

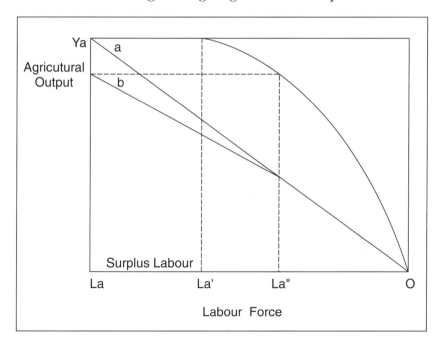

Note that even with LaL_a" labour leaving the agricultural sector, agricultural output does not fall below L_aA, since surplus labour in agriculture is still available. Any further reduction in the agricultural labour force beyond OL_a", will mean that agricultural labour with positive marginal product will be leaving the agricultural sector. This will then lead to falls in agricultural output below L_aA. Labour shortages in agriculture will begin to appear and food prices will start to rise. The agricultural wage rate will also begin to rise to the right of point s in the middle section of the diagram. Point s is therefore a very important turning point in the development process and is known as the *shortage* point of the economy, since it is after this point is reached that shortages of labour and food begin to be felt.

As further development of the industrial sector proceeds, a point will be reached when labour shortages are so acute in the agricultural sector that the agricultural wage rate will be equal to that of industry (point c in the middle panel of the diagram). This is known as the *commercialization* point of the economy, since once this point is passed, the agricultural wage will exceed the industrial wage, and the agricultural sector will have to compete with the industrial sector for labour. In order to increase productivity, the agricultural sector will have to increase investment and use modern inputs and farming techniques – in short, to become a modern, commercialized agricultural sector. Sectoral dualism will thus eventually disappear.

In one respect, the above analysis depicts the process of the shift towards manufacturing in the Asian NICs with some degree of accuracy (Oshima 1986b:789–796). As Table 2.8 shows, all the Asian NICs (even the city-states) did experience a transfer of labour out of the agricultural sector. With the exception of Hong Kong, all Asian NICs also show an increase in employment in the industrial and services sectors. Table 2.9 shows that a similar sectoral transformation can be observed in the composition of output.

For all Asian NICs, there is a clear decline in the share of GDP accounted for by agriculture, and (except for Hong Kong), a

Table 2.8
Structure of Employment (% Total)

Country	1960	1990
Agriculture		
Hong Kong	8	2
Singapore	8	0
South Korea	66	21
Taiwan	50	14
Industry		
Hong Kong	52	39
Singapore	23	35
South Korea	9	34
Taiwan	21	42
Services		
Hong Kong	40	58
Singapore	69	64
South Korea	25	45
Taiwan	29	38

0 = Less than 0.5%

Source: Far Eastern Economic Review, Asia Yearbook, (various issues).

clear increase in the share accounted for by industry. The decline in the share of GDP accounted for by industry in Hong Kong reflects the fact that by 1960, Hong Kong already had a developed industrial sector (Chen 1985:134). It is also a reflection of the increasing relocation of Hong Kong industry to the Free Trade Zones of the Peoples' Republic of China, as a response to increasing wage rates and labour shortages in Hong Kong (Cheng and Taylor 1991; Economist 1991e:15). By 1990, manufacturing accounted for only 18% of Hong Kong's GDP, while services accounted for 73%, reflecting the rapid growth of its financial sector (Mondejar 1990:70). The share of GDP accounted for by industry in Singapore,

Table 2.9
The Composition of Output (% GDP)

Country	1960	1990
Agriculture		
Hong Kong	4	0
Singapore	4	0
South Korea	37	9
Taiwan	29	5
Industry		
Hong Kong	38	26
Singapore	18	37
South Korea	20	45
Taiwan	29	39
Services		
Hong Kong	55	73
Singapore	79	63
South Korea	43	46
Taiwan	43	55

0 = Less than 1%

Source: Same as Table 2.8.

South Korea and Taiwan is large by international standards. In 1988, the share of industry in GDP in Japan was 31%, in the USA it was 21%. In this sense, many Asian NICs are more industrialized than some of the advanced industrialized countries in the world. Their dependence on the manufacturing sector is far greater than that of Japan or the USA.

The Lewis Model, however, is at variance with one important aspect of the growth experience of the Asian NICs. In the two countries which had large agricultural sectors, South Korea and Taiwan, industrial development was preceded (rather than followed) by agricultural modernization and development (Liang and Lee 1976:287; Grabowski 1988:54–60; Scitovsky 1985:220).

Like Hong Kong and Singapore (but for different reasons), South Korea and, to a greater extent, Taiwan were not burdened with large, inefficient agricultural sectors by the time they were ready to embark on export-oriented industrialization in the early 1960s. The Lewis Model, in concentrating almost exclusively on the development of industry, ignores the fact that most industrialized countries began their development by developing their agricultural sectors first, or at least at the same time as the development of industry (Oshima 1986b:787–788,802).

From Import-Substitution to Export-Expansion

With the exception of Hong Kong, all the Asian NICs began their industrial development by adopting a strategy of import-substitution. Even Singapore, with its tiny domestic market, had a brief period in the 1960s when it too adopted import-substitution policies. In the 1950s and 1960s, import-substitution was seen as the path to industrial development. Even today, many countries are still implementing these policies. By the late 1950s, both South Korea and Taiwan began to realize that import-substitution was not a viable long-term industrialization strategy and started to implement a strategy of export-oriented industrialization. The turning point in Singapore occurred in 1965, when it was forced to leave the Federation of Malaysia.

Import-Substitution as a Development Strategy

In the 1950s and 1960s, many less developed countries adopted a strategy of import-substitution in order to (a) develop industry as a means of reducing their dependence on agriculture, (b) create employment in order to absorb a rapidly growing labour force, (c) increase incomes and standards of living and (d) save scarce foreign exchange in the face of deteriorating balance of payments positions.

The policies adopted included (a) imposing tariffs and other restrictions (such as quotas and foreign exchange controls) on the imports of selected (mainly) consumer goods, leaving the domestic market for local industry, (b) maintaining an over-valued exchange rate in order to facilitate imports of capital and other inputs required for local manufacturing industry and (c) providing financial incentives to local entrepreneurs to set up manufacturing enterprises.

The logic behind the imposition of tariffs and other restrictions on imports is demonstrated in Figure 2.9. Suppose the domestic demand for a certain product which is the target for import-replacement is DD'. The world price (which is the price at which the product can be imported) is P_w. Before import-replacement takes place, $0Q_3$ of the product is imported, satisfying the entire domestic demand. Domestic production is zero, since at a price of P_w domestic supply is zero. If local production were to take place, its average costs would be higher than the import price (because of diseconomies of scale due to small market size). The local supply curve SS' does not start at the origin. Before import-replacement begins, consumers benefit from the low import price. This is reflected in the large consumers' surplus P_weD in Figure 2.9.

In order to replace imports, a tariff is placed on imports so that the domestic price is $P_d = P_w$ + tariff. At this price, the quantity demanded falls to $0Q_2$. Domestic production (which is now profitable) rises to $0Q_1$ and imports fall to Q_1Q_2. Thus, import-replacement now satisfies most of the domestic demand.

Note that after import-replacement has been implemented, consumers are worse off since they have to pay a higher price for the locally-produced product. Consumers' surplus falls to P_dcD. Local producers gain, since for infra-marginal units between 0 and Q_1 they earn producers' surplus (shown by the area SP_db). The government also gains tax revenue equal to abcd. The areas P_wSba and cde are deadweight losses.

Note that exactly the same outcome could have been obtained by restricting imports to a quota equal to Q_1Q_2 (rather than imposing a tariff). The only difference is that no tariff revenue would have been collected by the government. Instead, importers

Figure 2.9
The Welfare Effects of Import-Substitution

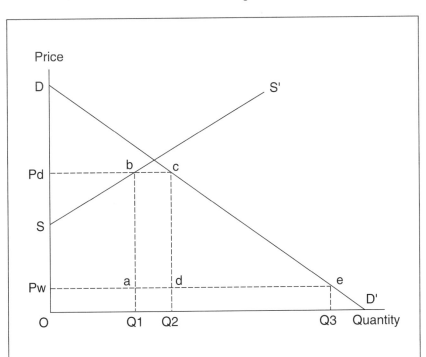

will gain, since they will be able to import Q_1Q_2 of the product at the world price, P_w, and sell this amount at the domestic price, P_d. The gain to importers is represented by the area abcd in Figure 2.9

The initial response to these policies was usually a rapid expansion of local manufacturing output. This is sometimes referred to as the "exhilaration phase" of import-substitution. In the Philippines, for example, manufacturing value-added grew by between 10% and 15% per annum during 1950–1955, as a result of import-substituting industrialization which was implemented after the Second World War. The import coefficient, measured by the ratio of consumer goods imports to total imports, fell steadily, from about 40% in 1950 to about 18% in 1965 (Paauw and Fei 1973:156). These indices, however, mask some deep-seated problems associated with import-substitution.

Import-Substitution as a Self-Terminating Strategy

By the early 1970s, many development economists were convinced that import-substitution was not a viable long-term development strategy (Little et al. 1970).

Once the domestic market was saturated, growth rates of the manufacturing sector fell dramatically. By 1965, the growth rate of manufacturing value-added in the Philippines had sunk to about 2% per annum. In addition, the employment generating effects of import-substitution turned out to be much smaller than had been expected, largely because of the adoption of capital-intensive technology. Between 1960 and 1967, manufacturing output grew by 6.1% per annum in the Philippines, while manufacturing employment grew by only 1.5% per annum (Griffin and Enos 1970:147).

In addition, the reduction in the import coefficient for consumer goods was usually accompanied by an increase in the import coefficient for producer goods. At the same time that the import coefficient for consumer goods fell from 40% to 18% in the Philippines (during 1950–1965), the share of producer goods imports in total imports rose from 50% to a peak of 70% in 1962 before falling to 63% in 1965 (Paauw and Fei 1973:156). The impact of import-substitution on total imports was to change the composition of imports. Very little foreign exchange was actually saved since local industry often had a very high import content.

The capital-intensive nature of local manufacturing industry also tended to give rise to a more unequal distribution of income as owners of capital, the small industrial labour force and those fortunate enough to obtain import licences, gained at the expense of the rest of the population.

By the early 1970s, economists began to realize that the true levels of protection placed on imports were, in many cases, much higher than suggested by nominal tariff rates (Corden 1971). When measured as the proportion to which value-added, measured in domestic prices, is allowed to exceed value-added, measured in world prices, the "effective" rate of protection (ERP) was often significantly higher than the nominal rate of protection. In some instances, domestic industries were so inefficient that the ERP was negative! (Appendix A2, at the end of this chapter presents a simple numerical and graphical explanation of these arguments). This indicates that it would have been much cheaper to import the product rather than manufacture it locally. The subsidization of local industry, when considered together with the fact that local consumers were often forced to pay domestic prices which were often much greater than world prices, pointed to a gross misallocation of scarce resources. In 1990, a locally-assembled car in the Philippines cost just under US$12,000. This was equivalent to 12 times the annual income of 80% of the population (Tiglao 1990:71).

High levels of protection also had another disadvantage. The combination of economies of scale and relatively small domestic markets meant that many firms operated at less than minimum efficient size. Their average costs were often much higher than the minimum average costs that would have been attained if their volumes were much larger. By sheltering high-cost, inefficient firms, import-substitution often resulted in manufacturing plants working with large excess capacity (in some cases, over 90% [Carver 1987:70]). This made any prospect of exporting remote, as these firms could not compete in world markets. Any attempt to reduce tariff protection was usually met with resistance from those with most to lose from such actions – entrepreneurs and workers in protected industries. Instead, rising costs over time made it necessary to increase levels of protection.

If this was not enough, high levels of protection raised the cost of production in agriculture, and this, combined with over-valued exchange rates, penalized agricultural exports.

By the end of the 1970s, most development economists and policy-makers were convinced that import-substitution was not a viable long-term development strategy. Manufacturing growth could not be sustained, employment creation was not large, income distribution often worsened and foreign exchange savings were slight, if any. The Asian NICs had appreciated these lessons 20 years before.

Export-Expansion as a Development Strategy

By the late 1950s, import-substitution, which had been implemented after the war in South Korea and Taiwan, was showing signs of market exhaustion and stagnation (Rabushka 1988:125; Byun et al. 1976:386). This, in addition to the announced intention of the USA to end foreign aid to both these countries by the early 1960s, made it necessary to consider alternative development strategies.

In the case of Singapore, its expulsion from the Federation of Malaysia in 1965 raised the question of its viability as an economic unit, given its very small domestic market and lack of natural resources. Selective import-substitution had already been implemented in the early 1960s when Singapore was preparing to be merged into its economic hinterland (the Malayan peninsular) in the Federation of Malaysia. Although this occurred, the merger proved to be short-lived and Singapore's separation from Malaysia was followed by further tariff and quota restrictions on imports from Malaysia (Lee 1973:26,94). Import-substitution, however, was never seen as a viable long-term industrialization strategy, given the small size of the domestic market. Since its founding in 1819, Singapore had always been an international centre of trade. By the late 1960s, it could no longer depend on its entrepot trade to continue to absorb its growing labour force, as neighbouring countries developed their own port facilities. To make things worse, the British Government announced, in 1966, its intention to withdraw all its military forces from Singapore within four years (British bases in Singapore had been an important source of employment for Singaporeans). In view of these developments, Singapore had little option but to embark on an export-oriented industrialization strategy when it was forced out of the Federation of Malaysia in 1965 (Lee 1973:46).

In the case of South Korea and Taiwan, import-substitution was showing all the classic signs of exhaustion by the early 1960s. In addition, the United States, which had financed much of the imports of both countries through its aid programme, announced its intention to discontinue foreign aid by the mid-1960s. In 1961,

General Park Chung Hee took over power in South Korea and launched the country into export-oriented industrialization. At about the same time, the Taiwanese government had fully appreciated the writing on the wall and switched to an export-oriented industrialization strategy.

Of all the Asian NICs, Hong Kong was the only one which did not embark on import-substitution industrialization. Since its inception, Hong Kong's main economic activity was to serve as an entrepot for trade between the rest of the world and China. The victory of the Communists in 1949 led to an economic blockade by Western countries which cut their trade and commercial links with China. Almost overnight, Hong Kong's main source of living was cut off. There was little alternative but to embark on export-oriented industrialization.

When a country has completed the first stage of import-substitution (concentrating on the replacement of consumer goods imports), there are two options which can be taken (Balassa 1988:S282–S284). The first is to continue the process of import-substitution into the second stage (concentrating on the replacement of producer goods imports). This is usually much more difficult than the first stage, since capital requirements are much higher, economies of scale are much larger, and technological expertise and requirements of skilled labour are also much greater. Very few less developed countries have taken this route successfully. The second option is to undertake a strategy of export-oriented industrialization. This was the route taken by the Asian NICs. The problem here was how to convert high-cost, inefficient industries, which had been used to years of sheltered protection under tariff and non-tariff walls, into efficient producers, capable of competing successfully with the best in world markets.

The neo-classical economist's answer to this question is in terms of a "market-oriented model" (Amsden 1991:283), which entails the dismantling of the various distortions in product and factor markets which were implemented in the course of import-substituting industrialization. The general policy prescription is to de-regulate markets, to "get prices right", so that relative prices, determined by demand and supply in well-functioning markets, can guide resource allocation efficiently into activities in which there is comparative advantage (Page 1994:3–4). This often requires dismantling tariff and other barriers to trade, allowing the market to determine the exchange rate, the rate of interest, the prices of inputs for industry and the price of labour. This does not mean that incentives should not be given to industry, but that they should be neutral, in the sense of not discriminating between imports or exports (Balassa 1988:S284) and stable, so that entrepreneurs can be confident that the system of incentives will not be reversed suddenly (Balassa 1988:S286).

In the market-oriented model, the role of government is thought to be minimal, being restricted to the provision of public goods (Economist 1990b:12), an economic environment which encourages investment and an efficient administration that helps, rather than hinders, exports (Balassa 1988:S286). Large, lumbering government bureaucracies and inefficient public enterprises are to be avoided. Commercial and industrial activity should, as far as possible, be left to private enterprise.

There is considerable debate about the extent to which the above account accurately describes the main features of the policy orientation of the Asian NICs in their pursuit of export-oriented industrialization. An alternative, "institutionalist" model (Amsden 1991:283), points out that, in reality, the governments of all the Asian NICs (even Hong Kong), intervened in the economy in various ways and continued to protect selected industries with tariff and other barriers to imports, in order to shield domestic firms (Wade 1988; Fanjzylber 1981:117–120). A more accurate picture is therefore one which portrays the transition of the Asian NICs, from import-substitution to export-oriented industrialization, as one which combines "an interaction of market forces and state intervention" (Amsden 1991:285). The experience of the Asian NICs suggests that their success is due to a combination of the provision of appropriate incentives, the development of increased production capabilities and the establishment of a number of institutions which support and nurture the process of industrial development. For example, considerable government intervention and influence persists in the South Korean financial sector, even though some wide-ranging "market-oriented" reforms were undertaken in the 1980s. While there has been some liberalization of financial markets, this does not mean that a completely market-driven system was put in place (Amsden and Euh 1993:379–390).

The role of government in orchestrating, promoting and encouraging industrial growth is central to the development effort. The Asian NICs differ in their combination of incentives, capabilities and institutions and in the extent to which their governments have actively led the development effort (Lall 1991:151–155). All have been characterized by "state intervention in the market, competently executed, and remaining within the broad parameters of a competitive market" (Fukuyama 1992:125).

The degree of government intervention in economic affairs varies considerably between the Asian NICs. Hong Kong is often regarded as occupying one end of the spectrum, where government intervention is thought to be minimal. The Hong Kong government's policy of "positive non-intervention" allows businessmen to get on with what they do best (making money) with minimal government interference. The main role of the government is to provide social infrastructure, maintain law and order, and foster an environment which does not hinder the creation of wealth (Leipziger and Thomas 1994:7).

In recent years, this view has come under attack. It is often pointed out that, even in Hong Kong, the government plays an important role in economic affairs through its control over Crown land, its provision of various economic services (such as export promotion) and its provision of public housing (Castells 1992:45–49).

At the other end of the spectrum are South Korea and Taiwan. Both these countries had been colonies of Japan until after the Second World War and had inherited the Japanese model of government administration and economic management. This involved government ownership of some key industries (banks in South Korea, public enterprises in Taiwan) and government control and guidance of key sectors of the economy which were privately owned. The South Korean government's control over the large industrial combines, the *chaebol*, through the provision of capital at subsidized rates, is an example of this. If Hong Kong lies at one end of the spectrum, with South Korea and Taiwan at the other end, Singapore occupies a position somewhere in the middle. Here the combination of a market-oriented economy with direct government participation in some industries and government control and supervision of the business sector has been developed into a fine art. Business is allowed to get on with the process of creating wealth and jobs without government interference, as long as certain well known boundaries are not infringed. For example, the pronouncements of the National Wages Council (which had the task of determining annual wage increases) were not mandatory (they were just "recommendations") but were always adhered to assiduously by both local and foreign-owned enterprises. The government participated directly in economic activity through the ownership of firms in the banking, manufacturing, public utility and service sectors. It supervised the activities of the banking and finance sector through its central bank (The Monetary Authority of Singapore), and successfully masterminded its export-oriented industrialization strategy through its Economic Development Board.

The extent of government intervention in economic affairs in the Asian NICs is therefore one of degree. The view that the Asian NICs are the epitome of the *laissez faire* system of economic organization is a myth. In South Korea and Taiwan, export-oriented industrialization was pursued at the same time as some sectors of the economy were under considerable protection (Liang 1992). All governments in the Asian NICs intervened in economic affairs. What distinguishes the Asian NICs from each other is the extent of government intervention and the degree of subtlety and finesse with which it was accomplished.

Risks of Export-Oriented Industrialization

Export-oriented industrialization appeared to solve most of the problems of import-substitution. Since tariffs were not required to protect domestic industry, the problem of supporting high-cost, inefficient industries is avoided. Export-orientation also exposes domestic firms (in the export as well as the non-export sector) to international competition and forces them to be efficient. In addition, export-oriented industrialization, based on labour-intensive manufactured goods, will avoid the problem of inappropriate capital-intensity and will generate employment. Industrialization based on exporting manufactured goods will also earn foreign exchange if it is not overly dependent on imported inputs or foreign capital (Linnemann 1987:180–222).

These advantages should be considered in the context of some disadvantages of export-oriented industrialization. First, an open economy, highly dependent on a few markets for its exports, is likely to be very vulnerable to "external shocks". The two oil crises in the 1970s and the severe recession which hit the Asian NICs in the mid-1980s, brought this painful lesson home to the Asian NICs. Second, changes in technology (robotization and computer-aided manufacturing in particular) may reduce a country's comparative advantage in manufactured goods based on relatively cheap labour. A country may also lose its comparative advantage in the manufacture of labour-intensive exports if other countries can offer even lower wages. Third, sudden changes in consumer demand may affect the exports of countries which specialize in the manufacture of certain types of consumer goods (such as toys and women's clothes). Fourth, increasing employment and incomes, coupled with declining fertility rates, will lead to upward pressure on wage rates as labour markets tighten. Fifth, success in exporting manufactured goods may make it increasingly difficult for a country to maintain its export performance, because it is likely to face increasing tariff and non-tariff barriers against its exports in its major markets and because increasing trade surpluses will put upward pressure on its exchange rate. In a sense, the very success of an export-oriented industrialization strategy makes its continuation difficult. These issues will be discussed in Chapter 6.

Changes in Income Distribution and Living Standards

The Kuznets' Hypothesis

The Kuznets' Hypothesis states that as countries move from less developed to developed country status, income distribution is likely to become more unequal first and then, at high levels of development, become more equal (Kuznets 1955). If income distribution is measured as the income share of the lowest 40% of income earners, this share would be expected to fall as economic development proceeds, reach a minimum point, and then rise at higher levels of economic development. If income inequality is measured by the Gini ratio and plotted against different levels of economic development (as represented by per capita income), the Kuznets' Hypothesis can be represented by an inverted U-shaped (or bell-shaped) curve. Charting the course of the income share of the lowest 40% of income earners at different levels of economic development would generate a U-shaped "Kuznets' curve". The principal reason for this non-linear relationship between income distribution and economic development is thought to be the operation of market forces. As labour is transferred from agriculture to industry (as in the Lewis model) during the process of industrialization, some workers (in industry) will earn much higher wages than others (in agriculture). This will tend to make the distribution of income more unequal. As more and more workers are transferred from agriculture to industry, labour shortages will eventually occur in agriculture. This will induce mechanization and the use of modern inputs such as fertilizers. Productivity and wages will tend to rise in agriculture. In industry, the influx of more and more workers will tend to have a dampening effect on wages. These developments will tend to make the distribution of income more equal at high levels of economic development.

Several statistical studies have been published which, using cross-section data, appear to confirm the Kuznets' Hypothesis (Ahluwalia 1976; Cromwell 1977; Papanek and Kyn 1986).

Critiques of the Kuznets' Hypothesis

The Kuznets' Hypothesis has been the subject of a vigorous debate amongst economists. Time-series analyses do not appear to support the existence of a U-shaped relationship between income distribution and economic development. Some countries exhibit increasing inequality of income distribution over time, whilst others exhibit the opposite pattern. There have even been some instances of a perverse relationship between income distribution and economic development, with some countries showing an improvement in income distribution followed by a deterioration (the opposite of the pattern suggested by the Kuznets' Hypothesis (Weisskopf 1976; Randolph 1990). The Kuznets' curve derived from cross-section data may tell us nothing about the pattern of income distribution of countries in the cross-section over time. In 1989, the share of income of the top 10% of income earners in Sri Lanka (whose per capita GDP was US$372) was 43%, while the share of the top 10% of income earners in Sweden (whose per capita GDP was US$20815) was 20.8%. There is no reason to believe that, as Sri Lanka develops and at some time in the future, attains Sweden's level of per capita income (US$20815), the share of the top 10% of income earners in Sri Lanka will decline to the same level as that observed for Sweden in 1989 (that is, 20.8%). The cross-section pattern of income distribution of many countries at one point in time tells us nothing about the pattern of income distribution of any particular country over time.

Figure 2.10 illustrates this argument. In Figure 2.10, income inequality is measured on the vertical axis by the Gini coefficient. Since inequality rises as the Gini coefficient increases, the Kuznets' curve is depicted as a *inverted* U-shaped curve. Suppose a cross-section of countries is taken at one point in time, say, 1970, and an inverted U-shaped curve is fitted to the data, thus supporting the Kuznets' Hypothesis. At a later point in time, say 1980, another cross-section of the same countries is taken and this also supports the Kuznets' Hypothesis. As Figure 2.10 shows, these cross-section analyses can be consistent with different patterns of income distribution over time. Some countries might exhibit continuously declining Gini coefficients (such as the path traced by the curve ab in the figure), whilst other countries might exhibit continuously increasing Gini coefficients (illustrated by the curve cd in the figure). Thus, empirical tests of the Kuznets' Hypothesis using only cross-section data may be quite misleading.

Even cross-section studies throw considerable doubt on the robustness of earlier statistical investigations, when different data sets are used. Excluding socialist countries, or countries with questionable data, from the sample often produces results that do not support the Kuznets' Hypothesis (Wright 1978; Saith 1983; Ram 1988).

The Asian NICs as Exceptions to the Kuznets' Hypothesis

Until the mid-1980s, the pattern of income distribution of the Asian NICs over time did not appear to conform to the Kuznets' Hypothesis. With the possible exception of South Korea during the 1970s, the distribution of income in the Asian NICs improved throughout much of their post-war history (Koo 1984; Islam and Kirkpatrick 1986; Rao 1988; Ranis 1985b; Chinn 1977; Hsia 1975; Lin 1978; Mizogouchi 1985). In 1965–1966, the Gini ratio of household income in Singapore and Hong Kong was 49.8% and 46.7% respectively. In South Korea and Taiwan it was 34.4% and 35.8% respectively. By 1981–1982, the Gini ratio had fallen to 44.3% in Singapore, 45.3% in Hong Kong and 30.8% in Taiwan. In South Korea, it had risen to 35.7% (Rao 1988:28). Thus, with the exception of South Korea, income distribution in the other Asian NICs improved (in most cases, steadily) during the 16 years of rapid economic growth since the mid-1960s. This led many to suggest that the Asian NICs were an exception to the Kuznets' Hypothesis (World Bank 1993:29–32). It has also led to the view that the sharing of the fruits of rapid economic growth enabled the governments of the Asian NICs to obtain the support and co-operation of all sections of their populations in the pursuit of export-oriented growth (Page 1994:5).

In the early-1980s, income distribution in Hong Kong appeared to have worsened slightly as a result of the rapid development of its financial services sector (Chen 1985:151; Bowring 1992:16–17). In 1981, the Gini ratio rose to 45.3%. A similar development can be observed in Singapore, where the Gini ratio rose to 47.4% in 1984 (Rao 1990:143–160). For Hong Kong and Singapore, levels of income inequality in the early-1980s were very close to what they were in the mid-1960s. The improvement in income distribution during the intervening years had almost completely reversed itself.

In Taiwan, the quintile ratio, which stood at about 5.0 in 1965, declined steadily to 4.17 in 1980, indicating a steady improvement in the distribution of income. Since 1980s, however, the quintile ratio has increase steadily, to reach a peak 5.18 in 1990, before declining slightly to 4.97 in 1991. As in the case of Hong Kong and Singapore, a change in the nature of the growth process resulted in deteriorating income distribution. By the mid-1980s, Taiwan had moved much of its labour-intensive industries to southern China in response to rising wages at home. From 1985 onwards, the services sector became the largest sector (in terms of employment) in the economy. In addition, speculation in real estate and on the stock exchange enabled large fortunes to be made in a relatively short space of time.

In the case of South Korea, income distribution has not been as equal as in the other Asian NICs because of a policy of encouraging a small number of large-scale industrial groups (the *chaebol*) and an attempt by the government to develop heavy industry in the 1970s by implementing import-substitution policies. Although income distribution improved (from a Gini ratio of 34.4% to 33.2%) between 1965–1970, it worsened throughout the 1970s as the government engaged in its heavy industry drive. In 1982, the Gini ratio in South Korea reached 35.7%. Since the 1980s, the South Korean government has begun to reverse its preferential policies toward its industrial groups (James et al. 1989:203). As a result, income distribution has improved. In 1988, the Gini ratio (at 33.6%) was of a similar magnitude to what it was in 1970.

Nevertheless, rural poverty remains a continuing problem in South Korea (Chung and Oh 1991).

For most Asian NICs, income distribution appears to have improved over long periods of time in the course of their development (Papanek 1988:56–63). There are several factors which account for this. First, effective land reform was implemented in South Korea and Taiwan when they were Japanese colonies. Land reform was intensified after the war, when these countries came under US influence. This, in addition to the modernization of the agricultural sector meant that South Korea and Taiwan had more favourable initial conditions (in the form of a more equal distribution of assets) than many less developed countries when they began their growth strategies. Hong Kong and Singapore never had to deal with the problem of an unequal distribution of agricultural land, or a large, stagnant farm sector. Second, all the Asian NICs invested heavily in education. Education is known to be positively associated with income equality (Ahluwalia 1976:131). By the 1980s, literacy rates in the Asian NICs were at the 90% level, while enrolments at the secondary school level were between 70% and 80%. These ratios are not very different from those of developed countries. In addition, the education of females was a prominent feature of the development of the Asian NICs. This was accompanied by an increase in the female participation rate in the labour force. Many women, who previously were unemployed, or had very low-paying jobs, were able to gain higher incomes. This helped to improve the distribution of income (Papanek 1988:70–72).

Third, all the Asian NICs experienced rapid fertility decline during the course of their development. This will be discussed in more detail in the next section. For the present, it is important to note that population growth has been identified as being a significant factor affecting income inequality. The higher the rate of population growth, especially in the rural areas, the more unequal the distribution of income (Ahluwalia 1976:132).

Fourth, the export-oriented industrialization strategy adopted by the Asian NICs involved labour-intensive manufacturing activities, which employed large amounts of labour (Fujita and James 1990).

Figure 2.10
Cross-Section Versus Time-Series Tests
of the Kuznets' Hypothesis

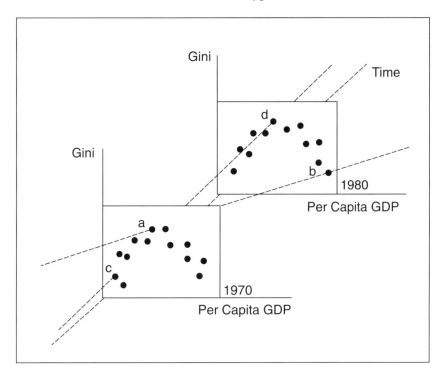

As mentioned above, female employment grew rapidly in all the Asian NICs. With the exception of South Korea, industrial development was based on the establishment of medium- and small-scale firms, avoiding the extreme concentration of wealth that is found in other countries.

The trend toward increasing equality of income distribution in the Asian NICs appears to be at variance with the Kuznets' Hypothesis. This is largely due to the fact that, in the Asian NICs, the initial distribution of assets was more equal, educational policies improved the income-earning capacity of the population, especially females, and the nature of the growth process generated employment through the growth of medium and small-scale firms. Thus, the relationship between income distribution and economic development may not always be as Kuznets had suggested, owing to the *nature* of the growth process and the configuration of initial conditions.

In the early-1980s, the nature of the growth process changed in Hong Kong and Singapore. Shortages of land and labour forced the movement of labour-intensive manufacturing industries off-shore (to southern China in the case of Hong Kong and to Malaysia, Thailand and Indonesia in the case of Singapore). In Singapore there was a move toward capital and skill-intensive industries. Another important development in both Singapore and Hong Kong, is the development of high value-added service industries (such as financial services, where large incomes can be earned). These changes in the nature of the growth process account for the increase in income inequality observed in Hong Kong, Singapore and Taiwan since the mid-1980s. The relationship between income distribution and economic development depends, not only on the level of development, but also on the nature of the growth process (Chen 1985:150).

Rising incomes and more equal income distribution over long periods of time in the Asian NICs are reflected in improvements in the standard of living. Singapore now boasts the highest standard of living in Asia, apart from Japan, and Hong Kong's standard of living is not far below that of Singapore. Life expectancy at birth in Singapore increased from 67 years in 1968 to 73 years in 1983. The infant mortality rate fell from 22 per thousand to 8 per thousand (World Bank 1990). Similar improvements can be observed in the other Asian NICs. As an illustration of material well-being, in 1989, the number of TV sets per 1,000 persons in Hong Kong was 426 and in Singapore, 315. The figure for South Korea was 278. This compares with a figure of 724 for the USA and 609 for Japan and a figure of 4 for Bangladesh (FEER 1990a:14).

Changes in Population Growth

Economic Development and Population Growth

Rapid population growth in less developed countries is commonly thought to be detrimental to economic development. It puts pressure on governments to provide social infrastructure in the form of educational and health facilities and may divert funds from productive investment in the short- to medium-term. High rates of population growth are also likely to aggravate the problem of unemployment and the inequality of income distribution, as well as put pressure on food production. The clearing of forests to increase food production is also likely to cause serious environmental problems. Productivity is also likely to fall unless investment in productive capital keeps pace with population growth. (Stavig 1976:735–750; Birdsall 1977:68–70; World Bank 1984:79–100).

There is another view, however, that argues that population growth may be beneficial to economic development because a larger population enlarges the domestic market and stimulates investment. In addition, economies of scale can be reaped with larger domestic markets. Population growth also provides labour for increased production and prevents problems associated with a rapidly ageing of the population (Simon 1986; Kelley 1988).

These divergent views are encapsulated in the notion of a *population paradox* (Thirlwall 1978:147–149). Rapid population growth may reduce output growth because it reduces productivity through diminishing returns and diverts resources away from investment. On the other hand, it may increase output growth by stimulating investment, enabling scale economies to be realized and increasing productivity. Empirical studies show that the medium- to long-term effects of population growth on output growth appear to be neutral. The negative effects of population growth on output growth appear to be offset by the positive effects (Thirlwall 1978:149–151). This does not mean that, in the short-term, rapid population growth does not cause severe problems for less developed countries. Poverty and rapid population growth appear to be closely inter-related in less developed countries (World Bank 1981:107–110; Clad 1988; Kamaluddin 1991).

Declining Fertility in the Asian NICs

In the process of economic development, fertility rates tend to decline. As standards of living rise, family size tends to become smaller for a number of reasons. Infant mortality rates normally decline with improvements in public health, the proportion of people engaged in agriculture falls with increasing urbanization, incomes and savings rise and educational attainments in the population as a whole (and particularly amongst women) increase. The increase in the educational attainments of women has been singled out as an important factor explaining the decline in fertility rates as a country develops (Jain 1981; Wong 1987).

All the Asian NICs experienced significant declines in fertility rates in the course of their rapid economic development. Between 1965 and 1973, the annual rate of population growth was 2% in Hong Kong, 1.8% in Singapore, 2.2% in South Korea and 2.4% in Taiwan. Between 1980 to the year 2000, the annual increase in population is expected to be 1.2% in Hong Kong, 1% in Singapore and 1.5% in South Korea. The rate of population increase in Taiwan was 1.7% between 1973 and 1985 and is expected to decline further by the year 2000 (World Bank 1986:229; Council for Economic Planning and Development 1986:4).

While increases in standards of living and education have been important in contributing towards the decline in fertility, all the Asian NICs have also implemented effective family planning programmes in order to accelerate fertility decline. Singapore and South Korea have "very strong" family planning programmes, whilst Hong Kong's family planning programme is regarded as "strong" by the World Bank (World Bank 1984:201). In 1983, the percentage of married women of childbearing age using contraception was 80% in Hong Kong, 71% in Singapore and 58% in South Korea (World Bank 1986:231).

Until recently, strict policies were implemented in Singapore in order to slow down its rate of population growth. These included a number of financial and non-financial disincentives (ranging from steeply rising fees in maternity wards depending on the birth-order of the child, to discriminatory treatment of third and subsequent children in the choice of school), as well as the provision of sterilization and abortion procedures at subsidized costs and upon demand (Chen 1978). These policies were so effective that, by 1990, Singapore's population growth rate had declined to less than 1% per annum and was expected to be as low as 0.2% per annum by 2025. The prospect of Singapore's population and labour force ageing rapidly and actually contracting in the first quarter of the twenty-first century led to a sudden reversal of policy. Singaporeans, particularly those with university degrees, are now being encouraged (with financial incentives) to have more children (Balakrishnan 1991a:55; Holloway 1985:42–43; Economist 1990c:33).

Improvements in Education

Education and Economic Growth

Education and economic growth are closely related. Countries with high levels of economic growth and development usually have high levels of education (Barro 1991:416–418). The link between the two lies in the effect of education on productivity (Tasker 1990:20–21). The higher the level of education and training in the work force, the higher the level of productivity is likely to be, as a result of an increased capacity to adopt, and adapt, new technology in productive activities (Meier 1989:450–454). This assumes that the supplies of different types of educated labour can be tailored to the needs of the economy, so that the problem of "graduate unemployment" can be avoided (Aznam 1987:10).

Educational Attainment in the Asian NICs

For the Asian NICs, a highly-educated and highly-trained labour force is of utmost importance, since the nature of their growth strategy involves learning, copying and adapting inventions and production processes which have been developed by other (advanced) countries. Until the late 1980s, industrial development in the Asian NICs was based on imitation rather on basic invention. As a result, governments of all the Asian NICs invested heavily in education.

In 1989, educational expenditures as a proportion of government expenditure ranged from 20% in Singapore and South Korea, to 13% in Taiwan (the figure for Hong Kong was 17%). With few exceptions, the figure for most other developing countries in Asia is in single digits. By the late 1980s, literacy rates in the Asian NICs were in the 80% to 90% range (FEER 1990b). In the early 1980s, the mean years of schooling in the work force were highest in the Asian NICs (between 6 to 8.5 years), compared with other developing Asian countries (FEER 1989:14), and the percentage of school children in primary and secondary schools was comparable with that of developed countries (World Bank 1990).

In addition to the provision of primary and secondary education, all the Asian NICs benefited from declining fertility levels, which resulted in smaller cohorts of children entering the education system. This enabled governments to provide more educational resources per child, thus increasing the quality of education (World Bank 1993:45,194). Another important feature of the provision of education in the Asian NICs is that between 65% and 83% of the government's education budget is devoted to providing basic (primary and secondary) education. This is far higher than in other countries, where a 30% share of the education budget devoted to basic education is not uncommon (World Bank 1993:199).

The abilities and performance of students in some of the Asian NICs for which data is available show that they are now of world standard. In 1989, Singapore high school students test scores in Biology, Chemistry and Physics ranked 1, 2 and 5 amongst a sample of 13 developed countries. The scores of Hong Kong students ranked 7, 3 and 2 (Johnston 1991:125). Test scores of 13-year-old students from Hong Kong were ranked 10 out of a sample of 20 countries, ahead of the scores of students from Scotland, the USA, Canada and England (World Bank 1993:71).

Although the provision of education at the primary and secondary school levels is high, the provision of tertiary education in the Asian NICs is mixed. In Singapore and Taiwan only about 6% of the work force had tertiary education in 1984 (Economic Committee 1986:119). In terms of the proportion of persons aged 20–24 years who were enrolled in higher education in 1983, the figure for Singapore and Hong Kong was 12%. For South Korea, it was 24% (World Bank 1986:237), while for Taiwan, it was 19%. At the tertiary level, there is a marked emphasis on the training of engineers and scientists. For example, between 1965 and 1990, an average of 52% of all university graduates in Singapore had engineering or science degrees. In Taiwan, about 33% of all graduates between 1965 and 1990 had engineering or science degrees. For Taiwanese graduates with overseas (mostly US) degrees, the proportion is even higher, 42%. These ratios are significantly higher than in less developed countries. In Indonesia, for example, the proportion of students in tertiary educational institutions studying science and engineering is about 16%.

South Korea is a good example of the rapid growth of education in the process of upgrading the quality of the work force. In 1951, the share of education in the government budget was 2.5%. Only 2% of the Korean population over 14 years of age had completed secondary school. By the 1980s, the share of education in the government budget had risen to 22%. This, however, represented only a third of total expenditures on education (the other two-thirds being borne by the private sector and by families). Between 1945 and 1986, elementary school enrolment increased by five times, secondary school enrolment increased by 28 times while enrolment in tertiary institutions rose by 150 times. Compared with the other Asian NICs, South Korea has the highest number of scientists and engineers per million people (Kim 1990:146–147). These advances in the provision of education are reflected in the increasing quality of the South Korean work force. The proportion of workers with secondary education increased from 7% to 49% between 1946 and 1983. In the manufacturing sector, the proportion of workers with secondary education was 66% in 1983 (Amsden 1989:222).

One important feature of the provision of education in the Asian NICs is that of the education of women. Data from Hong Kong show a pattern that is common in all the Asian NICs. In 1976, only 25% of women in Hong Kong completed secondary school. By 1986, 40% had completed secondary school and by 1992, the figure is expected to be 48%. Women with no education, or only some primary education, made up 33% of all females in 1976. This is expected to decline to 22.5% in 1992 (FEER 1990c:12). In the early 1980s, the enrolment rate among females in primary school was 107%. By contrast, in 1981, the female literacy rate in Pakistan was 14% for the country as a whole and as low as 3% in some provinces (Rashid 1989:40). Indeed, at the primary and secondary school level, the gender-gap (that is the difference in enrolments between males and females) has been eliminated in the Asian NICs (UNDP 1991:138).

By the end of the 1980s, labour shortages started becoming acute in the Asian NICs. As a result, they had to move from labour-intensive manufactured exports (in which they had become less competitive) into capital and skill-intensive, higher-technology manufactured exports and services (such as financial services). This required an even greater investment in education as this stage of industrial development required skilled labour (in the form of engineers and scientists) engaged in research and development. For the Asian NICs, the era of industrial development based primarily on learning and imitation had passed.

Conclusion

Since the 1960s, the Asian NICs have performed extremely well, in terms of economic growth and development. They have recorded rates of economic growth that are amongst the highest in the world. Within a space of 25 or 30 years, they have been transformed from poor, less developed countries (mainly agrarian or trading economies), to prosperous, semi-industrial countries. They are now important centres of world manufacturing activity and two (Hong Kong and Singapore) are important world financial centres. In terms of per capita income and living standards, Hong Kong and Singapore have surpassed several developed countries in Western Europe and are themselves on the verge of being declared "developed" by the world community.

This remarkable performance was achieved by a combination of favourable world trading conditions, good social infrastructure (developed over a long period of time), market-oriented economic policies which encouraged export-oriented manufacturing based on comparative advantage, prudent macroeconomic management of the economy which combined high growth with low rates of inflation and astute government direction and intervention which provided a stable policy environment and actively supported export-oriented industries.

There is some debate as to whether the emergence of the Asian NICs in the 1960s was a natural outcome of changing comparative advantage in the course of the development of the world economy, or the result of certain unique conditions. This is the subject of the next chapter.

The Effective Rate of Protection

The nominal rate of protection is measured by taking the ratio of the tariff on a product as a percentage of the price of the product. If a product can be imported at a world price of $1000 and a tariff of $300 is placed on it, the nominal rate of protection (NRP) is (300/1000) or 30%. This is a misleading indication of the true level of protection, since what is being protected by the tariff is not the world price of the product (the $1000), but the value-added which domestic producers can earn by making the product domestically under tariff protection (World Bank 1987:79). Value-added is defined as value of output less the cost of material inputs (that is, all inputs other than labour). Several different circumstances need to be considered when determining the true, or *effective* rate of protection (ERP).

The "Standard" Case

Suppose a product can be imported at a world price of $P_w = \$1000$. A tariff of $T = \$300$ is placed on its import. The domestic price of the product will be $P_d = \$1300$. Suppose, further, that domestic costs of production are $C_d = \$600$ and that no tariffs are placed on inputs used in the manufacture of this product. The value-added, measured in domestic prices is $VA_d = (P_d - C_d) = 700$, while the value-added, measured in world prices is $VA_w = (P_w - C_d) = 400$. Table A2.1 displays the relevant data.

The effective rate of protection (ERP) is defined as the amount by which value-added, measured in domestic prices, is allowed to exceed value-added, measured in world prices, calculated as a percentage of value-added, measured in world prices: $(VA_d - VA_w)/VA_w$. In the above example, the ERP would be: $(700–400)/400 = 75\%$, which is much higher than the nominal rate of protection of 30%. Note that the tariff is protecting value-added

Table A2.1

Value-Added in World and Domestic Prices

World price	P_w	1000
Tariff	T	300 (NRP = 30%)
Domestic price	P_d	1300 (P_w + T)
Domestic cost	C_d	600
Value-added (P_d)	VA_d	700 (P_d − C_d)
Value-added (P_w)	VA_w	400 (P_w − C_d)

Figure A2.1

The Effective Rate of Protection

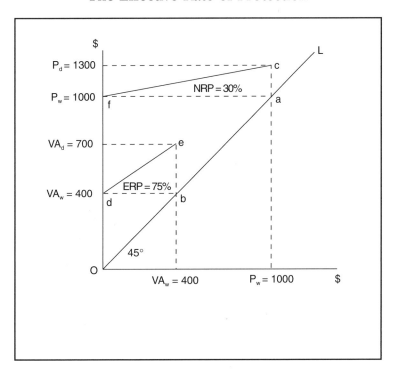

measured at domestic prices, since this is allowed to exceed value-added at world prices by exactly the amount of the tariff (VA_d−VA_w=T). Figure A2.1 illustrates this case.

Points a and b on the 45° line, OL, imply that $P_d = P_w$ and VA_d = VA_w (that is, no tariffs are imposed). The example above is depicted in the diagram as point e, where VA_d = 700 and VA_w = 400. The nominal rate of protection, NRP, is given by the slope of the ray fc, which is 30%. The ERP is given by the slope of the ray de, which is 75%. It is clear from Figure A2.1 that the ERP is much greater than the NRP. In the *standard* case, most products would fall in the upper part of the diagram, above the 45° line.

The "standard" case is also illustrated in Figure A2.2. In this figure, the "no tariff" case is shown in column A, while the "standard" case, with a tariff of $300 is shown in column B. NRP = 30%, but ERP is 75%.

The "Tariff on Inputs" Case

Suppose that the above example were amended to include the imposition of tariffs on inputs (not an uncommon occurrence). Table A2.2 displays the relevant data:

With tariffs on inputs of $400, VA_d = 300 while VA_w remains at 400. The ERP = (300–400)/400 = –100/400 = –25%. The ERP is negative because VA_d (although positive) is less than VA_w owing to the tariff on inputs. Tariff protection, in this case, has actually penalized local manufacturers. Figure A2.3 illustrates this case.

In Figure A2.3, the "no tariffs" case is depicted at point a. The nominal rate of protection, NRP, is given by the slope of the ray fc, which is 30%. The above example is depicted as point d in the Figure A2.3, where VA_d = 300 and VA_w = 400. In the "tariffs on inputs" case, products will fall in the section of the diagram below the 45° line. The ERP is given by the slope of the ray Oe, which is –25%. Again, the figure shows that the NRP grossly underestimates the ERP.

The "tariff on inputs" case is also illustrated in Figure A2.2, in column C, which shows that the tariff on inputs has reduced value-added at domestic prices to $300. Since this is less than value-added at world prices, the ERP is negative (–25%).

Table A2.2
The "Tariff on Inputs" Case

World price	P_w	1000
Tariff	T	300 (NRP = 30%)
Domestic price	P_d	1300 (P_w + T)
Domestic cost	C_d	600
Tariff on inputs	t	400
Value-added (P_d)	VA_d	300 (P_d − C_d − t)
Value-added (P_w)	VA_w	400 (P_w − C_d)

Figure A2.2
Nominal and Effective Rates of Protection

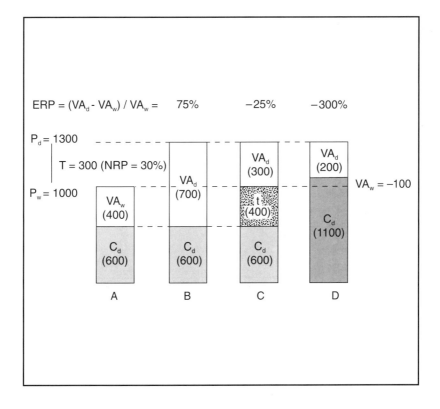

Table A2.3
The "Negative Value-Added" Case

World price	P_w	1000
Tariff	T	300 (NRP = 30%)
Domestic price	P_d	1300 (P_w + T)
Domestic cost	C_d	1100
Value-added (P_d)	VA_d	200 ($P_d - C_d$)
Value-added (P_w)	VA_w	−100 ($P_w - C_d$)

Figure A2.3
The "Tariff on Inputs" Case

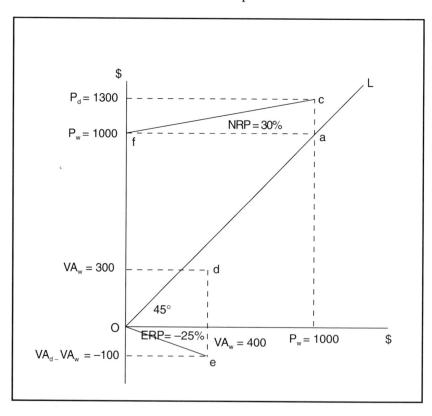

The "Negative Value-Added" Case

In the above example, suppose that there are no tariffs on inputs, but the domestic producer is so inefficient that domestic costs of production are $1,100. Table A2.3 displays the relevant data.

In this example, the domestic producer is so inefficient that VA_w is negative. In this case, the ERP = $(200 - 100)/-100 = -300\%$. The ERP is negative because VA_w is negative. Note that value-added is negative only when measured in world prices. Value-added measured in domestic prices is positive because the tariff allows the inefficient firm to survive. Industries with negative value-added measured in world prices (sometimes referred to as value-subtracting industries) have been observed in many less developed countries (Soligo and Stern 1965).

In this case, tariff protection is imposing a burden on the economy by having to support an inefficient producer. Since C_d is greater than P_w, it would have been cheaper just to import the product. Figure A2.4 illustrates this case.

In Figure A2.4, the "no tariffs" case is depicted at point a, on the 45° line. The nominal rate of protection, NRP, is given by the slope of the ray, fc, which is 30%. The above example is depicted as point d in Figure A2.4. Such cases usually fall in the left quadrant of the diagram. The ERP is given by the slope of the ray Od, which is −300%. Again, the NRP gives a very misleading picture of the true rate of protection.

The "negative value-added" case is shown in Figure A2.2 in column D. Domestic costs of production are greater than the world price, resulting in negative value-added at world prices ($VA_w = -100$). This implies that the ERP is −$300.

An appreciation of *effective* rates of protection suggests that the social costs of import-substitution under tariff protection may be much higher than might be suggested by nominal rates of protection.

Figure A2.4
The "Negative Value-Added" Case

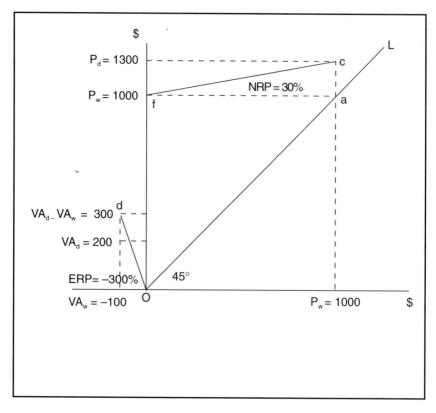

CHAPTER 3

The Emergence of the Asian NICs

Introduction

There are two main schools of thought about the emergence of the Asian NICs in the 1960s. On the one hand, what might be described as the *mainstream,* or neo-classical (sometimes referred to as the World Bank) view argues that the emergence of the Asian NICs in the 1960s was a natural outcome of the development of the world economy. As such, the Asian NICs should be regarded as only the first tier of countries which have progressed to semi-industrial country status. Other less developed countries can be expected to follow in their footsteps over time. On the other hand, what might be described as the *radical* (sometimes referred to as *revisionist)* view stresses that the emergence of the Asian NICs in the 1960s was due to a set of special factors. Because of this, it is unlikely that other less developed countries will be able to join the ranks of the Asian NICs.

The Mainstream View

The mainstream view of the emergence of the Asian NICs is associated with economists who are connected with the World Bank, which has consistently encouraged less developed countries to pursue export-oriented industrialization policies (World Bank 1987:8; World Bank 1991:88–108) as a means of accelerating economic development. Recently, economists associated with the

Asian Development Bank have also espoused this view (James et al. 1989:207).

According to this view, the emergence of the Asian NICs in the 1960s was a natural outcome of the development of the world economy. Perhaps the best-known exposition of this view is that of Balassa, in his *stages* theory of comparative advantage (1981b). Different countries have comparative advantages in producing different types of products at different stages in their development. Over time, they lose their comparative advantages in some products and concentrate on other products in which they have, or can develop, comparative advantage. The products which they can now no longer produce efficiently are taken up by other countries (at lower levels of development) which have comparative advantage in these products. The process can be thought of as countries ascending a ladder over time, moving from low technology products to higher technology products as their comparative advantage changes from the manufacture of unskilled labour-intensive products to skilled and capital-intensive products. For this reason, this argument might be described as the *technological ladder hypothesis* (Kaplinsky 1984:81).

The Technological Ladder Hypothesis

A succinct statement of this hypothesis can be found in James et al. (1989:216):

> The ever changing structure of comparative costs allows a given country to proceed up the ladder of comparative advantage from specialization in primary products to unskilled labour-intensive exports, to skilled labour-intensive exports, to capital-intensive exports, and to knowledge-intensive exports. As one country moves up the ladder, another country below is able to climb another rung: as Japan has risen on the ladder toward knowledge-intensive exports, the Asian NICs have replaced Japan as exports of skill-intensive manufactures and services and some heavy industrial goods. Similarly, as the NICs proceed through the various stages of comparative advantage, there is room for other countries to replace

them in the markets for the more labour-intensive manufactures and resource-based goods.

Similar accounts of this hypothesis can be found in Balassa (1981a:22–23), Athukorala (1989:111), OECD (1988:4), Griffith (1987:66–67) and Bruton (1989:1610–1611).

The process involved may be presented graphically, as in Figure 3.1.

Figure 3.1
The Technological Ladder Hypothesis

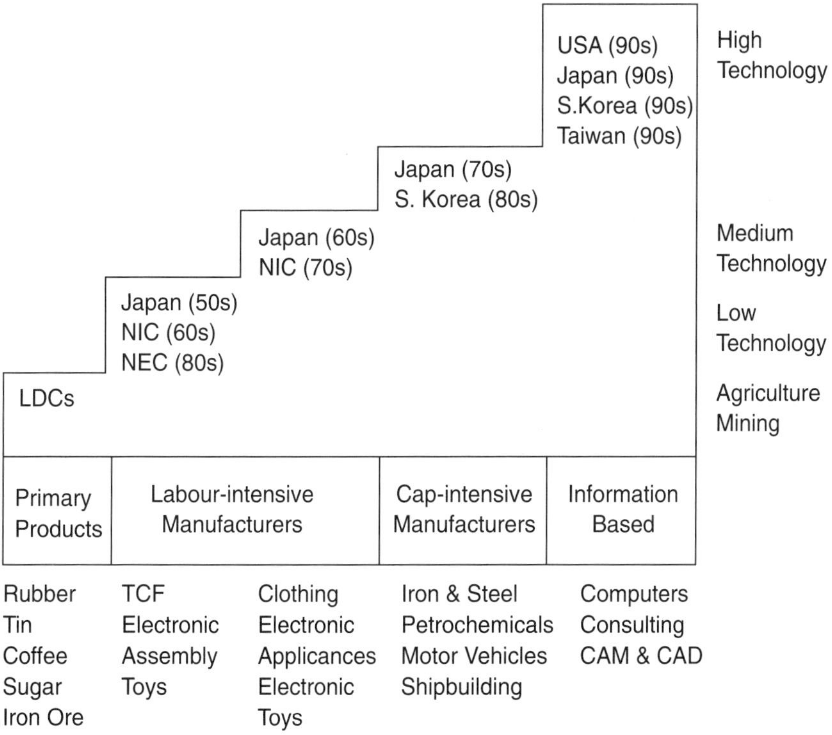

		USA (90s)	High
		Japan (90s)	Technology
		S.Korea (90s)	
		Taiwan (90s)	
	Japan (70s)		
	S. Korea (80s)		
Japan (60s)			Medium
NIC (70s)			Technology
Japan (50s)			Low
NIC (60s)			Technology
NEC (80s)			
LDCs			Agriculture
			Mining

Primary Products	Labour-intensive Manufacturers	Cap-intensive Manufacturers	Information Based
Rubber	TCF	Clothing	Iron & Steel	Computers
Tin	Electronic	Electronic	Petrochemicals	Consulting
Coffee	Assembly	Applicances	Motor Vehicles	CAM & CAD
Sugar	Toys	Electronic	Shipbuilding	
Iron Ore		Toys		

At the bottom of the technological ladder are the less developed countries of the world, which specialize in the export of primary products (mainly food, cash crops and minerals). In the 1960s, the advanced industrial countries (such as the USA, the UK and Japan) began to lose their comparative advantage in the production of labour-intensive manufactured goods (such as Textiles, Clothing and Footwear [TCF], simple toys, etc.). This occurred because of rising wage rates and declining productivity in these countries.

The USA provides an example of this. In 1960, the rate of inflation in the USA was about 1% per annum. By 1970 it had reached 6.5% per annum. Between 1963 and 1971, average real weekly wages in the USA grew by an average of 19% per annum, while labour productivity growth declined from 3.1% per annum during 1958–1967 to 0.4% per annum during 1967–1976. This made the production of labour-intensive goods unprofitable.

In the United Kingdom, wage inflation soared under the Wilson Labour Government, leading to severe balance of payments crises and the necessity to devalue the pound (for the first time in its history) in 1968.

In Japan, rising wages made labour-intensive manufactures, such as garments, uncompetitive by the mid-1960s. The decline in Japan's clothing exports and the rise in the clothing exports of the Asian NICs since the mid-1960s is a reflection of this (Nemetz 1990:9; Yamazawa 1993:1–8).

As a result of these changes, the developed countries had to move up to more sophisticated, middle technology goods (such as electrical appliances, higher value-added clothing, etc.). About this time, the Asian NICs (Hong Kong, South Korea and Taiwan initially, Singapore later on) took up the manufacture of labour-intensive manufactured goods (TCF products, electronic components assembly, etc.)

The movement of the production of labour-intensive goods from the advanced industrial countries to the Asian NICs was accomplished by the export of capital in the form of foreign investment and by the transfer of technology through licensing agreements. Indeed, foreign investment by the advanced industrial countries to the Asian NICs enabled the former as well as the latter to ascend the technological ladder (Riedel 1991:143).

By the late 1970s, the Asian NICs themselves were becoming less and less competitive in manufacturing labour-intensive goods, due to tightening labour markets and rising wage rates. This caused the Asian NICs to move up to producing middle-technology goods for export, whilst the advanced industrial countries moved up to producing capital-intensive goods. At the same time, some less developed countries had begun to become efficient at producing labour-intensive goods. These countries are known as the "New Exporting Countries" (NECs). In Southeast Asia, Malaysia and Thailand fall into this category of countries. Table 3.1 reflects these changes in comparative advantage:

Table 3.1
Changes in Export Structure
(% Total Exports)

Item	Textiles & Clothing			Machinery		
Year	1970	1980	1989	1970	1980	1989
Hong Kong	44.3	40.7	39.5	11.8	17.5	23.3
Singapore	5.6	4.3	5.0	11.0	26.8	47.0
South Korea	41.1	29.9	23.9	7.2	20.3	35.0
Taiwan	29.0	21.8	16.3	16.7	24.7	35.6
Indonesia	0.2	0.7	4.3	0.0	0.0	0.5
Malaysia	0.7	2.9	5.5	1.6	11.5	28.2
Philippines	2.2	6.7	7.9	0.1	2.1	9.7
Thailand	7.5	10.0	17.1	0.1	5.9	15.4
China	NA	10.0	17.1	0.1	5.9	15.4

Source: ESCAP 1991, Management of external sector policy, *Economic and Social Survey of Asia and the Pacific*, p. 151.

As the table shows, by the end of the 1980s, all the Asian NICs had reduced shares of textiles and clothing in their total exports and all had increased shares of machinery in their total exports. Over the same period of time, all the near-NICs and even China had rapidly rising shares of textiles and clothing in their total exports. Some near-NICs (particularly Malaysia, the Philippines and Thailand) had also begun to export various types of machinery in increasing proportions. Much of this increase in labour-intensive exports and in machinery exports, was due to the Asian NICs and Japan moving their production facilities into the near-NICs in order to take advantage of lower costs. As in the case of the Asian NICs, foreign investment was the transmission mechanism which facilitated the industrialization of the near-NICs.

In the 1980s, some Asian NICs (for example, South Korea), had begun to produce capital-intensive goods (such as motor vehicles and steel) for export (Nemetz 1990:10–13). By the 1990s, South Korea, Taiwan and Singapore had begun to export computers, computer peripherals and other information-based products.

This process can also be observed within a particular industry. In the electronics industry, for example, comparative advantage in the production of components shifted from the USA and Japan to the Asian NICs in the 1960s and 1970s, and from the Asian NICs to the near-NICs in the 1980s. A similar shift can be observed in the production of consumer electronics (radios, TV sets, etc.). By the late 1980s, even the production of some industrial electronic products (numerically-controlled machine tools, computer-aided manufacturing equipment, etc.) had moved from Japan and the USA to the Asian NICs (Chen 1990:51–60).

This process has been likened to the *flying geese* pattern of development, first suggested by the Japanese economist, Akamatsu (1962). According to this view, the developed countries are like the leader in a flock of geese flying in a V-shaped formation. The less developed countries are the followers, slowly catching up with the leader. By 1984, the Asian NICs emerged as major exporters of electronic products, with total exports of US$15.3 billion (twice their value in 1979). By the mid-1980s, exports of electronic products by the Asian NICs exceeded that of the EU, while the USA became a net importer of electronic products. By 1986, the production of most electronic products (TV sets, radios, audio tape recorders) by the Asian NICs exceeded that of Japan (Kang 1989:55). By the early 1990s, South Korea had begun to challenge Japanese domination in the production of video cassette recorders (VCRS). Clearly, by moving up the technological ladder, the Asian NICs maintained their dominant position in the production and exports of electronic products (Krommenacker 1986:396–397).

The technological ladder hypothesis therefore suggests that the development of the world economy is associated with some countries gradually losing comparative advantage in the production of certain commodities, and as a result, moving into the production of higher technology products. Their position, lower on the technological ladder, is taken by other countries which now have comparative advantage in producing the products which the countries above them can no longer produce. Over time, these countries too will start losing their comparative advantage and have to move up the technological ladder, while still other countries move in below them to take their previous position (Amsden 1983; Lin and Sung 1985; Jaffe 1988). In consumer electronics, this can be seen in the shifting of production of certain types of electronic products from Japan to the Asian NICs (such as South Korea and Hong Kong) in the 1970s and 1980s, and to the near-NICs (such as Malaysia and Thailand) in the 1980s and 1990s (Porter 1990:50,64).

Another interesting analogy which captures this sequential development is that of a relay race, given by Griffith (1987:66–67):

There is a view which suggests that over a period of time the more advanced of the less developed countries will lose their comparative advantage in the production of certain manufactures to a second tier of less developed countries which will in turn lose their comparative advantage to another tier of less developed countries lower down the ladder of development. It is a relay race ... in which the first tier of manufacturing developing countries to start, passes the baton to the second tier, and then limps behind.

The technological ladder hypothesis suggests that, over time, gaps will appear in the international trading system, as some countries lose their comparative advantage in the production and export of some commodities. This is a natural outcome of the development of the world economy and provides opportunities for other countries lower down on the technological ladder to move up and take over the production and export of those commodities which the countries above them are no longer able to produce competitively.

Not all countries will be able to take advantage of the opportunities which open up as a result of these changes in comparative advantage. Countries which are able to do so must satisfy a number of conditions. Not only must they have the adequate social infrastructure (transport and communications, an educated labour force, etc.) that comes with a certain level of development, but they must also implement a number of economic policies which make them attractive as production sites for the industries which the countries above them on the technological ladder can no longer support. This is what the Asian NICs did, and this explains why only a few countries were able to take advantage of the gaps which opened up in the international trading system in the 1960s.

The Pursuit of Market-Oriented Policies

According to the mainstream view, the Asian NICs were able to ascend the technological ladder in the 1960s by implementing a number of economic policies which enabled them to take advantage of the changes in the international trading system. One of these was the pursuit of market-oriented policies which involved, amongst other things, "getting prices right". This meant intervening in markets less (Economist 1991a:73) and allowing the forces of international competition to set relative prices. This enabled them to allocate their scarce resources efficiently into export-oriented industries (Page 1994:3–4). The correction of distortions in trade (tariffs and quotas), foreign exchange (over-valued exchange rates) and interest rates (under-valued), gives rise to a competitive domestic market economy and allows a country to specialize in areas in which it has comparative advantage. A good example of this, is the removal of quotas on imports in South Korea. In 1958, only about 5% of all import items in South Korea were not subject to quota restrictions. By 1984, this figure had risen to 85% of all import items (World Bank 1987:100). This does not mean that no import restrictions were maintained to protect selected domestic industries. In both South Korea and Taiwan, some import restrictions remained, but they did not result in excessive price distortions, and they diminished over time (OECD 1988:36,41).

In the financial market, "getting prices right" involved the liberation from financial repression (Economist 1993b:82). Under import-substituting industrialization, interest rates had been kept artificially low in order to stimulate investment (particularly in South Korea and Taiwan). One consequence of this was that savings were discouraged as real interest rates were often negative on account of high rates of inflation. In the mid-1960s, the shift to export-oriented industrialization was accompanied by financial reforms which allowed the rate of interest to rise above the rate of inflation. With positive real interest rates, savings were encouraged. The experience of South Korea provides an illustration of this. In 1960–1964, the real deposit rate averaged –0.7% while the average savings ratio was 4.9% of GNP. In 1965 a number of financial reforms were undertaken as South Korea adopted an export-oriented industrialization strategy. The Won was devalued and a single exchange rate replaced a system of multiple exchange rates. Major reforms in banking saw the official rates of interest on savings deposits rise from 15% to 30%. This stimulated savings and, coupled with increases in charges for government services, put less pressure on the government to finance its expenditures by printing money. As a result, the rate of inflation fell from about 20% per annum in 1960–1964 to 8% per annum in 1965–1969. The real rate of interest on savings deposits rose by between 11 percentage points to 26 percentage points, depending on maturity (McKinnon 1973:107–108). After the 1965 financial reforms, the real deposit rate averaged 14.3% over the period 1965–1969 and the savings ratio increased to 12.9%. The growth rate of the economy doubled between these two periods (Dornbusch and Reynoso 1989:205).

The importance of market-oriented policies should not be taken to mean that "getting prices right" is all that is required to ensure success in export-oriented industrialization (Krugman 1990:33-35). Indeed, some writers have argued that the role played by market-oriented polices in the success of the Asian NICs has been over-emphasized (Page 1990:413; Lall 1991:134). Amsden, in particular, argues that in the case of South Korea, "market-oriented" reforms in the financial sector did not mean that the government did not wield considerable influence in the allocation of investment funds (Amsden and Euh 1993:370–390). Other favourable factors need to be present as well. In addition to pursuing market-oriented policies in export industries, the Asian NICs also improved the quality of their factor endowments (mainly through education and training) and deployed them efficiently and effectively (through the use of competitive markets as a means of allocating resources) (Page 1994:3). In this sense, they not only took advantage of their factor endowments, but also improved their comparative advantage by upgrading the quality of their factors of production (Porter 1990:74–76). All the Asian NICs pursued an active policy of developing new products, finding new markets and of implementing the necessary policies which enabled them to take advantage of changes in the international trading system (Page 1990:412).

Export-Oriented Policies

All the Asian NICs adopted outward-looking export-oriented policies. For Hong Kong and Singapore, there was no viable alternative. Being city-states with small populations and small land masses, there was no option but to embark on export-oriented industrialization. Although South Korea and Taiwan have larger populations, they are resource-poor economies and have to export to pay for the imports they require in order to industrialize. In addition, per capita incomes in South Korea and Taiwan were so low in the early 1960s, that industrial growth and employment could not be sustained by producing just for the domestic market.

By concentrating on the export of manufactured goods, the Asian NICs were able to maximize their comparative advantage and benefit from the static and dynamic gains from trade (Krugman 1990:34). Exposure to the forces of international competition not only forced firms in the export sector to become efficient, but also put pressure on firms in the non-export sector (which supplied them with inputs) to become efficient. This enabled the industrial sector to move up to international best practice and enabled the Asian NICs to increase their productivity rapidly (Page 1991:50).

Although in theory, export incentives should be neutral, not favouring either imports or exports, in practice, many Asian NICs subsidized exports by giving export-oriented firms preferential treatment in such matters as the provision of finance, taxes on profits and access to imported inputs at world prices (Page 1994: 4–5; Leipzinger and Thomas 1994:7).

Export-financing was provided in the form of access to capital at subsidized rates of interest. In some Asian NICs, capital was directed to targeted firms and industries. Export-credit schemes and government guarantees on foreign loans were also used. Preferential access to foreign exchange to purchase imported inputs was also granted to export-oriented firms. South Korea is a particularly good example of these measures. The government, which took over the ownership of all the banks in the early 1960s, gave the large industrial combines, the *chaebols*, access to finance at heavily subsidized rates of interest (often 50% or more below market rates) on the condition that they met specified export targets. The South Korean government also guaranteed repayment of foreign loans taken out by exporting firms (Edwards 1988; Petri 1988; Wade 1988; Koo and Kim 1992:127,192).

Many Asian NICs also offered tax holidays to export-oriented firms, often exempting them from profit taxes for long periods of time. In Singapore, such firms were designated as "Pioneer firms", and given tax holidays of between five and ten years.

Taxes on imported inputs were often waived so that export-oriented firms could obtain their imported inputs at world prices. In order to ensure that these inputs were used only by export-oriented firms, Free Trade Zones and bonded warehouses were used to prevent the imported inputs from being made available to other firms. A well-known example of this is the Kaohsiung Free Trade Zone in Taiwan.

All the Asian NICs provided services which helped their export-oriented firms to penetrate foreign markets. This took the form of providing economic intelligence, subsidizing export promotion costs, establishing trade offices in their main export markets and the establishing of trading companies. For example, Singapore's Economic Development Board (EDB) has long maintained offices in all the major cities of Western Europe and the USA, gathering economic intelligence on export markets and promoting Singapore as an off-shore production site. The Singapore government also set up a trading company called INTRACO to facilitate exports.

Many Asian NICs subsidized the costs of export-oriented firms by giving them access to low cost land, factory space, water, gas, electricity and other amenities. These were usually provided in industrial estates in which infrastructure was provided at minimal or zero cost to export-oriented firms wishing to set up there. Singapore again provides an excellent example of this. Since the mid-1960s, a large number of industrial estates have been established in Singapore, the best-known is perhaps the Jurong Industrial Estate.

In order to attract export-oriented foreign-owned firms, as well as to ensure that export delivery dates are not jeopardized, many Asian NICs proscribed the role and function of trade unions and banned strikes. In addition, wages were kept low in order to keep labour-intensive manufactured exports competitive. In 1969, the South Korean government of General Park imposed wide-ranging restrictions on trade unions and banned strikes in foreign-owned firms. In Singapore, the National Wages Council which was established in the early 1970s, "recommended" annual wage rises (until the late 1970s) which were consistently below productivity increases. Wage rates were kept low and industrial disputation was minimized (in some cases, to zero) by the enactment of tough labour laws (the euphemism used for this is "disciplining labour") (Pang et al. 1989:129–130). By 1977, the number of man-days lost in Singapore due to industrial stoppages had declined from a peak of 410,891 in 1961 to zero.

The Role of Foreign Capital

Adopting export-oriented policies was only one of the ways in which the Asian NICs opened their economies to international influences. The other was their openness to foreign capital (in the form of foreign investment or foreign loans) and foreign technology (in the form of licensing agreements) (Duller 1992:45–54).

All the Asian NICs attracted foreign capital into their export industries. During 1970–1980, Singapore and Hong Kong were amongst the ten largest recipients of foreign investment amongst developing countries. In the period 1980–1990, Singapore was the largest recipient of foreign investment amongst all developing countries. Hong Kong and Taiwan were amongst the top ten largest recipients of foreign investment during this period.

In Hong Kong, South Korea and Taiwan, the dependence on foreign investment was relatively low (in 1978, between 10% and 20% of manufactured exports were from foreign-owned firms). South Korea, in particular pursued a policy of restricting foreign investment in industries where local investment could be encouraged. As a result, foreign investment was only 6% of total external borrowing in South Korea in 1983 (foreign loans made up the bulk of external borrowing) (Kim 1990:148). In Singapore, the dependence on foreign investment was very high (about 70% of manufactured exports were from foreign-owned firms) (Nayyar 1978; Chia 1989). In 1983, foreign investment in Singapore accounted for 92% of total external borrowing (Kim 1990:148).

Foreign investment brought not only capital, new technology, management skills and the training of labour, but in many cases, it also brought export markets. Foreign-owned firms usually had established markets in developed countries either for final products with established brand names, or for intermediate goods. For example, the Apple Computer Company manufactures Apple computers in Singapore and sells them throughout the world. On the other hand, Texas instruments produces computer chips in Singapore and ships them to its subsidiaries and to other firms throughout the world.

Foreign investment was only one of the ways in which the Asian NICs gained foreign technology. In South Korea, where foreign investment was not encouraged, foreign technology was acquired through the import of new machinery and through licensing agreements. During 1962–1983, South Korean firms entered into 2631 licensing agreements with foreign firms (mostly Japanese and American) (Amsden 1989:233). The high level of education in South Korea (and the other Asian NICs) facilitated the ability to learn and adapt new technologies.

The basic point about foreign investment and foreign technology is that the Asian NICs were open to foreign influences and were willing to accept them, learn from them and eventually improve on them. Unlike other countries, there was no hostility toward foreign ideas, foreign capital, and in some cases, foreign ownership. There is some empirical evidence to support the view that the degree of openness to foreign influences, in conjunction with the level of education, is positively related to economic growth (World Bank 1993:322–323).

Macroeconomic Stability

All the Asian NICs maintained macroeconomic stability by pursuing conservative monetary and fiscal policies.

Rates of inflation were (with few exceptions) kept relatively low and stable. Between 1965 and 1973, the rate of inflation was 6.3% in Hong Kong, 3.7% in Singapore, 11.3% in South Korea and 4.5% in Taiwan (Krause 1988:S47). In 1981–1990, the rate of inflation in the Asian NICs was 8.2% in Hong Kong, 2.3% in

Singapore, 6.5% in South Korea and 3.1% in Taiwan (Rowley 1991a:46). This compares favourably with other less developed countries which had significantly higher rates of inflation. For example, in the Philippines, the average rate of inflation during 1971–1980 was 15% per annum. For the period 1981–1990 it was 13% per annum. In addition, the rates of inflation in the Asian NICs were not only relatively low, but were also relatively stable. Unlike other less developed countries (those in Latin America come to mind), the rate of inflation did not exhibit wide fluctuations (World Bank 1993:110–112).

Government budgets were usually in surplus. When deficits were incurred, they were usually small and not allowed to persist for very long, or cause a crisis of confidence. As a result, inflation rates were kept low (Fry 1991a:27–29). During 1987–1992, a period of difficult trading conditions as a consequence of the world recession, Hong Kong and Singapore recorded a government budget surplus of 2.5% and 3.5% of GDP respectively. South Korea and Taiwan recorded government budget deficits of –0.2% and –0.6% of GDP respectively (most of the deficits occurring in 1991 and 1992, when the world recession began to bite). By contrast, over the same period, India and Pakistan recorded government budget deficits of –7.3% and –7.8% of GDP respectively. In the Asian NICs, government budget deficits, when they did occur, were kept small because governments did not prop up inefficient public enterprises or maintain large welfare programmes. Government-owned enterprises, whether they provide public utilities in a captive domestic market (such as telecommunications), or compete with other firms in the domestic or international market, are expected to operate as commercial firms and pay their own way. In this context, it is interesting to note that in 1992, the government-owned Singapore Airlines earned the highest profits (US$518 million) amongst all international carriers in the world. The Hong Kong-based Cathay Pacific Airlines and the Taiwan-based China Airlines were ranked second and fourth (US$391 million and US$143 million respectively) in terms of profitability (FEER 1993b:46). In 1989, government expenditure on housing, amenities, social security and welfare was 14% of government expenditure in Singapore and 10% of government expenditure in South Korea. The figures for Australia and New Zealand were 29% and 34% respectively (World Bank 1991:225).

Of the Asian NICs, only South Korea has borrowed from abroad (the other Asian NICs have no foreign debt). Between 1959–1961 and 1980–1983, public sector borrowing accounted for 56.4% of total foreign borrowing, while private sector borrowing accounted for 40% of total foreign borrowing (the rest was accounted for by foreign investment) (Amsden 1989:92). In 1970, South Korea's total foreign debt was US$2.2 billion and its foreign debt to GNP ratio was 25%. In 1980, this figure rose to US$27.4 billion (45% of GNP). By 1989, South Korea's foreign debt stood at US$33.1 billion and its foreign debt to GNP ratio stood at 15.8% of GNP. Its debt-service ratio in 1989 was 11.4%. In spite of South Korea's high level of international indebtedness in the 1970s and 1980s, it had no problems financing its debts and was never in a situation where it was plunged into a financial crisis because of an inability to replay its loans. The reason for this is that most of its loans went into export-oriented investment projects which earned foreign exchange. International creditors were always confident of being repaid and South Korea's international credit rating remained high. Indeed, by the end of the 1980s, South Korea had been able to bring its debt/GNP ratio down to relatively low levels (compared to other countries).

On the external front, the Asian NICs also managed to maintain relative stable real exchange rates. In the 1960s, the currencies of the Asian NICs were linked to the British Pound or the American Dollar. By the 1980s, all had moved to a managed floating exchange rate which was operated to ensure parallel movements *vis-à-vis* the US Dollar, the currency of their major trading partner. Although South Korea and Taiwan did devalue their currencies occasionally in order to keep their exports competitive, their real exchange rates were still relatively stable, compared with many other less developed countries. During the 1980s, the currencies of all the Asian NICs appreciated as a result of growing trade surpluses. However, the magnitude of the appreciation of their currencies was modest, when compared to that of some African and Latin American countries (World Bank 1993:114–115).

There were periods in the 1970s and 1980s when external shocks affected the Asian NICs. The two oil crises in the 1970s caused large balance of payments deficits and sharp rises in inflation in all the Asian NICs (and in many other countries in the world). The Asian NICs responded to these crises swiftly and effectively by containing inflationary pressures through tight monetary and fiscal policy and by intensifying the promotion of exports. In some Asian NICs (for example, South Korea) the exchange rate was devalued in order to give exports a further boost. In others, a freeze was put on wages so as not to aggravate inflationary pressures. Within a few years, these policies, although painful, had their intended effect and restored macroeconomic stability. Indeed, the Asian NICs were amongst the first countries to be adversely affected by external shocks, but were also amongst the first countries to recover.

The maintenance of macroeconomic stability over long periods of time was conducive to growth. Low and stable rates of inflation and stable real exchange rates encouraged foreign capital inflow as did the avoidance of external debt crises. What distinguishes the Asian NICs from other less developed countries is that they got not only prices right, but they also got basic economic fundamentals right. By maintaining macroeconomic stability, they fostered an economic environment which was conducive to high saving and investment, and which was attractive to foreign investment. Their prudent monetary and fiscal management of the economy was seen as a mark of efficient public sector management which gave confidence to local as well as foreign investors.

The Role of Government

As pointed out in the previous chapter, the role of government is now considered to be much more central to the development of the Asian NICs than previously thought (Wade 1990; Fanjzylber 1981:120–126). Governments of all the Asian NICs intervened in economic affairs by subsidizing costs, investing directly in industrial enterprises, supervising and guiding firms in their investment decisions and orchestrating and co-ordinating the export effort. Only the nature and extent of government intervention in economic affairs varies between the Asian NICs. The centrality of the role of government in the emergence and success of the Asian NICs is no longer in question (Castells 1992:55; Islam 1992:69–101)

The importance of the state in the emergence of the Asian NICs has been traced to a number of factors. One is the need to legitimize military dictatorships (as in the case of South Korea and Taiwan) (Koo and Kim 1992:144). Even in Singapore, there was a need to show that the popularly elected PAP government was better in delivering higher standards of living and increasing prosperity than the Communists which it had defeated. Another factor is military competition between states which made it necessary for governments to accelerate economic growth and industrial development in order to ensure military preparedness (Harris 1992:75). The fact that in all the Asian NICs, the government did not face opposition from other groups in society (for example, a landed gentry, an unsympathetic civil service or militant trade unions) which it had either eliminated or neutralized, made it relatively easy for the state to assume a central role in economic affairs (Castells 1992:54–55).

One important aspect of government intervention in the Asian NICs is that it was done through the operation of market signals, and monitored so that certain goals were achieved. In addition, civil servants in the Asian NICs were largely insulated from pressure groups, so that government policy was not hijacked to serve the interests of narrow interest groups. In South Korea, the provision of finance at subsidized rates of interest was made on condition that the recipients of these funds met certain specified export targets. Firms often had to compete for these funds. In Singapore, the granting of tax holidays was linked to export performance and employment creation. In both South Korea and

Singapore, wages were kept low in order to stimulate the demand for labour. So although governments did intervene, they did so by manipulating variables which affected market outcomes. This is quite different from government intervention which attempts to impose outcomes by replacing markets, or which attempts to impose outcomes which are contrary to the logic of markets. On the occasions when some Asian NICs did attempt to do this (the policy of the Singapore government to raise wages substantially during 1979–1983 is an example), the folly of such policies soon became apparent and they were quickly reversed.

Governments in the Asian NICs provided the social infrastructure needed for rapid industrialization. This included basic physical infrastructure such as an efficient road, rail, air and sea transport networks, telecommunications facilities, industrial estates and export-processing zones. In addition, governments also provided a favourable and supportive environment for business, one that encouraged the creation of wealth. Another important function of government in the Asian NICs was to provide education and training of the labour force which enabled new technology to be absorbed and which increased productivity (Page 1994:3).

The Success of the Asian NICs

The mainstream view explains the emergence and subsequent success of the Asian NICs in terms of the implementation of appropriate policies in four major areas. "Getting prices right" in the sense of establishing a competitive market-oriented economy imposed the discipline of the market in both the micro and macro levels of decision-making. Stable macroeconomic management encouraged the inflow of foreign capital and increased the ability of the economy to withstand external shocks (such as the two oil crises). Export-oriented trade policies enabled the Asian NICs to take advantage of their comparative advantage, encouraged the import of new technology and made policy mistakes highly visible. The provision of social infrastructure, particularly education, led to the rapid absorption of new technology and increased productivity (World Bank 1991:52–87).

The main implication of the mainstream view is that the success of the Asian NICs can be repeated by other less developed countries, if they adopt similar policies. The emergence, and subsequent success, of the Asian NICs, was not due to special factors, and can be emulated by other countries (Economist 1991a:73).

This view of the emergence and success of the Asian NICs appears to be consistent with Porter's theory of the determinants of international competitiveness. According to this view, countries are most likely to succeed as home bases for successful international firms if they excel in four major attributes, which Porter calls the national "diamond". These are:

- Internal factor conditions, such as skilled labour, or good infrastructure.

- Domestic demand conditions for the products and services of various industries.

- Supporting industries which are internationally competitive.

- Firm strategy, structure and rivalry, which determines how firms are created, organized, managed and the nature domestic rivalry.

The national "diamond" is a mutually reinforcing system. Advantages in one determinant (for example, good infrastructure) will also create, or improve advantages in others (for example, the competitiveness of supporting industries). In addition, countries need to excel in all the four determinants of international competitiveness, not just a few, in order to achieve and sustain success in global markets.

Two other factors are important in determining the success of nations in international competitiveness: chance and the role of government. Chance events are developments outside the control of firms. If favourable, they may create opportunities for one country's firms to capture global market share and dominate the world market for certain products. The elements of chance, which affected the Asian NICs favourably, are discussed below.

Government policy can help or hinder a country's prospects

for success in international competition. Investment in physical and human resources, policies which encourage competition, prudent financial and monetary management of the economy, are some of the ways in which governments can help a country to excel in all the determinants of international competitiveness which are depicted in the national "diamond" (Porter 1990:71–73). Porter argues that all the elements of the national "diamond" can be observed in the rise of the Asian NICs, particularly in the development of South Korea (Porter 1990:453–479).

The Radical View

The mainstream explanation of the emergence of the Asian NICs, in the 1960s, is not accepted by what may be described as the *radical* view of the emergence of the Asian NICs. Not all the authors who subscribe to this view are radical in the sense of being neo-Marxist (although some are). The term *radical* is used here to connotate an *anti-establishment* or *revisionist* view.

The radical view of the emergence of the Asian NICs should be seen in the context of dependency theories of under-development. According to these, less developed countries are caught in the stranglehold of the rich countries in the world capitalist system which needs to exploit them in order to prosper. The growth and development of the rich countries is at the expense of the poor. Development in the world economy is a zero-sum game. Wallerstein (1979:73) states this view succinctly:

> ... it is not possible theoretically for all states to "develop" simultaneously. The so-called "widening gap" is not an anomaly but a continuing basic mechanism of the operation of the world economy. Of course, some countries can "develop". But the some that rise are at the expense of others that decline.

The apparent ability of the Asian NICs to escape from underdevelopment and to industrialize successfully, presents something of a problem to those who hold the above view (Fukuyama 1992:101). One response is to characterize the growth of these countries as different, in important respects, from that of the developed countries (Cardoso 1973). Another is to explain the emergence of the Asian NICs as a unique event, due to special factors (Amin 1976:213):

> The installation of "runaway industries" originating in the United States, Japan, and Britain, in these territories (South Korea, Taiwan, Hong Kong and Singapore), has been sufficiently systematic to ensure, during the 1960s, a growth of manufacturing industry at exceptional rates ... But the very fact that they are concentrated in a few underdeveloped countries rules out the possibility of this being a development that could be extended to all the countries of the Third World.

The emergence of the Asian NICs is thus explained as a special case, unlikely to be repeated by other less developed countries (Frank 1983:331–333; Bienefeld 1981:82–83). A number of special factors are usually invoked to support this view. These may be discussed under the headings of History, Geography and Luck.

Historical Factors

South Korea and Taiwan were colonized by the Japanese from the beginning of the twentieth century up to the Second World War. Singapore was colonized by the British from the early nineteenth century up to 1957. Hong Kong is still a British colony, but is due to be returned to China in 1997. According to Reynolds (1983), Japan and Britain stand out, amongst the world's colonial powers, as being those which had most interest in helping their colonies develop. This development was undertaken primarily in the interests of the imperial powers, rather than of the colonies. Nevertheless, Japanese colonization of South Korea and Taiwan, and British colonization of Hong Kong and Singapore, developed the basic infrastructure, and created economic conditions which laid down the foundations for future development.

Japanese colonization

After the Sino-Japanese war of 1895, Taiwan (or the island of Formosa, as it was known then) came under the control of Japan. Korea became a Japanese colony after 1910. Following the Japanese victory in its war with Russia in 1905, Japan declared Korea as its protectorate and annexed it five years later. Both countries remained Japanese colonies until the end of the Second World War.

Although the people of Korea and Taiwan suffered great hardship under Japanese rule (Halliday and McCormark 1973:146–147), the Japanese did develop both agriculture and industry in these two countries. These foundations were very important in enabling South Korea and Taiwan to embark on export-oriented industrial growth in the 1960s (Wu 1987:378; Eckert 1990).

The development of the Taiwanese economy during the period of Japanese colonization provides an illustration of this view. The Japanese were interested in developing Taiwan as a source of food for Japan. With this in mind, the Japanese undertook the modernization of Taiwanese agriculture. Land reform was implemented, high-yielding seeds were introduced, irrigation systems were laid down and improved farming techniques were encouraged. In addition, the Japanese improved health and education on the island and developed social infrastructure, especially transport and communications. Industry was developed, although this was mainly concerned with food processing. By the time the Second World War broke out, Taiwan had an efficient agricultural sector, good social infrastructure and considerable industry. This colonial experience was quite different from many other colonized countries in Asia and Africa, which were of interest to the imperial powers only as a source of raw materials. Because of this, their native economic and social systems were destroyed and replaced with plantations and mines (Grabowski 1988:55–60; Fei et al. 1979:21–26; Nolan 1990:48; Oshima 1988:S109).

Agricultural development in Korea under the Japanese was not as successful (compared with Taiwan). The Japanese exploited

Korean agriculture by levying high agricultural taxes which eventually squeezed the peasantry. Although agricultural output did rise (by 2.3% per annum between 1910 and 1941), the standard of living of the majority of the Korean people fell. Korean industrial development was more successful under the Japanese, with the establishment of heavy industry in the north of the peninsular in 1930. This was done as part of Japanese preparations for war (Amsden 1989:52–54). As in Taiwan, the Japanese also established a system of education according to the Japanese model (indeed, during this period Koreans and Taiwanese were not allowed to study their own languages) and a system of centralized government and administration, some of the essential features of which survive to this day. The Japanese also created a modern infrastructure in terms of transport and communications and laid the foundation of a finance and commercial sector (Amsden 1989:31–35; Oshima 1988:S109).

British colonization

Hong Kong and Singapore were colonized by the British in the nineteenth century for the purpose of expanding British trade in the Far East. As a result, basic social infrastructure, particularly education, transport and communications, was developed. In addition, all the financial, insurance, banking and logistic services which are involved in international trade were established in these two colonies. An efficient civil service was established to provide effective government administration.

By the time Hong Kong and Singapore were ready to embark on export-oriented industrialization in the 1960s, they had highly developed transport and communications facilities, a well-developed financial sector, a highly-educated work force which was proficient in the language of international commerce, science and technology, an efficient government administration and over 100 years experience of trading with the rest of the world (Oshima 1988:110).

Geographical Factors

Geography also plays an important part in the emergence of the Asian NICs. All of them are in strategic locations and became important to the major powers in their quest for hegemony in the Far East. It was in the interests of these powers (Japan in the nineteenth century, the USA in the twentieth), to control and develop these countries. In addition, all the Asian NICs are in important economic locations. South Korea and Taiwan are close to the rapidly expanding Japanese economy. Hong Kong is the gateway to China, while Singapore is situated at the confluence of major world trade routes, and is the hub of the Southeast Asian region (Krause 1987:2–3).

Strategic location

In the nineteenth century, Korea and Formosa were perceived by Japan to be vital to her strategic interests (Mayo 1973:212–221). As explained above, this led to substantial economic development of these two countries after they came under Japanese control after 1895. In the twentieth century, South Korea and Taiwan were regarded by the USA as important bulwarks against the spread of Communism in Asia (Wang 1977:48–50; Fajnzylber 1981:127–128; Woo 1990). Between 1951 and 1965, the USA poured about US$100 million per year of aid into Taiwan (Liang and Lee 1976:296). In South Korea, US aid was of the order of about US$260 million per year between 1954 and 1963 (Krueger 1979:210). While most of this aid was in the form of military aid, some of it was instrumental in the development of infrastructure and local industry. In both South Korea and Taiwan, American aid financed the import of machinery and raw materials during their import-substitution phase (Nolan 1990:47).

The strategic location of all the Asian NICs also meant that, during their growth phase, they were sheltered under the defence umbrella of the major superpowers (the USA in the case of South Korea and Taiwan, Britain in the case of Singapore and Hong

Kong). This meant that these countries did not have to divert large amounts of resources to maintaining large defence forces and could concentrate on productive investments. In South Korea, defence spending as a proportion of GDP fell from 7.3% in 1956 to 3.3% in 1973. Even in the 1990s, military expenditures as a percentage of GDP in the Asian NICs was of the order of 4%–5%, well below that of other Asian countries (such as Pakistan, Burma and North Korea) which devoted between 6% and 9% of their GDP on military expenditures (Tai 1991:52).

Economic location

All the Asian NICs are also in important economic locations (Nolan 1990:46; Oshima 1988:S111). South Korea and Taiwan are geographically close to the major growth pole in the East, Japan. As will be discussed in Chapter 4, they have benefited from the ripple effects of the rapid economic growth of the Japanese economy in the post-war period. Hong Kong, lying at the foot of China, is the gateway to this large and important economy. Much of China's trade with the outside world passes through Hong Kong. Singapore lies geographically on major world trade routes. Most seaborne and airborne trade between Japan and Europe passes through Singapore. Singapore is also the economic hub of the Southeast Asian region and has become the centre of manufacturing and distribution activities of multinational firms servicing the entire region. In recent years, Singapore has also become the regional administrative centre of many multinational firms managing their operations east of the Suez (FEER 1991d:91). In addition, both Hong Kong and Singapore lie in time zones which enable them to deal with international financial centres around the globe on a 24-hour basis. This has greatly aided their development as world financial centres.

Political Factors

A number of special political factors appear to be associated with the emergence of the Asian NICs. The perception of external threat to survival and the nature of internal government have been thought to be important.

Siege mentality

After the Second World War, all the Asian NICs were faced with problems which threatened their very survival (Oshima 1988:S115–116). South Korea continually faced the possibility of invasion from the North. Taiwan was threatened with frequent pronouncements of the intention of the Communists to "liberate" it (Wu 1987:379; Soo 1984:105). Singapore, after its expulsion from the Federation of Malaysia in 1985, faced the real problem of its viability as an independent nation state without an economic hinterland, an island of predominantly Chinese people in a potentially hostile Malay region. Hong Kong's status as a British colony was always accepted as a temporary one, as it was due to be returned to China in 1997. With the victory of the Communists on the mainland in 1949, and the outbreak of the Korean War in 1951, the Western powers placed an economic blockade on China, thus depriving Hong Kong of its main source of livelihood – as an entrepot for Western trade with China. Like Singapore in 1965, Hong Kong was cut off from its economic hinterland, creating grave doubts about its long-term economic survival. The flood of refugees from China in the 1950s and 1960s and the intense competition for personal survival, underlined the precarious nature of economic existence in Hong Kong.

Like Japan on the eve of the Meiji Restoration, it was the threat of outside danger which put the survival of the Asian NICs into question. They were motivated to develop as quickly as possible in order to establish their claims as viable economic and political entities. Like Japan, all the Asian NICs are examples of "defensive modernizations" (Fukuyama 1992:74). The need to survive provided the incentive which propelled them into the quest for rapid economic growth (Castells 1992:58–59).

Authoritarian but efficient governments

A further factor which is often cited to explain the emergence and successful development of the Asian NICs is the nature of their governments. All the Asian NICs are governed by authoritarian governments. South Korea and Taiwan have, until recently, been governed by military dictatorships. Singapore, since its independence, has been governed by one political party, the PAP. Hong Kong has been under direct rule by Britain since its founding as a colony. Like Japan, there has been no change of government in Singapore and Taiwan since the Second World War (Economist 1991c:15; Robinson 1991; Woo 1990). Until the late 1980s, South Korea was ruled by a military dictatorship.

Authoritarian government, by itself, does not necessarily guarantee that correct policies will either be selected, or effectively implemented. The Third World is littered with the wrecks of economies which have been ruled by corrupt, inefficient, authoritarian governments. However, when authoritarian government is combined with capable, honest and efficient administration, and one that is not beholden to any particular interest group, the results can be startling (Brown 1993:50). Difficult policy decisions can be made and acted upon quickly and effectively (an important requirement in very open economies which are highly vulnerable to sudden changes in the economic environment in which they operate) without having to go through endless debate, or to avoid offending particular interest groups (Hamilton 1987:1243; Chen 1985:142). Of course, this can end up in catastrophe if the wrong decisions are taken, but even in this situation, authoritarian governments are better able to implement corrective policies because they do not have to worry about the support of sectional interests (Griffith 1987:77). An example of the opposite case is the Philippine government, which has recently diluted legislation designed to reduce tariff barriers in order to make domestic industry more competitive. Under a previous proposal, the average maximum rate of tariff protection was to be 30%, but this has been put aside in favour of maintaining a tariff rate of 50% on a large number of imports. Large import-substituting firms will be the main beneficiaries of this decision (Tiglao 1991:62–63).

Authoritarian governments in the Asian NICs have been coupled with efficient and honest public administrations. In a survey of the extent of bribery and corruption in public life, the Asian NICs were in the top six countries, with Singapore achieving a perfect score of 100. This should not be construed to mean that there is no corruption amongst public officials in Singapore or any of the other Asian NICs. On the contrary, some celebrated cases have come to light in all the Asian NICs. However, the extent of corruption in public life in the Asian NICs is generally regarded to be much less compared with other less developed countries.

Some writers have argued that it is the combination of market-oriented economic systems and paternalistic authoritarian governments which go a long way in explaining the emergence and success of the Asian NICs (Fukuyama 1992:238,241,243).

The prevalence of authoritarian governments in the Asian NICs has had another salutary effect on economic development. By maintaining long periods of political stability, they have provided a secure and predictable environment which encourages long term investment, particularly foreign investment. There is some evidence to support the view that political stability is positively related to economic growth (Barro 1991:432; Pennar 1993a:26–29).

Cultural Factors

There is considerable debate in the literature about the importance of cultural factors, particularly values, in the success of the Asian NICs. All the Asian NICs are inhabited by people of Chinese stock and all embrace the basic values of Confucianism in its various forms. This may have something to do with their economic success (Krugman 1990:35; Kim 1990:151; Koh 1987:38–39). In addition, an explanation of the economic success of the Asian NICs, couched exclusively in economic terms, appears to many to be unsatisfactory (Clegg et al. 1990:37).

The values of a society and its economic success may be

linked in two ways. Values, particularly those which emphasize achievement, may affect the quantity and quality of entrepreneurs which a society can produce. This will eventually affect economic performance. Values may also affect the work ethic of a society, as well as the attitude of people towards education and training. This will affect the quality of the labour force and ultimately, the growth performance of the economy. The quality of a country's workforce will affect the effectiveness with which it absorbs, disseminates and adapts new technologies (Oshima 1988:S106). This is particularly true of the Asian NICs, since their industrialization is based, not on basic invention, but by learning and adaptation (Amsden 1989: 3–10; Oshima 1988:S106).

The two links between values and economic performance are shown in Figure 3.2. The connection between values and economic success was first raised by Weber (1958), who argued that the rise of capitalism in Western Europe was related to the presence of people of the Protestant faith (instead of the Catholic faith). Weber argued that there were some values of the Protestant religion (for example, diligence, thrift, non-aversion to the accumulation of wealth) which favoured economic success.

The idea of a connection between values and economic success was further refined and given scientific status by the psychologist McClelland (1961), who made the link between values and entrepreneurship. McClelland argued that certain values inculcated in childhood (particularly those which stressed achievement), if prevalent in a society, would result in the creation of entrepreneurs, whose activities would be related to subsequent economic performance. A closely related theory, formulated by Hagen (1962), put a sociological element into this idea. According to Hagen, entrepreneurs usually came from elites whose path to upward mobility had been blocked by those at the very top of the social pyramid. These "blocked elites" suffered a sense of frustration and rejection which focused their energies toward excelling in commerce and industry. More recently, Porter (1990:129) has argued that cultural factors cannot be separated from economic outcomes, as they are closely intertwined with economic factors.

Cultural factors affect the environment facing firms and are important influences on the determinants of competitive advantage.

Empirical support for the view that values are related to economic growth is mixed. Some authors claim to have found statistical evidence to support this link (McClelland 1961; Teikener 1980; Freeman 1976), while others refute these claims (Scatz 1965; Mazur and Rosa 1977).

With respect to the Asian NICs, it was Kahn (1970:118,122) who first suggested that the Confucian value system of Taiwan and South Korea (Hong Kong and Singapore can be added to this list) has played a pivotal role in their economic success since the 1960s. Kahn argued that Confucianism, in its emphasis on harmonious relationships, diligence, loyalty, obedience and respect for education and learning, inculcates values which are very conducive to modern economic growth. Diligence and seriousness towards one's tasks gives rise to a work force that is hardworking, reliable and thrifty. This is often supported by the observation that workers in the Asian NICs endure the longest working hours in the world (Rowley 1991b:60). In 1985, the average number of hours worked per week in the manufacturing sector was 54 hours in South Korea, and between 44 and 48 hours in the other Asian NICs (Kim 1990:151). In addition, the Confucian work ethic also emphasizes the present rather than the life hereafter and places a high value on self-reliance (and a low value on public handouts) (Oshima 1988: S108–109,S117). The Confucian work ethic as been likened to the Protestant work ethic and the Jewish work ethic (Scitovsky 1985: 219–220). Loyalty and obedience can explain why people in the Asian NICs put up with authoritarian governments which often deprive them of basic human rights. The emphasis on harmonious relationships and loyalty explains why management and labour in the Asian NICs work together in the pursuit of national goals and regard each other as partners rather than adversaries (Tai 1989: 24–27; Waters 1990). Moreover, this harmony also extends to the relationship between government and business (Chen 1985:141). The respect for education and learning explains why the Asian NICs have some of the most educated and trained work forces in the world (Chen 1985:142; Porter 1990:465; Kim 1990:151). As Chen puts it, the success of the Asian NICs can be explained by "triangular interactions between absolutism, Confucianism, and capitalism" (1985:155).

In the case of Hong Kong, Singapore and Taiwan, which are populated by people of Chinese origin, the loyalty and trust between people of the same dialect and/or kinship group facilitates business dealings and enables a huge international network of contacts to be tapped (Mackie 1993:51,55,58).

The view that cultural values are important in explaining the emergence and economic success of the Asian NICs stresses the link between cultural values and the quality of the work force and the work ethic, rather than the link between cultural values and the quantity and quality of entrepreneurship (although the business

Figure 3.2
Values and Economic Performance

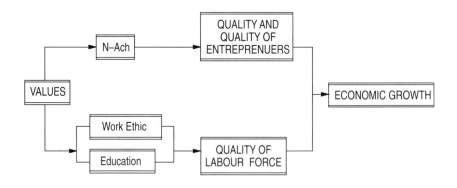

N-Ach; values emphasizing achievement

acumen of the Overseas Chinese is legendary) (Bond and Hofstede 1990:383–390). However, it should not be forgotten that Hong Kong and Taiwan benefited from the influx of entrepreneurs and industrialists who fled Communist China after 1949. Even Singapore benefited from this flow of entrepreneurial talent, although to a lesser extent. South Korea benefited from the influx of entre-preneurs from the north (which was the location of heavy industry) after the Korean War. The post-war industrialization of Hong Kong and Taiwan owes a considerable debt to the presence of these entrepreneurs (Nolan 1990:48).

The case of Singapore merits a little more attention. Much of its export-oriented industry is dominated by foreign-owned firms. This should, however, not be interpreted as a refutation of the view that cultural values are important in explaining Singapore's economic success (Chowdhury and Islam 1993:34) since this view stresses the link between cultural values and the quality of the work force rather than the link with entrepreneurship. In addition, with the exception of Japanese-owned firms, the management (even at the highest levels) of many foreign-owned firms in Singapore is now in the hands of locals.

Recently, Fukuyama (1992:224) has argued that differences in economic performance between countries can only partially be explained by differences in economic policies. Some of the differences may be attributed to differences in culture, and in particular, the work ethic. Moreover, Fukuyama argues that the experience of the Asian NICs (and Japan) suggests that individualistic self-interest (which is the basis of McClelland's theory) may be inferior to that of Confucian societies which extol the interest of the group as paramount. On the contrary, excessive individualistic self-interest may be detrimental to society as a whole (Fukuyama 1992:233). In this regard, Fukuyama echoes Kahn's arguments that the superiority of the Confucian value system is a vehicle for rapid economic growth.

An interesting example of Fukuyama's argument that differences in economic policy are only part of the explanation of the success of the Asian NICs is a comparison between Latin

America and the NICs of Asia. There is little doubt that a major reason for the slower growth of Latin American countries since the 1960s is that they did not implement the "appropriate", outward-looking, market-oriented policies which were implemented in the Asian NICs (Adams and Davis 1994:8–26). Why were the Latin American countries not able to appreciate, or to implement, the superiority of export-oriented industrialization policies? Adams and Davis, at their end of their survey of the relative economic performance of Latin American countries and the Asian NICs, puts this down to historical and cultural factors (Adams and Davis 1994:26).

Many scholars dispute the importance of cultural values in the explanation of economic success. The thrust of their critique is that it is the implementation of appropriate economic policies, not differences in values, that explains differential economic performance (Lall 1988:198; Woronoff 1986:178–184; World Bank 1993:79; Jones et al. 1993:100). Entrepreneurship is a matter of education, training and skills, not cultural heritage (World Bank 1991:57). There is no necessity to invoke superior cultural values; indeed, some see this as a sign of analytical weakness (Balassa 1988:S274). Economic factors alone can explain the emergence and success of the Asian NICs (Chowdhury and Islam 1993:33). The problem with this view is that it does not explain why only a few less developed countries in the 1960s were able to implement and sustain the economic policies which propelled them into rapid export-oriented industrialization. If it were just a matter of implementing the "right" economic policies, why did many more other less developed countries become NICs?

In addition, the view that cultural values are an important determinant of economic success smacks of cultural determinism, whose implications are unacceptable to many people. This inference is a *non sequitur*, since the work ethic which is characteristic of Confucian societies can be taught without a wholesale conversion to Confucianism (Oshima 1988:S117). Nevertheless, many people feel uneasy with the implied suggestion of cultural superiority which is associated with the view that cultural values are an important determinant of economic success (Galbriath 1979:22).

There is also the argument, that until the successful growth of the Asian NICs, their economic backwardness (in the 1950s) was often put down to the rigid, stifling straight-jacket of Confucianism, which retarded China's economic development for centuries (Pan 1988:47; Pan 1991:243; Soo 1984:105) (however, the brand of Confucianism which characterizes the Asian NICs and Japan, may be quite different from the "classical" Confucianism of ancient China (Sayle 1987:46)). Moreover, the people of Hong Kong, Singapore, South Korea and Taiwan have been Confucians for generations. Yet, they languished in stagnant, poverty-stricken, economies for decades before they embarked on export-oriented industrialization in the 1960s. Since Confucianism did not change, it must have been the change in economic policies which was the catalyst for economic growth (Balassa 1988:S276).

In countries such as Singapore, where large numbers of Overseas Chinese have settled and become economically successful, their high achievement drive may be more a function of their status as immigrants rather than their cultural values (Pan 1991:243). Indeed, with increasing economic prosperity, there has been a decline in the work ethic of the younger generation in Singapore, a prospect which is a cause for great concern to the Singapore government (Economist 1993a:29; Holloway 1987: 60–61).

A large number of trees have been cut down in the quest for an answer as to whether it is cultural values or correct economic policies that is the cause of the emergence and economic success of the Asian NICs. The answer, surely, is that it is a bit of both, plus favourable external economic conditions. It is unlikely that cultural values can be shown to be the *only*, or even the *main*, reason for the success of the Asian NICs. Appropriate values by themselves are not sufficient to generate sustained economic growth. They must be supported by the appropriate institutions which provide the opportunities for people to enter and excel in business (Lubeck 1992:192).

Cultural values which are conducive to economic growth will be of no avail, if inappropriate economic policies are implemented, or institutions are established which negate them. The economic history of China during periods of fervent Maoism attests to this. On the other hand, appropriate policies implemented in a setting in which values conducive to economic growth are absent will not be successful either. Attempts by various governments to raise the economic well-being of disadvantaged groups are an example of this.

It is more likely that a combination of favourable cultural values, in conjunction with appropriate economic policies which present opportunities for economic advancement, explains the success of the Asian NICs. This also explains why the Chinese who migrated from southern China to Southeast Asia, did not become economically successful until after they left their homeland (Wu 1983:113–114). Even in Southeast and East Asia, economic success through modern industrial growth did not begin until changes in economic policy opened up opportunities for their development.

In the case of the Asian NICs, favourable external economic conditions (to be discussed in the next section) were also crucial.

Cultural factors are an important part of the explanation of the emergence and economic success of the Asian NICs. However, this is only one of the many elements of the explanation. It is the combination of cultural factors and other favourable conditions which explains the success of the Asian NICs (Little 1979:463).

Luck

Porter (1990:73) suggests that chance events, if favourable, can play an important part in enabling firms to take advantage of new opportunities and to excel in international competitiveness. A case can be made for the view that the Asian NICs did benefit from some favourable developments which were largely outside their control. Just at the time when they had reached a level of development which enabled them to embark on export-oriented industrialization, a number of important changes took place in the international trading system. In a sense, the Asian NICs happened to be at the right place at the right time, and were able to seize on opportunities which were not open to other less developed countries (Oshima 1988:S111).

The 1960s saw four major "revolutions" in transport and communications and in manufacturing technology. The first was the development of containers for the transport of goods. The Asian NICs were amongst the first in the Third World to build container terminals to take advantage of this technology, which lowered unit transport costs. Hong Kong has the world's largest container port, while Taiwan has the world's third largest container port (Harris and Cotton 1991:112). In 1993, container-port traffic in Hong Kong was 9.2 million 20-feet equivalent units, while that of Singapore and Kaohsiung (in Taiwan) was 9.0 million and 4.6 million respectively.

The second major development was satellite communications. This made it much easier for the head offices of multinational corporations to monitor the financial position of their subsidiaries in other parts of the world and to issue corrective instructions, should this be necessary. The speed with which this could be done lowered the risks of foreign investment considerably and encouraged the large outflow of foreign investment in the 1960s.

The third development was miniaturization. Manufacturing technology (particularly in the electronics industry) enabled products to be reduced in size considerably (compare the size of the radio in the 1950s with the 1990s). In the 1960s and 1970s, it was said that a successful manufacturer of electronics goods was often forced to move to *smaller* premises. This development, combined with the container revolution in transport, reduced unit transport costs. By the 1960s, many products (for example, the manufacture of transistors and diodes in the electronics industry) had reached such a stage that relatively unskilled labour could be used in their production. This also encouraged the offshore movement of manufacturing plants by multinational companies. This was aided by the fact that by the late 1960s, the developed countries (particularly the USA and Britain) were experiencing high levels of wage inflation and declining productivity. Many labour-intensive goods could no longer be made competitively in these countries (Bienefeld 1981:91–92).

In addition to the above, the entire post-war period, from 1950 to 1973, was one in which world trade was increasing. In the 1950s, world trade was expanding by about 8% per annum (Broad and Cavanagh 1989:56) In these circumstances, the developed countries of the world, particularly the USA and countries of Western Europe, were hungry markets for manufactured goods. This aided the export-oriented industrialization strategies of the Asian NICs considerably. It has also been suggested that some Asian NICs received preferential treatment for their exports by the USA (Fajnzylber 1981:128–129).

The Asian NICs were fortunate that, just at the time when they had reached a level of development which made them ready to take advantage of the gaps in world trade and enter into export-oriented industrialization, important developments in transport and communications, manufacturing technology and world trade were taking place, which would aid them in their goals. In this sense, they happened to be at the right stage of development at the right time. Their governments were astute enough to seize the opportunities before them, and their people were willing to work hard to achieve their national goals.

In addition to the above, Taiwan (like Japan) benefited from the outbreak of the Korean War, whilst Singapore and Hong Kong benefited from the escalation of the Vietnam War. In both cases, the countries concerned received an economic boost from being part of US military supply routes (for example, Singapore was an important source of petroleum and aviation fuel for the US Air Force operating in Vietnam) and destinations for US Marines going on Rest and Recreation leave.

Conclusion

There is no single explanation for the emergence and subsequent success of the Asian NICs. Neither the mainstream, nor the radical view provides a complete explanation of their success. Both views contain some elements of truth. The mainstream view explains how, in the 1960s, changes in the international economy opened up opportunities for other countries to enter into export-oriented industrialization. The radical view explains why only a few countries in the less developed world managed to take advantage of these opportunities. In this sense, the mainstream view and the radical view are complementary to each other rather than mutually exclusive. The story of the emergence and subsequent success of the Asian NICs should be likened to that of a jig-saw puzzle. The picture makes sense only when all the major pieces have been put in place. A single piece, on its own, cannot tell the whole story. Or to use another illuminating analogy, it is only when all the tumblers fall into place, that a combination lock can be opened (Riedel 1988:2–3).

Little, in his analysis of the emergence and success of the Asian NICs, concluded that "everything can be attributed to good policies and good people" (1981:43). In the light of the above discussion, one might add "good luck" as well.

Introduction

Singapore's transition from less developed country (LDC) to Newly Industrializing Country (NIC) provides an illuminating case study which illustrates the interplay of factors which explain the emergence of the Asian NICs in the 1960s.

Founded in 1819 by Sir Stamford Raffles, it rapidly grew from a small, largely uninhabited, island to a bustling city port, soon overtaking Penang and Malacca as the centre of international trade in Southeast Asia. Its rapid growth was so spectacular that Sir Stamford Raffles was to write (Pan 1990:27):

> In little more than three years, it has risen from an insignificant fishing village to a large and prosperous town, containing at least ten thousand inhabitants of all nations actively engaged in commercial pursuits.

From its inception, the port of Singapore was established on the principle of free trade as it was to be the conduit through which international trade flowed between East and West. With the discovery of tin and the establishment of rubber plantations in surrounding countries, Singapore quickly became an entrepot, collecting and processing raw materials from its economic hinterland for export and distributing imported manufactured goods from the West to its neighbours. Trading with the rest of the world was therefore the *raison d'être* of Singapore's existence, from the beginning.

Singapore as a Less Developed Country

Colonial heritage

The British ruled Singapore for about 135 years. During this period, considerable development took place in the form of social infrastructure, public administration, education, health, law, finance and other services. A deep water harbour was established, road and rail links with the Malayan peninsular were built, an well-maintained internal road network was established and, as befits a centre of international commerce, international communications links were forged. The British also established an efficient public administration (based on the British Civil Service) and a system of education patterned along British lines, using English as the medium of instruction. University education was provided with the establishment of a medical college (later named the King Edward VII Medical College) in 1905 and Raffles College in the 1920s.

These developments were later to play an important part in the economic development of Singapore, as they laid the foundations for its transition from LDC to NIC.

A commercial and trading centre

Trade and commerce have been the life-blood of the Singapore economy since its beginning. British firms were instrumental in the development of Singapore as a centre of world trade. The great trading firms, such as Boustead, Sime Darby, Guthrie and many others, were the link between raw material producers in Malaya and other countries in the region and importers and manufacturers in Britain. They were often sole agents for manufactured goods of industrial firms in Britain. Local trading firms, run mainly by Chinese businessmen, acted as middlemen between the large British trading houses and small indigenous traders.

Around this organization of merchandise trade grew various financial institutions, such as banks, insurance firms and finance companies, as well as large shipping firms and ship-chandlers which supplied ships with all their provisions. Many of these supporting services were established by British firms. Over time, however, many Chinese firms were established to service the needs of the rapidly expanding entrepot. The foundations of the economy, as a world centre of trade and finance, had been laid.

A relatively developed city-state

By the time Singapore was granted self-government from the British in 1959, it had developed into a relatively modern, city-state. After about 135 years of development under British colonial rule, it had become a world centre of trade and finance. It boasted a world-class deep water port, excellent international communications, good social infrastructure, a well-educated, mainly English-speaking work force and an efficient public administration. In 1956, the per capita income of Singapore was estimated to be S$1,200, making it a relatively wealthy (compared with other less developed countries) LDC. Table A3.1 shows some comparative data for the 1960s to illustrate this point.

It is clear from the table above, that, the standard of living in Singapore in the 1960s was well above that of its regional neighbours. By less developed country standards, Singapore was already a relatively well developed country by the early 1960s.

However, a number of economic and political problems began to emerge. Singapore's entrepot trade, which had been the

Table A3.1
Indicators of Development, 1967

	Singapore	Malaysia	Philippines	Thailand	Indonesia
GNP/Pop (US$)	646	335	278	155	104
Pop/Doctor	1910	6220	1310	7230	31820
Pop/Nurse	600	1320	1130	5020	6500
Newspapers*	325	75	27	22	7
Telephones*	59	15	6	3	2
TV sets*	55	11	5	6	1
Cars*	62	19	6	4	4

* per 1,000 population

Source: F Felix 1972, *World Markets of Tomorrow*, (New York: Harper Row), pp. 308, 271, 295, 319, 251; World Bank, *World Development Report*, (various issues).

mainstay of the economy for over a century, began to stagnate and decline as neighbouring countries, such as Indonesia, Thailand, Malaya and the Philippines began to develop their own ports in order to trade directly with the West. This was an early warning signal that Singapore was unlikely to be able to rely on entrepot trade as the main engine of its growth. A diversification of economic activities had to be found. Manufacturing, which had been discouraged by the British because of potential competition with their manufactured exports, was limited to a few products which enjoyed natural protection due to high transport costs (for example, soft drinks, canned foods and building materials). In any case, the domestic market was considered too small to support a viable manufacturing sector. As an economic unit, Singapore had always been considered part of the Malayan peninsular, its economic hinterland. An obvious solution would be to create a single political unit, made up of Malaya and Singapore in order to take advantage of their economic complementarity. While this made impeccable economic sense (Singapore, for all intents and purposes had been the New York of Malaya), the political obstacles to this scheme proved eventually to be insurmountable.

Political uncertainty, 1959–1965

The main problem which lay in the way of a merger between Malaya and Singapore was that the vast majority of the inhabitants of the city state (over 75%) were Chinese. The Chinese also made up a significant minority (about a third) of the population of Malaya. The fear amongst the Malays was that, after merger, the Chinese would dominate economic life and later encroach on the political dominance held in Malaya by the Malays (the Chinese would, in fact, make up the majority of the total population of a merged Malaya and Singapore).

This fear was heightened by the fact that there was a pro-Communist faction in the Peoples' Action Party (PAP), the ruling party in Singapore, and that the leaders of this pro-Communist faction had attained high office within the PAP. This caused considerable anxiety in Malaya, which had been fighting a Communist insurgency since 1948. In order for the path toward merger to be clear, the PAP had to rid itself of the pro-Communists within its ranks.

An internal power struggle erupted within the PAP, leading to a split between the two factions, and the eventual defeat of the pro-Communists who later broke away to form the Barisan Socialis (Socialist Front). In Malaya, these events were watched with nervous intensity, as Singapore veered away from the brink of being governed by a Communist-dominated PAP. The possibility of this unthinkable event occurring at some time in the future was too horrendous to contemplate. A merger between the two countries appeared to be the way of preventing such a catastrophe.

In 1961, the then Prime Minister of Malaya, Tengku Abdul Rahman, proposed a Federation of Malaysia, which would comprise Malaya, Singapore, Sarawak, North Borneo and Brunei. This larger federation, it was thought, would reduce the dominance of the Chinese, by including the Malay and other indigenous peoples of Sarawak, North Borneo and Brunei. After a referendum in Singapore and a Commission of Inquiry in Sarawak and North Borneo (the Cobbold Commission) showed that the majority of the population in the territories concerned was in favour of such a merger, the Federation of Malaysia was formed in 1963.

Unfortunately, no one had consulted the Indonesians about this dramatic change in the political map of Southeast Asia. Indonesia had long since considered itself the leader of the Non-aligned Movement, a champion of anti-colonialism and the natural leader in Southeast Asian affairs. Now, all of a sudden, boundaries were being re-drawn, and political entities re-moulded, at its very doorstep. An enraged President Sukarno, beset by internal political problems of his own, unleashed his policy of *Konfrontasi* (Confrontation) against the new Federation of Malaysia by dropping paratroopers in the Malayan peninsular, sending commandos to Singapore to carry out acts of sabotage and instigating an armed revolt in Brunei, which eventually opted not to join the Federation after all.

Meanwhile, political friction began to surface between the PAP and the United Malays National Organization (UMNO), the ruling party in Peninsula Malaya. These came to a head after the PAP challenged UMNO directly, by contesting the general elections in Malaya in 1964. Political and racial tensions between the Malays and the Chinese reached a crescendo and threatened to break out in widespread inter-communal violence. The only way of averting such a catastrophe was to have Singapore leave the Federation. This it did, reluctantly, on 9 August 1965. About the same time, the internal struggle between the Communists and the military in Indonesia erupted in a failed coup attempt, the ousting of President Sukarno and the termination of the policy of confrontation against Malaysia.

The years 1959–1965 were marked by political turbulence and great uncertainty. The economic impact of these factors on the Singapore economy was dramatic. Trade with Indonesia (one of Singapore's largest trading partners at that time), slowed to a trickle. Foreign investment was hesitant and economic growth sluggish.

The Growth Phase 1965–1973

Expulsion from Malaysia

This year1965 marked the beginning of Singapore as a sovereign nation state. Cut off from its economic hinterland, its economic prospects and long-term viability were clouded in uncertainty.

With a very small land area (at that time, about 530 square kilometres at low tide), a small, but rapidly-growing population (just under 2 million people, but growing at about 4% per annum) and no natural resources to speak of, Singapore's long-term survival as an independent nation state appeared to be in serious doubt. The only things going for Singapore at that time were its superb geographical location, its well-educated and hard-working population, its long years of experience in international commerce and finance, its superb infrastructure, its efficient public service and its very able, highly intelligent political leadership. However, its separation from Malaysia and its already declining entrepot trade meant that new ways had to be found for it to earn its living.

Withdrawal of British forces

To make matters worse, the British government suddenly announced in 1966 its intention to withdraw all is forces from its military bases in Singapore by 1971. The British economy, by this time, had gone into serious decline, with severe balance of payments crises leading to the devaluation of the Pound Sterling in 1968, and Britain could no longer afford to maintain its overseas military forces in the Far East.

Although the withdrawal would not begin until 1968, it would eventually mean the displacement of some 20,000 civilian jobs, and the loss of some 14% of Singapore's GDP. This could only compound the problem of unemployment that was looming as a result of a rapidly growing labour force. Some major changes in economic strategy were required to meet these challenges.

The import-substitution phase

For a relatively brief period between 1959 and 1965, Singapore embraced a strategy of selective import-substituting industrialization through the imposition of quotas, and later tariffs, on imports of selected manufactured goods. At that time, this made good sense, since a merger with Malaya was anticipated and the resulting larger domestic market would be large enough to sustain some import replacement industries in Singapore.

With Singapore's exit from the Federation, import-substituting industrialization lost its rationale. Although one of the first consequences of the separation was a rise in import barriers in Singapore (to prevent a flood of manufactured goods from across the causeway), it was soon realized that, given its small domestic market, import-substitution did not make any economic sense in Singapore. Long-term viability lay in an industrialization strategy that was based on the export of labour-intensive manufactured goods aimed at world markets. This required a reversal of economic policy.

Export-oriented industrialization

The export-oriented industrialization strategy that was to be the corner-stone of Singapore's future development, required eliminating existing import barriers and encouraging labour-intensive export-oriented manufacturing firms to set up their operations in the city state. The Economic Development Board (EDB), originally established in 1961 to oversee Singapore's industrial development, was charged with this important task.

With the assistance of foreign (mainly United Nations) experts and a local staff of talented technocrats, the EDB set about its tasks with vigour and determination. Its main functions were to promote foreign investment in Singapore, to help in the financing and management of industrial enterprises, to underwrite the issue of shares and to guarantee loans raised by industrial enterprises, to develop industrial estates and to provide technical assistance to firms. As the operations of the EDB grew over time, many of these functions were hived off to specialist organizations. For example, development financing was later taken over by the Development Bank of Singapore and the management of the Jurong Industrial Estate was taken over by the Jurong Town Corporation.

After Singapore's separation from Malaysia, the EDB began to promote Singapore as a manufacturing platform for foreign-owned firms. The concept of Singapore as a "global city" was promoted, in order to emphasize its important position in the international grid of trade and commerce.

Singapore's geographical position, low-cost labour, excellent infrastructure, financial services and "one-stop" processing of foreign investment applications, made it an attractive location for multinational firms. Through the EDB's many overseas offices (located in most of the advanced industrial countries), large manufacturing firms were persuaded to locate their labour-intensive manufacturing operations in Singapore. In order to make such a move attractive, the government offered various financial incentives (such as tax holidays, often geared to degree of export orientation, accelerated depreciation allowances, tax deductions for export promotion expenses, etc.) and low-cost factory space in industrial estates. Often, these incentives were given in the form of a "package deal", so that potential foreign investors would deal with only one government agency when applying to set up manufacturing facilities in Singapore. The government also removed all restrictions on the flow of funds in, as well as out of Singapore, made it easy for foreign executives to work in Singapore, signed double-taxation agreements with many countries so that foreigners working in Singapore would not have to pay income tax twice and through strict labour laws and the establishment of the National Wages Council, ensured that wage rises and industrial unrest would be minimal. In addition, political stability, which also meant certainty with respect to government "open door" policy toward foreign investment, and an efficient and honest public service, also enhanced Singapore's reputation as an attractive destination for foreign investment.

Aided by favourable international conditions (rapidly growing world trade, rising inflation and growing industrial unrest in many developed countries), the various financial and other incentives offered by Singapore led to large inflows of foreign investment, leading to a massive expansion of export-oriented manufacturing, after 1965. Between 1965 and 1973, value-added in the Singapore manufacturing sector increased by an average of 23% per annum. By 1975, foreign-owned firms and firms with minority foreign participation accounted for over 70% of gross manufacturing output and over 80% of manufactured exports. Most of these investments were in labour-intensive industries, such as textiles, clothing and footwear, shipbuilding and shiprepairing, and electronic components assembly. In the 1960s, industry accounted for only 18% of GDP. This increased to 30% in 1970 and 41% in 1980. Manufactured exports, which accounted for 30% of total exports in 1965, grew to some 60% of total exports in 1975. Since most manufactured exports were made up of labour-intensive goods, employment in the manufacturing sector increased significantly, from 110,000 in 1969 to 412,000 in 1992. Total employment, however, grew from 399,000 in 1969 to 1,576,000 in 1992. Much of this was due to the expansion of other labour-intensive sectors of the economy, such as banking and finance, construction and the tourism and hospitality industries. The rate of unemployment, which stood at about 6% in the late 1960s, declined steadily to reach a low of 2.5% in 1984 and has remained around that level ever since. Indeed, by the early 1970s, labour shortages started appearing in some sectors of the economy (such as construction, manufacturing and domestic services), making it necessary for the government to allow the import of foreign workers from neighbouring countries. By 1973, some 13% of the workforce was made up of foreign workers. Singapore had moved from a labour-surplus economy, to a labour-deficit economy.

Rapid economic growth after 1965 was reflected in rising per capita incomes, increasing standards of living and a more equal distribution of income. In the 1960s, per capita incomes were growing at about 5% per annum. This doubled to just over 10% per annum in the 1970s. Real per capita GDP was about US$500 in 1960. By 1970 it was US$1,320 and reached US$5,379 in 1980. At the same time, income distribution improved, mainly due to the fact that economic growth was labour-intensive and that many labour-intensive industries (textile, clothing and footwear and electronics assembly) employed women. The female participation rate in Singapore increased from 21% in 1960 to 32.5% in 1980. In some age-groups (for example, 20–24 years and 25–29 years), the female participation rates were as high as 75%. In 1990, Singapore's quintile ratio (the ratio of the share of income of the top 20% of income earners to that of the bottom 20% of income earners) was about 7.0, putting it in the same category as South Korea, Hong Kong and Taiwan.

Emergence as an NIC, 1979–1984

By the late 1970s, Singapore had emerged as an NIC. By this time, the Singapore economy had displayed all the characteristics of an NIC – sustained, rapid economic growth, a high degree of industrialization, a concentration on the exports of manufactured goods, full employment, steadily increasing per capita incomes and rising standards of living.

Singapore now boasts the highest standard of living in Asia, apart from Japan. By the early 1990s, Singapore's per capita income had already exceeded that of some European countries (such as Ireland, Spain, Greece and Portugal) and is expected to exceed that of Australia in the mid-1990s. Other indicators of living standards, such as the percentage of households which own their own homes, electrical appliances and other physical indicators of well-being, all show indices of between 78% (washing machines) and 99% (TV sets). In the case of education, some 14% of the relevant age-group are in universities, while some 24% are in polytechnics (*Straits Times* 1992c:24).

By the late 1980s, Singapore began to experience all the characteristics of a mature NIC – declining birth rates, labour shortages, appreciating currencies and declining international competitiveness in labour-intensive exports. These are problems, however, that many other less developed countries would love to have.

Factors explaining Singapore's emergence as an NIC

The history of Singapore's transition from LDC to NIC lends support to the view that there is some element of truth in both mainstream and radical views about the emergence of the NICs.

The importance of taking advantage of one's comparative advantage in order to move up the technological ladder, the implementation of market-oriented economic policies, the pursuit of sound monetary and fiscal policies, the de-regulation of financial and other markets: all these factors fall within the prescriptions of the mainstream view.

On the other hand, government intervention in export promotion as well as in the labour market, favourable international trading conditions, good infrastructure and public administration inherited from colonial times, a highly-educated workforce, an energetic and diligent workforce imbued with an appropriate work ethic, an authoritarian government – are all factors which are emphasized by radical writers.

The Singapore experience illustrates that it is a blend of these two sets of factors that explain its transition from LDC to NIC. For this reason, it is possible that the experience of Singapore's emergence as an NIC (and, indeed, of any of the other NICs) may not be easily replicated by other less developed countries wishing to embark on the same journey.

CHAPTER 4

The Role of Japan in the Rise of the Asian NICs

Introduction

The rapid growth and development of the Japanese economy after the Second World War has had important positive effects on the growth of the Asian NICs. The rapid growth of export-oriented manufacturing capability of the Asian NICs has been aided by Japan's foreign investment and trade policies toward them. These have been aimed at developing increasing complementarity between the Japanese economy and the Asian NICs. Manufactured goods which could not be made efficiently in Japan have been transferred to Japanese overseas subsidiaries. This has comprised final consumer goods as well as producer goods. In some instances, the division of labour between Japan and the Asian NICs occurs in the same product group. Japan specializes in high quality, up-market products, whilst the Asian NICs specialize in the same product, but in the lower quality end of the market. In recent years, Japan has also been an increasingly important market for the exports of consumer goods from the Asian NICs.

Economic Complementarity

Economic complementarity refers to the degree to which trading partners become less specialized in the products they exchange through international trade. One way of measuring this is to construct trade specialization ratios.

Consider the following example. Japan exports, say, motor cars to Singapore. The trade specialization ratio of Japan with respect to Singapore, for cars, can be measured as:

$$SR_{g, c} = \frac{(EXP_{g, c} - IMP_{g, c})}{(EXP_{g, c} + IMP_{g, c})}$$

where SR = Specialization ratio
        EXP = Japanese exports
        IMP = Japanese imports
        g = the product concerned, cars, in this case
        c = the trading partner, Singapore, in this case

If Japan is completely specialized in the export of cars to Singapore, it will export cars to Singapore, but not import cars from Singapore. In this case, $IMP_{g, c} = 0$, $EXP_{g, c}$ will be some positive number, and $SR_{g, c} = 1$. Singapore, on the other hand, imports cars from Japan, but does not export cars to Japan. In Singapore's case, $EXP_{g, c} = 0$, $IMP_{g, c}$ will be some positive numbers, and $SR_{g, c} = -1$. If trade in cars between Japan and Singapore happens to be completely balanced in the sense that Japan exports, say, US$30 million of cars to Singapore, and also imports US$30 million of cars from Singapore, then $EXP_{g, c} = IMP_{g, c}$, and $SR_{g, c} = 0$.

The specialization ratio therefore takes the following limiting values. If a country is completely specialized in the export of a product *vis-à-vis* its trading partner, the specialization ratio will be 1. If a country is completely dependent on imports of a product from its trading partner, the specialization ratio will be –1. If trade is balanced, the specialization ratio will be 0.

Over time, decreasing specialization (or increasing complementarity) in trade between two countries will be reflected in a specialization ratio that will be declining, from a value of 1 towards a value of –1. Thus, in the case of the trade in cars between Japan and Singapore, if over time Singapore begins to export cars to Japan, the specialization ratio of Japan *vis-à-vis* Singapore in cars will decline from 1 to say, 0.8, 0.7 etc., over time. This is a clear indication of increasing complementarity because it means that there are some types of cars which Japan specializes in manufacturing and exporting to Singapore, whilst there are other types of cars which Singapore specializes in manufacturing and exporting to Japan.

Empirical studies of the specialization ratio of a number of commodities traded between Japan and the Asian NICs over time, do show increasing complementarity. In 1965, there were only 12 export items whose specialization ratio between Japan and the Asian NICs were between +0.5 and −0.5. By 1978, there were 26 export items whose specialization ratio fell between +0.5 and −0.5. This indicates increasing complementarity in trade between Japan and the Asian NICs (Watanabe 1980:395). Between 1965 and 1978, there has been increasing complementarity between Japan and the Asian NICs in such product groups as textile yarn, printing and publishing, chemicals, metal products, electronic equipment, etc. Most of these are producer goods rather than consumer goods. This is particularly true of Japan's trade with South Korea, which has the most developed heavy industry sector amongst the Asian NICs (Watanabe 1980:398–405). In electronics, South Korea specializes in products whose production technologies have been standardized (for example, condensers and integrated circuits). Japan, on the other hand, specializes in high technology products (for example, transducers, machine parts and audio parts) (Watanabe 1980:406).

Another interesting measure of the degree of complementarity between Japan and the Asian NICs is the index of the horizontal division of labour (Watanabe 1980:398). The index, between say, Japan and Singapore, for a product (say, TV sets), is defined as:

$$H = \frac{EXP_{g,c} + IMP_{g,c} - \mid EXP_{g,c} - IMP_{g,c} \mid}{EXP_{g,c} + IMP_{g,c}}$$

where H = index of the horizontal division of labour
         EXP = Japanese exports
         IMP = Japanese imports
           g = the product concerned, TV sets, in this case
           c = the trading partner, Singapore, in this case

If a country is completely specialized in the export of a product (that is, it does not import the product), $IMP_{g,c} = 0$, and the index of the horizontal division of labour will be 0. If a country is completely dependent on the import of a product (that is, it does not export the product), $EXP_{g,c} = 0$, and the index will also be 0. Therefore, completely unbalanced trade, either in exports or in imports, will be reflected in an index having a value of 0. If trade is completely balanced, in the sense that a country exports and imports the same amount of a product, $EXP_{g,c} = IMP_{g,c}$, and the index will be 1. Increasing complementarity between two countries, will therefore be reflected in the index of the horizontal division of labour increasing over time, towards a value of 1 (or 100%).

Many products which are traded between Japan and the Asian NICs do show an increasing value of the index of the horizontal division of labour. For example, for textile yarns, the index was 11.5% in 1965, 39.6% in 1970, and 41.9% in 1978. For printing and publishing, the index was 13.7% in 1965, 14.3% in 1970 and 90.2% in 1978. Most of the products traded between Japan and the Asian NICs show this pattern (Watanabe 1980:398). This shows that the degree of complementarity between these countries has been increasing over time.

The degree of economic complementarity between two countries can also be measured by trade intensity indexes. For any two countries, say, Japan and Singapore, the index of trade intensity is defined as:

$$I = \frac{\left(\dfrac{EXP_{j,s}}{EXP_{j,w}}\right)}{\left(\dfrac{IMP_s}{IMP_w}\right)}$$

where I = index of trade intensity
       EXP = exports
       IMP = total imports
          j = Japan
          s = Singapore
          w = world

If the index of trade intensity between Japan and Singapore is greater than 1, this means that the share of Japanese exports to Singapore as a proportion of total Japanese exports is greater than total Singapore imports as a proportion of world imports. This suggest that there is some economic complementarity between the two trading partners. In 1987, the trade intensity index between Japan and the Asian NICs was 2.207 (Singapore), 3.893 (South Korea), 3.937 (Taiwan) and 2.209 (Hong Kong). These indexes were much higher than the trade intensity indexes between the USA and the Asian NICs (Yamazawa, Hirata and Yokota 1991: 218–219).

There is, thus, a division of labour between Japan and the Asian NICs, according to comparative advantage. This can be seen in the pattern of imports into Japan from the Asian NICs. Between 1970 and 1980, 45% of Japan's imports from the Asian NICs were made up of (mainly labour-intensive) manufactured goods. The most important of these were textiles, yarns, fabrics and clothing, machinery, transport equipment, resource-based manufactures and miscellaneous manufactures. In 1981, the Asian NICs accounted for 26% of all textile, yarn and fabric imports into Japan, 46% of all clothing imports, 15% of all electrical machinery imports and 13% of all miscellaneous manufactured goods imports (Sazaname 1990:80–83). The division of labour between Japan and the Asian NICs is one in which the latter specializes in labour-intensive consumer goods and some producer goods. Japan, on the other hand, specializes in capital-intensive consumer and producer goods, which it exports to the Asian NICs. South Korea, for example, is dependent on imports for 60% of the materials and equipment in the shipbuilding industry. In metal cutting machinery, its import dependence is 80% while in textile machinery, it is 86%. Most of South Korea's imports of producer goods come from Japan (Nakajo 1980:465-66; Stillitoe 1985a:71).

In recent years, some Asian NICs have begun to export some producer goods to Japan, as their skills in producing these products efficiently have increased. In 1986, Asian NICs (mainly Taiwan and South Korea) exported ¥40 billion of machine tools to Japan. By 1990, this had increased to just under ¥80 billion. Taiwan can now offer machine tools, of comparable quality, to Japan, at prices up to 40% lower than those offered by Japanese firms. In 1989, exports of machine tools from Taiwan to Japan increased by 100%. By 1990, Taiwan accounted for about 8% of all machine tool imports into Japan. South Korea's machine tool industry is not as well developed as Taiwan's. In 1990, it accounted for only about 3% of total imports of machine tools into Japan. The increasing exports of machine tools from the Asian NICs to Japan is yet another indication of the increasing economic complementarity between these countries (do Rosario and Clifford 1991:62).

Trade between Japan and the Asian NICs

Trade patterns between the Asian NICs and Japan reflect their economic complementarity. A good example of this is the pattern of trade between South Korea and Japan. Table 4.1 shows the exports and imports of South Korea *vis-à-vis* Japan.

Japan is South Korea's main source of imports, buying US$6 billion worth of Japanese (mainly capital) goods in 1989. At the same time, South Korea is also Japan's second-largest source of imports. South Korea imports most of its component requirements from Japan and exports finished products to the USA, EU and other countries. While it has acted as a source of lower quality Japanese-style goods in the past, South Korea has, in recent years, upgraded the quality of its products and now competes with some Japanese products in world markets.

As Table 4.1 shows, nearly 33% of South Korea's imports from Japan, in 1990, were made up of machinery and a further 29% were made up of electronic products. Steel and chemicals accounted for another 31%. On the export side, 27% of South Korea's exports to Japan, in 1990, were made up of textiles, whereas food, timber and minerals accounted for 22%, electronic products 18% and steel 15%. There is therefore considerable intra-industry trade between South Korea and Japan, indicating a high degree of complementarity between the two economies. Many Japanese consumer goods are not allowed into South Korea. Apart from trying to reduce its dependence on the Japanese economy, the

Table 4.1
South Korea's Trade with Japan, 1987

Imports	% Total
Machinery	23.7
Electronic	29.1
Chemicals	19.5
Steel	11.2
Textiles	3.9
Consumer goods	0.9
Other goods	2.8
Exports	% Total
Textiles	27.0
Food products	22.4
Electronic	17.8
Steel	15.4
Consumer goods	6.3
Machinery	3.9
Leather goods	3.6
Chemicals	3.5

Source: United Nations, *World Commodity Trade Statistics*, (various issues).

South Korean government is also anxious to reduce its huge deficit with Japan. In 1988, this stood at about US$4 billion, but rose to about US$6 billion in 1990 (Clifford 1991a:40; Baum and Shim 1991:34). In 1990, Japan accounted for only 15% of Singapore's total trade. Singapore imports capital goods from Japan, and exports refined petroleum products. Some 68% of Singapore's imports from Japan in 1990 were made up of machinery and transport equipment, while 52% of Singapore's exports to Japan were made up of petroleum products. Machinery made up 26% of Singapore's exports to Japan and miscellaneous manufactured goods made up only 6%. Over the years, Singapore, like the other Asian NICs, has experienced a widening trade deficit with Japan. In 1980, this trade deficit was S$6.3 billion, but by 1990, it had grown to S$16 billion (FEER 1991d:91).

In the case of Taiwan, although Japan is Taiwan's fourth largest trading partner, most of this trade is "invisible", in the sense that it is carried out by Japanese trading companies which import Taiwanese goods and market them under Japanese brand names. Very few of Taiwan's large manufacturing companies have set up offices in Japan. Although Taiwan's exports to Japan totalled about US$7 billion in 1990, most Japanese consumers are unaware that many goods they purchase are actually made in Taiwan. Japan is also a principal supplier of capital and intermediate goods to Taiwan. In 1990, about 60% of Taiwan's imports from Japan were made up of industrial components for Taiwan's export-oriented industries. Less than 10% of Taiwan's imports from Japan are made up of consumer goods. As in South Korea, many Japanese consumer goods are not allowed into Taiwan. In 1990, tariffs on some Japanese goods were raised by 50% and state-own corporations were not allowed to import from Japan if local sources were available. Even Japanese films have been kept out of Taiwan by a US$18,500 import surcharge. The import of Japanese cars and liquor has been totally prohibited for some time (Baum and do Rosario 1991:40–42; Baum 1991b:43).

The Asian NICs accounted for an average of 14% of Japanese trade in 1985–1989. Japan has always recorded a trade surplus with the Asian NICs. The reason for this is that the Asian NICs import much of their requirements of producer and consumer goods from Japan, but export most of their manufactured goods to the USA and EU. In 1973, Japan had a trade surplus of US$2.9 billion, but by 1986, this had grown to US$17.5 billion. In 1990, Japan's trade surplus with the Asian NICs had grown to US$31 billion. This was only slightly less than Japan's trade surplus with the USA (which stood at US$37 billion in 1990). In terms of volume, Japan's trade with the Asian NICs in 1990 was greater than Japan's trade with the EU (Rowley 1991f:48–49).

Trade between Japan and the two East Asian NICs (South Korea and Taiwan), totalled US$50.3 billion in 1988. This was about half Japan's volume of trade with the USA in that year (which amounted to US$132 billion). Considering the relative sizes of the South Korean and Taiwanese economies compared with that of the USA, this is a remarkable achievement (Holloway, Clifford and Moore 1989:55). Over the years, Taiwan, like South Korea, has experienced a widening trade deficit with Japan. In 1991, Taiwan's trade deficit with Japan stood at US$7.8 billion (up from US$3.5 billion in 1986). South Korea's trade deficit with Japan was US$7 billion. In 1991, the Asian NICs as a group had a trade deficit of US$36 billion (slightly larger than the USA's trade deficit with Japan, which was US$34 billion in 1991). Taiwan and South Korea have recently held talks aimed at increasing bilateral trade, as a means of reducing their trade deficits with Japan (Baum and Shim 1991:34).

The Role of Japanese Foreign Investment

The pattern of complementarity between Japan and the Asian NICs has been fostered by Japanese foreign investment. By 1983, the accumulated stock of Japanese investment in the Asian NICs was US$2,063 million. The bulk of this was in the manufacture of chemicals (27%). Textiles accounted for 14%, machinery 12%, electrical machinery 17% and other manufactures 14% (Sazaname 1990:78–79).

In 1988, over 80% of the accumulated stock of Japanese investment in Taiwan was in the manufacturing sector. In Singapore and South Korea, about 50% was in the manufacturing sector. In Hong Kong, nearly 90% was in commerce and services (Smith and do Rosario 1990:48).

Japanese foreign investment in South Korea has averaged about half the total foreign investment flowing into the country each year. Between 1962 and 1976, cumulative Japanese investment in South Korea totalled US$433 million and accounted for 65% of total foreign investment in that country. Most of this was in textiles (23%) and electrical machinery (16%) (Westphal, Rhee and Pursell 1979:359–388). In 1988, foreign investment in South Korea reached a peak of US$1.3 billion, of which Japan accounted for US$0.6 billion (USA foreign investment was US$0.3 billion). Since then, foreign investment in South Korea has declined slightly, reaching about US$0.8 billion in 1990. Japanese investment in South Korea is concentrated in motor vehicle manufacture (all major South Korean car firms are part-owned by large Japanese car makers), petrochemicals (between 1969 and 1975, Japanese petrochemical companies invested US$110 million in South Korea) and electronics (in the late 1980s, the Hitachi company announced a major transfer of technology which would enable the Goldstar group to manufacture 1mb and 4mb memory chips) (Clifford 1991a:40–41).

A significant proportion of the trade between Japan and the Asian NICs is made up of intra-firm trade (that is, imports and exports between Japanese firms and their subsidiaries in the Asian NICs). In 1975, 27% of all imports of manufactured goods into Japan were made up of imports from the subsidiaries of Japanese firms, while 14% of all exports were made up of exports to subsidiaries of Japanese firms. These proportions had doubled over the previous ten years (Nakajo 1980:470). In 1975, some 60% of all Japanese foreign investment in Asia was involved with the transfer of some part of a company's production process overseas. As Japan becomes less efficient in some areas of manufacturing, these are transferred to other countries, such as the Asian NICs, which are more efficient in these areas (Nakajo 1980:474–479).

In recent years, more than half of all direct foreign investment by multinational corporations went to Asia, with the Asian NICs being important recipients. This pattern is also a reflection of the rise of Japanese multinationals in the world economy. The UN Centre on Transnational Corporations has suggested that Japanese multinationals have set up "regional core networks" in Asia and other regions, in order to achieve an optimum global manufacturing strategy (Rowley 1991d:57). A good example of this can be seen in the foreign investment strategies of the Japanese textile industry (do Rosario 1991b:66–67).

For example, the Toray company has 28 major subsidiaries in Southeast Asia and another ten in other parts of the world. Its largest investments are in the near-NICs, Malaysia, Thailand and Indonesia. Toray recently invested ¥10 billion in a plant in Malaysia (the biggest of its kind outside Japan), to produce special plastics. In Thailand, it is building a ¥13 billion plant to product polyester filament, while in Indonesia, it is building a ¥300 million factory to produce nylon yarn. Many other Japanese textile companies have moved offshore to Southeast Asia because of rising costs in Japan. In the 1970s, some 40% of Japan's total foreign investment was in textiles.

Most of the production of Japanese textile firms in Southeast Asia is concentrated in commodity fibres. Technology-intensive special fibres are produced in Japan. These include artificial suede, fabrics which change colour under different lighting and temperature conditions, extra-thin synthetic fabrics, etc. There is thus a clear division of labour in the international operations of Japanese textile firms. Increasing competition for low-cost manufacturers (such as South Korea, Hong Kong and Taiwan) has forced Japanese textile companies to move their low-technology, labour-intensive operations offshore and to concentrate on up-market, high-technology productions at home (do Rosario 1991b:66).

A good example of the division of labour between Japan and the Asian NICs can be seen from the manufacture of synthetic fibres in South Korea. In 1968, South Korea was completely dependent on imports of synthetic fibres (its specialization ratio was −1). This is not unusual, as the manufacture of synthetic fibres is very capital-intensive. In that year, it was also completely specialized in the export of apparel (its specialization ratio was 1) as the manufacture of clothing is a very labour-intensive process. In synthethic fabrics, South Korea's specialization ratio was 0 in 1968 (completely balanced trade). Almost all South Korea's imports of synthetic fibres came from Japan.

Between 1968 and 1981, South Korea's specialization ratio increased steadily from −1 to 0, and in 1980, for the first time, South Korea was a net exporter of synthetic fibres. In synthetic fabrics, its specialization ratio increased from 0 in 1968 to 0.7 in 1981, indicating that South Korea had also become a net exporter of synthetic fabrics. Its specialization in the export of apparel was maintained throughout this period. Measured in terms of production/consumption ratios, South Korea produced only between 10% (polyester staple) and 50% (acrylic staple) of its requirements of various synthetic fibres in 1968. By 1980, its production/consumption ratio for most synthetic fibres had exceeded 100%, and by 1985, it was producing between 10% and 30% more of synthetic fibres than it consumed.

This transformation from net importer to net exporter of synthetic fibres was accomplished by a policy of import-substitution, based on Japanese technology obtained through foreign investment or through licencing agreements. Beginning in 1969, all the major synthetic textile manufactures entered into joint-ventures, or licensing agreements with major Japanese synthetic fibre producers. South Korea's dependence on Japanese technology and expertise was not long-standing, however. By 1986, most Japanese joint-venture partners had substantially reduced their equity participation in South Korean textile companies, and by 1984, most South Korean textile companies had begun to undertake their own research and development activities. Most South Korean synthetic fibre manufactures had caught up with their Japanese counterparts, in terms of quality, in standard synthetic fibres. Their costs of production were lower than in Japan, and as a result, South Korea could export these synthetic fibres in competition with Japanese companies. In 1970, domestic prices of some synthetic fibres (such as polyester staple) in South Korea were about 1.8 times higher than import prices. By 1981, this ratio had been reduced to 1.1 times higher. This reflects the growing efficiency of the South Korean synthetic fibre manufacturing industry (throughout this period, productivity increased substantially in this industry). While South Korea had become internationally competitive in the export of standard synthetic fibres by 1981, it was still unable to compete with Japan (in terms of price and quality) in differentiated synthetic fibres. There is thus a division of labour, with South Korea specializing in standard synthetic fibres and Japan specializing in differentiated, high quality, synthetic fibres (Tran 1988: 306–402).

Japan has played an important part in the development of the Singapore economy since 1960. Apart from being a major participant in the construction sector, Japanese firms also play a major role in manufacturing activities. In 1990, there were about 1,500 Japanese firms operating in Singapore and they employed about 70,000 workers. Japanese foreign investment in Singapore totalled over S\$708 million in 1990 and accounted for about 32% of total foreign investment in that year. In 1980, Japan accounted for only 11% of foreign investment in Singapore. The cumulated stock of foreign investment owned by Japan, as of 1990, was S\$6,496 million. This represented 29% of the total stock of foreign investment and was the second largest share (behind that of the USA). Apart from the manufacturing sector, much of Japanese foreign investment in Singapore goes into the real estate sector.

Between 1952 and 1990, Japan invested US\$3.7 billion in Taiwan (accounting for about one-third of all foreign investment). Most of this has gone into the manufacturing sector, where Japanese influence in car manufacture, plastics and chemicals is strong. In

1990, there were some 1,200 Japanese firms operating in Taiwan, with hundreds more operating through Taiwanese agents (Baum 1991b:43).

The Upvaluation of the Yen

By the mid-1980s, persistent Japanese trade surpluses with the USA and EU caused trade frictions between these countries. In 1980, Japan recorded a trade surplus of US$7.2 billion with the USA and US$9.5 billion with the EU. These surpluses grew to US$40.2 billion, and US$11.7 billion respectively, by 1985. With respect to the USA, over a third of this surplus was accounted for by the export of Japanese motor vehicles, one quarter was accounted for by the export of high technology products and the rest was due to the export of other manufactured goods (Smith 1987a:70–71).

In September 1985, the "Plaza Agreement" was signed by the Group of Five (USA, Britain, Japan, West Germany and France) (Hultman 1986:287–293). This led to the upvaluation of the Yen relative to other major currencies. In 1985, the Yen-US Dollar exchange rate stood at about ¥260:US$1. By 1988, it had soared to about ¥130:US$1, a 100% appreciation in three years. While the value of the Yen depreciated against the US$ in 1989 (primarily because of interest rate differentials), it began to appreciate again in 1990. In the early months of 1990, the Yen appreciated against most currencies by at least 25%, as Japanese trade surpluses continued to rise and the Japanese government implemented a tight monetary policy. In 1991, some financial observers suggested that the Yen may continue to appreciate and reach ¥120:US$1 at the end of 1991 (Economist 1991h:100). This proved to be a gross underestimate. By April 1994, the Yen had appreciated to a value of ¥104:US$1!

The rapid appreciation of the Yen had a number of important effects on the Japanese economy in the short term (Kohama and Urata 1988). The volume of exports declined in 1986 and 1987, while the volume of imports increased. Between 1985 and 1989, the volume of manufactured imports into Japan increased by 60%. Import penetration ratios rose (up to over 50% in some imports). The Asian NICs benefited from this. Imports from South Korea and Taiwan more than doubled in value (measured in US Dollars), between 1986 and 1987. Consumer electronics and clothing exports from these countries grew dramatically as a result of the appreciation of the Yen (Kohama and Urata 1988:328–333).

Profitability of export activities fell (by as much as 25% in some items). In 1987, when ¥140 was equal to US$1, it was thought that if the Yen-US Dollar exchange rate rose to ¥120:US$1, no manufactured goods could be exported from Japan to the USA at a profit (in the last quarter of 1986, when the Yen was at ¥160 to US$1, the Nissan motor car company exported 2 million cars, but did not make any profit (Sayle 1987:44,51)). These pessimistic views turned out, eventually, to be mistaken, as Japanese companies began reacting to the higher value of the Yen by restructuring, increasing productivity, squeezing their suppliers and moving offshore.

The decline in profitability led to a decline in employment in many sectors of the economy. The hardest hit were coal products, textiles, chemicals, metal products and machinery, which suffered a decline in employment of about 4% between 1985 and 1988 (Kohama and Urata 1988:336–337). In 1987, the Japanese steel industry expected to suffer a loss of US$2.5 billion and to shed some 6,000 jobs.

As a consequence of these unfavourable effects on the Japanese economy, Japanese firms started moving unprofitable production facilities offshore, to the Asian NICs, to developed countries such as the USA and EU and to the less developed countries (particularly the ASEAN countries) (Smith 1986a: 66–67). In 1985, Japanese foreign investment stood at about US$10 billion. By 1987, it had climbed to US$30 billion and by 1989, had reached US$68 billion. Relatively low technology, energy-inefficient, labour-intensive manufacturing processes were moved to the Asian NICs, and the ASEAN countries in order to take advantage of lower production costs. Some high technology, capital-intensive processes were moved to developed countries, in order to avoid protectionist barriers (Kohama and Urata 1988:332–333,339). One indication of this movement is that Japan now has only one aluminium plant producing 200,000 tons of aluminum a year. Ten years ago, Japan produced 1 million tons of aluminum ingot. Following the rise of the Yen, Japanese investment grew by 50% a year in the Asian NICs, and by 100% per year in the ASEAN countries (Smith and do Rosario 1990:47–48). Between 1986 and 1988, Japanese foreign investment increased by 152% in Hong Kong, 147% in Singapore, 158% in Malaysia, 162% in Indonesia and 592% in Thailand (FEER 1990d:95; Smith 1989b:59).

Table 4.2 shows the volume of Japanese foreign investment in the Asian NICs and some near-NICs. As can be seen from the table, Hong Kong and Singapore have been the main recipients of Japanese foreign investment since 1985, each recording nearly US$2 billion in 1989. Amongst the near-NICs, Thailand is the main recipient of Japanese foreign investment, receiving about US$1.2 billion in 1989. As economic recession hit the world economy, the volume of Japanese foreign investment in all Asian NICs and near-NICs declined in 1990.

Table 4.2

Japanese Foreign Investment in Asian NICs and Near-NICs
(US$ billion)

Year	HK	SIN	SK	TAI	MAL	THAI	INDON
1985	0.1	0.3	0.2	0.1	0.1	0.1	0.4
1986	0.5	0.2	0.5	0.2	1.5	0.2	0.2
1987	1.0	0.5	0.5	0.2	1.6	0.2	0.5
1988	1.7	0.7	0.4	0.3	0.3	0.7	0.5
1989	1.8	1.9	0.6	0.4	0.6	1.2	0.6
1990	1.7	0.7	0.5	0.2	0.7	1.0	1.1

Source: FEER 1991f, Capital – a scarcer commodity, *Far Eastern Review*, September 26, p. 49.

For the Asian NICs, the upvaluation of the Yen was a mixed blessing. The upvaluation of the Yen gave the Asian NICs a competitive advantage in export markets (do Rosario 1991a:57). As the Yen rose in value, Japanese exports became less competitive. Since the currencies of the Asian NICs were linked to the US Dollar and remained virtually unchanged in value, the exports of the Asian NICs increased as the value of the Yen rose. The inverse relationship between the exports of the Asian NICs and the value of the Yen is clearly seen in Figure 4.1. The growth rate of the exports of the Asian NICs is inversely related to the change in the value of the Yen relative to the value of the US Dollar.

In the first ten months of 1987, the value of Japanese manufactured goods imports rose by 30%, while textile imports increased by 44%. Imports of knitwear increased by 70% over the same period. Much of this came from the Asian NICs. South Korean exports of synthetic fibres to Japan increased ten-fold in 1987. Hong Kong exports of clothing increased by 86%. By 1987, textile imports had accounted for 32% of domestic sales, and were expected to continue to rise to 40% (Smith 1987b:40–41).

This rise in exports was tempered by the fact that many Asian NICs depend on Japan for most of their inputs (for example, half of the inputs required for the manufacture of video tape recorders in South Korea come from Japan). The rise in costs has reduced the impact of the upvaluation of the Yen on the export competitiveness of the Asian NICs. In third markets, such as the USA and EU, the competitive advantage of the Asian NICs *vis-à-vis* Japan, is counter-balanced by the fact that the product range of the Asian NICs is relatively narrow. In addition, Japanese exporters, in a bid to retain market share, reduced their profit margins, by holding prices virtually constant in the face of the appreciating Yen. For example, Japanese car makers increased prices in the USA by only 3%–4%, when the Yen appreciated by a further 20% in December 1985 (Smith 1986b:58–61).

The appreciation of the Yen after 1985 did not reduce Japanese trade surpluses in the short run. Although exports did decline and imports did rise, Japan's trade surplus with the USA continued to increase in years following the Plaza Agreement. The reason for this was the "J Curve" effect. Although relative prices changed immediately with the appreciation of the Yen, volumes did not change immediately. US imports of Japanese goods (encouraged by persistent US government budget deficits) began to cost more in terms of US currency. Between the end of 1985 and the end of 1987, the Japanese trade surplus with the USA increased by an additional US$30 billion. Japanese exporters, who initially held prices down when the Yen started appreciating, began passing the full impact of the currency appreciation to consumers, as cost-cutting and other efficiency measures were exhausted. There was even concern that the burgeoning trade surplus would trigger another round of upvaluation of the Yen *vis-à-vis* the US Dollar, and generate a vicious spiral (Smith 1988:88–89). At the same time, Japan's trade surplus with the EU also continued to increase (Islam 1988:93). The appreciation of the Yen did not last very long. From the end of 1988, the Yen began to devalue relative to the US Dollar (because of high interest rates in the USA and large outflows of Japanese foreign investment). By the first quarter of 1990, it had depreciated to ¥155:US$1, causing concern that Japan's trade surplus with the USA would continue to cause frictions between the two countries (Rowley 1990b:57). This was reinforced by the fact that, as the Yen rose between 1985 and 1988, Japanese firms undertook a major restructuring of their operations and by the end of 1988, had become more efficient, reducing unit costs by 45% and increasing value per unit of exports by 68% (Holloway 1989a:101). The events of 1985–1988 made the Japanese even more efficient as they faced the prospect of living with *endaka* (the era of the strong Yen). Japan's trade surplus in 1991 is expected to top US$90 billion and its current account balance is expected to exceed US$70 billion (Rowley 1991c:46). It appears that the Japanese have, indeed, learnt to live with *endaka*!

Conclusion

There is a close relationship between Japan and the Asian NICs. The economies of the Asian NICs are complementary to that of Japan. They import most of their capital and producer goods from Japan and export finished (most labour-intensive) goods to Japan, the USA and EU. In recent years, the growing industrial sophistication of the Asian NICs has enabled them to export some capital and sophisticated consumer goods to Japan. The complementarity between the Japanese economy and the Asian NICs has been fostered through Japanese foreign investment and technology transfer. It is reflected in the pattern of trade between Japan and the Asian NICs.

The upvaluation of the Yen in 1985 had positive, as well as negative, effects on the Asian NICs. On the one hand, the Asian NICs benefited, as they gained a competitive advantage in their export markets. In addition, the upvaluation of the Yen increased Japanese foreign investment in the Asian NICs, as unprofitable manufacturing activities were moved off-shore. The appreciation of the Yen also stimulated Japanese demand for the exports of the Asian NICs. On the other hand, the appreciation of the Yen increased the costs of the imports of capital and producer goods from Japan, which was the main supplier of such inputs to the Asian NICs. As a result, profit margins of the exporters in the Asian NICs were reduced.

Figure 4.1
Yen-US$ Exchange Rate and NIC Exports
Percentage Changes, 1971–1091

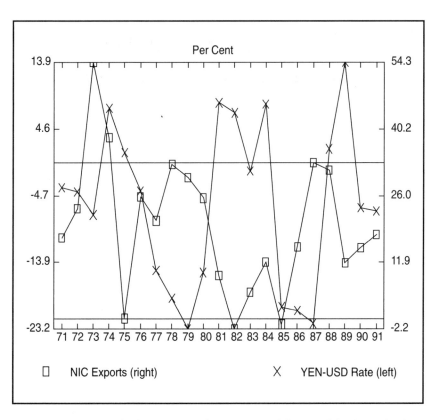

Source: International Monetary Fund, *International Financial Statistics*, (various issues); International Monetary Fund, *Direction of Trade Statistics Yearbook*, (various issues).

CHAPTER 5

The Risks of Export-Oriented Industrialization

Introduction

While export-oriented industrialization has many advantages, it also contains a number of risks. Countries with a high degree of exposure to the international economy (such as the Asian NICs) are highly vulnerable to sudden, unpredictable changes in international trade and finance. These external "shocks" may take the form of sudden, large changes in the prices of essential imported inputs (such as petroleum), or in the movement of interest rates, exchange rates, etc., and are largely outside the control of individual countries.

Dependence on one or two developed countries for exports of manufactured goods may also result in a sudden reversal of fortunes if the demand for their products suddenly vanishes. This may be due to a recession in the importing country, or to a change in demand (in the case of products, such as toys or clothes, for which consumer preferences can change rather quickly).

Countries which base their export strategy on the manufacture of labour-intensive products can see their comparative advantage undermined by a number of factors. Sudden changes in technology (such as robotization, computer-aided design and manufacture), may significantly reduce the competitive advantage of labour-intensive methods of production, relative to capital-intensive methods of production. In addition, a low-wage country specializing in labour-intensive manufactures may suddenly find that another country is able to offer even lower wages. This will erode the comparative advantage of the former country rather quickly.

Changes in technology may also reduce the comparative advantage of countries which base their export-oriented industrialization strategy on the production of components for manufacturing plants in other countries. Computer-aided inventory systems, the development of lean production processes and the need for flexibility in production runs, make it necessary for manufacturers to have their component suppliers nearby. This will reduce the attractiveness of parent companies locating their components factories thousands of kilometres away, even though labour costs may be lower there.

The more successful a country is in the export of manufactured goods, the more likely it is that increasing pressure in its principal markets will result in the imposition of import barriers to its products. In addition, growing balance of trade surpluses, which are the result of a successful export-oriented strategy, are likely to put upward pressure on exchange rates. In a sense, being too successful an exporter generates economic and political pressures which make it difficult for the success of such a strategy to be maintained.

The NICs of Asia are good examples of the view that, while export-oriented industrialization has many advantages, it also involves a number of risks which are associated with very open economies. Such countries are highly vulnerable to "external shocks", sudden changes in the international trading system, which are largely outside their control and often unpredictable.

The First Oil Crisis

The first serious occurrence of this vulnerability took place in 1973, when OPEC increased the price of crude oil by three times. In 1972, the price of OPEC crude oil was about US$2 per barrel. By the end of 1973, it was about US$6 per barrel. This sudden tripling of oil prices caused severe balance of payments difficulties to all the Asian NICs, since they were all net oil importers. Indeed, some of the Asian NICs were amongst the first to see the adverse impact of the rise in oil prices on their external accounts. This took the form of large balance of payments deficits, caused by soaring import bills and stagnating exports, as the rest of the world reeled under the impact of the rise in the price of oil.

In 1974, South Korea's trade deficit increased by 8.5% of GNP, while the trade deficits of Singapore and Taiwan increased by 18.4% and 10.2% of GNP respectively. The increase in oil prices also led to inflationary pressures and significant declines in the growth rates of GDP in all the Asian NICs. Between 1972 and 1973, the rate of inflation in Hong Kong increased from 6.1% to 18.2%, while the rate of GDP growth declined from 16.4% in 1973 to 1.8% in 1974. In South Korea, the rate of inflation reached 24% in 1974 (compared to 3% in 1973), while the growth of GDP declined from 8.3% in 1974 (from 15.3%) in 1973. A similar pattern can be observed in the case of Singapore. The rate of inflation rose to 22% in 1974 (it was 2.1% in 1972) and the rate of growth fell to 4% in 1975 (from 13% in 1972). Perhaps the largest adverse impact of the 1973 oil crisis was felt in Taiwan, where inflation reached over 40% in 1974 (from 3% in 1972) and the growth rate of GDP fell to just 1% in 1974 (from 13% in 1972) (Balassa 1981c).

The Asian NICs responded to the adverse effects of the first oil crisis by implementing contractionary monetary and fiscal policies in an effort to contain the inflationary impact of the rise in oil prices. The share of government expenditures in GDP was also reduced in order to restrain the growth of aggregate demand. At the same time, all the Asian NICs intensified the promotion of their exports. These included such measures as increased investment in export-oriented industries and, in some cases, currency devaluation. As a result of these efforts, most of the Asian NICs recovered from the impact of the first oil crisis by 1976.

The Second Oil Crisis and the Recession of the Mid-1980s

In the mid-1980s, this lesson was brought home again to all the

Asian NICs in the form of a severe economic recession. After about 20 years of sustained and rapid (in many cases, double-digit) economic growth, all the Asian NICs experienced substantial reductions in their growth rates. Singapore even suffered negative rates of economic growth. The problems which the Asian NICs faced following the 1973 oil crises, paled in comparison.

The Depth of the Recession

The depth of the recession of the mid-1980s can be seen from the data in Table 5.1.

In 1983, all the Asian NICs were recording double-digit growth rates of GDP. Just two years later, Hong Kong recorded a growth rate of –0.1% and Singapore, a growth rate of –1.6%. This was the first time negative growth rates had been experienced in two decades. Taiwan's growth rate fell, from 12% in 1983, to 4.4% in 1985, while South Korea's growth rate fell from 13% in 1983 to 6.9% in 1985.

Table 5.1
Growth Rates of GDP, 1983–1990 (% per annum)

Country	1983	1984	1985	1986	1990
Hong Kong	11.2	9.4	–0.1	12.1	2.3
Singapore	13.1	8.3	–1.6	1.8	8.5
South Korea	12.8	9.4	6.9	13.0	8.5
Taiwan	12.0	9.6	4.4	18.0	5.2

Sources: Asian Development Bank, *Key Indicators of Developing and Asian Countries,* (various issues); Asian Development Bank, *Asian Development Outlook,* (various issues); World Bank, *World Development Report,* (various issues); World Bank, *World Tables,* (various issues), Far Eastern Economic Review, *Asia Yearbook,* (various issues), Republic of China, *Statistical Yearbook of the Republic of China,* (various issues).

These dramatic declines in economic performance were mirrored in the growth rate of exports. These are shown in Table 5.2.

With the exception of Singapore, all the Asian NICs were recording double-digit growth rates of exports in 1983. However, by 1985, Singapore's exports decreased by 24%. In the following year, Hong Kong's exports declined by 7%, South Korea's by 10.5% and Taiwan's by 39%. Figure 5.1 shows the growth rate of the exports of all the Asian NICs between 1984 and 1989. The severe decline in the growth rates of exports between 1984 and 1985 is evident from this graph.

This decline in exports can also be seen in the growth rates of specific export items. Table 5.3 shows that in all the major export items, both South Korea and Taiwan registered negative growth rates in 1985.

For South Korea, exports to the USA declined by 4% in 1985, while exports to the EU declined by 5%. In the same year, Taiwan's exports to the USA declined by 2%, while its exports to the EU declined by 4%. Hong Kong was even more adversely

Table 5.2

Growth Rates of Exports (% per annum)

Year	Hong Kong	Singapore	South Korea	Taiwan
1982–1983	43.8	11.9	5.3	20.9
1983–1984	19.0	27.2	18.5	28.1
1984–1985	3.9	−0.6	−10.5	−5.2
1985–1986	−7.2	−24.0	−10.5	−39.3
1986–1987	40.7	32.7	9.1	36.0

Sources: Hong Kong Department of Statistics, *Exports*, and *Imports* (various issues); Ministry of Finance, Taipeh, *Monthly Statistics of Exports*, and *Monthly Statistics of Imports* (various issues); Singapore Trade Development Board, *Singapore Trade Statistics* (various issues), World Bank, *Yearbook of International Trade* (various issues).

Figure 5.1
Average Export Growth, 1984–1989

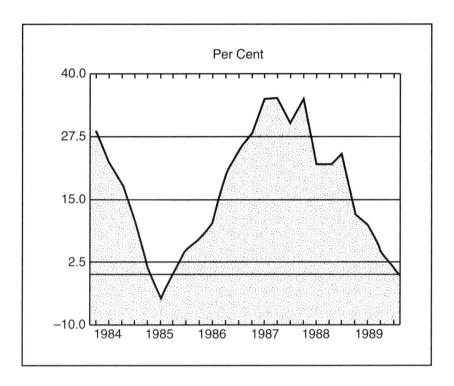

Source: International Monetary Fund, *Direction of Trade Statistics Yearbook*, (various issues).

Table 5.3
Export Growth Rates, 1985 (%)

Item	South Korea	Taiwan
Electrical	–5.1	–0.1
Footwear	–1.5	–2.7
Iron & Steel	–8.3	–16.6
Textiles	–5.1	–2.5

Source: Ensor P and Rowley A 1985, Performing twins on a greasy pole, *Far Eastern Economic Review*, September 26, p. 101.

affected. Its exports to the USA and Japan declined by 11% in 1985, while its exports to Britain and Germany declined by 18% and 21% respectively. (Ensor and Rowley 1985:101; Bowring 1985:102). Since the USA and the EU were the major export markets of these countries, the negative growth rates of exports to these countries had a severe contractionary effect on the economies of the Asian NICs.

Singapore provides an example of this. Figure 5.2 shows the growth rate of Singapore's GNP between 1979 and 1987. Between 1979 and 1984, Singapore's GNP growth was in double digits (averaging 14.8% per annum). In 1985 and 1986, Singapore's GNP growth registered –1.2% and –1.8% respectively, the first time in 20 years that the economy experienced negative GNP growth.

As shown in Figure 5.2, the effects of the recession on the labour market were also severe. In Singapore, for example, employment in the manufacturing sector had been increasing steadily up to 1980. Between 1980 and 1985, manufacturing employment fell by 13% (World Bank 1990:489). Some 90,000 jobs were lost in 1985 alone (Economic Committee 1986:39). The unemployment rate, which stood at 2.6% in 1982, rose to 6.5% in 1986.

Causes of the Recession

The causes of the recession in the mid-1980s can be attributed to external, as well as internal factors. Although the recession was trigged off by external factors, internal factors aggravated the depth of the recession in many Asian NICs. While the external factors were beyond the control of the Asian NICs, some of the internal factors were self-inflicted.

Figure 5.2

Singapore: GNP Growth Rate and Unemployment Rate,
1979–1987

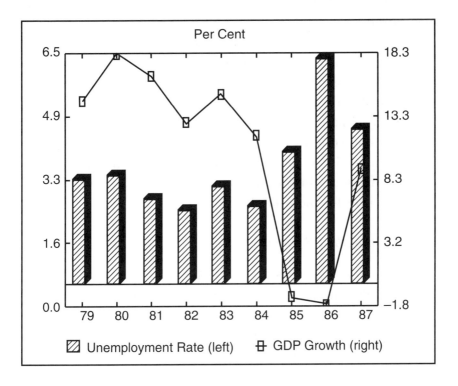

Source: Department of Statistics, *Yearbook of Statistics, Singapore* (various issues).

External Causes

The 1979 oil crisis

In 1979, OPEC raised oil prices again. In 1978, the price of crude
oil was about US$16 per barrel. In 1979, it rose to about US$29,
and peaked in 1981, at US$38 per barrel. This increase of over
100% in three years caused tremendous problems in the world
economy as oil-importing countries struggled to adjust to huge
balance of payment deficits. All the Asian NICs are net oil-importers
and were hit hard by the rise in the price of crude oil. For example,

South Korea's imports of crude oil increased by 53% in 1979 and 69% in 1980. In absolute terms, South Korea's import bill for crude oil increased from US$2.2 billion in 1979 to nearly US$6 billion in 1980. This increase accounted for more than 80% of the deterioration of South Korea's current account balance between 1978 and 1980 (Roberts 1985:20). However, the full impact of the 1979 oil price hike was not felt until the mid-1980s, when the USA and other industrial economies began to slow down. By this time, the price of crude oil also began to decline because of the inability of OPEC to limit supply and because of reduced demand by oil-importing countries. By the mid-1980s, the full impact of the 1979 oil price rise on the oil-importing countries was aggravated by a fall in revenues in oil-exporting countries. This had dramatic consequences for the Asian NICs.

Slow-down of the US economy

In the first quarter of 1984, the growth rate of GDP in the USA was just over 8% (over the previous four quarters). Starting in the second quarter of 1984, it declined steadily, reaching 3% in the third quarter of 1985 and after a brief recovery, fell to a low of about 1.8% in the first quarter of 1987. The decline in the growth rate of the USA is mirrored, almost exactly, in the decline in the growth of exports of the Asian NICs (Figure 5.3).

The reason for this is that the USA represents the largest export market for most of the Asian NICs. In 1986, exports to the USA, as a proportion of total exports, accounted for 31% in Hong Kong, 23% in Singapore, 40% in South Korea and 48% in Taiwan. It is therefore not surprising that a marked slowdown in the growth of the US economy would have dramatic consequences for the Asian NICs. Even Singapore, whose dependence on the US market is the least amongst the Asian NICs, felt the impact of the slowdown of the US economy. In 1984, the growth rate of Singapore's GDP was 8.2% per annum. In 1985, 1986 and 1987, it was −1.8%, −0.5% and −1.8% respectively. Industrial production, which registered a growth rate of 8% in 1984, declined by 8% in 1985.

The decline in the growth rate of the US economy between 1984 and 1987 was also accompanied by a slowing of the economies of the major industrial economies, as the full impact of the 1979 oil crisis took its toll. As a result of this, the Asian NICs had no alternative markets on which to fall back when the US economy started to falter in 1984.

Exchange rate appreciation

Since the Plaza Agreement in 1985, the currencies of all the Asian NICs have been appreciating against the US Dollar (Balakrishnan 1989a:77). This has meant a loss of competitiveness in the US market *vis-à-vis* other countries. In 1985, the South Korean Won stood at 900 Won to the US Dollar. By 1989, it appreciated to 600 Won to the US Dollar. Similarly, in 1985, the New Taiwanese Dollar stood at NT$40 to US$1. By 1989, it had appreciated to NT$28 to US$1. Between 1985 and 1989, the South Korean Won appreciated by 50% against the US Dollar. The New Taiwanese Dollar appreciated by 42% against the US Dollar. The Singapore and Hong Kong Dollars appreciated by smaller amounts, 20% and 1.5%, respectively.

Even in the EU, exports of the Asian NICs have been performing poorly, partly due to currency appreciation. The South Korean Won, for example, appreciated against the Deutsche Mark by 50% between January 1988 and June 1989 (Clifford 1989a: 84–85).

Changes in consumer demand

By the middle to late 1980s, the consumer electronics boom in the USA had begun to cool off, mainly due to market saturation. By this time, nearly 60% of all households in the USA owned personal computers, although most were using them either as baby-sitters or expensive typewriters. In 1984, the US semiconductor industry forecast that demand for microprocessors (which grew by 50% in 1984), would have zero growth in 1985, and that it would take at least six months to run down excess inventories. This affected the

Asian NICs which produced and exported memory chips and other components used in the manufacture of home computers. At the end of 1984, several electronics firms in Singapore began laying off workers as a result of reduced demand for electronics components (Kulkarni 1985a:68–69).

Consumer preferences in clothing also took a turn for the worse as far as textile manufacturers in the Asian NICs were concerned. The post-war baby boom had led to a generation of "yuppies", who by the mid-1980s had caused a shift in the demand for clothing. Wealthier and more discerning consumers were

Figure 5.3
Recession in the Mid-1980s

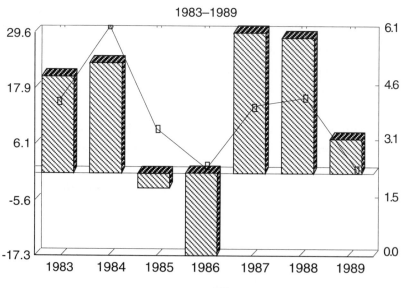

Source: International Monetary Fund, *Direction of Trade Yearbook*, (various issues); Council on Economic Development and Planning, *Taiwan Statistical Yearbook 1992*.

demanding higher quality (fashion) clothing and were willing to pay higher prices for them. This led to significant declines in the exports of countries such as Hong Kong, which specialized in the export of low-priced low-end of the market clothing to the USA (Goldstein 1988b:107).

The oil crisis of 1979 also affected the demand for refined oil products, the demand for oil exploration equipment and the demand for tankers. With the price of crude oil peaking at US$38 per barrel, it became more economical to build oil refineries in the Middle East and transport refined oil products to countries such as Japan. This reduced the demand for Singapore's oil refining capacity (the third largest in the world) and shipbuilding industries. Between 1975 and 1979, the output of Singapore's petroleum industry grew by an average of 29% per annum. In 1983, it grew by –5% per annum. Similarly, the average rate of growth of Singapore's shipbuilding industry in 1975–1979 was 14% per annum. In 1983, it grew by –15% per annum (Economic Committee 1986:222; Krause 1987:10–11). The reason for this was a marked decline in the demand for oil tankers. In 1973, world deliveries of oil tankers stood at about 70 million deadweight tons (dwt). After the first oil crises, this fell to a low of about 17 million dwt in 1979. After a brief recovery in 1982, world deliveries of tankers fell to about 6 million dwt. Even the world merchant fleet, which totalled 425 million gross tons in 1982, declined to a low of 401 million gross tons in 1988. These changes affected the Singapore shipbuilding and shiprepairing industry adversely.

Decline in other markets

After hitting a peak of about US$38 per barrel in 1981, the price of crude oil began to fall as a result of over-production by some OPEC countries and the declining demand from oil importing countries, as a result of substitution to other sources of energy (solar and wind powered electricity generation), increased production of North Sea oil, conservation in oil usage and the slowdown in economic activity. In 1989, the price of crude oil had come down to about US$15 per barrel. This reduced the demand for the exports of the Asian NICs in the oil-producing countries, which had accounted for about 6% of their total exports. Countries like South Korea were hit hard by the cancellation of large construction projects in the Middle East.

In addition, the decline in oil prices was accompanied by a general decline in all commodity prices. This reduced demand for the exports of the Asian NICs from less developed countries which depended on commodity exports as a major source of foreign exchange. This was aggravated by many less developed countries seeking industrial self-sufficiency in the face of a marked reduction in the capacity to import (Bowring 1985:99).

Internal Causes

While external factors triggered off the recession of the mid-1980s in the Asian NICs, internal factors aggravated it. Some of these internal factors were common to all the Asian NICs, others were peculiar to specific countries.

End of the construction boom

Between the 1960s and the early 1970s, the rapid growth of the Asian NICs was aided by a boom in construction. All the Asian NICs engaged in building infrastructure after the Second World War, and after the 1960s, they engaged in the construction of container terminals, free trade zones, office space, etc. This gave a big boost to the rate of economic growth. In 1965–1969, the share of construction expenditures in GDP was about 11% in all the Asian NICs. By 1983, it had grown to about 20% for all the Asian NICs, except Taiwan. South Korea, in particular, had by this time, developed a thriving export industry in large-scale construction works, particularly in the Middle East (Oshima 1986a:208-210,214–215).

In 1985, the construction boom ended. In all the Asian NICs, the construction sector (which had registered double-digit growth rates up till then) began to slow down considerably. The main reason for this was market saturation resulting from over-building (Holloway 1986a; Holloway 1986b; Cottrell 1986; Ensor 1986; Goldstein 1986). In Hong Kong, for example, the slowdown in the construction sector had begun in 1983. In that year, property loans were 37% of total bank loans. This declined steadily to a trough of about 29% in 1987 (Taylor 1991b:48). Singapore, in particular, was affected very badly by a similar decline in the construction sector as a result of over-building. Table 5.4 shows the demand and supply conditions for various types of property in Singapore.

As Table 5.4 shows, considerable excess supply had developed in Singapore by 1985 and, in most sectors of the industry, was expected to persist for several years. Total contracts for new construction dwindled, from about S$3.3 billion in 1981, to S$1

Table 5.4

Singapore: Demand and Supply for Property

Year	Cumulative Supply	Cumulative Demand	Balance
OFFICE SPACE (1000 sq m)			
1985	2261.0	2049.5	211.5
1987	2678.4	2104.7	573.7
INDUSTRIAL (1000 sq m)			
1985	5512.0	4659.4	852.6
1987	6301.3	5121.7	1179.6
RETAIL (1000 sq m)			
1985	1415.0	1170.2	244.8
1987	1546.0	1205.9	340.1
PRIVATE RESIDENTIAL (No. Units)			
1985	99496	91021	8475
1987	103650	98235	5415

Source: Kulkarni G 1985b, Building for a boom that did not come, *Far Eastern Economic Review*, March 14, p. 70.

billion in 1985. Private contracts fell from about S\$2 billion to almost zero (Economic Committee 1986:199). Rentals for office space and residential housing fell by 32% in one year, prices of private apartments fell by 30% (Kulkarni 1985b:71).

Rising costs

All the NICs of Asia began to experience upward pressure on wages by the mid-1980s, as labour markets started tightening due to rapid economic growth and falling fertility rates. In 1985, manufacturing wages in South Korea were rising at a rate of 10% per annum while productivity was rising at 8% per annum. By 1989, South Korean manufacturing wages were rising by 25% per annum, while productivity growth remained at about 8% per annum.

Rising wage costs were deliberately given a boost in Singapore between 1979 and 1983 through a "wages correction policy". After years of holding wage increases down through the "recommendations" of the National Wages Council, projected labour shortages prompted the government to increase wages substantially. The aim of this policy was to provide incentives to firms to shift to higher-technology, capital-intensive operations. Between 1979 and 1983, average weekly earnings of the Singapore work force increased by 76%. General salary increases between 1984 and 1985 averaged 10% (productivity grew by 6%) and contributions to the Central Provident Fund (a compulsory retirement scheme) were raised to 25% of wages, for both employers and employees. In addition, employers had to pay a 2% payroll tax and 4% of wages towards a Skills Development Fund. Executive salaries in Singapore were between 50% and 100% higher than in Hong Kong in 1985 (Kulkarni 1985c:71). Between 1979 and 1984, wages rose by about 12% per annum, while productivity rose by 5%. As a result, Singapore's competitive position deteriorated *vis-à-vis* other Asian NICs (Economic Committee 1986:43). This, combined with the downturn in external markets, caused considerable unemployment.

Slow-down in tourism and other industries in Singapore

In the recession of the mid-1980s, Singapore was hit hardest compared with the other Asian NICs. Some factors which account for this were peculiar to Singapore.

The tourist industry, which had been booming in the 1970s, suddenly collapsed in the early 1980s. Since 1978, there had always been more tourists arriving in Singapore every year than there were Singaporeans. In 1982, tourism accounted for 14% of Singapore's GDP. Several factors explain the sudden decline in the number of tourists coming to Singapore after the early 1980s. First, the strong Singapore Dollar, in addition to rising costs, made Singapore a relatively expensive shopping destination (Hong Kong and Thailand were much cheaper for this purpose). Second, rapid urban renewal replaced many famous tourist spots in Singapore (for example, large parts of Chinatown, the famous Bugis Street, etc.) with high-rise apartment blocks or gleaming office towers. The reasons for tourists wanting to visit Singapore diminished by the day. Third, by the early 1980s, Singapore had established a reputation for being a puritan society (at one time, male tourists with shoulder-length hair were not allowed to enter the country without first visiting a barber). Fourth, surrounding countries (such as Indonesia, the Philippines and Malaysia) began to impose stiff departure taxes and high levies on imported goods. Since, these countries were an important source of visitors to Singapore, an important component of the country's tourist flow was stemmed. The growth of tourist arrivals (which had stood at 10% per annum in 1981) fell to –3.5% in 1983. Hotel occupancy rates slid from 81% in 1982 to 55% in 1985, while an additional 4,500 hotel rooms were added in that year (bringing the total number of hotel rooms to over 30,000) (Kulkarni 1985d:66–67).

There is also some evidence to suggest that the severity of the recession in Singapore was aggravated by its pro-cyclical fiscal policy and by an unintended contraction in its money supply in the mid-1980s (Krause 1987:11–14; Lee 1987:132–142). In Singapore, many public services, which in other countries would be carried out by government departments, are carried out by statutory boards and other government-owned entities, which conduct investment, construction and other activities independently of the government budget. Since the government has no direct control of these bodies, it cannot prevent them from contracting their investment and other activities during an economic downturn. For example, during an economic downturn, the Housing Development Board (HDB), would normally curtail its activities, thus aggravating the economic downturn. In other countries, the government would probably stimulate the construction sector in order to counteract the contraction of general economic activity during an economic downturn.

There is also some evidence to suggest that Singapore experienced a sharp reduction in money supply in 1984–1985. This was partly caused by a sharp increase in Central Provident Fund (CPF) contributions. The increase in the surplus of the CPF was not offset, either by outflows from the CPF, or by injections of domestic currency into the economy by the Monetary Authority of Singapore (MAS). This contributed to a decline in the money supply in 1985 and aggravated the economic downturn.

The severity of the recession in Singapore in the mid-1980s was therefore the result of a coincidence of a number of factors. The recession affected all the "pillars" of the Singapore economy simultaneously. Tourism declined considerably by the mid-1980s, both oil-refining, and shipbuilding and shiprepairing were badly affected by the second oil crisis, construction (another major sector of the economy) declined significantly as supply exceeded demand and, to make things worse, the recession affected other countries in Southeast Asia (such as Malaysia, Thailand and Indonesia) badly, thus further aggravating the economic downturn in Singapore (since neighbouring countries, such as Malaysia and Indonesia, are important trading partners of Singapore).

There is no doubt that Singapore could not have avoided the 1984–1985 recession (Lim 1989:214–215). Given its very open economy, there was no way of avoiding the effects of a recession in its major overseas markets. A more important question is whether Singapore could have, with better economic foresight, ameliorated the effects of the recession, rather than aggravated it.

Large-scale firms in South Korea

In South Korea, the government had attempted, between 1973 and 1980, to develop a large-scale manufacturing industry in certain key producer-goods through a policy of import-replacement under tariff protection. In January 1973, President Park announced the Heavy and Chemical Industrialization Plan, which was to develop six strategic industries (steel, electronics, petrochemicals, machinery, shipbuilding and non-ferrous metals) (Fujita and James 1989:235–250). The main vehicle for this ambitious plan was the large-scale combines, the *chaebols*. Large-scale borrowing from foreign sources were used to finance the huge investments which were necessary. These funds were channelled to the *chaebols* by the government in return for meeting production targets. This forced smaller firms to seek finance for their expansion from the higher-cost "curb" market.

As a result of this policy, investment in heaving industry increased by 2.4 times between 1973 and 1980 and the heavy industry share of investment rose from 46% to 56%. The concentration on the development of heavy industry resulted in a decline in share of capital going to other sectors of the economy, particularly light industry and agriculture. This led to a decline in their growth, from 22.5% to 10.5%, during this period (Oshima 1986b:797,799).

By the early 1980s, this policy was considered to be a failure. The second oil crisis caused a sudden and significant deterioration of South Korea's trade balance (which increased to US$887 million), and exports started slowing down. Heavy foreign borrowing (which reached US$47 billion in 1985) had caused the foreign debt to GDP ratio to climb from 23% in 1970 to 53.6% in 1985. The debt-service ratio reached a dangerously high level of 22% in 1985 and was still increasing. To make things worse, the upvaluation of the

Yen, which began in 1985, increased the value of South Korean debt, since much of this was denominated in Yen. The downturn in the world economy resulted in high levels of excess capacity in many of the heavy industries which had been set up. The rise in oil prices also resulted in a significant increase in the rate of inflation, which climbed to 29% in 1980. Wage increases reached a peak of 36.6% over the previous year in 1979, while productivity growth was only 15%. Interest rates also increased significantly. By the late 1970s, the South Korean economy was in deep trouble. A number financial failures occurred as firms, both large and small, struggled with rising costs and falling exports. In 1979, the government undertook corrective polices under a stabilization plan. This attempted to bring the rate of inflation down and to increase exports by implementing a wage-freeze and liberalizing key sectors of the economy (such as the financial sector). This did not, however, prevent the collapse of South Korea's sixth-largest *chaebol* (the Kukje group), which was dismembered and absorbed into the other *chaebols.*

The dominance of the largest ten industrial groups (the *chaebols*) in South Korea's export-led growth since the 1960s, has also had some disadvantages. In 1987, the sales of these ten largest *chaebols* accounted for 69% of South Korea's GNP. Fierce competition for market-share between these groups has led to excessive duplication of investments, large management bureaucracies and paper-thin profits. In 1990, total profitability of the Hyundai group was only 5.8% of net worth. Debt as a proportion to sales for the group as a whole was 73%. Some Hyundai subsidiaries (such as Hyundai Securities) had debt to sales ratios of over 400%. Most *chaebols* are highly diversified, producing everything from oil tankers to refined sugar. High-profile brand names (such as Daewoo, Hyundai, Samsung and Goldstar) have become easy targets for protectionist lobbies in export markets, such as the USA and EU. The government's policy of channelling capital at low cost to these *chaebols* has starved smaller firms of finance, or forced them to borrow from the higher cost "curb" market, making them highly vulnerable.

The net outcome of these structural problems in South Korea made it difficult for the country to respond to the economic downturn when it occurred in the mid-1980s.

Small-scale firms in Taiwan

Taiwan elected to chose a different path to industrialization. Unlike South Korea, it fostered the growth of small-scale firms which produce components, or manufacture finished goods for well-known foreign firms. Small- and medium-sized firms accounted for 90% or more of firms in each sector of the economy, and account for 61% of manufactured exports (World Bank 1993:161–162). Apart from a few brand names such as Acer or Logitec, most Taiwanese firms are unknown outside the country, although they produce many goods which sell under famous brand names.

The concentration of small-scale firms which supply foreign firms has made Taiwan very vulnerable to fluctuations in external demand. A downturn in the US economy (which takes nearly 50% of Taiwan's exports) usually affects Taiwanese firms first. In addition, the small size of the average Taiwanese firm makes it difficult for them to move up-market into higher technology, more capital-intensive products. Most do not have the capacity to undertake any research and development activities.

Since the early 1980s, Taiwan has run vast current account surpluses as a result of its successful export-oriented policies. Taiwan's foreign reserves, which stood at US$9 billion in 1982, shot up to US$45 billion in 1986 and reached US$78 billion in 1987. This led to a significant increase in the money supply. With excess liquidity, property prices soared and the Taiwan stock exchange boomed. Investment in shares competed for attention with productive investment. It was even estimated that some 100,000 workers left their jobs to speculate on the stock market full time (Economist 1990a:20).

In the mid-1980s, Taiwan was beset by another problem. The EU recognized the Peoples' Republic of China and withdrew recognition of Taiwan. This made it difficult for Taiwanese businessmen to travel to Europe because of visa restrictions. By the late 1980s, Taiwanese textile exports to the EU dwindled to almost zero compared with its 35% to 40% share a few years earlier.

Economic Recovery

The recovery of the US economy in 1987 revived the depressed economies of the Asian NICs. This recovery did not last long. The stock market crash of 1987 sent shock waves throughout the international financial community. US growth rates began to slide again during 1988. By 1990, the US economy was heading for a recession which it reached in 1991.

Recovery of the US Economy

The fortunes of all the Asian NICs took an abrupt turn for the better in 1987 when the US economy revived. The upswing in exports to the USA raised growth rates to 13.6% in Hong Kong, 8.8% in Singapore, 12% in South Korea and 11% in Taiwan. Export growth rates soared to 40.7% in Hong Kong, 9.1% in Singapore, 32.7% in South Korea and 36% in Taiwan. For the Asian NICs as a group, export growth recovered from a low of –5% in 1985, to 35% in 1987–1988 (Rowley 1990c:54). For a time, it looked as if the Asian NICs would once again achieve, and maintain, double-digit growth rates.

Slower Growth in the 1990s

Throughout 1988, the growth rate of the US economy began to weaken. From a level of 5% in the first quarter of 1988, US GDP growth declined steadily to 1% in the last quarter of 1990. By the first quarter of 1991, the US economy was in recession, partly due to the after effects of the world-wide stock market crash of 1987, and the Gulf War in 1990. Other countries in the OECD, such as Canada and Britain also moved into recession in 1991 (Holloway 1991b:41). In addition, by 1990, all the Asian NICs were more dependent on the US market for their exports than they were a decade earlier (Holloway 1990:54).

The general deterioration of the economic health of the world economy suffered another setback in mid-1991, when the Japanese economy began to slow down (from 6% growth in 1990) to 3% growth in 1991 and 0.2% growth in 1993.

In line with this general slowdown, the export growth of the Asian NICs as a whole declined from 34.2% in 1987 to 8.4% in 1990. In South Korea, export growth declined from 36.4% in 1987 to 2.8% in 1990, while in Taiwan it declined from 34.8% to 1.4%. Singapore's export growth declined from 38.3% in 1988 to 6.0% in 1992. Even though Hong Kong managed to maintain double-digit growth rates of exports, it experienced a decline from 36.8% in 1987 to 12.3% in 1990.

By 1992, GDP growth rates in the Asian NICs had declined to 5.0% in Hong Kong, 5.8% in Singapore, 4.5% in South Korea and 6.6% in Taiwan. Apart from the general decline in world economic growth, the Asian NICs were, by this time, experiencing increased protectionism in their major markets, rising rates of inflation, increasing social unrest (especially in South Korea and Taiwan), and political uncertainty (especially in Hong Kong). The prognosis for the 1990s was that the era of double-digit growth for the Asian NICs had passed irrevocably into history.

Conclusion

The recession of the mid-1980s affected all the Asian NICs severely. Growth rates of GDP and of exports, which were in double-digits only a few years prior to 1985, fell dramatically, many into negative figures. Unemployment rose, as firms started laying off workers.

While the sudden slowdown of the US economy triggered off the recession in the Asian NICs, internal factors aggravated the depth of the recession. Government inspired wage increases of substantial proportions reduced the international competitiveness of Singapore labour. Even in South Korea and Taiwan, where wage rises were not as high, tightening labour markets were putting upward pressure on wages. Most Asian NICs experienced upheavals in their domestic financial markets, as many firms collapsed in the wake of the 1987 stock market crash.

After a brief recovery in 1987, the US economy started to slide again in 1988, descending to 1% growth in 1990 and moving into recession in 1991. Other OECD economies followed. Even the Japanese economy slowed down to what its Finance Minister called "cruising speed", 3% growth in 1991. By 1993, Japanese growth had slowed to 0.2%. As a result of the general slowdown of world economic growth, the growth of exports of the Asian NICs as a group descended to 8.4% per annum in 1990. GDP growth rates of all the Asian NICs were about 6% per annum (except for Hong Kong, which registered 3.5% in 1991). With more difficult trading conditions expected to continue throughout the 1990s, the heady days of double-digit growth for the Asian NICs appeared to have gone for good.

By 1992, most of the major OECD countries were in recession. Even the Japanese economy, which was expected to pull the rest of the world into higher growth rates, hovered at the brink of negative growth. Although all the Asian NICs were affected by this general decline in economic conditions in their major markets, none had suffered the severe declines in output and employment experienced during the 1984–1985 recession. For example, the Singapore economy, which experienced a growth rate of about 7% in 1991, was expecting growth in 1992 to be in the range of 5% to 7% per annum (Ministry of Trade and Industry 1991:25). In fact, the economy grew by 5.8% in 1992. One reason for this is that the coincidence of unfavourable internal and external factors, which accounted for the severity of the recession in the mid-1980s, did not prevail in the early 1990s.

CHAPTER 6

Prospects for the Asian NICs in the 1990s

Introduction

The 1990s ushered in a period of slower growth for the world economy. By 1990, a seven-year expansion in the world economy came to a virtual halt. A large number of industrial economies in the OECD showed signs of slowing down as they implemented tight monetary policies in response to rising inflation. The slowdown in world economic activity became more pronounced and widespread with the outbreak of war in the Persian Gulf in August 1990. By the end of the year, average real GDP growth in the major industrial countries had slowed to 2.6% per annum (compared to 4.5% in 1988), and several large economies (the USA, UK and Canada) were in the throes of a recession. Even the Japanese economy started slowing down (Holloway 1991b:41; World Bank 1991:21-23), and looked set to enter a recession (Rowley 1991e:120).

The prospects for world economic growth in the 1990s do not look bright. Uncertainty over a successful conclusion of the Uruguay Round of GATT talks, which dragged on until the end of 1993, caused many major trading nations to adopt protectionist stances. The unification of the EU in January 1993 suggests a more inward-looking Europe, while the proposed establishment of a free trade area in North America is likely to mean reduced access to the US market by other countries. The demand for international finance is expected to increase from such countries as Germany, the countries of Eastern Europe, as well as the less developed countries of the Third World. At the same time, the supply of international finance is shrinking, as Japan (the major creditor nation in the world) moves toward a recession. All this indicates a much more difficult economic environment for world economic development in the 1990s. In addition, the competitive advantage of the Asian NICs is being eroded by technological changes in manufacturing processes (Drucker 1986; World Bank 1991:26).

At the same time, all the Asian NICs are experiencing upward pressures on their exchange rates *vis-à-vis* their major trading partners. This, combined with rising costs, makes their exports less competitive in world markets. The net result of all this is a slowing down in the growth rates of GDP and of exports in all the Asian NICs. For the first time since the early 1980s, the growth rate of exports of the Asian NICs in 1989 was lower than that of the average export growth rate of all Asian countries. This gap widened in 1990, and is expected to persist in 1991 and 1992 (FEER 1991e:57). In a sense, the very success of the Asian NICs in export-oriented industrialization has led to increasing difficulties in maintaining their success (Stutchbury 1990:75; Economist 1990e:65).

More Difficult Trading Conditions

Slow Down in World Trade

In the 1950s and 1960s, world trade grew at about 8% per annum. During the 1970s, it grew at about 4.5% per annum, while in the 1980s, it slowed down to less than 3% per annum (Broad and Cavanagh 1989:56). The long post-war boom, which ended in 1973, marked the beginning of an era of slower growth in world incomes and world trade and was accompanied by increased protectionism and friction between trading partners (Choo and Ali 1989:14–25). Trade can no longer be relied upon to be the engine of growth (Lewis 1980). Between 1968 and 1973, the growth of imports into the USA averaged 9% per annum. In 1988, it was 7.3% but declined to –1.5% in 1991. For the EU, the growth of imports in 1968–1973 averaged 8% per annum. In 1991, it was 3.2%. In 1991, imports into the UK declined by –5.8%, and in the following year, imports into France declined by –1.2% (IMF 1993:403,56,400,177). World trade is expected to continue to slow down in the 1990s. In 1991, imports of the industrial countries grew by only 1.5%. In the following year, imports recovered somewhat and registered a growth of about 4.9% (IMF 1993:6). As a result of the general slowdown in world trade, economic growth of the Asian NICs is expected to be lower. However, they are still expected to perform better than most other countries in the world (Williams 1989:74).

Recession in Major Trading Partners

The stock market crash of 1987 was followed by an economic recession in some of the major industrial economies. This was accompanied by the collapse of a number of major financial and non-financial institutions in the USA and elsewhere. Between 1989 and 1991, the US economy moved from a growth rate of 2.5% per annum to –1.2% per annum. The UK economy declined from 1.8% per annum to –2.1% per annum. Canada, which registered a growth rate of 3% per annum in 1989, slid to -1.1% in 1991. Even the Japanese economy, on which hopes of a world recovery had been pinned, slowed down from 5.6% in 1990 to 3.6% in 1991 (Holloway 1991b:41; Kaplinsky 1984:77), and was expected to experience negative growth in 1992 (Rowley 1991e:120). In fact, Japan registered a growth rate of 1.5% in 1992, but in the second quarter of 1993, the growth rate of the Japanese economy hit 0.2%. In 1992, the industrialized countries of the world as a group, registered a growth rate of only 0.5%.

The general slowdown in the world economy was reflected in lower growth rates for the Asian NICs. In 1990, GDP growth per annum was 3.2% in Hong Kong, 8.3% in Singapore, 9.2% in South Korea and 4.9% in Taiwan. The very low growth rate of the Hong Kong economy was largely due to political uncertainties about the future of Hong Kong following the 1989 Tiananmen massacre in Beijing. By 1992, the growth rates of GDP in the Asian NICs were 5.0% in Hong Kong, 5.8% in Singapore, 4.5% in South Korea and 6.6% in Taiwan. Only a few years before in 1987 and 1988, the Asian NICs were posting double-digit growth rates.

Increasing Protectionism

Recession in the major advanced industrial economies and more difficult trading conditions, have been associated with increasing protectionism, particularly in the USA and the EU, which have had persistent trade deficits with Japan, and the Asian NICs. Protectionism has taken the form of tariff, as well as non-tariff barriers. GATT has identified over 600 different types of non-tariff barriers, while UNCTAD has listed over 21,000 product-specific restrictions against imports (Kaplinsky 1984:78). During the period 1966–1986, the share of imports restricted by non-tariff barriers increased by 20% in the USA, 40% in Japan and 160% in the EU. By 1987, some 28% of all trade in industrial countries was affected by non-tariff barriers (World Bank 1991:105).

In the USA, increased protectionism has taken the form of a trade law, called "Super 301". This is a provision under the Omnibus Trade Act of 1988, which requires the US administration to identify "unfair" trade barriers (including copyright and patent infringement) with are most harmful to US exporters (the USA determines what is "unfair"). Following this, the administration has 12 to 18 months to negotiate the removal of these barriers. If these talks are unsuccessful, the administration can levy tariffs of up to 100% on selected imports from an offending country.

On 25 May 1989, the US administration named Japan, India and Brazil as the top offenders. South Korea and Taiwan only avoided being named as "unfair traders" by making last-minute concessions to the USA to open up their markets to US exports. Taiwan, for example, had agreed to reduce its trade surplus with the USA by 10% per annum between 1989 and 1992, and to cut import tariffs by 3.5% in 1992.

Furthermore, the US administration put eight countries

(which included India, China, South Korea, Taiwan and Thailand) on a "watch list" because of their alleged failure to protect US patents and copyrights. They faced retaliation within 21 months. Seventeen other countries were put under "special attention" while their negotiations with the US were in progress (Chanda 1989:99).

In addition to this, the USA (which had earlier signed a free trade agreement with Canada in January 1989) began negotiations (in 1991) to include Mexico in such a scheme. A North American Free Trade Area (NAFTA), which included Mexico (and eventually other Latin American countries) would severely affect access to the US market by the Asian NICs. Since most Asian NICs depend heavily on the US market for their exports, alarm bells started ringing in East Asia. Even the possibility of gaining access to NAFTA by moving production facilities to countries such as Mexico was blocked by strict rules of origin (Awanohara 1991a:42,44).

In the EU, the impending removal of all internal trade barriers in January 1993 signalled that preferential access to the EU by developing countries, after that date, would become increasingly difficult (in 1989, Asian NICs such as Hong Kong, Singapore and South Korea had already been denied access to the EU market in some products) (Islam 1990a:38-39). Recent estimates indicate that, with the exception of Hong Kong, all the Asian NICs would be adversely affected by the removal of internal trade barriers in the EU after January 1993 (Davenport 1991:69). Of more importance is the real prospect of the diversion of investment by EU companies away from the Asian NICs to member countries of the EU. Rather than a German company investing in Hong Kong or Singapore, it is likely to find it more attractive to invest in one of the EU member countries itself (Hughes Hallet 1994:121–146).

In 1990, there was serious concern in East Asia that the EU was going to restrict imports further unless "linkages" with exports from the EU were agreed upon. Countries such as Japan and South Korea, for example, would only be allowed to export cars to the EU if European banks were allowed to operate in these countries. In addition, "transplant" factories operating in the EU after January 1993 would have to meet stringent "local content" requirements and would be monitored for six years to make sure that they did not exceed an EU-wide market share (Rowley 1990d:63). On 26 July 1991, the EU announced that Japanese cars made in "transplant" factories in the EU would be regarded as imports and that the Japanese share of the EU car market would be limited by an EU-wide share, as well as specified shares in particular European countries. This rule has so far not been applied to imports of cars from South Korea, because the volume of such imports is small (Islam 1991b:54–55).

On 21 April 1991, a group made up of the leading European electronics companies asked the European Commission for protection against East Asian imports. Apart from tariff protection and anti-dumping investigations, the companies also asked for East Asian "transplant" factories to be treated differently from European-owned electronics plants operating in the EU (Islam 1991a:38). The EU is also continuing to put pressure on some NICs (such as South Korea) to give EU exporters better access to their markets in exchange for less obstruction into the EU (Islam and Clifford 1991:67).

Increasing protectionism in the EU towards the Asian NICs can be illustrated by the case of South Korea. In 1981, the EU placed no restrictions on the imports of TV sets from South Korea. In 1988, 36% of South Korean imports into the EU were subject to import restrictions. In the import of footwear, the EU had imposed restrictions on 70% of imports from South Korea in 1981. By 1988, this ratio had risen to 88% (Leipziger 1988:127).

Even Singapore came under the scrutiny of the EU's Executive Commission, as nine EU producers of electronic weighing scales (for example, those used in supermarket checkouts) charged it with dumping imports at below cost of production and grabbing 14% of the EU market for the product (*Straits Times* 1992b:40).

The uncertainty about a successful conclusion of the Uruguay Round of the GATT talks during 1990–1992 has also given rise to fears that world trade may be breaking up into regional trading blocks, one in North America and the other in the EU. Should this occur, the trade prospects for the Asian NICs would be bleak, since they depend on these markets for most of their exports. This pessimistic outlook has renewed interest in, and underlined the urgency for, the establishment of a trade bloc in the Pacific (centred on Japan). The proposals for such a regional trading group in the Pacific will be discussed in Chapter 8 (Islam 1990b:57).

Currency Re-alignments

Rising Trade Surpluses

All the Asian NICs have been recording rising trade surpluses as a result of their successful export-oriented policies. Before the mid-1980s, Singapore's current account surplus was usually negative. Since 1985, however, it has been consistently positive, reaching US$1.6 billion in 1988. A similar pattern can be observed in South Korea. Before 1986, its current account balance was always negative, but in that year it recorded a surplus of US$4.6 billion. By 1988, this had grown to US$14.1 billion. South Korea's trade surplus did not last long, however. Hong Kong has been earning trade surpluses for most of the last 20 years. In 1988, its current account surplus was US$1.2 billion (World Bank 1990). This pattern is also true of Taiwan. Apart from the 1973 oil crisis, it has always recorded a surplus on its current account. This reached US$18 billion in 1987, but has declined somewhat in recent years (Council for Economic Planning and Development 1990). In per capita terms, Singapore had the highest level of foreign reserves in the world in 1988 (US$6459 per head), followed by Switzerland (US$4881) and Taiwan (US$4012).

Of more importance, is the fact that all the Asian NICs have been recording increasing trade surpluses with their major trading partner, the USA. In 1984, the trade balance with the USA was US$35 billion for Hong Kong, US$1 billion for Singapore, US$2 billion for South Korea and US$7 billion for Taiwan. In 1987, these had soared to US$70 billion for Hong Kong, US$4.5 billion for Singapore, US$8 billion for South Korea and US$16.5 billion for Taiwan (Chanda 1987:99; Economist 1990e:65).

Appreciation of Currencies

The large trade surpluses of the Asian NICs are partly due to the fact that, up to the 1980s, their currencies had been under-valued (Economist 1990e:65). Their rising trade surpluses with the USA have resulted in a steady appreciation of all the currencies of the Asian NICs *vis-à-vis* the US Dollar. Between 1985 and 1989, the Hong Kong Dollar appreciated by 1.5%, the Singapore Dollar by 10%, the South Korean Won by 20% and the New Taiwanese Dollar by 55% against the US Dollar. The US administration has put constant pressure on the Asian NICs (especially South Korea and Taiwan) to revalue their currencies in the light of their growing trade surpluses with the USA (Awanohara 1990:56).

The upward trend in the exchange rates between the currencies of the Asian NICs and the US Dollar has blunted the competitive edge of the exports of the Asian NICs. Since the late 1980s, the real effective exchange rates of all the Asian NICs have been moving upward (Economist 1990d:124). This has been compounded by rising wage costs in all the Asian NICs (discussed below). The prospects for continued rapid expansion of exports in the 1990s, (particularly of labour-intensive manufactures) looks bleak.

Another factor contributing to this pessimistic view, is the likelihood of a continued upward movement in the value of the Yen relative to the US dollar. Trade frictions between Japan and her major trading partners (the USA and EU) do not appear to be abating. This is likely to give rise to renewed pressures to upvalue the Yen. While this has some advantages for the Asian NICs, since their exports become more competitive relative to Japan's (as explained in Chapter 4), it also has the effect of raising the costs of production of these countries, since much of their inputs are imported from Japan. This will diminish the competitive edge of the exports of the Asian NICs to the USA and EU.

Changes in Technology

In the 1990s, there is likely to be an acceleration of technological change in manufacturing that will make cheap labour less and less important in the production of manufactured goods. Capital-intensive techniques (for example, the use of robots), and computer-aided manufacturing processes (for example, in the textile industry), are likely to make the production of some (previously labour-intensive) products more efficient in the developed countries, rather than developing countries (Drucker 1986; World Bank 1991:26). Off-shore production in the Asian NICs and other less developed countries is likely to be affected adversely.

Robotization

Although robots were in use in some manufacturing processes in the 1970s, their widespread use developed in the 1980s. In the electronics industry, the introduction of robots in the various aspects of manufacture has reduced labour costs, increased productivity and increased product quality. This has reduced the comparative advantage of the Asian NICs in the labour-intensive operations. For example, in the assembly of semiconductors in the 1970s, production costs (using manual labour) in Hong Kong were 66% lower than those in the USA. In the early 1980s, the introduction of semi-automatic technology reduced Hong Kong's cost advantage to 36% below that in the USA. By 1983, the introduction of fully automated assembly lines reduced Hong Kong's cost advantage further, to 8% lower than that in the USA (Kaplinsky 1984:81).

Computer-Aided Manufacturing

Another important technological development of the 1980s is computer-aided-manufacturing (CAM) and computer-aided-design (CAD). Owing to its flexibility and programmability, it has reduced the importance of scale economies and enabled production to be undertaken closer to final markets. This has made off-shore production in faraway countries less and less important. Second,

CAM and CAD have reduced costs of production in some previously labour-intensive manufacturing operations. A good example of this is in the cutting stage of garment manufacture. In this industry, labour costs in less developed countries in the 1970s used to be only 5% of labour costs in developed countries. However, CAM/CAD technology has now removed much of this competitive advantage. (Hoffmann 1985).

Computer-Aided Inventory Control

The "Just-in-Time" (JIT) system of computer-aided inventory control is another instance of technological change eroding the comparative advantage of the Asian NICs and other less developed countries. The essence of this system is to keep inventories to a minimum, so as to keep production flexible and amenable to changes in product line. In the motor car industry, copies of a computer printout of the specifications of a particular model are distributed to spare parts suppliers as well as the main assembly line. All the components of that particular model are synchronized to meet at the right time and place on the assembly line (Ohmae 1982:194–195). The importance of this system of "zero-inventory" is that parts suppliers have to be located close to the final assembly plant, rather than thousands of kilometres away in other countries. This therefore reduces the importance of off-shore production in countries such as the Asian NICs.

The impact of these new technologies in manufacturing is that they have, once again, begun to make the manufacture of some products efficient in the developed economies. In some cases, such as the production of television sets and the assembly of electronic circuits, unit costs of production in developed economies are now lower than those of the Asian NICs. This has led to a movement of production processes back to the developed countries (Kaplinsky 1984:83–84; Junne 1987). Nevertheless, there is some doubt about the effects of technological change on industrial location. Chen (1990:66–69) has recently argued that technological change is unlikely to cause much investment and trade reversal in the electronics industry because, foreign firms have already invested large amounts of fixed capital in developing countries, which have large potential markets for their products, and that in any case, automated manufacturing technology requires skilled personnel who are much cheaper to hire in less developed countries. In other industries, such as textiles, there is some evidence to confirm that technological change in production processes have already offset the comparative advantage of the less developed countries and shifted production back to the developed countries. The use of computers in carding and combing machines has increased output by 300% or more, whilst reducing labour input. Similar increases in productivity have been achieved in other aspects of textile manufacture, such as knitting and weaving. By the mid-1980s, productivity in textile manufacture was higher in the USA, EU and Japan than in many developing countries, in spite of much lower wages in the latter (Velasco 1990:97–104).

Changes in Consumer Preferences

Kaplinsky (1991:29–35) has argued that, in the 1990s, changes in consumer preferences are also causing the Asian NICs (and other less developed countries) to lose their attractiveness as off-shore production platforms of multinational companies.

Kaplinsky's view is that consumers are now less concerned with price and more concerned with quality and fashion. This makes it necessary for firms to be flexible and to be able to respond quickly to changes in consumer preferences. In some products such as fashion clothing, shoes, and women's leather goods, firms have to be able to respond quickly to changes in style, colour and other product characteristics in order to meet consumer demand. This makes it necessary for all the firm's production processes (everything from design to manufacturing to the supply of inputs) to be located nearby. The clothing industry is a prime example of this. The moment a shift in consumer preferences for a certain colour or style is detected (for example, from plain-coloured polo-necked jumpers to multi-coloured V-necked jumpers with geometric designs), a firm's entire (jumper) product line will be shifted toward producing the current styles (Clifford 1994b:78).

For the Asian NICs (as well as for other less developed countries) this means that multinational firms will be less interested in spreading their production facilities across the world, in order to take advantage of low-cost labour. Price, in any case, is no longer the major consideration in the minds of consumers. The implication of this is that, in the 1990s, the Asian NICs (as well as other less developed countries) cannot expect to see large increases in foreign investment, as multinational companies in certain product groups will try to keep all the parts of their production processes near to each other.

Rising Costs

Tightening Labour Markets

By the end of the 1980s, the rapid growth and development of the Asian NICs was giving rise to increasing wages. Rising incomes, higher levels of education and the increasing employment rate led to declining fertility rates, tightening labour markets and rising rates of inflation.

South Korea provides a good example of this phenomenon. Many firms in South Korea are now turning down export orders because of the lack of workers to fill them. In 1991, the Ministry of Labour estimated that there was a shortage of 166,000 workers in the manufacturing sector. This is reflected in the fall in employment in the Kuro Industrial Complex outside Seoul, from 69,000 in 1988 to 55,000 in 1991. The main reason for this shortage of labour is the stabilization of the growth of the labour force. During the 1970s and 1980s, the labour force grew because of the "baby boom" of the 1950s. This has now stabilized and the number of new young workers is likely to decline in the future. Even though the female participation rate rose from 40.7% in 1984 to 47.2% in 1991, this has not been able to ease the shortage of labour in South Korea (Clifford 1991:30-31). These problems are expected to persist into the year 2000 (Park 1988).

In Taiwan, the government Council on Economic Planning and Development estimated that, by the end of 1991, there would be a shortage of 120,000 unskilled workers in Taiwan (assuming a GDP growth rate of 6%–7%). The construction sector needs an additional 45,000 workers just to complete projects already under way. Many construction projects are already falling behind schedule. For example, Taipei's MRT system is likely to be short of 20,000 workers in the next two or three years. The main reason for this shortage is a slowdown in population growth. Taiwan's labour forces declined in 1990 for the first time. In addition, labour force participation rates have dropped to 58.2%, the lowest level in five years. The unemployment rate has stayed at 2% for the last five years. Wages have shot up by 12.2% annually for the past four years. Productivity has been increasing by only 8.3%. In 1990, wages rose by 13.5%, while the economy grew by only 5.3% (Baum 1991a:36-37).

In Hong Kong, inflation has been rising steadily in recent years. Between March 1988 and March 1989, the CPI increased by 12.9%. As a result, Hong Kong's trade position has been deteriorating steadily. The main reason for this deterioration in economic performance is rising wages as a result of a tightening labour market. In 1990–1991, wages in the manufacturing sector rose by 19%, while those in the construction sector rose by 18%. Service sector wages rose by 13%. These increases are much higher than the rate of inflation and indicates that the CPI will continue to rise steadily. Hong Kong's loss of competitiveness, as a result of rising inflation can be seen in the low rate of growth of exports, 4.4% in 1990, while imports grew by 22.6% over the same period. Production of manufactured goods increased by only 3.1% in the last three months of 1990, after declining by 3.7% during the 12 months ending in the first quarter of 1990. Many manufacturing firms in the textile and plastics industries reduced their labour force by 10% during the 12-month period ending in February 1991 (Taylor 1991a:66). Wages in Hong Kong are now five times higher than the Shenzhen Free Trade Zone, just across its border with China. While labour shortages are a major cause of inflation in

Hong Kong, "positive non-intervention" by the Hong Kong government has allowed the growth of liquidity to fuel inflationary pressures (Taylor 1991c:44).

Singapore's population of 2.7 million in 1990 is growing at less than 1% per annum (compared with 5% per annum in the 1950s). By 2025, population growth may be as low as 0.2% per annum. Singapore's labour force, which was growing at 4% per annum in the 1960s, is now growing at less than 1% per annum and is likely to contract after 2010. Productivity growth, which averaged 3%–4% in the late 1980s is also likely to slow down in the 1990s, as the Singapore economy moves toward a more services-oriented economy. Economic growth is expected to be at around 5% per annum in the 1990s, compared with just under 10% per annum in the late 1980s (Balakrishnan 1991a:55). As a result of these trends, Singapore has been losing its comparative advantage in certain types of manufactures because of rising wages. In the third quarter of 1990, unit business costs (which include wages, service charges and government levies) rose by nearly 8% over the previous year. Wages in the manufacturing sector rose by 10% in 1990, while productivity growth lagged behind. Wages in the financial sector rose by 20% in 1990 (Balakrishnan 1991b:44).

An example of the impact of rising labour costs in Singapore can be seen in the increasing trend of local firms moving their low value-added manufacturing activities to countries such as Malaysia, Indonesia, Thailand and even China, where wages are very much lower. In January 1992, the Lam Soon Oil and Soap Manufacturing Company, one of the largest in Singapore, announced its intention to close down its entire manufacturing operation in Singapore, and relocate it to Malaysia and China. The Singapore operation would concentrate on warehousing, finance, sales and marketing activities and had the intention of moving into biotechnology (*Straits Times* 1992a:38).

Loss of Competitiveness

By the late 1980s, all the Asian NICs were losing their competitive edge in products, which a decade earlier were their major export items. For example, exports of radios, tape recorders and record players from the Asian NICs (mainly South Korea and Taiwan) to Japan boomed between 1985 and 1988, reaching a peak of just under 17 million units in 1988, but falling sharply after that. Rising costs and appreciation of currencies relative to the Yen were the main reasons for this. Between November 1988 and June 1990, the New Taiwanese Dollar rose from ¥4.33 to ¥5.64 to the NT$. This was a 30% increase in six months. The South Korean Won, during the same period, appreciated by ¥17.7 per 100 Won to ¥21.6 per 100 Won (a 22% appreciation) (do Rosario 1990:53; Rowley 1990e:54). By the late 1980s, all the Asian NICs were experiencing increasing rates of inflation. Between 1983 and 1988, inflation ranged from 1% per annum in Taiwan to 5% per annum in Singapore. By 1990, the rate of inflation was 12% in Hong Kong, 9% in South Korea and between 4% and 5% in Taiwan and Singapore. For the first time in many years, inflation in the Asian NICs was higher than the average (4% per annum) for the seven biggest OECD countries which are their main export markets (Economist 1991f:89–91).

Meeting the Challenges of the 1990s

The Asian NICs are gearing up to meet the challenges they face in the 1990s and beyond. Many are seeking to reduce their dependence on their major markets (the USA and EU), and are developing new markets in the less developed countries and in Eastern Europe. The larger of the Asian NICs (South Korea and Taiwan), are also concentrating more on their domestic markets than they have been in the past. Another strategy being undertaken is to move production offshore, either to the developed countries (in order to overcome protectionist measures), or to the less developed countries, especially the near-NICs in Southeast Asia (in order to take advantage of lower wage rates). By the late 1980s, the Asian NICs were the major sources of foreign investment in the ASEAN countries and accounted for a larger volume of foreign investment than even Japan. For example, in 1988, the Asian NICs invested US$490 million in Indonesia (24% of the total foreign investment in that country), while Japan invested US$169 million (8% of the total). A similar pattern can be observed in the other ASEAN countries (Smith 1989b:59). In addition, most of the Asian NICs are trying to move up the technological ladder into more skill-intensive, higher-technology products which would enable them to sustain their higher wage rates. Some are also importing foreign labour in an effort to keep production costs down. There are also moves to set up a regional trading bloc in the Pacific as a response to increasing protectionism in the USA and EU. The most recent of these, was the Seattle summit meeting of leaders from the Asia Pacific region to discuss the formation of APEC (the Asia Pacific Economic Community).

In the framework of Porter's analysis (1990:566–567), the Asian NICs are preparing to meet the challenges of the 1990s, by moving from factor-driven and investment-driven development, to innovation-driven development. This is being done by a process of upgrading the factors which affect their international competitiveness (Porter 1990:560–562).

Reduced Dependence on the USA and EU

All the Asian NICs are trying to reduce their high levels of dependence on the USA and EU for their exports. Many are seeking to increase their trade with other less developed countries, particularly those with higher per capita incomes (such as Malaysia, Thailand and Indonesia). With the ending of the Cold War, South Korea and Taiwan have been cultivating Eastern European countries as markets for their exports (Rowley 1989a; Baum 1990a; Clifford 1990a).

Developing Domestic Markets

The Asian NICs with relatively large domestic markets have also been turning their attention to developing their domestic markets. With rising incomes, domestic sales could offset declines in export markets. The South Korean car industry is a good example of this. In 1977, car sales in South Korea were 100,000 units, while exports were also about 100,000 units. In 1987, car exports were 1 million units, while domestic car sales were only 380,000 units. By 1989, car exports reached 1.8 million units, while domestic car sales were 750,000 units (Clifford 1989b:63). In 1990, due to disappointing sales in the USA and Canada, South Korean car exports actually fell below domestic car sales (Holloway 1991c:51).

Moving Offshore

Rising domestic wages and rapidly appreciating exchange rates have also prompted the Asian NICs to move off-shore. Some of this movement is to the developed industrial countries of the OECD (such as the USA and EU), where the aim is to get under protective barriers by setting up "transplant" factories. Another form of this off-shore movement is to the less developed countries (especially the near-NICs of Southeast Asia) where wages are much lower. The outflow of foreign investment from the Asian NICs also helps to reduce their balance of payments surpluses and upward pressures on their exchange rates.

Transplanting production to the developed countries

Foreign investment by South Korea and Taiwan has increased rapidly in the late 1980s. In 1984, South Korean foreign investment stood at US$57 million. By 1988, it had grown to US$212 million. The increase in foreign investment is even more pronounced for Taiwan. In 1984, Taiwanese foreign investment was US$39 million. In 1988 it was US$219 million. Since 1987, some 2,500 Taiwanese companies have set up manufacturing plants in Southeast Asia, while about 1,100 companies have done the same in the Peoples' Republic of China (FEER 1991h:225; Baum 1993:44–45).

South Korea has set up production plants in the EU in an attempt to combat increasing protectionism in Western Europe. Samsung has consumer electronics plants in Britain and Portugal; Daewoo manufactures microwave ovens in France and video tape-recorders in Northern Ireland. Goldstar manufactures the same products in Germany; Hyundai builds cars in Canada (Clifford and Moore 1989:89; Wilson 1988).

Moving production to the less developed countries

Many Asian NICs are also moving production facilities to the less developed countries, particularly the near-NICs of Southeast Asia. In the late 1980s, countries such as South Korea, Taiwan and Singapore increased their investments in Thailand, Malaysia and Indonesia many-fold (Holloway 1989b:71). Singapore, in particular, has been actively promoting the concept of two "growth triangles", one in the south (involving the Riau islands, Singapore and the Malaysian state of Johor), and the other in the north (involving Medan in northern Sumatra and the island of Penang) (Vatikiotis 1991a; Vatikiotis 1991b; Lee 1991). The cost of unskilled labour in Johor was about 43% that of unskilled labour in Singapore. For Batam, one of the main islands in the Riau group of islands, the differential is 26%. For an economy facing acute labour shortages, the logic of the southern "growth triangle" is clear (Lee 1991:9).

Singapore is also embarking on a strategy of "internationalizing" its domestic corporations in a bid to escape from increasingly unfavourable demographics at home (Balakrishnan 1991a:55–56).

Another good example of this development is the movement of Hong Kong industry into southern China, particularly the province of Guangdong. Labour costs in the Shenzhen Free Trade Zone are the highest in Guangdong province. Yet they are only 20% that of Hong Kong. A 50-year lease on undeveloped industrial land in Hong Kong is up to 50 times higher than in Shenzhen. As a result, Hong Kong has moved much of its labour-intensive manufacturing into southern China. Hong Kong companies now employ 4 million factory workers in southern China, while employing only 550,000 workers in Hong Kong itself. Increasingly, Hong Kong is being transformed into a high-wage service economy (Clifford 1994a:68–69).

In South Korea, wages have been rising at an average rate of 15.8% per annum since 1987. Labour shortages and rising costs have prompted many firms to move off-shore in search of lower costs. In 1993, South Korea's outward foreign investment reached US$1.8 billion (a 54% increase over the previous year). Half of this went to Asia, where South Korea's main targets for off-shore production are located (mainly in Indonesia and China). Most of South Korea's outward foreign investment (82%) was made by small- and medium-sized companies in search of lower production costs, and were in small- to medium-scale projects. However, after a slow start, foreign investment by South Korea's *chaebols* has begun to take off, with many large scale projects (ranging from cement, glass and steel to automobiles) established in China (Paisley and Kiernan 1994:53–57).

Moving up the Technological Ladder

A further strategy for coping with rising wages and increasing protectionism is to move up the technological ladder. All the Asian NICs have been pursuing this strategy vigorously.

In South Korea, industrial restructuring has been taking place, with the aim of closing down manufacturing operations that are no longer sustainable and moving into higher technology products (Paisley 1992:29–34). Instead of making labour-intensive garments, South Korean firms are concentrating on capital-intensive polyester and cotton spinning, as well as sophisticated consumer electronic products, such as 16 megabit DRAMs (Clifford 1991c: 66–69). In Hong Kong, garment manufacturers are moving up-market into fashion garments (Stillitoe 1985b). The Hong Kong government has also financed the establishment of the Hong Kong Industrial Technology Centre in a bid to assist Hong Kong's attempt to move up the technology ladder (Clifford 1994a:68–69). In Taiwan, the movement has been away from labour-intensive manufactures to high value-added services (particularly financial services) and electronics (Clifford 1989c:86–87; Clifford 1990b:42–43). Similarly, Singapore has been moving up the technological ladder, into wafer fabrication and voice-input computers (Goldstein 1988c; Balakrishnan 1991c; Johnstone 1991; Balakrishnan, Awanohara and Burton 1992). Singapore's movement up the technological ladder can be seen in the higher skill-intensity of its exports and the increase in capital-intensive inputs in its exports (Sandilands and Tan 1986).

All the NICs are increasing their research and development activities. In South Korea, for example, R&D expenditure in the electronics industry more than doubled, from Won 292 billion in 1985 to Won 832 billion in 1989. Total R&D expenditures rose from 0.58% of GNP in 1980, to 1.9% of GNP in 1989. By the year 2000, this is expected to reach 5% of GNP (Clifford 1991c:67). Taiwan is also moving in the same direction. Between 1991 and 1995, it plans to triple public and private R&D expenditures, and intends to concentrate on such high technology products as high-definition television (HDTV), aerospace, computers and tele-communications equipment (Business Times 1992a:9). In addition, many Asian NICs are now attempting to market their products internationally, under their own brand names, rather than act as suppliers to established international companies (Goll 1992:62–63). In some cases, firms in the Asian NICs have bought foreign firms with established brand names, with the intention of marketing their own products under these well-known brand names. The purchase of the Singer Sewing Machine company by the Hong Kong-based SemiTech is an example of this. In other cases, firms in the Asian NICs are promoting their own brand names internationally. The Taiwanese computer manufacturer, Acer (which is thought to have spent US$1 million searching for a suitable name), is an example of this (Goldstein 1991:52–53).

The gradual upgrading of the Asian NICs technological base can be seen in their exports to the OECD. In 1964, 82% of the OECD's imports from the NICs (including Brazil and Mexico) were made up of low-technology manufactured goods, while 18% were made up of middle and high technology products. By 1985, the proportions had changed to 53% and 47% respectively (OECD 1988:24).

All the Asian NICs face two major problems in trying to move up the technological ladder into capital and skill-intensive products. The first is the lack of managerial personnel. Most of the Asian NICs have adopted an elitist higher education system which turns out a relatively small number of university graduates each year. While this may not have caused major problems in their labour-intensive export phase, this is not the case in the next phase of their development. Technology and skill-intensive manufacturing require highly-trained management which all the Asian NICs are short of (Worthy 1991:81–89). The move into higher-technology manufactures also requires an adequate supply of engineers and technicians. While this may not be a problem for South Korea and Taiwan (where over 30% of university students study engineering), it is a major constraint for Singapore and Hong Kong.

In addition, skill and knowledge-intensive industrial development requires creative thinking. Instead of merely following instructions handed down from above, people need to develop new ideas, new ways of solving problems. Creative thinking, however, is in short supply, especially in the Asian NICs. After 30 years of doing what one is told to do, it is difficult to be spontaneously creative (Economist 1990g:77). People in the Asian NICs have been used to being persuaded to letting their leaders do their thinking for them. This problem was captured succinctly in a headline of one of the issues of the Singapore *Straits Times*, which tried to move its readers with the message: "Have fun spontaneously – here's how". The dearth of creative thinkers in the Asian NICs is also reflected in their low levels of achievement in the arts. Very few artists, film directors, novelists, musicians, etc. of world class have emerged from the Asian NICs. The few that have, usually have had to go abroad to develop their talents.

Importing Labour

Some of the Asian NICs are also importing labour in an attempt to deal with labour shortages and rising costs. In order to ease labour shortages, the Taiwanese government is allowing the import of foreign workers, mainly from Thailand and the Philippines.

However, trade union pressure has kept the number of imported workers down to a mere trickle. In addition, the government has tacitly allowed firms to retain their illegal workers. For example, some 3,000 illegal workers in the textile industry have been granted a temporary amnesty in order to aid the Taiwanese textile industry. Without migrant workers, it is estimated that half the firms in the industry would close down (Baum 1991a:36–37; Economist 1991c:34). The Roman Catholic Church in Taiwan estimated that, in 1990, there were at least 200,000 illegal workers on the island, mainly from labour-surplus Asian countries such as the Philippines and Indonesia (Baum 1990b:16).

Similarly, Singapore, which has imported unskilled labour in the past, has been trying to attract skilled labour from Hong Kong by offering preferential conditions for migration (Balakrishnan 1989b:35).

Setting up an Asia-Pacific Trading Bloc

In the late 1980s, there was renewed interest in the establishment of a trading bloc in the Pacific. This interest was rekindled by developments in North America and the EU, which indicated that regional trading blocs were being established there. At the same time, difficulties encountered in trying to conclude the Uruguay Round of the GATT negotiations gave rise to fears that the world trading system was going to break up into a number of trading blocs. This led to considerable interest in establishing a trading bloc in the Asia-Pacific region.

One proposal, which was sponsored by Australia, was to set up an Asia-Pacific Economic Cooperation forum (APEC). Another, suggested by Malaysia, was to set up an East Asian Economic Group (EAEG). After much discussion, EAEG (renamed East Asian Economic Caucus, EAEC) will now be a sub-grouping of APEC. These proposals will be discussed in Chapter 8.

After frenzied last-minute negotiations, agreement on the major proposals of the Uruguay Round was finally reached in late 1993, and the trade agreement was signed by members of the GATT on 15 April 1994. The GATT itself will be replaced by a new World Trade Organization (WTO).

Under these agreements, tariffs will be reduced by a weighted average of 61% in Japan, 37% in the EU and 34% in the USA. Tariffs on semiconductors, computer components and machinery for manufacturing computer chips will be cut to between 50%– 100%. Tariffs on chemicals will be reduced and harmonized at a maximum level of 6.5%. Most of these tariff reductions will be phased over a five-year period, although tariff reductions on pharmaceuticals will take effect immediately. These changes are expected to benefit the Asian NICs considerably (Waller 1994b:66).

Under the GATT agreement, the Multifibre Agreement (MFA), which set quotas for imports of textiles and clothing into the developed countries from less developed countries, will be phased out within ten years. At the same time, quotas will expand at increasing rates until they are eventually abolished. This will be of significant benefit to some Asian NICs (South Korea, Hong Kong and Taiwan).

Tariffs on agricultural products will also be reduced by 37% over six years in industrial countries and by 24% over ten years in developing countries. Asian NICs such as Taiwan and South Korea will face greater competition from imports in their agricultural sectors.

The new GATT agreement also has provisions which prohibit subsidies of various kinds. Subsidies on agricultural exports have attracted wide attention as they were one of the main reasons for the protracted negotiations which took place at the end of the 1980s. While industrialized countries will cut export subsidies by 36% over six years, developing countries will cut their subsidies on agricultural exports by 24% over ten years. Of greater relevance to the Asian NICs is the prohibition of subsidies on non-agricultural exports and the provision to impose countervailing duties where these subsidies occur.

In addition, the new GATT agreement also protects intellectual property. Copyrights, patents, trade-marks, trade secrets, integrated circuits, computer programs, sound recordings and motion pictures will be protected for periods ranging from 20 to 50 years. Such protection will be implemented within one year in developed countries and within five years in developing countries. These provisions may have considerable impact in some Asian NICs (Hong Kong and Taiwan, in particular).

Most studies of the impact of the new GATT agreement indicate that countries in Southeast and East Asia will be major beneficiaries of the changes in the world trading system, provided that they can take full advantage of the opportunities which will open up as a result of the tariff reductions which will take place over the next five to ten years (Waller 1994a:65; Waller 1994b:66). This augers well for the Asian NICs.

Conclusion

In the 1990s and beyond, the prospects of continued rapid growth of the Asian NICs looks bleak. Recession in the major OECD countries, increasing protectionism in North America and the EU, appreciating exchange rates and rising domestic costs, all threaten the maintenance of high growth rates for the Asian NICs.

In the late 1980s and early 1990s, a number of writers suggested that the Asian NICs had run out of steam, and were entering a period of decline. Daley and Logan (1989), as well as Bello and Rosenfeld (1990), argued that the internal and external problems facing the Asian NICs were causing them to enter a prolonged period of economic crisis. This was of sufficient importance to cause some doubt as to whether the Asian NICs would ever regain their position as the fastest growing economies in the world. By the late 1980s, it did look as if they were in economic decline (Stutchbury 1990:75).

These views may have been overly pessimistic. The NICs of Asia have responded to the challenges they face by developing alternative export markets, moving production facilities off-shore, restructuring and moving into higher-technology products, importing labour and seriously considering the establishment of a regional trading bloc in the Pacific. Whether these responses will adequately meet the challenges the Asian NICs face remains to be seen. Most informed observers are of the view that, in spite of the difficulties the Asian NICs face, they will continue to be amongst the fastest growing economies in the world. While it is likely that the Asian NICs will experience growth rates which are lower than those they have been used to, their pragmatism and flexibility, which have enabled them to surmount considerable difficulties in the past, will stand them in good stead in the future (World Bank 1993:115–117).

By the end of the eighties, most Asian NICs had already begun to show signs of a resurgence. Singapore's GDP growth, which had registered 5.8% in 1992, reached an impressive 9.8% in 1993. This almost double-digit growth rate was much higher than expected, and was the highest in Asia. The Hong Kong economy, which grew at 5% during 1992 (and 4.2% in 1991), registered a 5.5% growth rate of GDP in 1993, in spite of continuing difficulties between the Hong Kong Governor and Beijing over the nature and extent of political reform in the colony as it approaches 1997. The continuing high rate of growth in the Peoples' Republic of China, and the growing signs of economic recovery in the USA in early 1994, all suggest that Hong Kong's economic performance will continue to improve. In the case of Taiwan, economic growth has been steadily rising since 1990, when its GDP growth rate hit a low of 4.2%. By 1993, its growth rate had recovered to 6.8% even though investment growth and government spending on infrastructure projects were lower. Of all the Asian NICs, South Korea has had the slowest growth rate in recent years. In 1992, the growth rate of GDP in South Korea reached a low of 4.2%. In 1993 this edged up to 5%. A change to a popularly-elected civilian president was followed by an anti-corruption drive against businessmen and politicians. In addition, there was a change in government policy away from favouring the *chaebols*, and towards small- and medium-sized firms. These dramatic changes have combined with a relatively high rate of inflation and an appreciating currency to keep South Korea's GDP growth rate at about the 5%

level. However, some economic indicators, such as the increase in personal consumption and the increase in machinery import-licences during 1993, suggest that South Korea could look forward to higher rates of economic growth in future.

CHAPTER 7

More NICs in Time?

Introduction

According to the mainstream view, all countries can be thought of as being on different rungs of a *technological ladder*. In the 1960s and 1970s, the Asian NICs were at a stage where they could produce labour-intensive manufactured goods efficiently. Over time, however, they began to lose this comparative advantage as wages started rising and exchange rates started appreciating. By the 1980s, the Asian NICs were ascending the technological ladder and moving into higher technology, more capital-intensive products. This has opened up opportunities for some less developed countries to fill the gap left by the Asian NICs, and to ascend the technological ladder themselves, by taking up the manufacture of labour-intensive manufactured goods (Economist 1994a:73; Riedel 1991:143). The Asian NICs were, therefore, just the first tier of NICs to emerge in the 1960s. There is a second tier of countries, just below them, waiting in the wings, as it were, for the time when they too could emerge as *new* NICs. Some authors are of the view that, by the 1980s, there was sufficient empirical evidence to confirm the existence of this second tier, or *near*-NICs. Some have even singled out certain countries, for example, Malaysia, Indonesia and Thailand, as the new NICs or Asia (Schlossstein 1990). If there is, indeed, a second tier of countries which are just about to become NICs, this would lend empirical support to the mainstream view that, over time, other less developed countries would join the ranks of the Asian NICs. Others are highly sceptical of this.

Optimistic Views

In 1982, two World Bank economists, Havrylyshyn and Alikhani, published a paper which suggested that there was some empirical evidence to support the view that there was a second tier of less developed countries which were likely to join the ranks of the then NICs (Havrylyshyn and Alikhani 1982). They identified 12 less developed countries, which they refer to as *New Exporting Countries* (NECs), which had higher growth rate of manufactured exports than even the NICs. These NECs were Sri Lanka, Cyprus, Thailand, Indonesia, Peru, Jordan, Uruguay, Malaysia, Tunisia, Philippines, Colombia and Morocco. For the period 1970–1979, the NECs, as a group, recorded an average growth rate of 37.7% per annum of manufactured exports (some NECs, such as Indonesia and Thailand, achieved close to 50% per annum growth in manufactured exports). This was much higher than the growth of manufactured exports of the NICs (which was 28.7%) over the same period. Other less developed countries recorded a 22.2% growth of manufactured exports (Havrylyshyn and Alikhani 1982:653). The export performance of the NECs is even more remarkable when it is remembered that the 1970–1979 period was a difficult period for the world economy, as it spans the oil crisis of 1973. Although the growth rate of manufactured exports of the NECs did slow down after the oil crisis, it was, nevertheless, well above that of the NICs and of other less developed countries (Havrylyshyn and Alikhani 1982:655–656).

The data also show that in the late 1970s, the NECs were exporting the same types of labour-intensive manufactured goods that the NICs had concentrated on a decade earlier. Of the top seven products which the NECs exported in 1979, five (textile yarns and fabric, clothing, electrical machinery, non-metal mineral manufactures and miscellaneous manufactures) were in the top seven products exported by the NICs in 1970. In fact, the NECs, in 1979, relied more on textiles and clothing (39% of their total exports) than the NICs did in 1970 (27% of their total exports) (Havrylyshyn and Alikhani 1982:656). In addition, by 1979, the NICs were becoming less dependent on labour-intensive manufactures (textiles and clothing accounted for a smaller share of their manufactured exports) and were moving into more sophisticated, less labour-intensive products (such as transport equipment, electrical machinery, non-electrical machinery and iron and steel) (Havrylyshyn and Alikhani 1982:656–658). The NECs, therefore, appear to be taking over the more labour-intensive manufactures which the NICs are no longer able to produce efficiently, and the NICs themselves appear to be moving into less-labour intensive, more technologically sophisticated products. In other words, the NECs appear to be ascending the technological ladder and filling the place vacated by the NICs, with a lag of five to ten years. This conforms with the mainstream view of the emergence of the NICs.

Havrylyshyn and Alikhani also make the point that the NECs have been exporting manufactured goods to the same markets as the NICs. In fact, the share of NEC exports going to the industrial countries increased from 49% to 58%, between 1970 and 1979, while the share of NIC exports going to the industrial countries declined slightly from 64% to 62% (Havrylyshyn and Alikhani 1982:659–660). This is also in accordance with the view that the second tier is following in the footsteps of the NICs. Havrylyshyn and Alikhani conclude that "The evidence ... does quite clearly say that many other countries besides the NICs can and have followed the same path to successful exporting as had the NICs earlier" (Havrylyshyn and Alikhani 1982:661).

The optimism of Havrylyshyn and Alikhani was shared by Shinohara (1983), who argued that more countries could be expected to join the ranks of the NICs over time. Apart from a record of high growth rates of income and exports, Shinohara pointed to other favourable factors such as high savings and investment rates, as well as high rates of educational attainment, in such countries as Malaysia and Thailand. Moreover, high investment rates and high export growth rates were likely to be mutually reinforcing, since high export growth would provide the increase in income and resources that would generate higher savings and investment for export-oriented industries. It was this virtuous circle of investment and exports that would propel some less developed countries into the ranks of the NICs (Shinohara 1983:66–67). Thus, the emergence of new NICs over time could be expected, as more and more less developed countries reach a level of development, which would enable them to join the ranks of the NICs.

A thorough examination of the factors which need to be examined, before any conclusions can be made about the emergence of new NICs, was provided by Hamilton (1989). Hamilton argued that this involved an examination of the international economic environment, internal economic conditions and domestic power structures (Hamilton 1987:1227).

In the late 1980s, the international economic environment appeared to be unfavourable to the emergence of new NICs. World markets were much tighter, as more contenders vied for a world market that was slowing down. The volatility of raw material export prices made it difficult for less developed countries which depended on such exports to sustain high levels of investment and economic growth. Easier access to technology and international finance has made it possible for more less developed countries to enter into the already crowded market for manufactured exports (Hamilton 1987:1229–1230).

In terms of internal economic conditions, Hamilton points to the importance of high domestic savings rates, the degree of internal financial development, the absence of heavy debt burdens or large military expenditures and the access to foreign credit and financial institutions. In addition, the quality of the work force (in terms of education and training) and the level of wages relative to other countries are important. Countries with better physical infrastructure, and which have fewer market distortions (in terms of tariffs and other types of market interventions), are also likely to achieve high growth rates. The importance of an efficient agricultural sector is also stressed (Hamilton 1987:1230–1240).

Hamilton also emphasizes the importance of the absence of political dominance of classes which derive wealth from unproductive activities. Governments should have the political as well as economic power to take difficult decisions which are required for export-oriented industrialization. In addition, government administrations should be efficient and honest so that government policies can be implemented effectively (Hamilton 1987:1240–1243).

After considering several countries in Asia, Hamilton concludes that only two, Malaysia and Thailand, are likely to join the ranks of the NICs, since they meet the conditions for rapid economic growth more fully than other less developed countries. Of the two countries, Hamilton's view is that Thailand has the best prospects of becoming the next Asian NIC (Hamilton 1987:1256).

Hirata (1988) provides additional support for Hamilton's conclusions, and shows that both Malaysia and Thailand have implemented export- promotion policies since the late 1960s. These have included tax incentives, export credit schemes and the establishment of free trade zones. This has resulted in a rapid expansion of the export of labour-intensive manufactures in both countries since the 1970s (Hirata 1988:426–430).

The list of potential NICs is extended by Holloway (1991d:72). In addition to Thailand and Malaysia, Indonesia and the Philippines are thought to have good prospects of becoming NICs. Three reasons are given in support of this view. First, with the exception of the Philippines, all the countries mentioned have been recording rates of economic growth which are higher than the current Asian NICs. In 1988–1991, for example, Thailand recorded a GDP growth rate of 9.8% per annum, while Singapore recorded a GDP growth rate of 7.9% per annum (the highest amongst the Asian NICs). The higher rates of growth of countries like Thailand and Malaysia are also associated with accelerating industrialization. Second, Thailand, Malaysia, Indonesia and the Philippines all have higher rates of population growth than the Asian NICs, and will therefore be able to keep wages low. For example, in the 1990s, the labour force in Malaysia is expected to grow at 2.9% per annum, five times faster than that of Singapore. Third, countries such as Thailand and Malaysia have, in recent years, been the recipients of large inflows of foreign investment (much of this from the Asian NICs and Japan). In 1991, Malaysia was the third-largest recipient of foreign investment amongst developing countries, whilst Thailand and Indonesia were the fifth and seventh-largest recipients (Leipziger and Thomas 1994:7). This has contributed to their high growth rates and is laying the foundations for the rapid expansion of manufactured goods in the future. For these reasons, the prospects of new NICs emerging in Southeast Asia appear to be good. This view is also endorsed by other observers (Economist 1990f).

Pessimistic Views

Not all authors are as optimistic about the likelihood of other less developed countries joining the ranks of the NICs as those surveyed in the previous section. About the same time as Havrylyshyn and Alikhani were expounding their optimistic views, Cline (1982) was pointing out that there was a fallacy of composition in the argument that more and more less developed countries would enter the ranks of the NICs over time. If all less developed countries were to achieve the same degree of import penetration in developed country markets as the NICs had done, strong protectionist measures would immediately be provoked. Thus, while one or two less developed countries might ascend into the ranks of the NICs, the probability of a large number succeeding in a similar vein, was extremely small. The fact that this argument is based on some rather unlikely assumptions, has not been missed by other writers (Ranis 1985a:91–104; Nolan 1990:52–53).

In 1989, Broad and Cavanagh (1989) argued that, for a number of reasons, it was highly unlikely that any more NICs would emerge in the near future. First, the international economic environment was no longer favourable. World trade was slowing down and protectionism in developed countries was on the rise. Second, many less developed countries were struggling with huge debt burdens which was preventing them from increasing their savings and investment rates. In addition, these countries were often forced by international financial agencies (through conditionality clauses) to implement contractionary monetary and fiscal policies, which only contributed to global stagnation. Third, important technological breakthroughs were causing substitution away from natural products into synthetics. This had the effect of reducing the export income of many less developed countries and reducing their ability to attain high rates of growth. Fourth, the microprocessor revolution was increasing output but reducing employment, contributing to recession in many developed, as well as less developed countries. For these reasons, Broad and Cavanagh are of the view that, with the possible exceptions of Thailand and Malaysia, no other less developed country has come close to emulating the success of the NICs (1989:56; Sicat 1983:55–56). This view is echoed by Page who argues that, by the late 1980s, exports markets and the supply of external finance have become considerably less accessible. This has made it more difficult for less developed countries to withstand and adjust to the external shocks which they face and makes it unlikely that many of these countries will be able to make the transition to NIC status. Export-oriented industrialization strategies have given way to an emphasis on structural adjustment in the face of an uncertain, and often hostile, international trading environment (Page 1990:381).

None of the pessimistic views outlined above, question the empirical evidence put forward by Havrylyshyn and Alikhani. It was left to Athukorala (1989) to provide this critique.

Athukorala points out that the very high growth rates recorded by the NECs during 1970–1979 should be considered in perspective, since in most cases, they start from very low bases (1989:95). This was, however, recognized by Havrylyshyn and Alikhani (1982:656). In addition, the share of the NECs in the total imports of the OECD had risen from 0.6% in 1970 to 1.7% in 1979, and have since remained at that level. In contrast, the share of the Asian

NICs in total OECD imports has increased steadily, reaching 7.8% in 1983. Athukorala suggests that this implies that the NECs are more vulnerable to hostile international market conditions (1989:98). Another important characteristic of the NECs, is the important part played by a few countries, notably Malaysia, Thailand and the Philippines. These countries account for over 50% of NEC exports of manufactured goods and almost 90% of NEC exports of machinery. This may be related to their geographical proximity to the Asian NICs. The other NECs export mainly primary products and textiles (Athukorala 1989:103–107).

Furthermore, Athukorala suggests that there is no clear evidence of product substitution (that is, of the NECs taking over the production of labour-intensive manufactured goods from the NICs). In only three product categories (textiles, apparel and semiconductor devices) has the increase in the market share of the NECs been accompanied by a decline in the market share of the NICs. Even in these product categories, the NICs still have a dominant world market position. In other product categories, the market share of both NICs and NECs has risen. For example, between 1975 and 1984, the NICs market share of photographic apparatus and equipment rose slightly, from 85.6% to 86%. During the same period, the market share of the NECs rose by a larger margin, from 6.7% to 9.3%. Athukorala concludes that "contrary to the prediction of the theory of stages of comparative advantage, there is a substantial overlap in the commodity composition of manufactured exports of various developing country groups" (1989:111). It is debatable, however, whether the stages theory of comparative advantage does indeed imply product substitution, since in certain product categories, the market share (at the two or three digit level of aggregation) of both the NICs and NECs may be rising at the same time, as the former are concentrating on the higher-technology end of the market, whilst the latter are taking over the lower-technology (as in the case, for example, of electronics products).

Athukorala, however, is of the view that "the experience of the NECs during the period under investigation does not permit us to be optimistic about the prospects of export-oriented industrialization in developing countries" (1989:115).

Distinguishing Features of an NIC

While high rates of growth of manufactured exports are an important feature of NECs, they are only one aspect of the development of these economies. Havrylyshyn and Alikhani make the point that many of the NECs in their study had very high rates of growth of manufactured exports, but very low rates of GDP growth (1982:654–655).

With the benefit of hindsight, it is now clear that Havrylyshyn and Alikhani were a little too optimistic about the prospects of many of the NECs in their sample. Of the 12 countries mentioned in their paper, several (for example, Sri Lanka, Cyprus, Philippines, Colombia and Peru) have been embroiled in violent internal warfare, or political instability. Others, (such as Jordan) have had a reversal of fortunes after the 1990 Gulf War. Of the 12 countries studied by Havrylyshyn and Alikhani, only a few remain as likely candidates for NIC status. Thailand and Malaysia are frequently mentioned, even by authors who are pessimistic about the prospects of more NICs emerging.

If Havrylyshyn and Alikhani were overly optimistic about the likelihood of new NICs emerging, others, such as Broad and Cavanagh, as well as Athukorala, may have been much too pessimistic. While it is true that the international economic environment has been less favourable in recent years, it may mean that only a few less developed countries are likely to become NICs in the near future (as opposed to none at all). The question then, is which of the countries in the less developed world are likely to be the next one or two to emerge as NICs. Most observers are of the view that only Thailand and Malaysia are likely to make this transition in the 1990s. The reasons for this view will become clear once the distinguishing features of an NIC are laid out. Export performance is but one such feature, and there are many others.

A study of the historical development of the Asian NICs suggests that NICs have a number of distinguishing features. Some of these are economic in nature, whilst others are political. The more important of these appear to be:

- A sustained record of economic growth for the last 10 or 15 years

- High savings and investment ratios

- Good physical infrastructure

- High levels of education and training in the labour force

- A more equal distribution of income over time

- An efficient agricultural sector

- Structural transformation of the economy towards the manu-facturing sector

- Adoption of an export-oriented industrialization strategy

- An increasing share of labour-intensive manufactured goods in total exports

- A concentration on industrial country markets for their manu-factured exports

- Relatively low wages

- Little industrial unrest

- Low rates of inflation

- Strong government, able to take difficult decisions without having to consider the claims of special interest groups

- An efficient, honest, public administration

- Political stability

Malaysia as the Next NIC of Asia

Most observers believe that Malaysia has most of the features suggested above. Indeed, some are of the view that, on the basis of some criteria (such as per capita income, or the proportion of manufactured exports in total exports), it is already an Asian NIC. It is just a matter of time before international bodies give its status official recognition (Balakrishnan 1989c:96).

Malaysia has had a sustained record of high economic growth for the last two decades. During 1980–1988, Malaysia recorded an average rate of growth of GDP of about 5% per annum. This rose to an average of 9% per annum between 1989–1991 (Holloway 1991b:72). In the 1960s and 1970s, Malaysia economic growth was fuelled by the expansion of primary product exports (rubber, palm oil, tin and petroleum). In recent years, the export of labour-intensive manufactured goods (especially electronics) has been significant. In 1970, Malaysia's per capita income was US$380. This increased four-fold to US$1,563 in 1980, and rose to US$2,277 in 1990. By the year 2020, Malaysia's per capital income is expected to read US$7,380 (Tsuruoka and Vatikiotis 1991a:60). By the year 2020, the government vision is that Malaysia will have a fully developed industrial economy.

Malaysia's high rate of economic growth has been accompanied by high savings and investment ratios, compared to other less developed countries. Between 1970 and 1981, domestic savings in Malaysia averaged 25% of GDP. This rose to an average of 32.9% of GDP during 1981–1988. In 1990, Malaysia's savings rate reached 34.8%, and was higher than that of South Korea and Taiwan. Gross domestic investment averaged 26.7% of GDP between 1970 and 1981. During 1981–1984, gross domestic investment reached an average of 35% of GDP, but fell to an average of 26%, in the latter half of the 1980s, after the recession of 1985. In spite of this, Malaysia's record of savings and investment performance is one of the best amongst less developed countries.

Malaysia has good physical infrastructure. It is amongst the more highly urbanized countries in Southeast Asia. Its roads, telephones and schools are more evenly distributed than in many other less developed countries. Malaysia's infrastructure is so good that it is almost up to developed country level and it is not only concentrated in the capital, Kuala Lumpur (Balakrishnan 1989c:96). This has been achieved through the public expenditures in the various development plans. In 1985, public investment accounted for 55% of total investment. Much of this was directed toward upgrading infrastructure, education and other related areas (Fong 1989:72).

Educational attainment in Malaysia is high, compared with other less developed countries. In 1980, the literacy rate was 60%. In 1987, primary school enrolment was 102% and secondary school enrolment was 56%. The enrolment rate in tertiary education was 7%. While not as high as the Asian NICs, these indices are much higher than many less developed countries in Asia. Moreover, the labour force is not only well-educated, but English-speaking and relatively cheap (wages are about half that in Singapore). This has made Malaysia a favourite destination for foreign investors. In the late 1980s, Malaysia began to develop labour shortages, as a result of the rapid demand for labour generated by high rates of economic growth. Between 1987 and 1992, employment grew at an average of 3.6% per annum, while the labour force grew by 3.1% per annum. Over the same period, the rate of unemployment fell from 8.2% to 5.4%. By this time, Malaysia had begun to experience labour shortages in many sectors of the economy (Vatikiotis 1992:46–47).

Malaysia does not have a large rural population engaged in subsistence agriculture. Per capita incomes in the rural sector have been rising steadily over the years, as have standards of living. Although rural incomes have not risen as fast as urban incomes, the incidence of poverty in rural households has declined over time (Snodgrass 1980:79–80). Malaysian agriculture is relatively efficient, as it is made up of an efficient plantation sector and a small-holder sector that has been continually upgraded with new technology (in rice as well as rubber production). In 1981, paddy yields in Malaysia were about 3 tons per hectare, the second highest in Asia.

Over the last 10 to 20 years, the Malaysian economy has been undergoing a steady transformation, away from agriculture, toward industry. This is shown in Table 7.1.

Between 1970 and 1990, the share of agriculture in GDP declined from 29% to 19%, while that of manufacturing increased from 14% to 27%. If construction is included, the industrial sector's share of GDP increased from 17% in 1970 to 31% in 1990. Over the same period, agriculture grew by 1% per annum, while manufacturing grew at twice this rate (Tsuruoka and Vatikiotis 1991a:16). Between 1986 and 1990, the manufacturing sector grew by an average of 12% per annum. As a percentage of GDP, Malaysia's manufacturing sector is now comparable with that of the Asian NICs.

After a brief period in the early 1980s in which Malaysia tried to develop heavy industry under import protection, the government has begun to promote manufactured exports. In 1970, average tariff levels in Malaysia were already very low. Tariff revenue was 3.4% of GDP. By 1980, this ratio had fallen to 2.7%, and by 1990, to –1.2%. Although primary product exports are still important, manufactured goods made up 49% of total export earnings in 1988. By 1991, this proportion had increased to 64%, partly because of the decline in commodity prices. The structure of Malaysia's exports and her major export markets are shown in Table 7.2.

Table 7.1
Structural Change in the Malaysian Economy
% GDP

Year	1970	1980	1990
Agriculture	29.0	22.9	18.7
Mining	13.7	10.1	9.1
Manufacturing	13.9	19.6	27.0
Construction	3.8	4.6	3.5
Services	36.2	40.1	42.3

Source: Ministry of Finance, *Economic Report*, (various issues).

Between 1973 and 1985, manufactured exports grew by more than 15% per annum. In 1991, 57% of Malaysia's manufactured exports were made up of electrical appliances and components. Other manufactured goods, such as textiles, transport equipment, etc., account for less than 10% each of total manufactured exports. The structure of Malaysia's manufactured exports is shown in Table 7.3.

Malaysia's manufactured exports are therefore highly concentrated in one commodity group. In 1983, Malaysia was the largest single source of semiconductor imports into the USA (22.4%

Table 7.2

Malaysia's Major Exports and Export Markets
% Total exports, 1991

Major Exports	% Total
Manufactured goods	64.1
Crude petroleum	10.7
Timber	7.2
Palm oil	5.2
Liquid natural gas	4.0
Rubber	3.1
Tin	0.8
Other	4.9
Major Markets	% Total
Singapore	23.0
Japan	17.0
USA	16.1
EU	15.2
Other ASEAN	5.8
South Korea	4.3
Other	18.5

Source: Same as Table 7.1.

Table 7.3
Malaysia's Manufactured Exports
% Total, 1991

Electrical machinery	57.3
Other manufactures	9.0
Textiles (clothing and footwear)	7.6
Transport equipment	5.6
Chemical products	4.0
Food products	3.6
Wood products	3.3
Metal products	3.2
Rubber products	2.8
Petroleum products	1.8
Non-mineral metal products	1.6
Growth per annum (1980–91)	24.2
Growth per annum (1986–91)	30.7

Source: United Nations, *World Commodity Trade Statistics,* (various issues).

of total imports). By the early 1990s, Malaysia had become one of the world's largest exporters of some electrical appliances such as air-conditioning units. Between 1980 and 1991, Malaysia's manufactured exports grew by 24.2% per annum. This accelerated to 30.7% per annum between 196 and 1991.

Although Malaysia exports its manufactured goods to the industrialized countries, unlike the Asian NICs, its export markets are more diversified and balanced. As Table 7.2 shows, no single country takes up more than about a fifth of Malaysia's exports. In 1991, Malaysia's largest trading partner was Singapore (23% of exports), followed by Japan (17%), USA (16%) and the EU (15%).

In recent years, Malaysia has been experiencing large inflows of foreign investment, mainly from Japan and the Asian NICs. Between 1985 and 1990, total foreign investment approvals increased by more than 18 times, from M$959 million to M$17,629.

In 1991, Malaysia was the third largest recipient of foreign investment in the less developed world, accounting for 8.7% of the US$168 billion invested by developed countries in less developed countries. This is a reflection of these countries shifting their labour-intensive manufacturing plants to Malaysia, in order to take advantage of lower wages (as suggested by the technological ladder hypothesis). Japanese investment alone increased from less than M$500 million in 1980, to M$4.2 billion in 1990. In 1989, Japan was the largest foreign investor in Malaysia (31.3% of total foreign investment), followed by Taiwan (24.7%) and Singapore (10.6%) (Tsuruoka 1990:34–35). Between 1988 and 1989 alone, Japanese foreign investment in Malaysia increased by 120%, while that from Taiwan, Singapore and Hong Kong increased by 155%, 117% and 229% respectively. By the early 1990s, the world recession, which had engulfed most of the OECD countries, finally affected the Japanese economy. As a result of this, Japanese foreign investment declined significantly. The dominance of Japanese foreign investment in countries such as Malaysia is bound to be affected by this. Unlike, Thailand, foreign investment is not concentrated in the capital of Malaysia (Kuala Lumpur), but is spread from Penang and Butterworth in the north, to Johore in the south. In addition, industrial land is relatively cheap and close to good transport networks. Malaysia's currency is also undervalued. This not only encourages foreign investment but also exports.

Malaysia's relatively small population (about 17 million in 1992) also means that the amount of capital needed to accelerate industrialization is smaller than that required in more populous countries. Moreover, Malaysia's labour force is growing at just under 3% per annum. Between 1970 and 1990, the proportion of people between the ages of 15 and 64 increased from 52% to 59%. This growth in the labour force is likely to keep wages from rising too fast. The government has announced its desire to see Malaysia's population rise to 70 million at some time in the future, as it considers this the optimum level of population for the country (Economist 1991d:30). If this were to be the case, Malaysia could look forward to maintaining relatively low wage rates for some time to come. Much depends on the rate of economic growth. In the early 1990s, growth rates were so high that the demand for labour began to outstrip its supply.

Industrial relations in Malaysia have been relatively harmonious. Although there are a large number of labour unions, they are not militant, and Malaysia has not had serious industrial unrest for some years. In the free trade zones which concentrate on the production of electrical appliances and components, union activity is regulated by the government. While labour unions in Malaysia are not as docile as those in Singapore, they are also not as militant as those in, say, South Korea. Hamilton, however, takes a different view (1987:1256).

Malaysia has also been able to maintain relatively low rates of inflation. During 1970–1980, in spite of the rise in oil prices, Malaysia's rate of inflation averaged 6% per annum. Between 1980 and 1990, it declined to 3.3% per annum (partly due to the recession in the mid-1980s) but in 1992, rose to 5% per annum. This compares very favourably with some of the Asian NICs, as well as with other less developed countries in Southeast Asia.

While Malaysia appears to have many of the features that seem to be associated with NIC status, there are some aspects of its development which are not as favourable. The pattern of income distribution in Malaysia over time shows increasing inequality. Between 1957 and 1970, income distribution became more unequal. This was primarily due to capital-intensive industrialization policies (Snodgrass 1980:65–88). Between 1968 and 1976, income distribution became more equal initially, but started deteriorating after 1972. Capital-intensive industrialization policies were again thought to be the main cause of this (Randolph 1990:15–32). In respect of income distribution, therefore, the performance of the Malaysian economy is quite different from that of the Asian NICs, most of which experienced improving income distribution over long periods of time. The implementation of capital-intensive industrialization policies and the disparities between rural and urban incomes are thought to be the cause of this.

While government in Malaysia is not as authoritarian as in

the Asian NICs, it is not weak and indecisive, as in some less developed countries. The 1980s saw some deep divisions with the ruling Malay party (UMNO) as well as within the governing party (the National Front). There is also constant tension between the federal government and the member states in East Malaysia. These problems, which surface from time to time, have never caused any doubts about the ability of the central government to deal with them without recourse to the use of force. While the problems with the East Malaysian states are still simmering, divisions with UMNO and the National Front appear to have been resolved. Nonetheless, the government still has problems with limiting what Hamilton refers to as "zero-sum activities". There is also some question of whether the government is strong enough to resist the demands of the dominant racial group (the Malays) in the interests of accelerating economic growth (Hamilton 1987:1247,1256). The release of the New Development Policy and the Second Outline Perspective Plan on 17 June 1991, gives some basis for optimism on these matters (Tsuruoka and Vatikiotis 1991b:16–17).

On most comparisons, Malaysia is often regarded as having a relatively efficient public service. Hamilton, however, is of the view that corruption and nepotism was already significant under the New Economic Policy (1969–1990), and was likely to increase over time, as there is no politically powerful, cohesive, technocratic bureaucracy to counter sectional interests (1987:1247). This should be viewed in perspective. In a recent survey of the extent of bribery and corruption in public life, Singapore scored 100 (which represented negligible bribery and corruption), Malaysia scored 45 and India scored 17.

Malaysia is regarded by most observers as a politically stable country. Even though racial tensions between the Chinese and Malays simmer beneath the surface, there has been no major outbreak of racial violence in Malaysia for over 20 years. On the contrary, Malaysia is often held up as a model of inter-racial co-operation and harmony amongst developing countries. Recent power struggles with the Malay ruling party (the United Malay National Organization, UMNO) appear to have been resolved and its military is not politicized. The National Front government appears to have things under control. Malaysia has also been able to achieve changes in political leadership without loss of continuity of government policies or administrative capability.

While the general level of educational attainment of the labour force in Malaysia is relatively high, there is an acute shortage of skilled labour. It has been estimated that by the 1990s, Malaysia would have a shortage of 15,000 industrial managers and a substantial number of systems analysts and engineers. This situation is aggravated by a large outflow of skilled migrants to Australia, Canada and the USA (Fong 1989:77). As was pointed out earlier, in the late 1980s, Malaysia began to experience labour shortages (even in unskilled labour), as high rates of economic growth began to meet constraints in the supply of labour (Vatikiotis 1992:47; Hanneman 1992:10). This has caused some concern about Malaysia's ability to continue to attract investment in labour-intensive manufacturing industries in its headlong dash towards NIC status.

Lubeck (1992:176–198) has recently argued that Malaysia's prospects for becoming the next NIC of Asia are over-rated because it does not have two important features which are found in the Asian NICs: a developmentalist state with a comparatively autonomous technocratic elite, and the institutionalization of a close relationship between government and business. Lubeck's argument is that the civil service in Malaysia is weak and fragmented into a large number of competing agencies. State industrial policy is characterized by inconsistency, inefficiency, political patronage and corruption (Lubeck 1992:181). Unlike the Asian NICs, Malaysia has failed to establish key political institutions or an indigenous class of industrialists (Lubeck 1992:176). There are deep structural imbalances in Malaysian industry, with very few backward linkages to domestic industry and a high degree of dependence on foreign investors. In addition, the separation of economic power (held by the Chinese) and political power (held by the Malays) has resulted in an ethnic competition which pervades Malaysian economic life (Lubeck 1992:181–184). According to Lubeck, Malaysia may have adopted many of the export-oriented policies which were implemented by the Asian NICs. However, its chances of becoming the next NIC of Asia are not good because it has failed to develop the political institutions which played an important role in the success of the Asian NICs.

While there may be little disagreement about the Malaysian civil service not being as strong and as autonomous as its counterparts in the Asian NICs, the view that there is no close relationship between government and business in Malaysia is open to serious question. Many leading enterprises in manufacturing, banking, finance, agriculture and trade are now owned and run by Malays, either through government-controlled agencies, or privately. There is a close relationship between the Malay-dominated part of the business sector and government. Even the Chinese-dominated part of the business sector has close links with government, either at the state or federal level. This is accomplished either through the acquisition of Malay business partners, or through Chinese members of parliament, some of whom are government ministers. These close relationships between government and business have been institutionalized by the granting of honorary titles by rulers (at the state and federal levels of government) to businessmen. In addition, many politicians are invited to the board of business enterprises. The view that the relationship between government and business in Malaysia is not close is open to question.

In spite of some question marks, most observers are of the view that Malaysia is on the brink of being declared an Asian NIC. Its track record of economic development and export-oriented industrialization indicates that it is well-placed to join the ranks of the Asian NICs in the near future.

Thailand as the Next NIC of Asia

Thailand is regarded by the World Bank as a middle-income, less developed country. In terms of its level of per capita income, in the late 1980s, it is broadly comparable to such countries as Nicaragua,

Nigeria, Zimbabwe and Cameroon. In 1990, Thailand's per capita GNP was US$1160 (about half that of Malaysia at that time). This had been growing at an average of 6% per annum during 1980–1987, and accelerated to 10.5% per annum during 1988–1991 (Holloway 1991d:72). Since 1988, when Thailand's growth rate reached 13% per annum, the expansion of the economy has been slowing down, as the world economy slid deeper into recession. In 1992, Thailand recorded a growth rate of 7% per annum.

Thailand's savings rate averaged 22% of GDP throughout the 1970–1988 period. It reached a peak in the mid-1980s (to 26%), but fell back to the 22% level in the late 1980s. Gross domestic investment averaged 26% of GDP throughout the 1970–1988 period). Thailand's record of savings and investment is therefore not as good as Malaysia's. It is of the same magnitude as other less developed countries in the region (such as Indonesia and the Philippines).

In recent years, Thailand has experienced large inflows of foreign investment, which has enabled it to achieve very high rates of economic growth. In 1987, foreign investment in Thailand totalled about Baht 100 million. By 1990, this had increased to about Baht 350 million (Holloway 1991d:72). In 1991, Thailand was the sixth largest recipient of foreign investment in the developing world, accounting for 5.7% of total foreign investment in less developed countries. As in the case of Malaysia, much of this came from Japan and the Asian NICs. This is evident from Table 7.4.

In 1991, Japan was the largest source of foreign investment in Thailand (30.5% of the total), followed by Hong Kong (22.6%). Between 1984 and 1991, Japanese foreign investment increased by 17.2 times, while foreign investment from Hong Kong increased by 63.7 times. By 1991, even Singapore had become an important foreign investor in Thailand, accounting for 12.5% of total foreign investment. In 1991 the three Asian NICs (Hong Kong, Singapore and Taiwan) accounted for a larger share of foreign investment in Thailand than Japan. This is a reflection of the need of the Asian

Table 7.4

Foreign Investment in Thailand

Country	1984 Baht(mil)	1984 % Total	1991 Baht(mil)	1991 % Total
Japan	904	36.1	15570	30.5
USA	294	11.7	5900	11.5
Taiwan	248	9.9	2750	5.4
Hong Kong	181	7.2	11530	22.6
Singapore	3	1.2	6370	12.5
UK	101	4.0	230	0.4
Others	772	30.8	8720	17.1
Total	2503	100.0	51070	100.0

Source: Bank of Thailand, *Quarterly Report*, (various issues).

NICs to shift their labour-intensive manufacturing industries to low-wage countries.

Although Thailand has a very high literacy rate (86% in the late 1980s), educational levels are not very high. In 1983, only 29% of the relevant age group of children were in secondary schools (compared with 70%–80% for the Asian NICs) (Fairclough 1993: 25–26). This puts Thailand on a par with countries such as India (34%), Indonesia (37%) and Nepal (24%). The average years of schooling of the workforce in 1980 was about four years (compared with between six and seven years in the Asian NICs). The percentage of university students in the total population in Thailand was 0.07% in 1987. In the Asian NICs, the percentage was 2.2% in Taiwan, 1.8% in Singapore and 22.9% in South Korea. Every year, about 2,500 students graduate in science and technology. The demand for such graduates is about 8,000, implying a shortfall of 5,500 graduates per year. Under present trends, this shortage is expected to grow to about 30,000 per year, assuming a 5% growth rate of the economy (Handley 1988a:96–97). In 1987, there were

60 engineering graduates in Thailand per one million of population. This compares with 679 in South Korea and 425 in Taiwan (Tambunlertchai 1989:96).

Physical infrastructure is rather poor in Thailand (anyone who has tried to drive in Bangkok can attest to this). Roads, ports, airports and public utilities (such as electricity) are in short supply. For example, demand for electricity was growing at 15% per annum (twice the forecast rate) in the late 1980s. In 1986, the electricity generating authority had 40% spate capacity. By 1988, this had gone down to 25%. Telephone services, road transport and domestic airline services are all running at excess demand. Domestic airline passengers are subject to long delays and frequent cancellation of scheduled services. (Handley 1988b:94–95). To make matters worse, the government has recently reduced import duties on cars. Imported cars with engines of over 2300cc capacity had their import duties reduced from 300% to 100%. Cars assembled from imported kits had their duties reduced from 112% to 20%. This is expected to increase substantially the number of new cars added to the roads each year (in 1990, 400 new cars and trucks were added to Bangkok's roads each day). Peak hour traffic, which now crawls at an average of seven km/h in Bangkok, is expected to move at four km/h. Parents taking their children to school have to start at 5.30 am, and arrange for their children to have breakfast *en route* to school (Economist 1991k:30). A 10 km journey to work takes two hours on an average day. On bad days, it takes up to four hours. Most people who travel on Bangkok's roads (some call them parking lots) have to carry a portable toilet with them (in the form of a plastic bottle), in case they feel the call of nature whilst sitting in a three-hour traffic jam (Handley 1993:68).

Thailand is still a predominantly agricultural economy. In 1987, 61% of the population were engaged in (mainly subsistence) agriculture. As a share of GNP, industry accounted for 29% in 1987. Although, in recent years, the growth of the agricultural sector has been declining (from 6.6% per annum in 1989 to 2% per annum in 1991), and the manufacturing sector has been expanding (15% per annum in 1989, and 11% in 1991), much of

Thailand's industrial development is located in the greater Bangkok regions. Economic development has been very uneven, with many areas, particularly in the north-east of the country, untouched by industrialization (Tambunlertchai 1989:96; Tasker and Handley 1993:46–48).

Since 1972, Thailand has pursued an export-oriented industrialization strategy. It de-regulated the economy and set up an Investment Promotion Board to attract foreign investment. An Export Credit Scheme (which finances some 50% of all exports) was established in 1972 (Hirata 1988:430–434). The success of Thailand's export-oriented industrialization strategy can be seen from the changes in its export structure. This is shown in Table 7.5.

In 1963, agricultural exports accounted for most of Thailand's exports. The four main agricultural exports, rice, rubber, maize and tapioca accounted for 67.5% of all exports. Manufactured goods accounted for only 15% of total exports. By 1987, manufactured goods accounted for 68.5% of all exports, while the share of agricultural exports fell to 22.6%. Thailand's principal manufactured exports in 1987 were textiles (16.2%), clothing (15%)

Table 7.5
Thailand's Principal Exports
% Total

Year	1963	1973	1983	1985	1987
Rice	35.4	11.2	13.8	11.6	7.6
Rubber	18.7	14.2	8.1	7.0	6.8
Maize	8.9	9.2	5.8	4.0	1.3
Tapioca	4.5	7.9	10.5	7.7	6.9
Textiles	0.0	2.1	10.0	12.2	16.2
Integrated circuits	0.0	0.0	4.0	4.3	5.1
Other manufactures	15.8	34.8	27.5	35.5	47.2

Source: United Nations, *World Commodity Trade Statistics*, (various issues).

and footwear (2%), (33.2% of the total), consumer goods (16%), electronic products (17%), machinery (12%) and miscellaneous manufactures (19%). Integrated circuits, which were not exported until 1983, accounted for 5% of total exports in 1987.

Table 7.6 shows that manufactured exports grew very rapidly during 1970–1979, (averaging 48.5% per annum), but slowed down during 1980–1985 because of the effects of the second oil crisis. During 1985–1987, the growth rate of manufactured exports recovered to an average of 33.8% per annum.

Some 62.1% of Thailand's exports were sent to advanced industrial countries in 1987. Japan took 29% of Thailand's total exports, the EU took 19.2%, other ASEAN countries took 14.7% and the USA took 13.9%.

Thailand has a large pool of low cost labour to transfer from the agricultural to the industrial sector. The population, which totalled 53 million people in 1987, will continue to grow at about 1.7% per annum until the year 2000. This will mean a doubling of Thailand's population in about 30 years' time. Wages are low compared to the Asian NICs and some near-NICs. The average monthly salary of industrial workers in Thailand is about 40% that of South Korea, 70% that of Taiwan, 63% that of Singapore and

Table 7.6
Thailand's Exports
Growth Rates

Item	1970/80	1980/85	1985/87
Primary products	9.7	7.3	3.8
Processed foods	46.6	20.5	34.4
TCF and Electronics	68.6	10.6	20.1
Misc. manufactures	30.4	8.6	47.0
Other	Na	Na	Na
Total	24.6	7.7	24.5

Source: United Nations, *World Commodity Trade Statistics*, (various issues).

49% that of Hong Kong. It is also 40% lower than that of Malaysia (but double that of Sri Lanka and Indonesia).

Inflation in Thailand has been quite high, primarily because high rates of economic growth have led to excess demand. Between 1970 and 1980, the rate of inflation was 9.8% per annum. This slowed to 3.3% during 1980–1990 (primarily because of the mid-1980s recession), but returned to 8% per annum in 1991. Between 1973 and 1984, real wages in the manufacturing sector grew at an average of about 6% per annum.

Rapid economic growth in Thailand during the past 20 years has been accompanied by balance of payments deficits and rising debt. In 1989, the trade deficit was Baht 62 billion and it was growing at 22% per annum. Outstanding foreign debt stood at US$19 billion. The debt-service ratio was 20.3%.

The Thai government has played a modest role in economic activity. Government expenditure was only 18% of GDP in 1984 and the government spent only 19% of its revenues on economic services (the ratios for Malaysia were 35% and 26% respectively). Thailand has always suffered from endemic political instability. The *coup d'état* is a frequently-used method of changing government. However, unlike other countries, political instability in Thailand does not usually manifest itself in violence. In recent years, some unfortunate deaths have occurred, but this have been put down to some over-zealous officers ignoring the text books. Thailand is generally regarded as having a relatively weak government compared with other Asian NICs.

In the late 1980s, two important developments have put a dark cloud over Thailand's prospects of becoming the next NIC of Asia. The first is that AIDS is raging, almost out of control, in Thailand (Handley 1992:48). The bars, massage parlours and brothels of Bangkok are fertile grounds for the spread of the AIDS virus. At present rates of infection, it is estimated that Thailand will have one of the highest rates of HIV positive people in the world by the end of the 1990s. This will strain government resources which will have to be directed from other uses to deal with this massive problem. It will also put serious question marks on

Thailand's ability to supply a large pool of low-cost labour for export-oriented industries. The second major development is the acceleration of the implementation of market-oriented economic reforms in other countries in Southeast Asia (for example, Vietnam and Laos) where wages are even lower than in Thailand. This has already caused competitive pressures on textile firms in Thailand, which have had to mechanize in order to remain competitive (Tasker 1993:18). Thailand may be in the process of losing its comparative advantage in labour-intensive manufactured exports, even though its wages have not risen substantially.

Compared with Malaysia, Thailand's prospects for becoming an Asian NIC in the near future are not strong. It does not have many of the features which are regarded as important indicators of NIC status. However, compared with other less developed countries in Southeast Asia (apart from Malaysia), Thailand is much further down the track to becoming an NIC.

Indonesia as the Next NIC of Asia

It is of some interest to note that not all observers agree that Malaysia and Thailand are the most likely countries to become the next NICs of Asia. Schlossstein (1990) argues that Thailand is likely to be hampered by serious shortages of skilled labour and by adequate social infrastructure, in the form of a good communications network. It will take some time for Thailand to overcome these problems. Malaysia, according to Schlossstein, suffers from political and social instability, growing racial problems, and widespread corruption at all levels of government. In Schlossstein's view, Indonesia has the best chance of becoming the next NIC of Asia. It has vast natural resources, a large population and an authoritarian government which has been pursuing privatization and deregulation policies vigorously.

In 1989, Indonesia's per capita GNP was U$500, the lowest in ASEAN. This puts Indonesia in the category of a low-income, less developed country. Between 1965 and 1989, Indonesia's per capita

GNP grew at about 4.4% per annum. In 1989, countries with approximately the same level of per capita GNP as Indonesia included Lesotho, Mauritania and Angola. Since the mid-1980s, Indonesia's GNP has grown by about 7% per annum. With the slowdown in world economic growth in the early 1990s, Indonesia's GNP growth registered 6.6% in 1992, still higher than most other countries in the world. However, these high growth rates are of relatively recent origin and are the outcome of important economic reforms undertaken in the early 1980s. Between 1980 and 1988, Indonesia's GNP grew by an average of 5% per annum, but accelerated to 7% per annum between 1989 and 1991.

This acceleration in the growth rate of Indonesia's GNP has been accompanied by rising savings and investment ratios. Between 1981 and 1990, Indonesia's saving ratio averaged 32% of GDP. In 1991, it rose to 36% of GDP, the second-highest in the world (after Singapore). By the mid-1990s, it is expected to reach 38% of GDP. In the 1970s, Indonesia's investment ratio averaged 27% of GDP. During the 1981–1990 period, it increased to an average of 31% of GDP. The gap between savings and investment has been filled by capital imports. This has mainly taken the form of foreign aid rather than foreign investment. Foreign investment in Indonesia has never exceeded 3% of Gross Domestic Capital Formation since the early 1980s (compared with about 20% in Malaysia and 36% in Singapore). However, since the mid-1980s, Indonesia has experienced large flows of foreign investment. In 1992, it received over US$10 billion of foreign investment. Of this, 14.6% came from Japan, 9.9% from Hong Kong, 8.9% from the USA, 6.0% from Singapore, 5.4% from Taiwan and 4.5% from South Korea. Foreign investment from the Asian NICs together was greater than from Japan (East Asia Analytical Unit 1994:43). Most of the foreign investment from the Asian NICs has been in labour-intensive manufactured exports, such as textiles and footwear.

Indonesia is a very large country, covering 1.9 million square kilometres and over a 100,000 islands. In view of the diversity and heterogeneity of the country, it is not surprising to find that the quality of social infrastructure is very uneven. It is at its best in the island of Java which is the most densely populated and the most urbanized. But even here, large urban populations and rapid economic growth have put strains on social infrastructure. One example will suffice to illustrate the problem. In 1992, Hong Kong, with a population of about 5 million people, had a network of 2.8 million telephone lines (or about 56 lines per 100 people). Indonesia, with a population of about 180 million people had 1.5 million telephone lines (or less than 1 line per 100 people). In 1986, there were only 763,000 telephones in the whole country. In recent years, economic growth has been so rapid that there has been a shortage of electricity in the large cities. Most of the infrastructural facilities are located in the large urban centres. In the rural areas, where most of the population live, social infrastructure is relatively under-developed. For example, in large urban centres such as Yogyakarta, there are 467 kilometres of paved roads per 1,000 kilometres, while in Iran Jaya, the figure is only 0.8 kilometres per 1,000 kilometres.

In terms of education and training, in 1988, primary school enrolments in Indonesia were 119% of the relevant age group. Secondary school enrolments were only 48% of the relevant age group. The enrolment rate in tertiary education was 7%. Of those in universities, only 16% were enrolled in Science and Engineering degrees (compared with 57% in Singapore and 48% in Hong Kong). In 1990, the literacy rate was 75%. While education attainment at the primary school level is very high, Indonesia does not score very well in educational attainment at the secondary or tertiary level.

In terms of agricultural development, Indonesia has performed well since the mid-1960s, when high-yielding varieties of rice were introduced in Indonesian agriculture. Between 1971 and 1983, rice production grew at an annual rate of 5.3 per annum. For some provinces, such as Lampung in Sumatra and East Kalimantan in Kalimantan, rice production grew much faster, at about 10% per annum. While the growth rate of rice yields (in quintals per hectare) averaged 3.8% per annum, some provinces recorded growth rates which were double this figure. Since the population was growing at an average of 2.2% per annum during 1971–1983, this meant that by the mid-1980s, the availability of rice per head of population was increasing. Table 7.7 shows that, in addition to rice, the availability of other foods was much higher in 1988 compared with 1969.

Up till the late 1970s, the growth of the Indonesian economy was based primarily on its exports of crude oil. In 1980, crude oil and natural gas production accounted for 22% of GDP, as the price of oil rose to US$38 per barrel following the second oil price rise by OPEC in 1979. By 1989, the price of oil had fallen to US$18 per barrel and crude oil and natural gas production accounted for only 10% of Indonesia's GDP. In 1979, crude oil and natural gas accounted for over 80% of Indonesia's total exports. By 1991, their share in total exports had fallen to 37.4%.

The decline in the price of crude oil, which began in the early 1980s, prompted the Indonesian government to diversify its exports by promoting manufactured exports. A number of market-oriented economic reforms were undertaken in the early 1980s. These included the reduction of tariffs and quantity controls on imports, a change from quantity controls to price as the main mechanism of resource allocation, the de-regulation of the banking and financial sector, the reform of the customs and excise administration (eventually privatizing it to a Swiss firm, the Society

Table 7.7
Food Production Per Head in Indonesia

Item	1969	1988
Rice (kg)	107	161
Meat (kg)	2.7	5.3
Eggs (kg)	0.5	2.7
Fish (kg)	10.7	16.4
Milk (litres)	0.3	1.5

Source: Sjahrir (1992:27).

General du Surveillance, SGS), the streamlining of government administration, the conversion of non-tariff barriers to tariff barriers and various financial incentives for exporters of manufactured goods (Sjahrir 1992:58–65). Since the early 1980s, the Indonesian economy has undergone considerable structural change. This is shown in Table 7.8.

Between 1983 and 1991, both the agricultural and mining sectors declined in importance, while the share of manufacturing and construction in GDP rose, from 18.7% in 1983 to 26.3% in 1991. At the same time, the share of manufactured exports in total exports rose to 51.7%, while that of crude oil and natural gas fell to 37.4%. Table 7.9 shows composition of Indonesia's manufactured exports in 1991.

Indonesia is now an important exporter of textiles on account of its low wages. In 1990, textile labour costs were approximately US$14 per hour in Japan, US$5 in Taiwan, US$3 in South Korea and US$0.2 in Indonesia. As a consequence of this, many textile firms from the Asian NICs (mainly Taiwan, South Korea and Hong Kong) have relocated in Indonesia (Thee 1991:55–88). Between 1982 and 1989, Indonesian exports of clothing grew by 37.7% per annum, while exports of yarns and fabrics grew by 88.2%

Table 7.8
The Indonesian Economy
% GDP

Year	1983	1985	1987	1989	1991
Agriculture	22.8	22.6	21.3	20.5	18.5
Mining	20.8	18.2	17.3	15.5	15.7
Manufacturing	12.8	15.9	17.2	18.7	20.2
Construction	5.9	5.3	5.1	5.4	6.1
Services	37.7	38.0	39.1	39.9	39.5
Total	100.0	100.0	100.0	100.0	100.0

Source: Economic Intelligence Unit, *Malaysia and Indonesia,* (various issues).

Table 7.9
Indonesia's Manufactured Exports, 1991

Item	% Total
Labour-intensive	57.7
Clothing	19.1
Fabrics	13.1
Footwear	8.4
Electronics	3.4
Yarns	1.7
Resource-intensive	29.5
Plywood	25.7
Capital-intensive	12.8
Fertilizer	2.5
Paper products	2.2
Steel products	2.1

Source: Economic Intelligence Unit, *Malaysia and Indonesia*, (various issues).

and 52.2% per annum respectively (Hill 1991:107; Hill and Suphalachalasai 1992:310–329). Indonesia has also become an offshore production site for the manufacture of high quality shoes. Many shoe manufacturers, such as Nike and Reebok, have moved substantial proportions of their production from South Korea and Taiwan to Indonesia, because of lower costs there (Clifford 1992a:56–57).

Indonesia is also making considerable progress in the development of heavy industry. The best-known of these is its ITPN aircraft industry. Indonesia is one of the few less developed countries which designs and builds its own aircraft. It has recently concluded a deal to export its CN-235 passenger aircraft to Malaysia (Vatikiotis 1993:54).

While market-oriented reforms have been implemented since the early 1980s, there are still a number of industries in Indonesia which are highly protected. Effective rates of protection in the flour milling industry were over 150% in the late 1980s. In a number of industries, such as cigarette manufacture, motor-cycle assembly and paper board manufacture, effective rates of protection ranged from 70% to over 150%. In many cases, these high rates of protection have served to confer monopoly rights on business conglomerates often (but not always) owned by ethnic Chinese businessmen.

Most of Indonesia's exports go to the advanced OECD countries. In 1989, Japan accounted for 42.1% of Indonesia's exports, the USA accounted for 15.8% and the EU accounted for 5.9%. While Indonesia's export orientation has always been toward the OECD countries, what is important is that in the 1990s, most of these exports are manufactured goods, rather than raw materials.

In terms of income distribution, Indonesia has fared better than either Malaysia or Thailand. Since the late 1970s, the distribution of income has become progressively more equal, both in rural as well as in urban areas, and the number of people living below the poverty line has fallen steadily. Between 1976 and 1987, the Gini ratio of personal incomes fell from 36% to 32% in the urban areas. In the rural areas, the Gini ratio fell from 31% to 26%. Over the same period, the proportion of the total population below the poverty line declined from 40.1% to 17.4% (Tjondronegoro et al. 1991:71,74).

Under President Suharto, Indonesia has had an authoritarian government since the mid-1960s and has been administered by a band of able technocrats. Under President Suharto's New Order, Indonesia has enjoyed political stability for 25 years. Beneath the surface, however, a number of potential conflicts lie suppressed by an authoritarian government. The relationship between the ethnic Chinese minority and the native population is one of these. Others include the relationship between Muslims and Christians, the suppression of Islamic fundamentalism and the regional rivalries between Java and the other islands. Irredentist movements in Aceh in northern Sumatra, Iran Jaya and on the island of Timor are a reminders of this. The question of the successor to President

Suharto (who is now in his sixth consecutive term as President) and what kind of government Indonesia would then have, is a subject of acute concern in Indonesia and elsewhere. The fear is that without a strong leader, latent conflicts which have been kept bottled up will suddenly explode to the surface.

The military is highly politicized in Indonesia, and several powerful interest groups and individuals have considerable influence over government policy formation. Government administration in Indonesia is not as efficient as in other countries in the region. Civil servants are paid relatively low wages and often have to take on two jobs to make ends meet. In a recent survey of the extent of bribery and corruption in public life, Indonesia scored 12 out of a maximum of 100 (for negligible bribery and corruption).

Thus, while Indonesia has made some important steps toward a market-oriented economy based on the exports of labour-intensive manufactured goods, there are a number of features of the Indonesian economy which will delay its ascension to NIC status.

Conclusion

The views of Havrylyshyn and Alikhani, in suggesting that there was a second tier of 12 countries which had good prospects of becoming NICs, appear to have been too optimistic. Changes in the international environment and within the countries themselves, suggest that all but a few of the countries in Havrylyshyn and Alikhani's list are unlikely to make the transition from LDC to NIC in the near future. This does not mean, as some writers have suggested, that no less developed countries will make the grade.

On most criteria, it appears that Malaysia is most likely to become the next NIC of Asia, followed by Thailand. If this occurs, the Asian Six will play a dominant role in world trade in the latter part of the 1990s, just as the original Asian NICs did, two decades earlier. In this context it is interesting to note that in a recently published survey of emerging economies, Malaysia and Thailand ranked fifth and sixth, just after the four Asian NICs (which were at the top of the list) (FEER 1992a:51). Indonesia's prospects of attaining NIC status appear to be more remote. Although it has made considerable progress towards an export-oriented manufacturing economy, relatively poor social infrastructure, the continued high level of protection for many industries and relatively low educational attainments (at secondary and tertiary levels) will hold it back from attaining NIC status for some time to come.

There is one other country which might lay claim to be the most likely country to emerge as the next NIC of Asia in the not too distant future: China. The rapid industrialization of China's southern coastal provinces (resulting in their very rapid economic growth), the growing economic integration between Hong Kong, Taiwan and China, and imminent return of Hong Kong to China in 1997, all point to the emergence of China as the next economic powerhouse of Asia (Riedel 1991:117). These aspects of China's recent development will be discussed in Chapter 8.

CHAPTER 8

The NICs in World Trade and Development

Introduction

The major markets for the exports of the Asian NICs are in the USA, EU and Japan. These countries are also the major suppliers of capital and technology to the Asian NICs. It is therefore not surprising that the USA, EU and Japan are the major trading partners of the Asian NICs. Developments in these countries, not only in terms of general economic health, but also in terms of protectionist tendencies, are of major concern to the Asian NICs. While economic links between the Asian NICs themselves, and between the NICs and other countries in the Asia-Pacific region (except Japan) are not as strong, they have been growing steadily in response to the threat of growing protectionism in the USA and EU. Trade and investment links between the Asian NICs and other developing countries in the region have been increasing over the last decade. The one exception to this appears to be Australia, whose trade and investment relations with the Asian NICs appear to be minimal. This is surprising, given Australia's geographical proximity to Southeast and East Asia.

The NICs and the USA

Trade Flows between the USA and the Asian NICs

For most Asian NICs, the USA accounts for between a quarter and half of total exports. The USA is also an import source of imports into the Asian NICs, accounting for up to a third of total imports in some cases. Table 8.1 shows the exports of each Asian NIC to the USA as a percentage of total exports, as well as the imports of each Asian NIC as a percentage of total imports:

Table 8.1
Exports and Imports of Asian NICs to the USA
1992, % Total

Country	Exports	Imports
Hong Kong	23.1	7.3
Singapore	21.2	13.9
South Korea	24.7	22.5
Taiwan	32.3	23.0

Source: United Nations, *World Commodity Trade Statistics,* (various issues); International Monetary Fund, *Direction of Trade,* (various issues); Republic of China, *Statistical Yearbook of the Republic of China,* (various issues).

As shown in the above table, the Asian NICs export between 20% and 30% of their total exports to the USA. South Korea, Taiwan and Hong Kong are most highly dependent on the US market. The dependence of the Asian NICs on the USA has been declining over time as the Asian NICs have sought to diversify their markets.

The Asian NICs export manufactured goods to the USA. Machinery, electrical machinery, miscellaneous manufactures, textiles, clothing and footwear, toys, plastics and transport equipment made up 70% of Taiwan's exports to the USA in 1990. Machinery, electrical machinery, transport equipment and miscellaneous manufactures accounted for nearly 90% of Singapore's exports to the USA in 1990. In the case of Hong Kong, apparel alone made up 51% of total exports to the USA in 1990. Other important items were miscellaneous manufactures (11%), watches and clocks (9%) – Hong Kong is the world's largest manufacturer and exporter of time pieces, accounting for some 45% of the world market in 1991 (everything from fake Gucci masterpieces to genuine McDonald's chronometers), electrical machinery (7%) and office machines (8%). The above five exports made up 86% of Hong Kong's exports to the USA in 1990.

The USA is also a major supplier of machinery and other producer goods to the Asian NICs. In 1990, machinery, electrical machinery, transport equipment and organic chemicals made up 43% of Taiwan's imports from the USA. Some 46% of Singapore's imports from the USA were made up of aircraft, electronic valves, parts for office machines, data processing machines, chemicals and precision instruments.

Although the USA represents the most important export market for most Asian NICs, the share of total US imports accounted for by the Asian NICs is small. In 1992, the Asian NICs accounted for 8.98% of total US imports (down from 13.6% in 1987), with the largest shares held by Taiwan (2.75%) and South Korea (2.64%). This does not, however, mean that some Asian NICs do not dominate certain markets in the US economy. Taiwan, for example, accounts for over 60% of the world's production of electronic mice, most of which are exported to the USA (where most of the electronic cheese is located). In 1985, the Asian NICs accounted for 18% of the US market for apparel and clothing. For electrical machinery and appliances, their share was 12%, for tele-communications and sound recording equipment, it was 11%.

Most Asian NICs have had persistent trade surpluses with the USA. This is particularly true of South Korea and Taiwan. In 1992, Taiwan's trade balance with the USA was US$10.6 billion. South Korea's trade balance with the USA was US$2.7 billion. Singapore had a trade surplus of US$1.9 billion in 1992, while Hong Kong had a small trade surplus (US$0.5 billion) with the USA. Taiwan and South Korea have been under pressure to reduce their trade surpluses with the USA, under the threat of trade sanctions. In 1986, Taiwan had a trade surplus of US$15.7 billion with the USA. South Korea's trade surplus was US$7.1 billion.

Capital Flows between the USA and the Asian NICs

Up till the mid-1970s, the USA was the main source of capital for the Asian NICs. Since then, the USA moved from being a net creditor nation to a net debtor nation as its balance of payments deficits mounted steadily. Japan is now the main source of capital for the Asian NICs. This can be seen from Table 8.2, below, which shows net investment commitments in the Singapore manufacturing sector.

Note that in 1985, the USA accounted for 38% of all net investment commitments in the Singapore manufacturing sector, while Japan accounted for 22%. By 1991, the shares are almost reversed, with the USA accounting for 26% and Japan 31% of net investment commitments in the Singapore manufacturing sector. Note also that, apart from the aberration in 1990, the US share of net investment commitments has been falling over time, while that of Japan has been rising. A similar pattern can be seen in most of the other Asian NICs, although foreign investment in Hong Kong, South Korea and Taiwan is much less important than in Singapore.

During 1985–1990, the USA's share in total foreign investment in Hong Kong fell from 36.4% to 30.1%. In Taiwan, the USA's share fell from 51.7% to 34.4% over the same period. In 1987, the

Table 8.2

Net Investment Commitments in the Singapore
Manufacturing Sector (% Total)

Country	1985	1986	1987	1988	1989	1990	1991*
USA	38.1	30.8	31.2	29.2	26.5	47.6	25.6
Japan	21.8	34.0	34.5	34.4	27.6	31.9	31.3
EU	16.1	14.1	13.8	17.2	26.8	17.8	19.5

* = First three quarters

Source: Ministry of Trade and Industry, *Economic Survey of Singapore*, (various issues).

USA accounted for 25.7% of total foreign investment in South Korea. By 1991, this had fallen to 22.3% (Chen 1993: 44–51).

As is to be expected, most foreign investment in the Asian NICs is in manufacturing and services (especially financial services). For example, in 1990, US foreign investment in Hong Kong was concentrated in wholesale trade (36.9%), finance and insurance (30.8%), manufacturing (10.8%) and banking (9.2%). Relatively little went into manufacturing because the rise in wages in Hong Kong has caused much of Hong Kong's low value-added manufacturing to be relocated to Southern China. In Singapore, foreign investment is concentrated in petroleum refining and chemicals, electronics and electrical appliances, transport equipment and metal products. In Taiwan, electronics and electrical appliances take up the bulk of foreign investment, whilst in South Korea, foreign investment is concentrated in petroleum and chemicals, electronics and electrical appliances, hotels and transport equipment (Chen 1993:44–51).

The North American Free Trade Area and the Asian NICs

In January 1989, the USA and Canada signed a free trade agreement, which was to be implemented over a ten-year period. In December 1989, the USA began negotiations to include Mexico in a wider North American Free Trade Agreement (NAFTA), which would eventually include other Latin American countries. Inclusion of Mexico alone would create a free trade area with a market of US$6 trillion and a population of some 360 million people.

The 1990s are generally regarded as the decade in which most Latin American countries are going to emerge from the "ten lost years" of the 1980s, when their economies were strangled by high debt, hyper-inflation and negative growth. This dramatic turn around in economic fortunes is the result of several factors. First, most Latin American countries have shed their military dictatorships and adopted democratic forms of government. Second, these popularly-elected governments have not flinched from implementing painful economic reforms, which have been necessary to put their economies in order. Third, many countries in Latin America have adopted market-oriented policies aimed at expanding manufactured exports. Indeed, many have used the Asian NICs as their role models. Fourth, the international financial community has resumed financial support from many Latin American countries, following their demonstrated determination to adopt economically responsible monetary and fiscal policies. As a result of these developments, many (but not all) Latin American countries appear to be on the way to economic recovery. For example, Mexico's real GDP growth is expected to rise from 1.3% per annum in 1988 to 3.9% per annum in 1990, while its rate of inflation is expected to decline from 114% in 1988 to 22% in 1991. Although this is still a high rate of inflation, it is a dramatic improvement from 1988, and the trend is for further improvement. Many other Latin American countries are experiencing similar improvements (Economist 1991j:21). These developments are causing some concern in the Asian NICs. Low cost labour in Latin America (especially in Mexico), combined with American technology, could present the Asian NICs with severe competition for the exports to their major market, the USA.

Although the NAFTA proposals have been promised to be consistent with GATT rules (suggesting that other countries will not be kept out of NAFTA), this is cold comfort for the Asian NICs, since tariff reductions within NAFTA would automatically put countries such as South Korea and Taiwan at a disadvantage. NAFTA will also prevent other countries from exporting to the USA through the back door (by investing in, say, Mexico) (Awanohara 1991c:44). Estimates of the likely impact of NAFTA on the Asian NICs indicate that their exports to the USA could decline by 5%. If non-tariff barriers are also reduced as a result of NAFTA, this figure could be higher by a factor of 2 or 3 (Krenin and Plummer 1992:1352–1353).

President Bush, in his 1992 Singapore Lecture, denied that this would occur, saying that NAFTA would not exclude non-member countries such as the Asian NICs from access to the US market. However, essence of a Free Trade Area is that member-countries would get preferential access over non-members. The strict rules of origin which are to be implemented in NAFTA serve to confirm this. There was some suggestion that South Korea and Taiwan might be invited to join NAFTA at some time in the future, but nothing concrete came from this.

In addition to trade-diverting effects, NAFTA may also have investment-diverting effects, as US companies would be expected to take advantage of low cost and proximity to shift some of their production from the Asian NICs to Latin American countries near by (Krenin and Plummer 1992:1362–1364). While the NAFTA arrangements are not expected to be fully implemented for another 10 to 15 years, they have caused considerable concern in the NICs of Asia.

The NICs and the EU

Trade Flows between the EU and the Asian NICs

For most Asian NICs, the EU is the second largest market for their exports after the USA. Within the EU, most of the exports of the Asian NICs go to three countries: the UK, Germany and France. Table 8.3 shows the percentage share of exports and imports of the Asian NICs to the EU.

As shown in the table above, between 12% and 16% of the exports of the Asian NICs go to the EU. The share of total exports of the Asian NICs going to the EU is much lower than their share of exports going to the USA. Apart from Hong Kong, most Asian NICs import between 11% and 14% of their imports from the EU.

As in the case of the USA, Asian NICs export mainly manufactured goods to the EU. Machinery, electrical machinery, miscellaneous manufactures, footwear and plastics accounted for 65% of Taiwan's exports to Germany in 1990. In that year, 57% of Taiwan's imports from Germany were made up of machinery, aircraft parts, organic chemicals and miscellaneous chemicals.

Table 8.3
Trade between the Asian NICs and the EU
1992, % Total

Country	Exports	Imports
Hong Kong	15.8	9.6
Singapore	14.3	13.2
South Korea	12.3	11.7
Taiwan	14.8	13.5

Source: Same as Table 8.1.

Similarly, 65% of Singapore's exports to the UK in 1990 were made up of electrical machinery, textiles, miscellaneous manufactures and transport equipment. In that year, about one-third of Singapore imports from the UK were made up of machinery, electrical machinery, transport equipment and metal manufactures.

Although the EU represents an important export market for the Asian NICs, their share of total EU imports is very small. In 1992, the Asian NICs accounted for only 2.8% of total EU imports. Their share of total EU exports is even smaller (2.4%). Nevertheless, in some product categories (textiles, for example), the Asian NICs have large shares of the EU market. In UK, to take one example, in 1985, the Asian NICs accounted for 24% of the market for apparel and clothing, 13% of the market for office machines and data processing equipment and 14% of the market for miscellaneous manufactures. This has prompted calls for voluntary export restraints and other protectionist measures from EU producers.

Two of the Asian NICs have maintained trade surpluses with the EU, but with the exception of Taiwan, these have not been as large as their surpluses with the USA. In 1992, Taiwan's trade surplus with the EU was US$6.3 billion, South Korea's was US$1.7 billion. Hong Kong and Singapore had small trade deficits with the EU in 1992.

Capital Flows between the EU and the Asian NICs

The EU has not been an important source of capital for the Asian NICs, compared with the USA or Japan. As Table 8.2 above shows, since the mid-1980s, the EU has accounted for a small, though slowly rising share of net investment commitments in the Singapore manufacturing sector.

EU foreign investment in Hong Kong rose from 9.1% of total foreign investment in 1985 to 16.9% in 1990. In Taiwan, the rise in the share of the EU in total foreign investment was of greater magnitude, from 3.3% in 1981 to 12.5% in 1991. In Singapore, the share of the EU in total foreign investment has remained fairly constant, at about 19%. It is in South Korea that the share of the EU in total foreign investment has risen significantly. In 1987, the EU accounted for 18.7% of total foreign investment in South Korea. By 1991, this had growth to 58.9% (Chen 1993: 44–51).

The Unification of the EU Market and the Asian NICs

In January 1993, all internal barriers to trade within the EU were removed, resulting in a unified single market in Western Europe. Firms within the EU will be able to gain from economies of scale, and some trade may be diverted from suppliers outside the EU (such as the Asian NICs) to those within it. This will be true, particularly, of manufactured goods. It is expected that all the Asian NICs will experience a reduction in their manufactured exports to the EU after 1992. Estimates for South Korea suggest that unification of the EU market will result in a reduction of South Korean exports to the EU by 5%. If the effects of dismantling non-tariff barriers are taken into account, the figure could rise by a factor of 2 or 3 (Krenin and Plummer 1992:1357). In addition, it is likely that some import quotas, which are presently bilateral in nature, will be replaced by EU-wide quotas. Exports from Asian NICs through other Southeast Asian countries, such as Malaysia or Indonesia, are also likely to be subject to quantitative restrictions. This is why many Asian NICs, particularly South Korea and Taiwan, are establishing production facilities in some EU countries, especially Britain. Even these strategies are now being blocked, as some countries in the EU (such as France) are insisting on counting goods produced by Asian NIC firms in the EU, as part of their exports to the EU (Davenport 1991:69; Islam 1991b).

Equally important is the possibility that EU foreign investment might be diverted from the Asian NICs to other member-countries within the EU, or to neighbouring European countries. Rather than invest in Hong Kong or Singapore, a unified market in Europe might result in multinational firms based in the EU and investing within the EU, or in such countries such as the Czech Republic, or Poland, where wages are relatively lower, and where there is a pool of skilled labour (Hughes Hallet 1993:121–146; Krenin and Plummer 1992:1362–1364).

The NICs and Australia

Australia's geographic position gives it a unique opportunity to participate in, and benefit from, the rapid economic growth of the Asian NICs to its north. Other countries in the region, particularly Thailand, Malaysia and Indonesia, have already been beneficiaries of the dynamic growth of the Asian NICs. Given its proximity, one might have expected that Australia would also be favourably affected by these developments. In fact, trade and investment links between Australia and the Asian NICs are relatively small. For all intents and purposes, the Asian NICs have by-passed the Australian market and Australian business has been slow to take advantage of investment opportunities in the rapidly growing countries to its north.

Trade Flows between Australia and the Asian NICs

Table 8.4 shows that the Asian NICs have been a small, but growing market for Australian exports. Although each of the Asian NICs accounted for a relative small share of total Australian exports, this share has increased by between 2.5 to 5 times between 1975 and 1988.

Table 8.4
Australian Exports (% Total)

Country	1975	1985	1990	1993
Hong Kong	1.1	1.5	2.6	4.3
Singapore	1.6	3.1	5.5	6.2
South Korea	1.5	3.9	5.9	6.5
Taiwan	1.1	3.0	3.5	4.4
NICs	5.3	11.5	17.5	21.4
China	2.8	3.9	2.5	3.7
Japan	20.5	26.0	26.3	25.0
NEAsia	38.5	41.1	46.3	50.1

Australian Imports (% Total)

Country	1975	1985	1990	1993
Hong Kong	2.3	2.1	1.6	1.3
Singapore	1.5	3.0	2.3	2.5
South Korea	0.6	1.5	2.4	2.8
Taiwan	1.4	3.4	3.5	3.7
NICs	5.8	10.0	9.8	10.3
China	0.9	1.2	2.7	4.3
Japan	17.9	23.1	18.8	18.9
NEAsia	24.6	34.3	31.3	33.5

Source: Australian Bureau of Statistics, *Foreign Trade Australia Exports*, and *Foreign Trade Australia Imports*, Catalog No. 5436.0 and 5437.0, (various issues).

The Asian NICs, as a group, increased their share of total Australian exports by four times, from 5.3% in 1975 to 21.4% in 1992. It is interesting to note that in the 1980s, Japan's share of Australian exports has remained virtually stagnant, at about 26% of the total. In 1992, it fell to 25% as Japanese growth rates fell. Indeed, the Asian NICs are the only group in the table whose shares of Australian exports have been growing rapidly. In 1993, Australia's exports to the Asian NICs (A$13,034,077) were only slightly lower than Australia's exports to Japan (A$15,204,194).

Although there are some similarities in the principal products Australia exports to the Asian NICs, there are also some interesting differences. Table 8.5 shows that Australia's main export to Singapore in 1992–1993 was non-monetary gold (50.4%). The next most important item was petroleum (Singapore is the world's third largest oil refinery), which accounted for almost 11.4% of Australia's total exports to Singapore. These two items accounted for nearly 61.8% of Australia's exports to Singapore. The other principal exports to Singapore comprise mainly food products, machinery (electronic equipment) and manufactured goods (iron and steel). Each of these accounts for a small proportion of total Australian exports to Singapore.

Table 8.6 shows that, in the case of Hong Kong, exports of gold made up more than half of Australia's exports to Hong Kong (which is one the world's largest markets for gold). Like Singapore, the other principal exports comprise food products, metals and photographic equipment, and each of these accounts for a small proportion of total Australian exports to Hong Kong.

Table 8.5
Australia: Principal Exports to Singapore, 1992–1993

Item	% Total*
Gold	50.4
Petroleum	11.4
Machinery	11.4
Manufactured goods	7.8
Vegetables	2.6
Other food products	5.0
Total	88.6

* % Total exports to Singapore
Source: Same as Table 8.4.

Table 8.6

Australia: Principal Exports to Hong Kong, 1992–1993

Item	% Total*
Gold	23.5
Manufactured goods	17.7
Food products	14.7
Machinery	12.1
Coal	6.9
Aluminium	5.7
Total	80.6

* % Total exports to Hong Kong
Source: Same as Table 8.4.

South Korea and Taiwan present a different picture because they are more heavily industrialized than Hong Kong or Singapore. Australia's principal exports to South Korea (Table 8.7) are made up of four items. Coal, non-ferrous metals (mainly aluminum), textile fibres (mainly wool), metallic ores, manufactured goods and non-monetary gold account for 87.4% of all Australian exports to South Korea. Similarly, coal, non-ferrous metals (mainly aluminum), textile fibres (mainly wool), metallic ores, meat and fish make up 70.8% of all Australia's exports to Taiwan (Table 8.8).

Australian exports to the Asian NICs have been growing rapidly over the last ten years. From 1983 to 1993, Australian exports grew at a rate of 15.6% to Hong Kong, 17.7% to South Korea, 22.4% to Singapore and 15.7% to Taiwan. This is a reflection of the rapid growth of the Asian NICs and their growing importance as expanding markets for Australia's exports.

Table 8.4 also shows that the Asian NICs account for a relatively small share of total Australian imports. Each of the Asian NICs accounts for less than 4% of total Australian imports and these shares have not been growing very fast over the last decade or

Table 8.7
Australia: Principal Exports to South Korea, 1992–1993

Item	% Total*
Coal	23.1
Metallic ores	17.8
Non-ferrous metals	15.6
Manufactured goods	13.6
Gold	9.6
Textile fibres	7.7
Total	87.4

* % Total exports to South Korea
Source: Same as Table 8.4.

Table 8.8
Australia: Principal Exports to Taiwan, 1992–1993

Item	% Total*
Non-ferrous metals	18.6
Coal	16.4
Textile fibres	8.5
Iron and Steel	8.4
Metallic ores	6.5
Fish	6.5
Meat	5.9
Total	70.8

* % Total exports to Taiwan
Source: Same as Table 8.4.

so. As a group, the Asian NICs accounted for 6% of Australian imports in 1975. This increased to 10% in 1985, but has remained at about that level since then. The Japanese share of Australian imports declined somewhat in the 1980s, reaching a level of 19% in 1993.

In recent years, Australian manufactured exports have been rising rapidly. These are made up primarily of basic manufactures, machinery and transport equipment. Between 1991 and 1992, Australian manufactured exports grew by 8%. This more than doubled (to 17%) in 1992–1993. Australian manufactured exports accounted for about 25% of total exports during this period. Less than 6% of total Australian manufactured exports went to each of the Asian NICs (East Asian Analytical Unit 1992b:286)

The Asian NICs also account for a small share of Australian imports (Table 8.9). However, with the exception of Hong Kong, this share has been rising steadily over time. Between 1975 and 1985, the Asian NICs, as a group, increased their share of Australian manufactured imports, from 6% to 11%. Taiwan registered the largest increase (from 1.8% to 4.6%). With the exception of Singapore, these shares fell in 1993, as the Australian economy was in recession.

Australia's principal imports from Hong Kong (Table 8.10) are made up of five items – miscellaneous manufactures, office machinery, electrical machinery, textiles and clothing. These five items account for 71.1% of all Australian imports from Hong Kong.

Australia imports mainly refined petroleum products and office machines from Singapore (Table 8.11). Electrical machinery is also important.

Table 8.9
Australian Manufactured Imports (% Total)

Country	1975	1985	1993
Hong Kong	3.0	3.0	1.7
Singapore	0.4	1.0	2.1
South Korea	0.7	2.0	1.1
Taiwan	1.8	4.6	3.4
NICs	5.9	10.6	8.3

Source: Same as Table 8.4.

Table 8.10

Australia: Principal Imports from Hong Kong, 1992–1993

Item	% Total*
Miscellaneous manufactures	21.5
Office machinery	15.7
Electrical machinery	13.2
Textiles	10.7
Clothing	10.6
Total	71.7

* % Total imports from Hong Kong
Source: Same as Table 8.4.

Table 8.11

Australia: Principal Imports from Singapore, 1992–1993

Item	% Total*
Office machines	24.7
Petroleum products	20.3
Electrical machinery	8.3
Total	53.3

* % Total imports from Singapore
Source: Same as Table 8.4.

Although machinery imports are the largest single item Australia imports from South Korea (Table 8.12), there are a large number of other important imports (which include textiles, road vehicles, and telecommunications equipment) which account for just under 10% each of Australia's imports from South Korea. Non-mineral metallic products, miscellaneous manufactures and footwear are also important items which Australia imports from South Korea.

This pattern is also true of Australia's imports from Taiwan (Table 8.13). Office machinery and miscellaneous manufactures are the two most important items which Australia imports from

Table 8.12

Australia: Principal Imports from South Korea, 1992–1993

Item	% Total*
Machinery	15.1
Textiles	9.9
Road vehicles	9.7
Telecommunications equipment	9.3
Non-mineral metallic products	6.5
Miscellaneous manufactures	5.3
Footwear	4.5
Clothing	1.7
Total	62.0

* % Total imports from South Korea
Source: Same as Table 8.4.

Table 8.13

Australia: Principal Imports from Taiwan, 1992–1993

Item	% Total*
Office machinery	24.5
Miscellaneous manufactures	12.4
Metal manufactures	8.9
Textiles	8.3
Electrical machinery	6.5
Footwear	1.7
Clothing	1.5
Total	63.8

* % Total imports from Taiwan
Source: Same as Table 8.4.

Taiwan. There are a large number of other items (ranging from metal manufactures to clothing) which make up Australia's principal imports from Taiwan.

Australia's imports from the Asian NICs (except Hong Kong) have been growing rapidly over the last ten years. From 1983 to 1993, the growth rate of Australian imports was 3.3% from Hong Kong, 16.5% from South Korea, 12.3% from Singapore and 10.1% from Taiwan.

The main products which Australia imports from the Asian NICs reflect the latter's comparative advantage in manufactured goods. The importance of refined petroleum imports from Singapore derives from that country's position as the third largest oil refining centre in the world. The predominance of the imports of office machines (electric typewriters, computers, printers and calculators) and electrical machinery (computer chips, electric motors, etc.) is a symptom of the position of countries such as Hong Kong, Taiwan and Singapore in world trade in these products. One interesting feature of Australian imports from the Asian NICs is the importance of machinery and road vehicles from South Korea. This is a reflection of the relatively advanced stage of the development of heavy industry in that country.

Textiles, clothing and footwear (TCF) make up an important sub-group of manufactured goods which Australia imports from the Asian NICs. Table 8.14 shows that, except for Singapore (which was never able to sustain a large export-oriented textile industry because of its relatively high wages), this has been an important group of items in Australia's imports from the Asian NICs. In 1975, more than half of Hong Kong's exports to Australia were made up of TCF products. For South Korea, the proportion was slightly less than half. These proportions have been declining over time, as the Asian NICs gradually lost their comparative advantage in the production of these labour-intensive manufactures. TCF has never been a large Australian import from Singapore, but even this small share has been declining over time. As a group, the Asian NICs have seen the share of TCF products in their exports to Australia decline by more than half.

Table 8.14

TCF in Australia's Imports from Northeast Asia, 1975–1993

Country	1975	1985	1993
Hong Kong	57.8	35.5	21.7
Singapore	5.2	1.5	0.7
South Korea	47.5	33.9	16.4
Taiwan	38.4	26.3	12.2
NICs	37.2	24.3	11.8
China	64.9	51.8	43.9
Japan	8.4	4.1	2.0
NEAsia	23.6	13.3	11.2

Source: Same as Table 8.4.

Although TCF products have been an important import item from the Asian NICs, the latter have not accounted for a very high share of total TCF imports into Australia (from all countries). Table 8.15 shows that, in 1975, TCF imports from Hong Kong accounted for 17% of all Australian TCF imports. This declined to 4.2% in 1993. South Korea and Taiwan increased their shares of total Australian TCF imports between 1975 and 1985, but in 1993, each of these countries accounted for less than 7% of the total. The Asian NICs, as a group, accounted for about 18% of all Australian TCF imports in 1993. Again, this is a reflection of the loss of competitiveness of the Asian NICs in the export of TCF products over time. The increasing share of China in total Australian TCF imports reflects that country's emergence as a major world exporter of TCF products. Much of this has been due to textile manufactures from the Asian NICs (particularly Hong Kong and Taiwan) re-locating their production facilities to southern China in search of lower wages.

In the USA and EU, TCF imports from the Asian NICs have been a major problem, as these have caused large-scale unemployment (usually concentrated in particular geographical

Table 8.15
Northeast Asia's Share of Australian TCF Imports,
1975–1993

Country	1975	1985	1993
Hong Kong	17.1	10.2	4.2
Singapore	0.9	0.5	0.3
South Korea	3.7	7.4	6.7
Taiwan	6.7	12.6	6.6
NICs	28.4	30.7	17.7
China	7.1	9.1	27.2
Japan	19.0	13.4	5.3
NEAsia	54.5	53.3	50.2

Source: Same as Table 8.4.

areas). As a result, TCF imports from the Asian NICs (and other less developed countries) have been subject to quantity restrictions under the Multi-Fibre Agreement (MFA). Import penetration of TCF products from the Asian NICs into the Australian market has been relatively small. In 1967, TCF imports from the Asian NICs accounted for 1.5% of domestic production. By 1982, this had increased to only 7.6% of domestic production. The reason for this is that, apart from a few years during the Whitlam Labour government when tariffs were reduced, TCF products have been highly protected in Australia, in order to preserve employment. In 1987, the effective rate of protection for the clothing industry was 176%. This is expected to decline to 117% in 1995. At present, only 3% of the output of Australian TCF products is exported. The Hawke Labour government declared its intention to reduce the level of protection on TCF products, as a group, to 30% by the year 2000, in an effort to restructure the industry and transform it into an export-oriented industry.

Australia's trade balance with the Asian NICs has changed over time. Since the mid-1980s it has been in surplus, except for the small deficit with Taiwan in 1985. In 1993, Australia had a trade surplus with all the Asian NICs. This is shown in Table 8.16.

The rapidly improving standard of living has stimulated demand for Australian food and other products (such as raw materials and manufactured goods). On the other hand, Australia's small protected domestic market does not allow these countries to export large volumes of manufactured goods to Australia. At present, Australian average nominal tariffs for traded goods are 15%. This compares with 14% in New Zealand, 13% in Taiwan, 11% in South Korea, 6.2% in Japan, and 3.3% in the USA (Korporaal 1991:39). Australia's trade surplus with South Korea is explained primarily by the latter's need for industrial raw materials. South Korea is the most heavily industrialized country amongst the Asian NICs. Taiwan also imports mainly industrial raw materials from Australia. However, Taiwan is much more advanced in the production of certain consumer goods (for example, electronic equipment such as personal computers and telecommunications equipment) than South Korea.

Australia's trade links with the Asian NICs are relatively small, in spite of having increased steadily over the last 10 or 15 years. This suggests that Australia has not been able to take full advantage of the rapid growth of the economies to its north (Bowring 1984:86).

Table 8.16
Australian Trade Balance* with Asian NICs, 1967–1993
(A$1,000)

Country	1967	1982	1985	1993
Hong Kong	30064	–63419	182553	1800526
Singapore	47778	–139307	70160	2278435
South Korea	6660	380408	683853	2273200
Taiwan	11710	–186694	–205843	468542

* Exports – Imports
Source: Same as Table 8.4.

In 1991, the Australian government took steps to rectify this. It announced that Austrade (the government agency responsible for increasing Australian trade) would re-locate all its representatives in its offices in the USA and Western Europe to Asia (Korporaal 1991:68). This was in recognition of the view that, by the year 2000, Asia would account for 75% of Australia's trade. By 1994, Australia's exports to Northeast and Southeast Asia are expected to reach A$37.4 billion (from A$24.2 billion in 1989). Japan and the Asian NICs are expected to account for two-thirds of this increase (Deans 1991:67). In 1990, the ASEAN-5 (Brunei, Malaysia, Indonesia, Philippines and Thailand), the Asian NICs and Japan, already accounted for 40% of Australia's total trade (exports + imports). By 1993, this proportion reached 63%. These changes have followed the efforts of the Hawke Labour government at reducing tariff protection for Australian industry, in a bid to make it more internationally competitive (Korporaal 1990:38–39).

Under the Keating Labour government, there has been an intensification of government policy to forge closer links between Australia and the rapidly-growing economies to its north. The rapid growth of the Asian NICs had fuelled their demand for Australian exports. By 1993, the share of total Australian trade accounted for by the Asian NICs exceeded that of Japan. Between 1991 and 1993, Australian exports to the Asian NICs grew by 41% (Westfield 1994:44).

Capital Flows between Australia and the Asian NICs

Australia has not been an important destination for foreign investment by the Asian NICs. As Table 8.17 shows, as a group, the Asian NICs accounted for about 6% of total foreign investment in Australia. For historical and other reasons, the USA and the UK have been the major sources of foreign investment in Australia. In recent years, Japan has also been an important foreign investor in the Australian economy.

Singapore and Hong Kong were much more important than South Korea and Taiwan as sources of foreign investment in

Table 8.17

Australia: Stock of Foreign Investment, 1991–1992

Item	% Total*
USA	19.38
United Kingdom	18.52
Japan	17.19
Singapore	2.24
Hong Kong	3.52
South Korea	0.07
Taiwan	0.07
NICs	5.90
Total	60.99

Source: Australian Bureau of Statistics 1991–92, *International Investment Position Australia*, Catalogue No. 5306.

Australia. The Asian NICs accounted for 5.9% of foreign investment in Australia in 1991–1992. Until recently, Australian foreign investment regulations, prohibiting majority ownership of assets by foreigners, have discouraged investment by the Asian NICS (entrepreneurs from these countries prefer to have control over their investments). In addition, the militant reputation of Australian trade unions and the vociferous objections of some xenophobic lobby groups, have not helped. Entrepreneurs in the Asian NICs prefer to do business in a more congenial environment. Furthermore, Australia does not have an industrial base, or the cost structure, that can support the sort of industries which entrepreneurs in the Asian NICs may want to establish. They are more interested in investing in countries such as Malaysia and Thailand, where they can take advantage of lower wage rates and where rates of economic growth are much higher. Investing to produce manufactured goods for the Australian domestic market is not attractive as the domestic market is too small.

The USA, UK and Japan were the three largest foreign investors in Australia in 1991–1992. These three countries accounted for just over 60% of the total foreign investment in Australia, in 1991–1992. Most of this investment is geared to serve the domestic market.

Australian investment abroad shows a similar pattern. Table 8.18 shows that, in 1991–1992, the Asian NICs as a group, accounted for only 6.89% of total Australian investment abroad. Hong Kong was the most important recipient of Australian investment in 1993. The largest two recipients of Australian overseas investment were the USA and the UK. Japan received only 5.33% of Australian overseas investment.

Although the data in Tables 8.17 and 8.18 pertain only to one year, a similar pattern can be observed for other years. The relationship between Australia, the UK and the USA has always been strong in terms of foreign investment. For example, in 1981, Australian investment in Hong Kong accounted for only 2.3% of

Table 8.18

Australian Stock of Total Investment Abroad, 1991–1992

Item	% Total*
USA	26.11
United Kingdom	19.32
Japan	5.33
Singapore	2.08
Hong Kong	4.37
South Korea	0.37
Taiwan	0.07
NICs	6.89
Total	57.65

Source: Australian Bureau of Statistics 1991–92, *International Investment Position Australia*, Catalogue No. 5306.

total foreign investment in Hong Kong. The USA accounted for 43.5% of the total, and Japan accounted for 35.1% (Cheng 1982:68). For some Asian countries such as Japan and South Korea, the level of Australian investment is a very small proportion of the total because foreign investment is not encouraged. However, even where foreign investment is actively encouraged (as in Singapore and Hong Kong), Australian investment in these countries is still very small. This suggests that Australian business has been relatively slow to take advantage of investment opportunities in these rapidly growing economies (Friedland 1989:52–53).

This situation is changing gradually as Australia re-orients its trade and investment priorities towards Asia. In recent years, many Australian firms in the manufacturing, mining, finance and utilities sectors have moved into Asia (Westfield 1994:48–49).

The Prospects for an Asia Pacific Economic Community

The idea of a regional trading bloc in the Pacific was first raised by Kojima (1966), when it was thought that the impending entry of the UK into the EEC (as it was called then) would adversely affect countries such as the USA, Japan and Australia. Kojima proposed that a Pacific Free Trade Area (PAFTA) be established, initially comprising the developed countries of the Pacific (the USA, Canada, Japan, Australia and New Zealand), but allowing developing countries in the Pacific to become associate members. As a free trade area, PAFTA would involve a reduction in tariffs between member countries, while they each maintained their own rates of protection *vis-à-vis* the rest of the world. This proposal, however, was not taken up, in spite of a large number of conferences held to discuss it. The USA was of the view that such a proposal would be contrary to the principles of free trade (of which it saw itself as a champion), and there was concern that such a grouping would be dominated by the Japanese (Drysdale 1988:208).

In 1976, Australia and Japan proposed the establishment of an Organization for Pacific Trade and Development (OPTAD). The USA, this time around, was much more favourable to such a scheme, particularly after a specially-commissioned Congressional report was published in 1979 (Drysdale and Patrick 1979). OPTAD was conceived as a vehicle for high-level consultation between governments on trade issues. Several task forces were set up to investigate trade, energy and other areas of potential regional co-operation (Rieger 1989:25).

In 1980, the Australian and Japanese governments set up a Pacific Co-operation Commission (PCC). Following this, a number of Pacific Economic Co-operation Conferences (PECC) were held to discuss how closer co-operation might be achieved between countries in the Pacific. These conferences involved government officials, businessmen and academics.

In the late 1980s, the declining growth of world trade, increasing friction between the USA and the EU in agricultural exports, signs of increasing protectionism in North America and the EU, and serious doubts about a successful conclusion to the Uruguay Round of the GATT negotiations, gave new impetus to proposals to establish a trading group in the Pacific. In 1989, the Australian Prime Minister proposed the establishment of APEC (Asia-Pacific Economic Co-operation Forum) (Rees 1989:10–11), and shortly afterwards, the Malaysian Prime Minister proposed another regional grouping, EAEG (East Asian Economic Group) (Holloway, Rowley, Islam and Vatikiotis 1991:52–53). While APEC included all the countries in the Pacific, EAEG specifically excluded the non-Asian developed countries, such as the USA, Canada, Australia and New Zealand. As in the case of OPTAD, both APEC and EAEG were intended to provide a forum in which trade and other regional issues could be discussed. While there is some discussion as to how APEC and EAEG relate to each other (whether as alternatives or complements), negotiations on the next stage of the establishment of such a regional grouping were held up for some time because of the problem of the "three Chinas" (Vatikiotis 1990:9). Some countries wanted to admit the Peoples' Republic of China as a member first, while others wanted Hong Kong and Taiwan to be admitted first. This problem was resolved at the Seoul meeting of APEC in 1991, when all three countries were admitted to APEC at the same time.

The economic rationale for the establishment of a regional trading group in the Asia-Pacific region rests on several arguments.

First, the rise of Japan as a world economic and financial power and the rapid growth of the Asian NICs, has made these countries the most dynamic part of the world. Other countries, such as those in ASEAN, are also beginning to be drawn into this momentum of growth (Yanagihara 1987:404–407). Indeed, some authors (Kahn 1979) argue that the centre of gravity of world economic activity has shifted from the Atlantic to the Pacific. Whereas the nineteenth and twentieth centuries were those in which countries bordering the Atlantic Ocean were dominant in the world economy, the twenty-first century is said to be the Pacific century, when countries bordering the Pacific Ocean will be dominant in the world economy (Sudo 1991). In addition, the realization in Australia and New Zealand that these countries' futures are more closely tied with Asia, than with Europe, plus the emergence of a reformed, market-oriented Chinese economy, has increased the need for consultation and dialogue amongst countries in the region (Kanapathy 1983:42).

Second, economic conditions in the Pacific region appear to be favourable for the establishment of a trading group. In terms of total market size, the East Asian countries (Japan, the Asian NICs and ASEAN), are likely to be about the same size as the EU and North America by the year 2000. By then, total GNP of the East Asian countries is expected to be US$5,308 billion (compared with US$5,940 billion for the EU and US$6,940, for the USA) (Rees 1989:10). In 1987, "developing Asia and Japan" already accounted for about 20% of world trade, a share that is higher than that accounted for by North America. Intra-regional trade in "developing Asia and Japan" accounted for just under 20% of total trade (for North America, the figure was about 12%) (Rowley 1989b:53).

If Japan, the USA, Canada, Australia, New Zealand, the Asian NICs, and ASEAN are included in the concept of a "Pacific Community", such a grouping now ranks as one of the major centres of world economic activity. In 1983, Pacific Community countries accounted for 54% of world GNP, 42% of world population and 36% of world trade (Drysdale 1988:60–63). In addition, considerable trade already occurs with the Pacific Community, with some 60% of total trade occurring within the Pacific Community. By 1992, Pacific Community countries accounted for 40% of world trade and intra-regional trade accounted for 66% of total trade. In addition, trade in the Asia-Pacific region was growing at a faster rate than that of the world as a whole (DFAT 1993:1).

The reason for this is that there is a considerable degree of economic complementarity between countries in the Pacific Community. There are a variety of economies in this group of nations. First, there are land-rich, resource-rich advanced economies (Australia, New Zealand, Canada and the USA). Then there are land-poor, resource-poor, advanced industrial, or semi-industrial economies (Japan and the Asian NICs). In addition, there are land-rich, resource-rich, developing economies (Malaysia, Thailand, Indonesia) (Yanagihara 1987:404). With increasing industrialization, the Asian NICs and other developing countries in the region require food and raw materials, which can be supplied by the land-rich, resource-rich countries. Increasing industrialization also requires capital imports, which can be supplied by the advanced industrial countries in the region. The emergence of Japan as the world's largest creditor nation is important in this respect. Increasing industrialization will increase the supply, and lower the cost, of manufactured goods, which are required by other countries in the region. On various standard measures of economic complementarity, the degree of complementarity between countries in the Pacific Community appears to be high. The reason for this is that different countries in the Asia-Pacific region have comparative advantage in different products because of different resource endowments.

Balassa's index of "revealed comparative advantage" (1965), is calculated as the share of each product group in a country's total exports, divided by the share of that product group in world exports. For example, if the share of agricultural exports in Australia's total exports is, say, 10%, while the share of world agricultural exports to world total exports is, say, 5%, then the index of "revealed" comparative advantage is 2. It indicates that Australia has a "revealed" comparative advantage in the export of agricultural commodities, since the share of these exports in Australia's total exports, is twice as high as that for the world. The higher the index, the greater the comparative advantage a country has in the export of the product concerned.

Empirical studies (Drysdale 1988:100) show that Australia has a comparative advantage in agricultural and mineral exports. North American countries have a comparative advantage in agricultural and heavy machinery exports. Japan's comparative advantage lies in manufactured goods of all kinds. China's comparative advantage is in agricultural goods, minerals, and light manufactures. The Asian NICs have comparative advantage in light manufactured goods, while the ASEAN countries have comparative advantage in agricultural exports, minerals and fuels. Considerable complementarity is revealed by these data, as different countries in the region can specialize in different exports.

Table 8.19 shows trade intensity indexes for APEC countries. The trade intensity index is defined as:

$$I_{ij} = \frac{(\dfrac{X_{ij}}{X_i})}{(\dfrac{M_j}{M_w})}$$

where X_{ij} = Exports of country i to country j, X_i = total exports of country i, M_j = total imports of country j, M_w = total world imports. For example, the exports of Australia to China as a proportion of total Australian exports in 1992 was 0.032. The total imports of China as a proportion of total world imports was 0.021. The trade intensity index between Australia and China is therefore 0.032/ 0.021 = 1.51. If there were no impediments to trade, or no particular economic complementarities between countries, the trade intensity

Table 8.19
APEC Trade Intensity Indexes, 1986 and 1992

Country		NEANIC	ASEAN	AUS	CAN	CHI	JAP	NZ	USA
NEANIC	1986	—	1.24	1.12	0.46	3.73	1.46	0.76	1.47
	1992	—	1.63	1.43	0.66	7.49	1.26	0.81	1.75
ASEAN	1986	0.93	—	1.21	0.18	0.94	2.12	0.64	0.94
	1992	2.44	—	1.90	0.30	1.04	2.77	1.37	1.41
AUS	1986	1.63	1.58	—	0.34	0.98	2.96	13.78	0.48
	1992	3.17	3.97	—	0.49	1.49	4.16	22.02	0.60
CAN	1986	0.18	0.17	0.38	—	0.68	0.66	0.27	3.15
	1992	0.43	0.26	0.40	—	0.63	0.75	0.27	5.42
CHI	1986	4.81	1.18	0.47	0.15	—	1.85	0.23	0.32
	1992	10.24	1.39	0.72	0.23	—	2.24	0.42	0.69
JAP	1986	1.95	1.61	1.56	0.45	1.33	—	1.09	1.52
	1992	3.82	3.37	1.95	0.63	1.66	—	1.37	1.98
NZ	1986	0.67	0.99	10.75	0.32	1.72	1.95	—	0.61
	1992	2.00	2.05	17.29	0.46	0.97	2.59	—	0.88
USA	1986	1.13	0.79	1.35	4.09	0.59	1.30	0.82	—
	1992	1.21	1.51	1.88	6.11	0.81	1.76	1.22	—

Key:
NEANIC = Hong Kong, South Korea, Taiwan
ASEAN   = Brunei, Indonesia, Malaysia, Philippines, Singapore, Thailand
AUS   = Australia
CAN   = Canada
CHI   = China
JAP   = Japan
NZ   = New Zealand
USA   = United States of America

Source: International Monetary Fund, *Direction of Trade Statistics Yearbook 1993*.

indexes between countries would be 1. An index greater than 1 indicates the existence of economic complementarities between trading partners, while an index below 1 shows the opposite.

The data in Table 8.19 shows, with some exceptions, a considerable degree of economic complementarity between APEC countries. The highest degree of economic complementarity occurs between China and the Northeast Asian NICs (primarily because of the large volume of trade between China and Hong Kong), Australia and New Zealand, and between the USA and Canada. The trade intensity indexes between these countries (or groups of countries) is significantly greater than 1. Geographical proximity and cultural affinity are important determinants of the high indexes of trade intensity between these countries. Table 8.19 also shows that there is some degree of complementarity between most of the other APEC countries. The Northeast Asian NICs and the ASEAN countries have high trade intensities with most of the other APEC countries. Australia has high trade intensities with the Northeast Asian NICs and ASEAN countries. Japan has high trade intensities with most APEC countries, except Canada. The USA has trade intensities of above 1 with most APEC countries, except China. However, this is misleading, as it does not take account of the fact that much of the USA's trade with China passes through Hong Kong. Of all the APEC countries, Canada stands out has having low trade intensities (with values well below 1) with all APEC countries except the USA. So, with few exceptions, there is a significant degree of economic complementarity between major APEC trading partners, and this is reflected in the pattern of trade within APEC. Table 8.19 also shows that between 1986 and 1992, the trade intensity indexes increased for most APEC countries. This is a reflection of the growing economic integration of the region.

The high degree of economic complementarity between the major trading partners in the Asia-Pacific region has also caused some problems. In particular, the increasing trade friction between the USA and Japan on one hand, and the USA and the Asian NICs, on the other, has highlighted the need for some regional forum in which to discuss these problems. Differences between Australia and the USA over subsidized wheat exports by the latter, are also causing concern. It is the view of some observers that, at present, there is no regional institution which can be used to resolve these differences, or to enable countries in the Pacific to speak with one voice in international trade negotiations (Drysdale 1989:14–19).

Third, political conditions now appear more favourable to the establishment of a regional trading group in the Pacific. The end of the Cold War in Europe has focused attention on Soviet activity in the Pacific. In addition, the unification of the EU in 1993, negotiations to establish a trading block in North America, growing trade frictions between the USA and Japan, and the uncertainties which occurred in the late 1980s and early 1990s over a successful conclusion of the Uruguay Round of the GATT negotiations, have all given more urgency to the establishment of a regional trading group in the Pacific (Awanohara 1991b:32–33).

Although there are strong arguments in favour of the establishment of a regional trading group in the Pacific, there are a number of arguments against it. Owing to historical and cultural differences as well as to geography, countries in the Asia-Pacific region have little in common with each other, apart from their dependence on Japan and the USA. Of the 15 countries in the region, eight have no common borders, three share a common border with one other regional neighbour, while only one country shares common borders with two other regional neighbours (Daly and Logan 1989:215). In addition, the countries in the Asia-Pacific region are of very different levels of economic development. This was not the case when the countries of Western Europe embarked on setting up a customs union. Studies of regional integration schemes have shown that when the levels of development of member countries of such schemes are very uneven, the benefits of such schemes are likely to be distributed unevenly. Countries which are more developed, are likely to benefit more from the reduction of intra-regional tariffs (Kahnert 1969; Pazos 1973). Furthermore, by the middle of the 1980s, important changes had taken place in the world economy which indicated that the dynamism of Japan and the Asian NICs was not likely to be maintained (Stutchbury 1990:75).

World trade had started to slow down, protectionism was on the rise, technological change was eroding the comparative advantage of the Asian NICs, and exchange rate re-alignments were causing serious problems of adjustment in Japan and some of the Asian NICs (such as South Korea and Taiwan) (Daly and Logan 1989: 221–225).

At the present time, the best prospects for the establishment of a regional trading group in the Pacific rest with the proposals for APEC, which now appears to have the support of both the USA and Japan (Smith 1989a:11–12). The summit meeting of APEC leaders in Seattle in 1992 signalled the commitment of the USA to such a group, and its willingness to play a leading role in its formation. At the Bogor Summit of APEC leaders, held in November 1994, APEC leaders agreed to reduce tariffs of developed APEC countries to zero by 2010. Less developed APEC countries would follow suit by 2020. Only Malaysia voiced reservations about its willingness to abide by this timetable, citing the possibility that it might not be ready to open its doors completely to intra-APEC imports by that time.

There is considerable debate over the precise form that APEC should take. Most participating countries favour an "open" regional grouping rather than a discriminatory trading bloc. In the former, reductions in tariffs and other impediments to intra-regional trade are made in such a way that there is no need for all member countries to agree on specific proposals at the same time. The process of closer economic integration is essentially determined by market forces. Bilateral agreements can be made between member countries so long as provisions are made to enable other member countries to join in such agreements. Tariff concessions made between any member countries should be made to all other countries. In addition, such agreements should not be detrimental to non-members. This will ensure that trade diversion will not occur as a result of tariff reductions. Through discussions and consultations between member countries, a series of such agreements could gradually encompass all member countries as well as not discriminating against non-member countries (Elek 1992:74).

The driving force underlying "open regionalism" is that each country's trade liberalization will increase the benefits of other countries if they also liberalize their trade. It will therefore be in the interests of all countries in the group to agree to removing tariffs and other impediments to trade. This is the opposite of the "Prisoner's Dilemma" in game theory (Drysdale and Garnaut 1994:51).

This approach, by its nature, tends to deal with relatively non-contentious issues first. The exchange of trade information, the harmonization of codes and the reduction of physical impediments to trade (for example, in transport and communications facilities) are examples where mutual benefits are readily apparent. While there is no doubt that co-operation in such matters will facilitate trade, the real test of open regionalism will come when difficult decisions affecting income and employment have to be made (for example, the reduction of tariff and non-tariff barriers in "sensitive" areas such as textiles, financial services, agricultural imports, etc.).

Open regionalism in the Asia-Pacific region faces a number of other difficulties. With some exceptions, tariff levels between the major trading partners within the region are already relatively low. This leaves little scope for large gains from further tariff reductions. In addition, the tariff levels of countries within the region vary considerably (from very low in Singapore and Hong Kong, to moderately high in Thailand and the Philippines), making it difficult to obtain agreement on tariff reductions across a large number of countries (Panagaryia 1994:19). While some countries such as the USA are keen on seeing APEC eventually taking the form of a Free Trade Area, other countries such as China, are opposed to this.

There was a time when the model for APEC appeared to be a loose arrangement of member countries, rather like the OECD (Rowley 1989c:12–13). However, recent developments in the institutional set-up of APEC (which include a ministerial council, and a secretariat to be established in Singapore) may be the first steps towards an organizational form based on the EU (Arndt

1994:97). The decision of the Bogor Summit to lay down a timetable for the removal of tariff barriers within APEC is another sign that the organization may be moving inexorably in this direction.

Australia and the NICs: Challenges and Opportunities

The economic growth and development of the Asian NICs presents both challenges and opportunities for Australia. Being close to the region, Australia can benefit from the dynamism of the Asian NICs by forging close trade and investment links with these countries. However, as pointed out earlier in this chapter, Australia's links with the Asian NICs are marginal. Very few Australian firms have been involved in the business boom that has been taking place in Southeast and East Asia. Australia is still either looking in, or looking West, when it should be looking North, and East (Cooper 1991:74). As a result, countries such as Singapore and Taiwan are expected overtake Australia and New Zealand, in terms of living standards, by the year 2000. South Korea is expected to do the same soon after. Australia, on the other hand, has been sliding backwards, in the world ranking of nations (Simson 1991:22).

The challenge facing Australia is how to participate in, and benefit from, the rapid growth of the countries to its north. This will involve a restructuring of the Australian economy, by reducing the high levels of protection which shelter inefficient firms. It will require enlightened management which monitors and understands developments in Asian economies and is ready to take advantage of them. It will require the co-operation of labour, in reforming industrial relations and work practices, in order to improve efficiency. Attitudes have to change. Here is where education plays an important role. Some important changes have already taken place with respect to the teaching of Asian languages (Eccles 1994:40–42), but more needs to be done. The more Australians learn about Asia, its peoples, languages, cultures and economies, the more likely are they to appreciate why their northern neighbours are racing past them in economic terms. And they are more likely to understand that, by forging links, instead of erecting barriers, they stand a better chance of not being left in the twentieth century, when their northern neighbours are in the twenty-first.

The broad contours of what needs to be done have been known by informed observers for some time. The problem lies in how to implement the policies that are required to make the necessary changes. As in the case of the Asian NICs, perhaps what is required, most of all, is strong government, able to take, and implement, difficult decisions, without caving in to narrow sectional interests. Some important changes have already take place as a result of policies implemented by the Hawke Labour government. However, some authorities are of the view that the pace of change is too slow (Simson 1991:25).

The choice facing Australians has been clearly articulated by Professor Helen Hughes (Hughes 1988:195):

> The billion and three quarters people living in East Asian countries will go on developing no matter what Australia does. Australia has a choice; it can either continue to be a raw material mine at the periphery of East Asian development or it can take part in East Asian economic growth and thus accelerate its own development ... It may be easier to wait another ten years to make the effort to trade with the rapidly growing countries of Asia, but by the year 2000 others will have become entrenched in Asian markets. It may be too late for Australia.

The NICs and China

Economic Links between China and the Asian NICs

There are several reasons to suggest that China will play an increasingly important role in the economies of the Asian NICs. China's large population and its vast pool of low-cost labour present the Asian NICs with a opportunity to overcome their problems associated with labour shortages. Already, many Asian NICs (especially Hong Kong), have transferred their labour-intensive manufacturing operations to China. In fact, the southern provinces of China (Guangdong, in particular), are rapidly emerging as important centres of world manufacturing activity. When Hong Kong reverts to Chinese control in 1997, Guangdong province, will have become an NIE (newly industrializing economy) in its own right (Riedel 1991:117). In 1978, agriculture accounted for 90% of Guangdong's economy, while industry accounted for only 10%. By 1990, these proportions were virtually reversed. In that year, industry accounted for Rmb 142.2 billion (87%), out of the province's total output of Rmb 164.3 billion. It is interesting to note that Guangdong province has a population of about 64 million people. This makes it larger than all countries in Western Europe, except Germany. Between 1980 and 1990, Guangdong province recorded an average growth rate of 12.5% per annum. In 1990, Guangdong province accounted for almost 20% of China's total exports. The per capita income in Shenzhen, its most well known Free Trade Zone, was US$2,000 in 1990. In that year alone, Shenzhen's industrial output and foreign investment inflow increased by 40%, its exports by 25%. On most indicators, the southern provinces of China are rapidly emerging as the new NICs of Asia (Economist 1991i: 21–22).

China has already emerged as the world's largest producer of toys and now accounts for some 20% of total world textile production. In addition to this, China's large population offers the Asian NICs a potentially large market for their products. By the year 2000, China's GDP is expected to be four times larger than its 1980 level, and reach US$85 billion. This will provide an expanding market for both investment and consumer goods from the Asian NICs.

Cultural affinity also makes economic relationships between the Asian NICs (especially Singapore, Hong Kong and Taiwan) relatively easy. It is far easier for a businessman from Singapore, Hong Kong or Taiwan to conduct business in China, than it is for one from Germany, the USA or Japan. Even the political problems between Taiwan and China are being resolved, so that Taiwanese foreign investment in China can be expedited. In one respect, one can see the increasingly close relationships between China and the Asian NICs, as a means of combining Japanese technology (through foreign investment by the Asian NICs) with Chinese low-cost labour. This is something the Japanese could not do directly, because of Chinese resentment of Japanese atrocities during the Second World War. If internal political developments in China do not impede this process of closer economic integration with the Asian NICs, East Asia, as a region, will emerge as an even more important centre of world economic activity than it is at present.

The Relationship between China and Hong Kong

Of all the Asian NICs, Hong Kong (for obvious historical, geographical and cultural reasons) has the closest economic links with China. In 1990, trade between Hong Kong and China amounted to HK$400 billion (US$50 billion), almost as large as Hong Kong's GDP (which was HK$490 billion in 1990). In 1989, 80% of Hong Kong's re-exports came from China, and re-exports made up 61% of Hong Kong's total exports. In addition, China was Hong Kong's second-largest export market (after the USA), in terms of value, accounting for some 18% of Hong Kong's total exports. China is also Hong Kong's major source of imports, accounting for 31% of the total in 1989 (Salem 1989b:52–53).

From China's point of view, Hong Kong is its third-largest trading partner, after the USA and Japan (Sung 1992:159). Hong Kong acts as an important entrepot for China. In 1990, Hong Kong accounted for 47.5% of China's exports, but of this, 39.7% was re-exported to other countries (mainly the USA). In that year, Hong Kong accounted for 38.1% of China's imports, but of this, 26.6% were re-exports from Hong Kong (Sung 1992:161).

By 1990, Hong Kong had transferred about 80% of its manufacturing activity to the Free Trade Zones in southern China (of which Shenzhen is the most well known) and is now concentrating specializing in financial services. Industry now accounts for only 18% of Hong Kong's GDP, while services account for 81% (Mondejar 1991:70). Hong Kong is already the major loan syndication centre in Asia. Rapidly rising costs of labour and property have forced Hong Kong firms to re-locate in southern

China. In Shenzhen, for example, wage rates are 20% of those in Hong Kong. In other parts of Guangdong province, wage rates are 10% of those in Hong Kong. Labour productivity, however, is just as high as in Hong Kong. Land costs, particularly industrial land, in Guangdong province are 2%–3% of those in Hong Kong. Land in Xiamen can be leased for 70 years at 35 US cents per square metre! (Economist 1991i:22). It is therefore not surprising that many Hong Kong firms have re-located to southern China.

In 1986, Hong Kong accounted for some 77% of all foreign investment in Guangdong province. While this has declined to 63% in 1990, Hong Kong still accounts for 95% of all foreign investment contracts signed (the differences in the percentages are explained by the smaller average value of Hong Kong's investment projects). Some 4 million Chinese workers in Guangdong province are employed in some 20,000 Hong Kong-owned factories. In the electronics industry alone, between 80% and 90% of Hong Kong firms have manufacturing operations in China. Every day, some 50,000 Hong Kong residents, cross the Chinese border to manage Hong Kong-owned factories (Cheng and Taylor 1991:64–67). Employment in manufacturing used to account for 45% of total employment in Hong Kong in 1980. By 1992, this had declined to 22%. In absolute terms, there were some 950,000 workers in the manufacturing sector in Hong Kong in 1980. By 1992, this had declined to 560,000. Hong Kong now concentrates on services as its main economic activity. This includes not only financial services, for which it is well know, but also services to its manufacturing operations in southern China, such as design, research and development and quality control (Clifford 1994a:68–69).

Between 1979 and 1989, Hong Kong accounted for 59% of total contracted foreign investment in the whole of China. In 1990 alone, Hong Kong's share of total foreign investment in China was 61%. Most of this is concentrated in small-scale, labour-intensive projects. However, Hong Kong entrepreneurs are also involved in several large scale infrastructural projects in China (Sung 1992: 172–73).

Hong Kong is also an important loan syndication centre for the region. In 1987, the share of China's external loans syndicated in Hong Kong reached a peak of 31% (Sung 1992:172–173).

Owing to its geographical position, Hong Kong is the gateway for China's tourist trade. In 1987, some 44% of visitors entering China went through Hong Kong, whilst 55% of visitors leaving China left through Hong Kong.

The Relationship between China and other Asian NICs

Tightening labour markets are causing other Asian NICs to look for alternative low-cost production sites. In the case of Singapore, geographical proximity has led to increasing investment in Malaysia, Indonesia and Thailand. However, Singapore has also been actively seeking investment opportunities in China, in such diverse fields as shipbuilding, residential construction and the hotel industry. While the volume of Singapore investment in China is small, it is expected to rise significantly in the next ten years (Paisley 1991: 60–61; Goad 1991:12).

Taiwan allows only indirect trade and investment (mainly via Hong Kong) with China. Before 1978, there was little, if any, economic contact between Taiwan and China (which considers Taiwan one of its provinces). In 1990, however, Taiwanese trade with China amounted to nearly US$4 billion. Of this (US$3.2 billion) was made up of China's imports from Taiwan through Hong Kong. China's exports to Taiwan through Hong Kong amounted to only US$612 million (Sung 1992:164). Taiwan trades with China through other countries, such as Japan and Singapore, but data on these trade flows are not available.

In 1990, Taiwanese investment in China amounted to about US$3 billion. Of the 4,000 foreign investment projects approved in Fujian province in 1990, one-third came from Taiwan. Taiwan was also the second-largest source of foreign investment in Guangdong province in 1990 (after Hong Kong) (Economist 1991i:22–24). Since 1987, over 1000 Taiwanese firms have set up manufacturing operations in China (FEER 1991h:225). Most of these are small-scale, labour-intensive operations, specializing in the production of consumer goods for export. A good example of this is footwear. Some 80% of Taiwan's footwear industry has re-located to southern China, in search of low-cost labour (Sung 1992:171).

In 1990, South Korea's trade with China amounted to US$3.6 billion. About 60% of South Korea's exports to, and 45% of its imports from, China went through Hong Kong in 1990. This proportion has been declining over time, as South Korea continued to develop direct trading links with China. South Korea's main exports to China are made up of electronic and electrical goods, textiles as well as chemical fertilizers and plastics (Sung 1992:166).

Before 1985, there was no South Korean investment in China. Since 1985, South Korean investment in China has increased significantly, from US$144,000 in 1985 to US$81 million in 1990. Most of this is in small-scale (predominantly under US$1 million) labour-intensive projects, such as electronics products, toys and textiles. Although South Korea's investment in China is relatively small when compared with Hong Kong and Taiwan, it has considerable potential as South Korea is the most advanced of the Asian NICs in terms of industrial technology (Sung 1992:170–171; Jun and Simon 1992:196–205).

The NICs and Eastern Europe

The Decline of Communism in Eastern Europe

The decline of communism in Eastern Europe, and the subsequent conversion to market-oriented economic systems has opened up opportunities, as well as challenges for the Asian NICs.

On the one hand, Eastern European countries now present excellent opportunities for Asian NICs to set up (through foreign investment), high-tech industries. The reason for this is that many Eastern European countries have low-cost, but highly skilled labour. This is a factor of production which many Asian NICs lack, but which they need in order to ascend the next rung of the technological ladder. In addition, many Eastern European countries may be able to supply the Asian NICs with important semi-finished industrial products. So there is a potential for closer economic ties between Eastern European countries and the Asian NICs (Rowley 1989a:84–85).

Some Asian NICs, particularly South Korea and Taiwan, have already begin to increase their trade with Eastern European countries, partly in response to the growing tide of protectionism in the USA and EU. Taiwan, for example, increased its trade with Eastern Europe by a factor of six, from US$54 million in 1986 to US$360 million in 1989. East Germany, Poland and the USSR were Taiwan's major trading partners in the region. Many Taiwanese trading companies now operate in Eastern Europe (Moore 1990: 46–47). South Korea has also followed suit. Trade between Eastern European countries and South Korea has increased significantly in recent years, reaching US$400 million in 1988. The USSR is South Korea's major trading partner in Eastern Europe (Clifford 1989d:88–90). As economic and political problems in Eastern Europe stabilize over time, it is likely that the Asian NICs will forge even closer links with countries in that region.

The liberalization of Eastern Europe also presents some challenges for the NICs of Asia. It is possible that the abundance of relatively cheap and skilled labour in Eastern European countries may result in a diversion of foreign investment from the EU to Eastern European countries. For example, a German manufacturer of high quality sports shoes may now decide to shift production to Czechoslovakia rather than to Hong Kong. There may even be instances of production facilities formerly located in an Asian NIC being re-located to Eastern Europe, where cultural affinity and wage and skill levels may make such a move attractive.

Once political and economy stability are achieved in Eastern European countries, it is expected that, in time, many countries in the region have the capacity to become Newly Industrializing Countries in their own right. For the Asian NICs, this means a new set of competitors in world markets for manufactured goods (Economist 1991g:71).

Conclusion

The Asian NICs have strongest economic links with the USA, EU and Japan, both in terms of export markets and sources of capital and technology. However, by the late 1980s, protectionist tendencies began to gain momentum in the USA and EU. The Japanese market has always been relatively closed to outsiders. This has prompted the Asian NICs, together with other countries in the Asia-Pacific region to seriously consider the establishment of a trading group of their own. Through the 1970s and 1980s, there had already been an increase in economic ties between countries in the Asia-Pacific region. This trend has been increasing in recent years, as trade frictions with the USA and the EU began to become more frequent. Between 1985 and 1990, exports from the Asian NICs to ASEAN increased by 210%, while intra-NIC exports increased by 160% (Business Times 1992b:9).

Australia appears not to have benefited much from the dynamism of the economies to its north and east. Whether considered in terms of trade or investment, Australia's economic links with the Asian NICs can, at best, be described as slight. As a result, Australia has not been able to participate in, or benefit from, the rapid growth of the Asian NICs (and more generally, the countries to its north).

Recent renewed interest in the establishment of a regional trading group in the Pacific, holds out some hope for increased economic contacts between Australia and her Asian neighbours. However, more positive steps need to be taken, as APEC has been conceived only as a forum for discussion and consultation.

Australia has the choice of making the necessary changes which will enable it to participate more fully in the growth of the economies of Southeast and East Asia, or be left behind, as these countries march towards prosperity.

CHAPTER 9

Conclusion

The Costs of Rapid Economic Growth

The spectacular success of the Asian NICs since the 1960s has focused attention on the causes of their success in an effort to isolate the economic policies that work from those which do not. Relatively little attention has been paid to the costs which have been incurred in the pursuit of the economic prosperity which the Asian NICs now enjoy.

The Suppression of Individual Freedoms

All the Asian NICs have been ruled by authoritarian governments. Until recently, South Korea and Taiwan were ruled by military dictatorships. Singapore has been ruled by one democratically elected political party since its formation as a nation state in 1965. Hong Kong has been under colonial rule since the end of the nineteenth century.

With the exception of Hong Kong, all governments in the Asian NICs felt it was necessary to suppress certain freedoms in order to create the conditions which would foster rapid economic growth. These include the subordination of trade unions, the prohibition of strikes, the implementation of compulsory arbitration in industrial disputes and the suppression of political dissent. Stability, both in the sphere of industrial relations and in internal politics, was considered to be essential in order to create the conditions conducive to rapid economic growth. This was particularly true of the Asian NICs which depended on foreign capital for their development strategy. Draconian laws were enacted in order to ensure internal political stability. Public criticism of government policy or political leaders, whether explicit or implied, was constrained by invisible boundaries. Those who transgressed these boundaries were dealt with severely (Economist 1994b:32). Access to information was often constrained by the banning of certain international news publications, a prohibition on the purchase and use of satellite dishes and by a docile national press. Governments legitimized these constraints on individual freedoms by the growing economic prosperity which their citizens enjoyed.

In the 1991 *Human Development Report*, published by the United Nations Development Programme (UNDP), 40 indicators of human freedom are used to construct a Human Freedom Index. These include the right to teach ideas and receive information, freedom from unlawful detention, freedom from censorship, the independence of print and electronic media from political control, peaceful political opposition, and the right to determine the number of one's own children (UNDP 1991:20). Based on these 40 criteria, the Asian NICs were placed in a group of countries with medium freedom ranking. Within this group, two of the three Asian NICs were placed in the bottom half of the scale.

As the Asian NICs attained high levels of prosperity in the 1980s and 1990s, a highly-educated, affluent, liberal-minded middle class emerged. With the problem of basic survival having been solved, people in the Asian NICs began to demand greater political freedoms (Castells 1992:66,139–40,144–45). In South Korea, demonstrations by university students, supported by the middle class and workers, eventually led to the replacement of military dictatorships by democratically elected civilian governments. In Hong Kong, the prospect of the colony's return to China and the 1989 student massacre at Tiananmen Square sparked off demonstrations for greater political freedoms. In Singapore, the retirement of Mr Lee Kuan Yew and the election of Mr Goh Chok Tong as Prime Minister, was viewed by many as the beginning of a change to a gentler, more liberal, caring society. Thus, by the beginning of the last decade of the twentieth century, the Asian NICs had developed to such a high level of economic development and prosperity that it was becoming increasing difficult for governments to maintain the high levels of authoritarianism which were characteristic of these societies in the previous 30 years.

There is some debate about the veracity of this view. In many cases, changes in political leadership in the Asian NICs have not led to any marked improvement in political freedoms. Many important groups in society are still excluded from the policy-making processes of government and political dissent is still suppressed. The changes that have taken place have been marginal (for example, the decision of the Singapore government to allow the screening of X-rated movies in the late 1980s). There is therefore considerable scepticism as to whether increasing economic prosperity and higher levels of education in the Asian NICs will eventually lead to the enjoyment of greater political freedoms (Cotton 1991:311–27).

Working Conditions

In the 1960s and 1970s, one of the frequent criticisms of the Asian NICs was that their rapid economic growth was achieved by exploiting workers by keeping wages low and by allowing poor working conditions to persist (Henderson and Appelbaum 1992:17; Manning and Pang 1990:66–67). Trade union activity was proscribed by strict labour laws, but in many cases, these was designed to control Communist-inspired labour unrest rather than to achieve specific economic goals.

While labour may have been repressed in the 1960s and 1970s, by the 1980s, most Asian NICs had reached full employment and some were experiencing labour shortages. Under these conditions, it was difficult for governments to keep wages artificially low. Real wages began to rise as a result of excess demand. In Singapore, for example, real wage increases were kept to less than 1% per annum until the late 1970s. From 1979 onwards, the government realized that it was no longer feasible or desirable to keep wages low as a result of growing labour shortages. A "wages correction policy" was implemented in order to encourage firms to move into more capital-intensive production techniques. As a result of this, real wages increased substantially between 1979 and 1985 (10.7% per annum in current values, 6.6% per annum in real terms). The recession in 1985–1986 resulted in a wage freeze as the government began to realize that its "wages correction policy" had backfired and aggravated the depth of the recession. However, between 1988 and 1992, real wages in Singapore grew by an average of 8.2% per annum.

In the other Asian NICs, real wages rose by between 4% and 9% per annum from the 1960s to the 1980s. In Taiwan, for example, the growth of wages in the manufacturing sector has been greater than the growth of productivity for most years since 1978. This is shown in Figure 9.1.

In South Korea and Taiwan, the lifting of martial law resulted in a sharp increase in labour disputes. In Taiwan, the number of labour disputes doubled, from 700 in 1980 to 1458 in 1986. In South Korea, the number of labour disputes increased by more than three times, from 407 in 1980, to 1532 in 1989 (Bello and Rosenfeld 1990:224,43).

While the repression of labour may have been a feature of industrial relations in the Asian NICs in the early phases of their export-oriented industrialization, by the 1980s and 1990s, this was no longer the case. Tightening labour markets caused by growing shortages of labour had made such a policy untenable.

The Poor and the Disadvantaged

One aspect of the rapid development of the Asian NICs has been the rather high degree of income inequality in the city states, Singapore and Hong Kong. After a period (in the 1970s and early 1980s) during which income distribution became more equal, the distribution of income reached a high degree of inequality by the late 1980s. In Singapore and Hong Kong, this coincided with growing labour shortages and a shift towards high value-added services (such as financial services). By the late 1980s, the Gini ratio in Hong Kong and Singapore had reached 50%. This indicates

Figure 9.1
Manufacturing Wages and Productivity Growth in Taiwan, 1978–1992

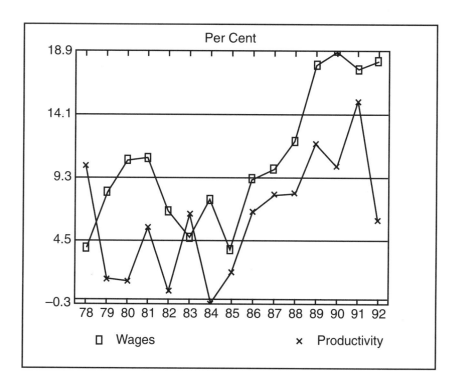

Source: Council for Economic Planning and Development, *Taiwan Statistical Data Book 1993*.

that in spite of rising prosperity, the increased wealth was not being shared equally. Even in South Korea and Taiwan, where income distribution was relatively more equal, poverty was not completely eliminated. In South Korea, income distribution worsened considerably in the 1970s. Although official statistics indicate that only 5.5% of the population were living below the poverty line in 1988, unofficial estimates suggest that the ratio is more like 20% to 30%. Poverty in rural areas is a particularly vexing problem (Clifford 1988b:86). The United Nations suggests that 16% were below the poverty line in 1980–1987 (UNDP

1991:152). While absolute poverty has declined over time, relative poverty has increased. Most small farmers (those owning less that one hectare of land) who rely entirely on farming for their livelihood, earn incomes below the poverty line (Chung and Oh 1991:96–97).

The problem of the poor and the disadvantaged in the Asian NICs is that there is no welfare net below which these cannot fall. Government expenditures on social welfare are low relative to other countries with similar levels of per capita income. Industrialization and increasing economic prosperity have not been accompanied by a parallel development of a comprehensive social security system (Chow 1981:366). In 1990, the proportion of government expenditure devoted to housing, social security and welfare was 12.2% in South Korea and 11.7% in Singapore (compared with 55.9% in Sweden and 48.2% in Austria and Germany) (World Bank 1993:239). Those who are unemployed, disabled or sick have to depend on relatives or charitable (often religious) organizations for help. In Asian societies, many are reluctant to do this as there is a strong aversion to relying on handouts from others. In a market-oriented economy based on merit, it is the young, the able, the well-educated and the healthy who stand to benefit most. The old, the less able, the poorly educated and the sick often have to fend for themselves, or rely on others (not the government) for their survival. Governments do not consider it their responsibility to care for the aged, the poor, the disadvantaged and the unemployed. This is epitomized by the fact that in Singapore and Hong Kong, there are few provisions (in the form of ramps) in government offices, office towers or shopping centres for people confined to wheelchairs.

Environmental Problems

The head-long dash for economic growth has led to serious environmental problems in the Asian NICs (Chong 1994:39; Pernia 1991:113–136). This is particularly true of South Korea and Taiwan, which have the most developed heavy industry sectors amongst the Asian NICs.

In Taiwan, the number of factories increased from 6,000 in 1950 to 90,000 in 1989. There were 2 million cars and 7 million motorcycles in Taiwan in 1989. This had resulted in high levels of atmospheric pollution. For example, in the Hsinchu Industrial Park, the level of atmospheric pollution is twice that of Los Angeles on most days. In the cities, people usually wear a face mask to protect themselves from the high levels of pollution in the atmosphere. Most of Taiwan's rivers are heavily polluted with chemicals. Water drawn from wells catches fire when exposed to a lighted match. Only 3% of Taiwan's population is served by a sewerage system. Although the Taiwanese government plans to spend US$33 billion on pollution control and solid waste disposal, it is not clear that this will solve the problem as most firms in Taiwan are too small and too strapped for cash to invest in pollution abatement technologies (Economist 1989c:63–64; Moore 1988a:52). Taiwan's environmental problems are not confined to the industrial sector. In agriculture, heavy use of fertilizers and pesticides has resulted in widespread pollution of Taiwan's rivers and waterways. This has caused widespread destruction of fish and other kinds of marine life (Bello and Rosenfeld 1992:197–204). In March 1985, copper sulphate poisoning of shellfish in southern Taiwan led to a steep decline in the price of oysters (farmed mainly for export to Japan). This came to be known as the "green oyster" affair (Reardon-Anderson 1992:12). Although Taiwan established an Environmental Protection Bureau (EPB) in 1983, it is not effective and often bypassed when large investment projects are considered (Reardon-Anderson 1992:6).

A similar situation can be observed in South Korea. In agriculture, heavy use of chemicals has led to widespread pollution of rivers and waterways, leading to high levels of heavy metals in sea food as well as crops. The development of heavy industry has resulted in high levels of atmospheric pollution in the major cities, with sulphur dioxide and carbon dioxide concentrations far above the acceptable levels. Like Taiwan, the development of nuclear power stations in South Korea poses an even larger threat to the environment (Bello and Rosenfeld 1990:94–110).

In both Taiwan and South Korea, increasing concern over environmental pollution has resulted in the emergence of a number of interest groups which have lobbied for more government action in cleaning up and preserving the environment. Popular protests have led to the postponement or cancellation of some large scale industrial projects. One of the most celebrated cases was the public protest movement organized by the people of Lukang village, which eventually led to the cancellation of a US$160 million titanium dioxide plant in central Taiwan (Reardon-Anderson 1992). Another was the decision of the Formosa Plastics Group to move some industrial plants offshore (to the USA) because of public pressure over environmental pollution (Moore 1988b:70–71). In South Korea, a number of boycotts have been organized by lobby groups against manufacturers who have been found to be guilty of acts of environmental irresponsibility (selling chemically contaminated products). Although the environmental movement in South Korea is smaller, and not as well organized as in Taiwan, it has had a number of successes (Bello and Rosenfeld 1990: 211–212,111–112).

In Singapore and Hong Kong, pollution from industry and from agriculture is not a serious issue, as there is little heavy industry or agriculture in these city states. The major environmental concerns have to do with urban congestion as a result of the shortage of space, the disposal of solid waste, and atmospheric pollution resulting from motor vehicles (Weiskel 1993:15). In 1988, Singapore's Greenhouse Index (measured in metric tons of carbon heating equivalents per capita) was 4.2, higher than all industrialized countries except the USA and Canada (UNDP 1991:162,191).

In Singapore, the government has dealt with the problem of traffic congestion with a number of market-oriented policies which would make a neo-classical economist beam with satisfaction. High registration fees have been imposed on motor vehicles. In addition, an auction system has been implemented so that those wishing to purchase cars have to bid for the right to do so. These COEs (Certificates of Entitlement) now cost more than what it would cost to buy a car in other countries. For example, in 1994, the COE for cars of 1600 cc engine capacity and above reached a peak of S$60,000. As a result of these policies, the cost of purchasing a motor car in Singapore is very much higher than in other countries. A four cylinder family saloon which costs A$30,000 in Australia, costs S$110,000 in Singapore (in 1994, $A1=S$1.12). This does not include the COE, which could add another S$60,000 to the cost of purchasing the car. In addition to the high cost of purchasing a car, the Singapore government has, since the 1970s, imposed a tax on those entering the Central Business District (CBD) by car. An Area Licence must be bought and displayed when driving in the CBD, between 7:30 am and 6:30 pm on weekdays, and from 7:30 am to 2:00 pm on Saturdays. Otherwise a hefty fine is imposed. At first this policy was enforced only during the morning rush hour. Now is it also imposed in the evening rush hour.

In spite of these strong measures, car ownership and use in Singapore continues to rise annually. Apart from the periods 1974–1977 and 1985–1987, when the number of registered private motor cars fell (as a result of economic recession), the growth rate of the number of private motor cars registered rose by 7% per annum during 1970–1990. The construction of a Mass Rapid Transport (MRT) underground rail system (completed in the late 1980s) is another aspect of Singapore's continuing attempt to deal with congestion on its roads.

During the 1960s and 1980s, the single-minded quest for economic growth resulted in a deterioration in the environment, particularly in South Korea and Taiwan. In Singapore and Hong Kong, the absence of large-scale heavy industry and a large agriculture sector using chemical inputs enabled these city-states to avoid the environmental problems experienced by the larger Asian NICs. However, Singapore and Hong Kong do have problems associated with urban congestion and the use of motor-vehicles, as well as with other forms of environmental pollution (Economist 1994c:26). With rising prosperity and a greater concern for the quality of life, environment groups have become active in South Korea and Taiwan, and to a lesser extent, in Singapore and Hong

Kong. The movement of all the Asian NICs into information and skilled-based industries and into high valued-added services will also aid in stemming the degradation of the environment. For South Korea and Taiwan, the current environmental situation may be so serious that it may prove to be impossible to repair.

Lessons from the Asian NICs

The success of the Asian NICs since the 1960s has prompted the search for lessons of their success, which may be useful for other less developed countries wishing to embark on an export-oriented industrialization strategy. Indeed, international agencies such as the World Bank (World Bank 1991, 1993), have urged less developed countries to emulate the policies adopted by the Asian NICs as a means of accelerating development.

There is no single East Asian model which other less developed countries might emulate. Instead, there is a wide variety of different policies which the Asian NICs have employed in their quest for rapid economic growth (World Bank 1993:347). Indeed Lall (1992) has argued that the Asian NICs represent four development models, rather than one. Hong Kong represents one end of the spectrum, with its adherence to "positive non-intervention" by its colonial government and its espousal of the free market. While the Hong Kong government has played a role in the economic affairs of Hong Kong, this role has been minimal, compared with that of the other Asian NICs. At the other end of the spectrum is South Korea, with its high degree of government intervention and direction in economic affairs, its fostering of large-scale combines (the *chaebol*), and its inhospitable attitude towards foreign investment. Taiwan and Singapore are intermediate cases, with the former closer to the South Korean end of the spectrum and the latter closer to the Hong Kong end of the spectrum.

In spite of the differences between the Asian NICs, reflection on the policies which they have adopted in their transformation from LDCs to NICs, suggests a number of lessons which may be useful to other less developed countries.

The Pursuit of Market-Oriented Policies

All the Asian NICs pursued market-oriented policies by deregulating their markets for inputs and outputs and allowing the forces of demand and supply to determine relative prices (Balassa 1988:S273-S290). In the foreign exchange market, this led to a depreciation of overvalued exchange rates and encouraged exports. In domestic financial markets, deregulation led to a rise in domestic interest rates, which stimulated savings and discouraged capital outflow. In the labour market, deregulation removed union pressure on wage rises and kept labour internationally competitive. "Getting prices right", in the sense of allowing prices to be determined by market forces, is often cited as one of the major policies pursued by the Asian NICs (Kuznets 1988:S11–S44). The use of markets, rather than administrative controls, allowed the Asian NICs to allocate their resources efficiently into export-oriented industries (Page 1994:3–4).

In some instances, governments deliberately manipulated prices to keep them below market-determined levels in order to use the market to stimulate demand (Amsden 1991). These interventions were aimed at affecting market outcomes, rather than supplanting them by administrative fiat. Low wages policies are good examples of this. Another good example is that of keeping interest rates low in order to subsidize the cost of capital to export-oriented firms. In most cases where these types of manipulations occurred, they were eventually discontinued in favour of market-determined outcomes. Even when they were in place, the distortions they created were much less when compared with other countries (World Bank 1993:112,116). One of the reasons for this is that firms which were given "directed credit", were carefully scrutinized, were subject to the forces of internal as well as international competition and were made to meet export performance targets (World Bank 1993:93).

Although some governments started off by granting special incentives to exporters, these became costly as the export drive succeeded, and an increasing reliance was placed on exchange rates and uniformity of incentives. In South Korea, for example, the real exchange rate for exports was within 6% of that for imports for every year after 1965 (Krueger 1990: 108–112).

Capitalizing on Comparative Advantage

All the Asian NICs capitalized on their comparative advantage and specialized in producing goods which they could make efficiently. In the 1960s and 1970s, this was labour-intensive manufactured goods, since this was the factor of production which was in large supply. "Getting prices right" allowed market forces to allocate resources according to comparative advantage. Since most of the Asian NICs had abundant quantities of labour, the market-determined wage was kept low and firms were thus encouraged to use labour-intensive methods of production. If wages had been allowed to rise above market-determined levels for any length of time, the Asian NICs would not have been able to produce labour-intensive manufactured goods at internationally competitive prices. When relative prices are distorted by, say, tariffs, they give the wrong signals to firms and lead to an inefficient allocation of resources.

Macroeconomic Stability

All the Asian NICs were able to maintain macroeconomic stability for long periods of time despite a number of external shocks which affected the international trading system. Prudent macroeconomic management kept government budgets in balance, or in surplus. Public enterprises were made to run like private firms. There was no subsidization of government-owned enterprises which made persistent losses. Welfare programmes, where they existed at all, were kept to a minimum. Inflation rates were kept low for long periods of time and the balance of payments were (with the exception of South Korea) usually in surplus. Even South Korea began to have a balance of payments surpluses in the late 1980s. In addition to the above, government commitment to export-oriented industrialization meant that there was stability and continuity in government policy toward business. The fact that the Asian NICs were governed by authoritarian governments also meant that political stability was virtually guaranteed. These conditions made the Asian NICs attractive for foreign investment and foreign loans and stimulated high rates of savings and investment.

High Rates of Saving and Investment

All the Asian NICs have developed on the basis of high savings and investment performance (Leger 1994:46–48). South Korea is a good example of this. South Korea has maintained a high rate of investment, an average of about 30% of GDP between 1970 and 1990. In 1991, the South Korean investment to GDP ratio reached 39.1%. Between 1965 and 1980, gross domestic investment grew at 15.9% per annum. Between 1980 and 1987, it grew at 10% per annum.

For much of this period, this high rate of investment was achieved through large capital inflows, mainly in the form of loans. External debt has increased steadily from about 30% of GNP in 1979 to over 50% of GNP in 1984. The important point about external finance is that South Korea used the inflows of foreign capital to revive economic growth before undertaking restrictive monetary and fiscal policies to bring down its current account deficit and rate of inflation. It was not until exports and output were booming that the government reversed its expansionary monetary and fiscal policies (Collins 1990:104–107).

Export-Oriented Industrialization

Export-oriented industrialization strategies have been the main feature of the rapid development of the Asian NICs since the 1960s. Exports contribute to resource allocation according to comparative advantage, allow a country to reap economies of scale, increase efficiency through competitive pressure and increase total factor productivity through spread effects. In all the NICs, exports have been encouraged by stimulating the private sector through various export incentives and removing administrative obstacles to exports (Balassa 1998:S273–290). Even in the more difficult world trading conditions since 1973, the NICs have performed much better than countries which have not implemented outward-looking development strategies. Other LDCs (the second tier) which have adopted outward-looking development strategies in the late 1970s or early 1980s (particularly Thailand and Malaysia) have also recorded much higher rates of economic growth than countries which have remained inward-looking. More difficult trading conditions in the 1980s have resulted in lower rates of economic growth in the NICs and near-NICs, but they have performed much better than other countries which remain inward-looking.

Export orientation imposes a discipline and a set of constraints that prevent the adoption of policies which hinder growth. The costs of policy mistakes become visible very rapidly. The policy of encouraging heavy industry in the 1970s and the Singapore policy of raising wages in the mid-1980s are good examples of this. The political penalties for adopting inappropriate policies are greater in the context of an ongoing outward-oriented strategy (Krueger 1990:108–112).

The Role of Government

The role of government has been to provide modern infrastructure, a stable incentive system and to ensure that government bureaucracy will help rather than hinder the private sector (Leger 1994:48–49). Public enterprises play a relatively small role in the Asian NICs. Governments need to be efficient (and honest), but not necessarily authoritarian (although they have been in most of the Asian NICs), in order to implement difficult policy decisions. Government services, including transport and communications were relatively efficient and low cost. Reactions to changes in the external environment (e.g. oil price rises) were swift and effective.

The share of government in economic activity is relatively low and usually a declining percentage of total economy activity

(Macomber 1987:476). Public consumption and expenditure ratios are well below those of the advanced industrial countries. Expenditures on health, social security and social welfare have been low. Expenditures on defence have been low, particularly in the 1960s when the NICs were in the "take-off" phase. The reason for this is that all the NICs were under the defence umbrellas of the super powers.

The role of government in the Asian NICs has been to reduce uncertainty, provide support for innovation and spur economic growth. The nature of government intervention has been to use market forces to achieve certain economic goals, rather than direct intervention in the workings of markets. While governments in the NICs have participated directly in economic activities (by entering into joint-ventures with local and/or foreign investors), they have always tried to work "with" the market, rather than against it (Balassa 1988:S273-290).

Sound macroeconomic policies and undistorted relative prices have enabled governments in the Asian NICs to overcome their mistakes quickly, while giving them the flexibility to change inappropriate policies. Loss-making industries are not perpetuated through subsidies. They are phased out quickly so that scarce resources are not wasted and can be released for new growth areas.

Powerful government agencies in the Asian NICs have forged close relationships with the private sector in order to facilitate the efficiency of policy implementation. Government and business do not consider each other as adversaries, but rather as partners pursuing the same national goals.

Compared with many LDCs, government administration is much more efficient and less corrupt in the Asian NICs. Political pressures from various interest groups have not been allowed to deter Asian NIC governments from making difficult policy choices in the national interest.

In the Asian NICs, authoritarian governments have facilitated economic growth by making it easier to implement appropriate economic policy through efficient government administration (Macomber 1987:474–481).

South Korea's experience of economic growth provides an example of relatively consistent, stable and sensible macroeconomic policies. It also provides an example of the reversal of inappropriate policies before they became too far out of line. Budget deficits have been kept small, averaging 2.3% of GNP between 1979 and 1984. Real interest rates have been kept relatively stable, averaging 2.5% between 1977 and 1987. The real exchange rate has also remained relatively stable. The standard deviation of South Korea's real exchange rate between 1975 and 1985 was 6.5, less than half that of other LDCs such as Brazil and Argentina (Collins 1990: 104–107).

Quality of the Labour Force

The quality of human resources, in the form of an educated and skilled work force, and entrepreneurial talent, has been crucial in the development of the Asian NICs. The willingness to take risks and to seize opportunities have been highlighted as important ingredients for the success of the Asian NICs. Enrolments in primary and secondary school have been equal to, or better than, those of the average for upper-middle income countries. Enrolments in higher education have been higher. There has also been a marked concentration in the training of scientists and engineers, particularly in South Korea and Taiwan. This is a reflection of the importance placed on education in the Asian NICs.

Another aspect of the quality of the labour force in the Asian NICs is the willingness to work hard. All the Asian NICs have longer average working hours per week than most other countries in the world, and fewer public holidays (Leger 1994:43).

In South Korea, during 1963–1972, the increase in the quantity and quality of factor inputs (capital and labour) accounted for 50% of the average annual rate of growth of output. Between 1972 and 1982, 80% of the growth of output was accounted by the increase in the quantity and quality of factor inputs (Collins 1990:104–107).

Flexibility and Pragmatism in Economic Policies

All the Asian NICs have adopted a flexible attitude toward policy implementation. Whenever economic policies were demonstrably incorrect, or inappropriate in the face of changed circumstances, they were discontinued or reversed. For example, in the late 1970s and early 1980s, the Singapore government embarked on a "wages correction policy", and increased wages across the board by substantial margins. By the mid-1980s, this was recognized to have been inappropriate, and a wages freeze was implemented in an effort to get the economy out of the recession of that time. Another example is that of the South Korean government, which tried to develop heavy industry behind tariff barriers in the 1970s. By the early 1980s, this was recognized to have been a mistake in the light of changed international economic conditions following the second oil crisis and the policy was discontinued. Flexibility was also shown in the ability of the Asian NICs to shift resources quickly from sectors, products and markets which are declining, to those which are expanding (Page 1990:414).

Dealing with the Risks of Export-Orientation

The experience of the Asian NICs has shown that there are a number of risks involved in adopting a strategy of export-oriented industrialization. Vulnerability to changes in the international economic environment, and the gradually eroding comparative advantage, are two of the most important problems such countries have to face. Diversification of exports, products and markets, can lessen a country's vulnerability to changes in the economic environment. This should be reinforced with vigilant monitoring of current or anticipated changes in trade and technology so that appropriate responses can be planned.

The Costs of Becoming Too Successful

One of the problems of being too successful as an exporter, is that other countries are likely to impose barriers to your exports. In addition, persistent balance of trade surpluses are likely to put upward pressure on your exchange rate. All the Asian NICs now face these problems, because they have been too successful at exporting manufactured goods. The lesson here is to ensure that balance of trade surpluses with major trading partners do not remain persistently large. This may require increasing foreign investment in trading partners and making domestic markets more accessible to imports from major trading partners.

The Growth of World Trade

The Asian NICs were fortunate in that world trade was expanding rapidly when they embarked on their export-oriented industrialization strategies. During periods in which world trade is slow, it will be difficult to achieve a rapid expansion of exports. Nevertheless, there may be niches in the international market which a country would fill and become a successful exporter, in spite of a general slowdown in world trade. The problem is to find those niches.

Computer-Aided Teaching

Introduction

One of the most useful tasks a computer can perform without complaining is repetitive teaching. This Appendix shows how a space-efficient, relatively fast, computer-aided teaching system can be implemented on most computer systems. The nature of the program makes it useful for teaching or testing students' grasp of factual material. This computer-aided teaching program and other teaching materials are available on disk from the author at the address shown below. These will enable students to revise the material covered in the various chapters of this book. Teachers will be able to set up their own revision exercises for *any* courses which they teach. This appendix contains instructions on how to set up revision exercises and other information files.

Using the Revise Program

If a hard disk is available, copy all the files on to the hard disk by following the steps below.

1. c: (log on to hard disk)

2. cd \   (select root directory)

3. mkdir teach   (make a new directory called "teach")

4. cd \teach   (select "teach" directory)

5. copy a:*.*   (copy all files from disk in drive A)

In order to begin a revision lesson (say, nic01), type the command **revise nic01**. The screen will clear and a set of instructions will be displayed. Read these carefully. At the bottom of the screen, you will be asked for your first name. Enter your first name, and press the RETURN key. The revision lesson will begin. To stop the revision exercise at any time, type **quit** at any of the input prompts.

If you do not have a hard disk, place the disk in drive A, and type **revise nic01**.

Note that the revision exercises which are provided on the disk have been encrypted, so it will not be possible for you to display them on the screen, or print them out on a printer. That would defeat the purpose of the revision exercises, as they are meant to be worked through interactively.

Students need not read the rest of this chapter, as the material is meant for teachers who may wish to set up their own revision exercises.

Setting up Revision Exercises with *Revise*

Before explaining how to set up your own revision exercises, it is useful to know something about the *Revise* program itself.

Revise is written entirely in the C programming language. Its major features are:

- It is a relatively small program, taking up only about 10K of code.

- Its input files are in ASCII (text) format, so they can easily be entered and edited with a text editor.

- Once the input files have been set up, they should be encrypted so that the student cannot see the answers to the questions. The encryption program can be obtained from the author. Details are given at the end of this appendix.

- There is no limit to the number of questions that can be set in a lesson.

- It can be used to teach (in the sense of presenting information to the student), or to examine (in the sense of testing the student). These two functions can be combined in one lesson. A lesson might start with a series of information frames which enable a student to revise key concepts, before going on to test the student's understanding with a number of questions.

- It is flexible in the sense that alternative answers to questions can be accepted. Answers are not confined to upper or lower case, or to a specific form or words (for example, the program can be set up to accept such alternatives as: Growth Rate, rate of growth, RATE OF INCREASE, etc.).

- Questions can be of different types, for example, multiple choice, true or false, entry of an answer by the student, etc. Different types of questions can be combined in a single test.

- Hints and comments can be embedded in each test. There is also a method of suppressing these hints and comments, if this is desired. Entire questions can also suppressed.

- The student is given three chances to answer each question (except for true or false questions). After each incorrect answer, a hint may be given. After the third unsuccessful attempt, the correct answer is given. This may be followed by a comment on why the correct answer is the right one. Or the comment may take the form of a reference to a book or journal article which explains the problem.

- Whenever a hint is given, marks are deducted for the help given.

- At the end of the test, a score is given to indicate how well or badly the student has performed.

- At any time during the test, the student can exit from the session by typing "quit" at any input prompt.

- The program can be used for a wide variety of purposes. Apart from teaching and testing, it can be used to display information of how to write essays, or how to do previous years' examination papers (the student can be taken through each examination question and told what a satisfactory answer involves).

- It is easy to set up, maintain and use. Questions are set up with a text editor in a simple format. Questions can be added or removed without having to worry about their numbering. Entire questions can also be suppressed (without being deleted from the file) or re-activated.

- Since the program is written in standard C, it can be ported to most computer systems. The executable file on the disk which is available from the author, is meant for MS-DOS computers. However, this program can also be compiled on UNIX and VAX systems. Source code of the *Revise* program, can be obtained from the author. For details, refer to the address, at the end of this appendix.

The format of the data file to be used with the *Revise* program must take the following form:

Figure A.1
Format of data file for the *Revise* Program

Answer on one or more lines (+ for an information frame)
  (one blank line)
Question on one or more lines (can be used to display information)
  (one blank line)
Hint 1 on one or more lines (can be suppressed if desired)
  (one blank line)
Hint 2 on one or more lines (can be suppressed if desired)
  (one blank line)
Comment on answer on one or more lines (can be suppressed)

Comments or hints can be suppressed by placing a # in the first column of the line where the comment would normally start. The advantage of this is that hints and/or comments can be suppressed in early versions of the revision lessons and then revealed at a later date by removing the # signs:

Figure A.2
Suppressing Comments and Hints

Answer on one or more lines
  (one blank line)
Question on one or more lines
  (one blank line)
#Hint 1 on one or more lines (suppressed)
  (one blank line)
Hint 2 on one or more lines
  (one blank line)
#Comment on one or more lines (suppressed)

A sample data file is shown below. Note that the format of this file conforms with the format shown in the above examples.

Figure A.3
Sample Data File for the *Revise* Program

complements
complementary goods

If the cross-price elasticity between two goods is negative, what sort of goods must they be?

Hint 1:   Think of what a negative cross-price elasticity implies.

Hint 2:   If the cross-price elasticity between two goods is negative, this means that as the price of one good rises, the quantity demanded of the other good falls. So what kind of goods are they?

Comment: When the price of good A rises, quantity demanded of A falls, and the demand for its complement B falls.

negative

less than zero

The income-effect of Giffen goods and Inferior goods is always ....

Hint 1:   When income rises, how would the demand for Giffen and Inferior goods be affected?

Hint 2:   Come on! It isn't all that difficult! When income rises, do you expect people to consume more or less Giffen or Inferior goods?

No comment

true

A demand curve normally slopes downwards from left to right? (True or False?)

#Hint 1:   No hint given

#Hint 2:   No hint given

Comment: As the price falls, more is demanded as real income increases and the product is relatively cheaper compared with close substitutes.

2

two

negative

less than zero

The own-price elasticity of demand for normal good is usually:

* ⟵ * required here to keep the whole question in one paragraph

(1)   zero

(2)   negative

(3)   positive

(4)   indeterminate

(5)   none of the above

Hint 1:   When the price of a normal good rises, what happens to the quantity demanded?

Hint 2:   If the price of a normal good rises, do you expect the quantity demanded to rise or fall?

Comment: As the price rises, quantity demanded of a normal good usually falls because real income has fallen, and the good in question has become relatively more expensive than its substitutes.

Different kinds of questions may be asked, true or false, multiple choice, etc. There is no necessity to restrict the answers to a single word. A long sentence may be used as well. Since the data file is a plain text file, new questions can be added to, or old questions deleted from, it from time to time. The program automatically numbers the questions, so additions or deletions to the data file do not affect the numbering.

The example file below is an amended version of the one shown above in that information frames have been added to the data file. The value of these information frames is that they not only allow the display of various kinds of information in the middle of a revision lesson, but also enable the program to be used as a pure teaching (rather than examining) device. An entire file can be made up of information frames which teach some basic principles, and this can then be followed by a revision lesson.

Figure A.4
Adding Information Frames to a Data File

+   (indicate that an information frame follows)

N O T I C E

This is a short revision exercise on microeconomic theory. You should not take more than 5 minutes to complete it.

#No Hint 1

#No Hint 2

#No Comment

complements
complementary goods

If the cross-price elasticity between two goods is negative, what sort of goods must they be?

Hint 1:   Think of what a negative cross-price elasticity implies.

Hint 2:   If the cross-price elasticity between two goods is negative, this means that as the price of one good rises, the quantity demanded of the other good falls. So what kind of goods are they?

Comment: When the price of good A rises, quantity demanded of A falls, and the demand for its complement B falls.

negative
less than zero

The income-effect of Giffen goods and Inferior goods is always ....

Hint 1:   When income rises, how would the demand for Giffen and Inferior goods be affected?

Hint 2:   Come on! It isn't all that difficult! When income rises, do you expect people to consume more or less Giffen or Inferior goods?

No comment

true

A demand curve normally slopes downwards from left to right? (true or false?)

#Hint 1:   No hint given

#Hint 2:   No hint given

Comment: As the price falls, more is demanded as real income increases and the product is relatively cheaper compared with close substitutes.

+   (indicate that an information frame follows)

CAUTION

The next question requires a bit more thought than the other questions so far. Take your time over it and answer when you are confident that you have got the right answer.

#No Hint 1

#No Hint 2

#No Comment

2
two
negative
less than zero

The own-price elasticity of demand for normal good is usually:
* ⟵ * required here to keep the whole question in one paragraph
(1)   zero
(2)   negative
(3)   positive
(4)   indeterminate
(5)   none of the above

Hint 1:   When the price of a normal good rises, what happens to the quantity demanded?

Hint 2:   If the price of a normal good rises, do you expect the quantity demanded to rise or fall?

Comment: As the price rises, quantity demanded of a normal good usually falls because real income has fallen, and the good in question has become relatively more expensive than its substitutes.

Before you are able to use this data file, it has to be encrypted with a program called **encode**, which is available from the author. The data file can be encrypted by typing the command **encode lesson > newlesson**. The *Revise* program can be now executed by typing:

revise newlesson

Note that it is the encrypted data file that is used with the *Revise* program, not the original data file. If you tried to use *Revise* with the original data file, by typing **revise lesson** you would just get gibberish on the screen.

When the lesson begins, a brief set of instructions is displayed and the student is asked to enter his or her first name. Then the first information frame will be displayed. After this, the student is asked the first question. If a correct answer is given, an appropriate word of encouragement is given and a comment (if any) on the correct answer is displayed. If an incorrect answer is given, some words or encouragement are uttered, a hint (if any) is displayed, and the student is asked to try again. If another incorrect answer is given, other words of encouragement are uttered, and another hint (if any) is displayed. After the third unsuccessful attempt, the correct answer is given, and a comment (if any) on the correct answer is displayed. The only exception to this procedure is that when "True or False" questions are asked, only one attempt is allowed (for obvious reasons). At any input prompt, typing **quit** will cause the computer to express genuine surprise and terminate the lesson.

When scoring for correct answers, the program will ignore information frames, but will deduct marks after each hint has been displayed. Each hint incurs a deduction of 1% of the total marks.

Suppressing Explanations Temporarily

One interesting use of the *Revise* program is to set revision or teaching exercises in which the explanations to the answers are not given till the end of the semester. In the version available to students at the start of the semester, no explanations to the answers are given. All that is required to suppress the explanations given in the comment paragraphs by inserting a # at the beginning of the comment. This will suppress the whole paragraph. At the end of the semester, another version of the exercise is made available to students, in which the # is deleted, so that all explanatory comments are displayed. In this way, the revision exercises can be used to force students to work things out for themselves first. Only at the end of the semester will they be given full explanations to the answers in the exercise. The following is a simple example of this:

Figure A.5
Suppressing Explanatory Comments

+   (indicate that an information screen follows)

A version with full explanations to answers for the more difficult questions will be made available at the end of the semester.

#No Hint 1

#No Hint 2

#No Comment

1/4
one quarter
one-quarter
one fourth
one-fourth
.25
0.25

A sample space consists of twelve numbers, 1 to 12 inclusive. A number is drawn at random. Let A be the event that the number drawn is a multiple of 4, and B that it is greater than 6.
*

P(A) = ...

Hint 1:   Figure out how many multiples of 4 there are in the sample space.

Hint 2:   Ouch! What struggle! What number times 4 equals 12?

#Comment: Since there are three multiples of 4 in the sample space the probability of picking one multiple of 4 is 3/12 or 1/4

1/2
half
.5
0.5

P(B) = ...

Hint 1:   How many numbers are there between 7 and 12 inclusive?

Hint 2:   Sure none of your fingers is missing? How many numbers are there between 7 and 12 inclusive?

#Comment: Since there are six numbers between 7 and 12, probability of picking one of this is 6/12 or 1/2

1/3
one third
one-third
0.3333
.3333

A sample space consists of twelve numbers, 1 to 12 inclusive. A number is drawn at random. Let A be the event that the number drawn is a multiple of 4, and B that it is greater than 1
*

P(A|B) = ...

Hint 1:   How many multiples of 4 are there between 1 and 12?

Hint 2:   Are all the multiples of 4 between 1 and 12 greater than 1?

#Comment: Since there are three events which are multiples (i. e., 4, 8, 12) and since all are greater than 1, P(A|B) = 1/3. (This whole comment will be suppressed as long as it starts with a # character).

false

Events A and B are mutually exclusive. (True or False?)

#No Hint 1

#No Hint 2

#Comment: Since the joint event AB is not empty, A and B cannot be mutually exclusive.

The obvious way to set up such an exercise is to write the data file with all the full explanations included, but with each comment paragraph starting with a # in order to suppress it. At the end of the semester, the # characters can be deleted using a search and replace facility of a good text editor.

Suppressing Questions

Entire questions can be suppressed in similar manner by turning them into comments. Supposing the following question is to be suppressed:

Figure A.6
Suppressing Questions

negative
less than zero

The income-effect of Giffen goods and Inferior goods is
always ....

Hint 1:   When income rises, how would the demand for Giffen
and Inferior goods be affected?

Hint 2:   Come on! It isn't all that difficult! When income rises,
do you expect people to consume more or less Giffen
or Inferior goods?

#Comment

– –

All that is required is to suppress the above question
is to make the following changes:

– –

+ ⟵—— (to indicate information frame follows)

#negative ⟵—— (# to suppress entire paragraph) less than zero
* ⟵—— (any character to join lines into a paragraph)
The income-effect of Giffen goods and Inferior goods is
always ....

#Hint 1:   When income rises, how would the demand for Giffen
and Inferior goods be affected?

#Hint 2:   Come on! It isn't all that difficult! When income rises,
do you expect people to consume more or less

Giffen or Inferior goods?

#Comment

Note that Hint 1, Hint 2 and Comment have all been turned
off by placing a # in the first column.

Once these changes have been made, the program will ignore the above question. The question can easily be "re-activated" by restoring it to its previous form.

Setting up a File of Instructions

Since the program can be used to display help screens, it can also be used as a teaching device (as opposed to a testing device) by having a data file made up of a series of help screens. The user can then page through the file, reading the instructions as they come up. The following is an example of this:

Figure A.7

A Data File of Instructions

+ (to indicate an information screen follows)

N O T I C E

This is not a revision exercise. It is designed to inform you of what is required to answer the various tutorial questions that are listed in the course handout. While the information in this file does not actually tell you how to write your tutorial essays, it does give you an indication of what the answers should cover.

#No Hint 1

#No Hint 2

#No Comment

+ (blank line)

The first set of tutorial questions are on the NICs of Asia.

#

\#

\#

+ (to indicate an information screen follows)

Question: 1

*

Examine, critically, the view that the rapid growth of the NICs of Asia in the post-war period was due primarily to the implementation of "laissez faire" market-oriented policies.

*

Comment:

The first thing you have to do in this question is to explain why market-oriented economic policies are thought to be an important ingredient of an export-oriented industrialization strategy. The reference by Balassa outlines the orthodox justification for this. The concepts of opportunity costs and comparative advantage need to be brought in here.

*

The second part of the essay should deal with the view (Fransman, Lim and Robison) that, as a matter of fact, there has been considerable government intervention in all the NICs (with the possible exception of Hong Kong, but even there, the government is beginning to take an active role). Outline clearly, how this has occurred, as explained by the writers mentioned above.

*

Last, you might address the question of whether the nature of government intervention matters. It may be that government intervention in NICs is different from the kind of government intervention in other countries.

\# (Suppress hint 1)

\# (Suppress hint 2)

\# (Suppress comment)

+ (to indicate an information screen follows)

Question 2

*

Discuss the major factors that explain the poor performance of the NICs in the 1980s.

*

Comment:

The major factors should be discussed in terms of internal and external factors. Several important external factors affected the NICs in the 1980s, for example, recession in their major markets, increasing protectionism, currency movements, technological change, increasing competition from other less developed countries, etc. Explain how each of these contributed to the problems faced by the NICs in the 1980s.

*

Internal factors are of two types: those which affected all NICs, and those which were peculiar to certain NICs. General internal factors were rising rates of domestic inflation, labour unrest, labour shortages, etc. There were also some internal factors peculiar to some NICs, for example, decline of tourism, over-building in the construction sector in Singapore, problems of large-scale units in South Korea, problems of small-scale units in Taiwan, etc. Explain each of these in some detail.

#

#

#

+ (to indicate and information screen follows)

Question 3

*

What are the arguments against the view that values play an important part in the explanation for the economic success of the NICs?

*

Comment:

First, briefly outline the view that values DO play an important part in the success of the NICs. Read the references by Kahn and Ruttan cited on page 4 of the course handout. Make the connection between values and entrepreneurship.

*

Second, outline the arguments against the view that values play an important part in explaining the success of the NICs. The papers by Pan, Soo and Wu discuss these arguments in some detail. The main point around which to build your arguments, is the view that there are other, equally plausible reasons as to why the NICs succeeded.

\#

\#

\#

+ (to indicate and information screen follows)

Question 4
*

What sort of economic policies might Australia implement, if it wanted to emulate the NICs and embark on an export-oriented industrialization strategy?

*

Comment:

First, you need to outline the main economic policies which the NICs implemented. The main point to work around here is the fact that all the NICs employed a combination of market-oriented policies and certain types of government intervention. Are there any lessons that Australia can learn here?

*

Second, tackle the question of whether any of these policies are currently being implemented in Australia? If not, why not? If they are, are the likely to work?

#

#

#

Suppose the above file is called **nic.exm**. Then typing **revise nic.exm** will display the above information frames, one at a time.

When the program pages through instruction screens as in the data file above, typing **quit** at any prompt will abort the session, so that it is not necessary to sit through the entire data file if that is not desired. When instruction screens are being displayed, the program will not show a score at the end of the data file. It just displays a message indicating that the end of the file has been reached.

There is another interesting way of using the above file. If the data file is long, using *Revise* to page through the program may not always be suitable. In order to read the information on, say, Question 20, the student will have to sit through the information on all the previous questions. A program, called **get**, which is available from the author, provides a means of selecting items from the data file. If the student wanted to read the information on Question, that needs to be done is to type **get nic.exm Question**. This will display the following information:

Figure A.8
A Data File of Examination Questions

Question
*

What are the arguments against the view that values play an important part in the explanation for the economic success of the NICs?
*

Comment:
First, briefly outline the view that values do play an important part in the success of the NICs. Read the references by Kahn and

Ruttan cited on page 4 of the course handout. Make the connection between values and entrepreneurship.
*

Second, outline the arguments against the view that values play an important part in explaining the success of the NICs. The papers by Pan, Soo and Wu discuss these arguments in some detail. The main point around which to build your arguments, is the view that there are other, equally plausible reasons as to why the NICs succeeded.

A data item might even be selected by an identifying string. In the above example, typing **get nic.exm values** would display the same information.

One other application of the above use of the get program is to set up a data file of essay assignments. A fragment of such a data file (dev.ess) is shown below:

Figure A.9
A Data File of Essay Questions

Bonnie Jenner

Discuss the extent to which the available statistical evidence supports the view that exports are positively related to economic growth.

This essay topic requires you to evaluate the results of various statistical studies of the relationship between exports and economic growth. Special attention should be paid to the quality of data and the methods used. First, summarize the models and the results reports by various writers in this field. Then offer a critical evaluation of their work.

Helen Head

Evaluate the theoretical bases of the various claims made by less developed countries for the establishment of a New International Economic Order.

This question is about the theoretical basis of the various claims underlying the demand for a NIEO. First, outline what the major demands are, for a NIEO. Then, discuss each of them, paying special attention as to whether they are supported by economic theory. For example, look at the demand for an Integrated Scheme for Commodities (ISC). What is it that the less developed countries want? Even if their demands were met, is it likely that an ISC would be successful, given what we know about the problems of operating buffer-stock schemes?

With a data file containing entries such as the ones shown above, the student Bonnie Jenner need only go to the computer terminal and type **get dev.ess Jenner** to read her essay assignment. Besides displaying information on what is required to answer the essay question, the data file could also contain a set of references pertaining to that question. If there are two or more students with the surname "Jenner" than the student would have had to type **get dev.ess "Bonnie Jenner"** to display his or her essay assignment. Note the double quotation marks around "Bonnie Jenner". These are required whenever the target string contains spaces.

Computer-Aided Essay Marking

Most students these days write their essays on a computer. They then print their essays out on paper and hand up the hard copy for marking. This has a number of disadvantages. First, students who use university printers to print out their essays usually complain that the printers are often busy, or not working. Second, in large classes of, for example, 700 students, carrying these printed essays around can be quite problem. Third, no matter how careful one designs a system to return the essays, some always manage to get lost. Fourth, once the essays have been returned, it is usually difficult to retrieve them if for any reason, it becomes necessary to look at them again. Most students who have been given the option to hand in their essays on disk, have commented that it is a much more convenient way of handing in essays.

A computerized essay-marking system solves all these problems. Since students hand in their essays on disk, there is no need to depend on university printers. Besides, think of the number of trees saved. Second, it is much easier to carry 700 3.5" disks around than it is to carry 700 printed essays around. Third, the computerized essay-marking program described below automatically saves a copy of each student's essay on your hard disk, so that it is always available, should the need arise to make another copy of the essay, or to look at an essay again. Finally, there is a bonus. When essays are submitted on disk, it is relatively easy to check for possible cases of plagiarism. A familiar-sounding paragraph can be searched for amongst all the essays stored on your hard disk. In my experience, merely announcing this possibility to students reduces the number of cases of plagiarism significantly!

My computerized essay-marking program, called *Essay*, starts by prompting the user for various details of the student (for example, the student's name, student number, course details, etc.). Once this has been entered, the program converts all text from lower to upper case (to preserve deterioration of eyesight), and puts the user in a text editor. The essays can now be read, and comments inserted at appropriate places in the essay. Once the essay has been marked, the user can transfer to another file which was created when the program was invoked. This is in the form of a summary sheet. An example is shown in Figure A.10 below:

Figure A.10
An Example of a Summary Sheet Generated by the Computerized Essay-marking Program

DATE MARKED : 5 JUN 1992
STUDENT   : 905286X MATTHEW HEAD
COURSE   : ECON 3002 ASIAN ECONOMIC
                   DEVELOPMENT
ASSIGNMENT   : ES

Appendix

TOPIC   : SECOND TIER NICS
LENGTH   : 3457 WORDS, INCLUDING BIBLIOGRAPHY
GRADE   : DN (Distinction)
COMMENTS   : (References may be made to: m_head.ess)
*

Despite some omissions, and the rather brief treatment of some important issues, this is a very good essay. You have shown an impressive grasp of the subject, and your knowledge of the relevant literature is most encouraging.
*

There are a number of places where you could have offered a bit more explanation, or provided some detail. For example, on line 77 of your essay (m_head.ess) where you mention H&A's arguments about the similarity of exports and trading partners, you could have provided more detail to show evidence of product substitution and dependence on the USA, EC and Japan as major markets. On line 162, you begin a discussion of agricultural development in Indonesia and the Philippines, but make no mention of agricultural progress in Malaysia and Thailand, the two most likely countries to become the next NICs of Asia. If you had looked into this, you would have found the agricultural growth in Malaysia and Thailand has been just as fast, if not faster, than that of Indonesia and the Philippines. Again on lines 305, you begin discussion of some of Athukorala's arguments, but do not discuss his criticisms in relation to "product substitution".
*

So although this is a good essay, both in coverage and in exposition, there are a number of places where a bit more care, and a bit more attention to detail, would have enhanced your essay considerably.

The summary sheet contains information about the student, the number of words in the essay (to check that the word-limit has not been exceeded), and allows the user to insert a grade, and some final comments of a general nature regarding the quality of the essay. When this has been done, the user exits from this screen,

331

and is then prompted to enter a (numerical) mark for the essay. When this is done, the program saves copy of the essay (with embedded comments, a copy of the summary sheet, and store the mark awarded in a separate file (this can be used to update a mark sheet). The student's essay (with comments embedded) and the summary sheet, can then be saved on the student's disk, which will be handed back to the student.

Versions of this computerized essay-marking program are available for MS-DOS computers, Unix and Vax systems.

Programs Available from the Author

The following programs are available from the author. They have been compiled for MS-DOS computers.

revise.exe	(*Revise* program)
encode.exe	(encryption program)
get.exe	(*Get* program)
essay.exe	(*Essay* program)

These programs may be purchased from the author for a cost of A$50 for all of them (programs are not available individually). Send all orders to:

> Gerald Tan
> School of Economics
> Flinders University
> G P O Box 2100
> Adelaide 5001
> South Australia

> Fax No: (08)-201-2566
> E-Mail: ecgt@cc.flinders.edu.au

State if you wish to receive executable files for MS-DOS computers, source code or both. Disk size should also be specified

(3.5" or 5.25"). The source codes of the above programs are also available from the author for A$50. You must have a C compiler to compile these programs, and you must know how to compile C programs.

For those who work in universities, colleges and schools, a large number of programs are available to carry out many tasks (from grading students' marks, to keeping a database of journal references, and more). These are described in Gerald Tan, *Unix Productivity Tools: For Teachers, Writers And Researchers* (Sydney: Addison-Wesley, 1991). The programs can be used on Unix, Vax, and MS-DOS computers.

Bibliography

Adams F G and Davis I 1994, The role of policy in economic development: East Asia and Latin America, *Asian-Pacific Economic Literature*, Vol. 8 No. 1, May, pp. 8–26.

Ahluwalia M S 1976, Income distribution and development: some stylized facts, *American Economic Review*, Vol. 66 No. 2, May, pp. 128–35.

Akamatsu K 1962, A historical pattern of economic growth in developing countries, *The Developing Economies*, Vol. 1 No. 2, March–August, pp. 3–25.

Amin S 1976, *Unequal Development* (Sussex: Harvester Press).

Amsden A H 1983, De-skilling, skilled commodities and the NICs emerging comparative advantage, *American Economic Review*, Vol. 73 No. 2, May, pp. 333–37.

Amsden A H 1989, *Asia's Next Giant: South Korea and Late Industrialization* (Oxford: Oxford University Press).

Amsden A H 1990, Third World industrialization: 'Global Fordism' or a new model? *New Left Review*, No. 182, July–August, pp. 5–32.

Amsden A H 1991, Diffusion of development: the late-industrializing model and Greater East Asia, *American Economic Review*, Vol. 81 No. 2, May, pp. 282–86.

Amsden A H and Euh Y D 1993, South Korea's 1980s financial reforms: Good-bye financial repression (maybe), Hello new institutional restrains, *World Development*, Vol. 21 No. 3, March, pp. 379–90.

Ariff M and Hill H 1985, *Export-Oriented Industrialization: The ASEAN Experience* (Sydney: Allen and Unwin).

Arndt H W 1983, Financial development in Asia, *Asian Development Review*, Vol. 1 No. 1, pp. 86–100.

Arndt H W 1994, Anatomy of regionalism, in R Garnaut and P Drysdale (eds), *Asia Pacific Regionalism: Readings in International Economic Relations* (Sydney: Harper Educational Publishers).

Asian Development Bank 1993, *Asian Development Outlook 1993* (Manila: Asian Development Bank).

Athukorala P 1989, Export performance of 'New Exporting Countries': how valid is the optimism, *Development And Change*, Vol. 20 No. 1, pp. 89–120.

Athukorala P 1993, International labour migration in the Asian-Pacific region: patterns, policies and economic implications, *Asian-Pacific Economic Literature*, Vol. 7 No. 2, pp. 28–57.

Australian Bureau of Statistics 1991–92, *International Investment Position Australia, 1991–92* (Canberra: Australian Bureau of Statistics), Catalogue No. 5306.

Auty J 1992, The macroeconomic impact of Korea's heavy industry drive re-evaluated, *Journal of Developing Areas*, Vol. 29 No. 1, pp. 24–71.

Awanohara S 1990, Currencies: manipulator's, beware, *Far Eastern Economic Review*, December 20, p. 56.

Awanohara S 1991a, Enter the Latin dragon: Asian exporters to the US fear threat from Mexico, *Far Eastern Economic Review*, July 11, pp. 42–3.

Awanohara S 1991b, A three-region world?, *Far Eastern Economic Review*, January 31, pp. 32–3.

Awanohara S 1991c, America's back door: Asian investors in Mexico will face strict rules of origin, *Far Eastern Economic Review*, July 11, pp. 44–6.

Aznam S 1987, The graduate farmers, *Far Eastern Economic Review*, August 27, p. 10.

Balakrishnan N 1989a, The south will rise: shifts in advantages tip the balance in Asia, *Far Eastern Economic Review*, May 4, pp. 76–7.

Balakrishnan N 1989b, The balancing act: immigration offer to Hongkong Chinese fuels debate, *Far Eastern Economic Review*, September 7, p. 35.

Balakrishnan N 1989c, The next NIC, *Far Eastern Economic Review*, September 7, pp. 96–8.

Balakrishnan N 1990, Liberalise the lair, *Far Eastern Economic Review*, July 12, p. 65.

Balakrishnan N 1991a, Lion on the prowl, *Far Eastern Economic Review*, May 23, p. 55.

Balakrishnan N 1991b, Losing the lustre: Singapore's competitive edge is under threat, *Far Eastern Economic Review*, February 21, p. 44.

Balakrishnan N 1991c, Singapore chips in, *Far Eastern Economic Review*, April 25, pp. 60–1.

Balakrishnan N 1992a, Gumboat diplomacy, *Far Eastern Economic Review*, January 16, p. 20.

Balakrishnan N 1992b, Reliant on Uncle Sam, *Far Eastern Economic Review*, February 6, p. 39.

Balakrishnan N, Awanohara S and Burton J 1992, Silicon implants: Singapore gambles on US technology ventures, *Far Eastern Economic Review*, February 6, pp. 45–6.

Balassa B 1981a, The process of industrial development and alternative development strategies, in B. Balassa, *The Newly Industrializing Countries In The World Economy* (New York: Pergamom Press).

Balassa B 1981b, A 'stages' approach to comparative advantage, in B Balassa, *The Newly Industrializing Countries In The World Economy* (New York: Pergamom Press).

Balassa B 1981c, The Newly Industrializing Countries after the oil crisis, in B. Balassa, *The Newly Industrializing Countries In The World Economy* (New York: Pergamom Press).

Balassa B and Michalopoulos C 1986, Liberalizing trade between developed and developing countries, *The Journal Of World Trade Law*, Vol. 20, pp. 3–28.

Balassa B 1988, The lessons of East Asian Development: an overview, *Economic Development And Cultural Change*, Vol. 36 No. 3, April, Supplement, pp. S273-S290.

Barro R 1991, Economic growth in cross-section of countries, *Quarterly Journal of Economics*, May, Vol. CVI, Issue 2, pp. 407–444.

Baum J 1990a, The barter business: Taiwan and the Soviet Union step up trade ties, *Far Eastern Economic Review*, December 20, p. 29.

Baum J 1990b, The work ethnics, *Far Eastern Economic Review*, September 13, pp. 16–7.

Baum J 1991a, Taiwan's building block: reliance on unskilled workers threatens economic development, *Far Eastern Economic Review*, May 2, pp. 36–7.

Baum J 1991b, Unequal partners: Taiwan goods fail to impress Japanese buyers, *Far Eastern Economic Review*, February 21, pp. 42–3.

Baum J 1993, Taipeh's offshore empire, *Far Eastern Economic Review*, August 18, pp. 44–5.

Baum J and do Rosario L 1991, The sumo neighbour: Taiwan fears and admires Japanese business, *Far Eastern Economic Review*, February 21, pp. 40–2.

Baum J and Shim J H 1991, Sibling rivals: Taiwan and South Korea try to reduce reliance on Japan, *Far Eastern Economic Review*, August 15, pp. 34–5.

Bello W and Rosenfeld 1990, *Dragons in Distress: Asia's miracle economies in crisis* (Harmondsworth: Penguin Books).

Bienefeld M 1981, Dependency and the Newly Industrializing Countries (NICs): towards a reappraisal, in D Seers (ed), *Dependency Theory: A Critical Reassessment* (London: J Pinter), pp. 79–96.

Birdsall N 1977, Analytical approaches to the relationship between population growth and development, *Population And Development Review*, Vol. 3 No. 1, March, pp. 63–96.

Birdsall N 1988, Economic approaches to population growth and development, in H B Chenery and T N Srinivasan (eds), *Handbook Of Economic Development* (Amsterdam: Elsevier Science Publications).

Bond M H and Hofstede G 1990, The cash value of Confucian values, in S R Clegg and S G Redding (eds), *Capitalism in Contrasting Cultures* (Berlin: Walter de Gruyter), pp. 383–90.

Bornschier V 1980, Multinational corporations and economic growth: a cross national test of the decapitalization thesis, *Journal Of Development Economics*, Vol. 7, June, pp. 191–210.

Bornschier V Chase-Dun C and Rubinson R 1978, Cross-national evidence of the effects of foreign investment and aid on economic growth and equality: a survey of findings and a re-analysis, *American Journal Of Sociology*, Vol. 84, November, pp. 720–38.

Bowring P 1984, Export opportunities lost as Asia gains ground, *Far Eastern Economic Review*, January 19, p. 86.

Bowring P 1985, Export-led downturn, *Far Eastern Economic Review*, September 26, p. 102.

Bowring P 1992, Crumbs for the poor: wage earners fall behind in wealth distribution, *Far Eastern Economic Review*, March 5, pp. 16–7.

Bradford C I Jr 1987, Trade and structural change: NICs and next tier NICs as transitional economies, *World Development*, Vol. 15 No. 3, March, pp. 299–316.

Broad R and Cavanagh J 1989, No more NICs, *Far Eastern Economic Review*, February 9, pp. 56–7.

Brown J 1993, *The Role of the State in Economic Development: Theory, the East*

Asian Experience, and the Malaysian Case (Manila: Asian Development Bank) Economics Staff Paper No. 52.

Bruton H J 1989, Import substitution, in H B Chenery and T N Srinivasan, *Handbook of Development Economics* (Amsterdam: Elsevier Science Publications) Vol. 2, pp. 1602–44.

Business Times 1992a, Taiwan planning big R&D drive to gain high-tech competitive edge, January 14, p. 9.

Business Times 1992b, Rise in trade seen among East Asian countries, January 14, p. 9.

Byun H Y, Chough S and Jeong K J 1975, Korea, in Ichimura S (ed), *The Economic Development Of East And Southeast Asia* (Honolulu: Univerity Press of Hawaii).

Cardoso F H 1973, Associated-dependent development: theoretical and practical implications, in A Stepan (ed), *Authoritarian Brazil* (New Haven: Yale University Press), pp. 142-76.

Carver L 1987, Too many players, *Far Eastern Economic Review*, March 5, pp. 70–1.

Castells M 1992, Four Asian tigers with a dragon head: a comparative analaysis of the state, economy and society in the Asian Pacific Rim, in R P Appelbaum and J Henderson (eds), *States and development in the Asian Pacific Rim* (Newbury Park, California: Sage Publications), pp. 33–70.

Chanda N 1987, Recession seems the only US option left, *Far Eastern Economic Review*, November 26, p. 99.

Chanda N 1989, Bark worse than bite: the US names its Super 301 "unfair" traders, *Far Eastern Economic Review*, June 8, pp. 99–100.

Chen E K Y 1985, The Newly Industrializing Countries in Asia: Growth experience and prospects, in R A Scalapino, S. Sato and J. Wanandi (eds), *Asian Economic Development – Present And Future* (Berkeley: University of California Press), pp. 131–60.

Chen E K Y 1990, The electronics industry, in H Soesastro and M Pangestu (eds), *Technological Challenge In The Asia-Pacific Economy* (Sydney: Allen and Unwin), pp. 51–73.

Chen E K Y 1993, Foreign direct investment in East Asia, *Asian Development Review*, Vol. 11 No. 1, pp. 24–59.

Chen P J 1978, Development policies and fertility behaviour: the Singapore experience of social disincentives, *Southeast Asian Affairs* (Singapore: Institute of Southeast Asian Studies).

Chenery H 1988, Industrialization and growth: alternative views of East Asia, in H Hughes (ed), *Achieving Industrialization In East Asia* (Cambridge: Cambridge University Press), pp. 39–63.

Chenery H B and Carter N G 1973, Foreign assistance and development performance, 1960–70, *American Economic Review*, Vol. 63 No. 2, May, pp. 459–68.

Chenery H B and Strout A M 1966, Foreign assistance and economic development, *American Economic Review*, Vol. 56, September, pp. 679–733.

Cheng E and Taylor M 1991, Delta force: Pearl river cities in partnership with Hongkong, *Far Eastern Economic Review*, May 16, pp. 64–7.

Cheng T Y 1982, *The Economy Of Hong Kong* (Hong Kong: Far East Publications).

Chia S Y 1989, The character and progress of industrialization, in K S Sandhu and P Wheatly (eds), *The Management Of Success: The Moulding Of Modern Singapore* (Singapore: Institute of Southeast Asian Studies).

Chia S Y 1993, Foreign direct investment in ASEAN countries, *Asian Development Review*, Vol. 11 No. 1, pp. 60–102.

Chinn D 1977, Distributional equality and economic growth the case of Taiwan, *Economic Development And Cultural Change*, Vol. 26 No. 1, October, pp. 65–79.

Cho U and Koo H 1983, Economic development and women's work in a Newly Industrializing Country: the case of Korea, *Development And Change*, Vol. 14 No. 4, October, pp. 515–32.

Choi W S 1991, High quality products key to survival, *The Korea Times Supplement*, November 30, p. 2.

Chong F 1994, Asia's economies may cost the Earth, *The Australian*, March 30, p. 39.

Choo H and Ali I 1989, The Newly Industrializing Economies and Asian development: issues and options, *Asian Development Review*, Vol. 7 No. 2, pp. 1–67.

Chow N W S 1981, Social security provision in Singapore and Hong Kong, *Journal of Social Policy*, Vol. 10 No. 3, pp. 353–66.

Chowdhury A and Islam I, 1993, *The Newly Industrializing Economies of East Asia* (London: Routledge).

Chung K W and Oh N W 1991, Rural poverty in the Republic of Korea: trends and policy issues, *Asian Development Review*, Vol. 10 No. 1, pp. 91–124.

Clad J 1988a, Genesis of despair: swelling numbers threaten hopes of climb out of poverty, *Far Eastern Economic Review*, October 20, pp. 24–5.

Clegg S R, Higgins W and Spybey T 1990, 'Post-Confucianism', social democracy and economic culture, in S R Clegg and S G Redding (eds), *Capitalism in Contrasting Cultures* (Berlin: Walter de Gruyter), pp. 31–78.

Clifford M 1988b, For those left behind ... a welfare state to help those left behind, *Far Eastern Economic Review*, November 24, p. 86.

Clifford M 1989a, Too high, too soon: South Korea ponders devaluation of the Won to boost exports, *Far Eastern Economic Review*, 7 September, pp. 84–5.

Clifford M 1989b, Local anaesthetic: domestic sales bouy up South Korean car makers, *Far Eastern Economic Review*, August 17, p. 63.

Clifford M 1989c, Down different roads: Seoul and Taipei struggle to stay competitive, *Far Eastern Economic Review*, March 16, pp. 86–7.

Clifford M 1989d, Bloc buying: Seoul uses economic power to strengthen ties, *Far Eastern Economic Review*, November 23, pp. 88–90.

Clifford M 1990a, Friends in need: South Korean-Soviet trade begins to bloom, *Far Eastern Economic Review*, September 20, pp. 86–7.

Clifford M 1990b, Away from wigs towards hi-tech, *Far Eastern Economic Review*, June 28, pp. 42–3.

Clifford M 1991a, Models of paradox: strong trade belies Japan-South Korea friction, *Far Eastern Economic Review*, January 31, pp. 40–1.

Clifford M 1991b, Running on empty, *Far Eastern Economic Review*, May 23, pp. 30–1.

Clifford M 1991c, Taking on the titans: South Korea's electronics makers are slowly catching up, *Far Eastern Economic Review*, October 31, pp. 66–9.

Clifford M 1991d, Integrated circuit: top South Korean electronics firms lead investment push overseas, *Far Eastern Economic Review*, December 26, pp. 66–7.

Clifford M 1992a, Spring in their step, *Far Eastern Economic Review*, November 5, pp. 56–7.

Clifford M 1992b, Pain in Pusan: South Korean shoe makers are losing their edge, *Far Eastern Economic Review*, November 5, pp. 58–9.

Clifford M 1992c, Labour on tap: foreign electronics firms flock to Indonesia, *Far Eastern Economic Review*, December 17, pp. 63–4.

Clifford M 1994a, Trading up: Hong Kong bends the rules for technology companies, *Far Eastern Economic Review*, May 26, pp. 68–9.

Clifford M 1994b, Check this out: Hong Kong stores cut costs the hi-tech way, *Far Eastern Economic Review*, June 16, p. 78.

Clifford M and Moore J 1989, Overseas attractions: entreprenuers shift production to low-cost countries, *Far Eastern Economic Review*, March 16, pp. 88–9.

Cline W R 1982, Can the East Asian model of development be generalized?, *World Development*, Vol. 10 No. 2, pp. 81–90.

Colman D and Nixson F 1988, *Economics Of Change In Less Developed Countries* (Oxford: Philip Alan).

Cooper K 1991, Australian groups cling to Britain, *Business Review Weekly*, April 26, pp. 74–5.

Corden W M 1971, *The Theory Of Protection* (Oxford: Oxford University Press).

Cotton J 1991, The limits to liberalization in industrializing Asia: three views of the state, *Pacific Affairs*, Vol. 64 No. 3, pp. 311–27.

Cottrell R 1986, Finally Hongkong gets back to business, *Far Eastern Economic Review*, June 5, pp. 60–2.

Council for Economic Planning and Development, *Taiwan Statistical Data Book* (Taipei: Council for Economic Planning and Development), various years.

Cromwell J 1977, The size distribution of income: an international comparison, *Review Of Income And Wealth*, Series 23, September, pp. 291–308.

DFAT 1993, *The APEC Region Trade and Investment* (Canberra: Department of Foreign Affairs and Trade).

Daly M T and Logan M I 1989, *The Brittle Rim: Finance, Business And The Pacific Region* (Ringwood, Victoria: Penguin Books Australia).

Davenport M 1991, Primary benefits, *Far Eastern Economic Review*, June 13, p. 69.

Davey B 1975, *The economic development of India: A Marxist view* (London: Spokesman Books), Chapter 6: The effects of foreign imperialism.

Deans A 1991, Hitching a ride: Australia makes its sales pitch to Asia, *Far Eastern Economic Review*, November 21, p. 67.

Dornbusch R and Reynoso A 1989, Financial factors in economic development, *American Economic Review*, Vol. 79 No. 2, May, pp. 204–9.

do Rosario 1990, No longer a bargain: Japan cools towards cheap NIC electronics goods, *Far Eastern Economic Review*, July 5, p. 53–4.

do Rosario L 1991a, Winning both ways: Japan's trade surplus with Asia is growing, *Far Eastern Economic Review*, August 1, p. 57.

do Rosario L 1991b, The ties that bind: Japan's Toray spins a web of foreign plants, *Far Eastern Economic Review*, 1991, September 5, pp. 66–7.

do Rosario L and Clifford M 1991, Tools of the traders: Asian machine market shows growing integration, *Far Eastern Economic Review*, May 30, p. 62.

Dowling J M and Hiemenz U 1983, Aid, savings and growth in the Asian region, *The Developing Economies*, Vol. 21 No. 1, March, pp. 3–13.

Drucker P 1986, The changed world economy, *Foreign Affairs*, Vol. 64 No. 2, Spring, pp. 768–91.

Drysdale P 1988, *International Economic Pluralism: Economic Policy In East Asia And The Pacific* (Sydney: Allen and Unwin).

Drysdale P 1989, Growing pains: new grouping could calm US-Asia friction, *Far Eastern Economic Review*, November 16, pp. 14–9.

Drysdale P and Garnaut R 1994, Principles of Pacific economic integration, in R Garnaut and P Drysdale (eds), *Asia Pacific Regionalism: Readings in International Economic Relations* (Sydney: Harper Educational Publishers), pp. 48–61.

Drysdale P and Patrick H 1979, *Evaluation Of A Proposed Asian-Pacific Regional Economic Organization* (Canberra: ANU Australia-Japan Research Centre) Research Paper No. 61.

Duller H 1992, The role of technology in the emergence of the newly industrializing countries, *Asean Economic Bulletin*, Vol. 9 No. 1, pp. 45–54.

East Asia Analytical Unit 1992a, *Australia's Business Challeng: South-east Asia in the 1990s* (Canberra: Department of Foreign Affairs and Austrade).

East Asia Analytical Unit 1992b, *Australia and North-east Asia in the 1990s: Accelerating change* (Canberra: Department of Foreign Affairs and Trade).

East Asia Analytical Unit 1992c, *Southern China in transition: the new regionalism and Australia* (Canberra: Department of Foreign Affairs and Trade).

East Asia Analytical Unit 1994, *Changing Tack: Australian Investment in*

South-east Asia (Canberra: Department of Foreign Affairs and Trade).

Eccles J 1994, Getting to know you: Australia brings Asia into its classrooms, *Far Eastern Economic Review*, November 10, pp. 40–42.

Eckert C J 1990, *Offstring Of Empire: The Koch'ang Kims And The Colonial Origins Of Korean Capitalism*, 1876–1945 (Seattle: Univeristy of Washington Press).

Economic Committee 1986, *The Singapore Economy: New Directions* (Singapore: Ministry of Trade and Industry), Report of the Economic Committee.

Economist 1989a, South Korea's miracle, *Economist*, March 4, pp. 83–4.

Economist 1989b, South Korea: a new society, *Economist*, April 15, pp. 25–8.

Economist 1989c, Pollution in Taiwan: filthy rich, *Economist*, July 15, pp. 63–4.

Economist 1990a, Taiwan and South Korea: two paths to prosperity, *Economist*, July 14, p. 18.

Economist 1990b, The modern Adam Smith, *Economist*, July 4, pp. 11–2.

Economist 1990c, Birth of another nation, *Economist*, March 10, p. 33.

Economist 1990d, Real effective exchange rates, *Economist*, November 3, p. 124.

Economist 1990e, Taming the little dragons, *Economist*, July 14, p. 65.

Economist 1990f, Southeast Asia's economies: sitting pretty, *Economist*, September 8, pp. 89-90.

Economist 1990g, A snappy little dragon, *Economist*, June 9, p. 77.

Economist 1991a, The path to growth, *Economist*, July 13, p. 73.

Economist 1991b, Freedom and prosperity: yes, they do march together, but sometimes out of step, *Economist*, June 29, pp. 15–8.

Economist 1991c, Illegal, but wanted, in Taiwan, *Economist*, March 2, p. 34.

Economist 1991d, Malaysia: baby boom, *Economist*, May 18, p. 30.

Economist 1991e, Asia: As close as teeth and lips, *Economist*, August 10, pp. 15–6.

Economist 1991f, Inflation in the NICs: Just like us, *Economist*, September 28, pp. 89–90.

Economist 1991g, Eastern Europe and the world, *Economist*, July 6, p. 71.

Economist 1991h, The yen – further to climb?, *Economist*, October 26, p. 100.

Economist 1991i, The South China miracle: a great leap forward, *Economist*, October 5, pp. 21–8.

Economist 1991j, Latin America's economic reforms: there is a better way and they have found it, *Economist*, October 19, pp. 21–4.

Economist 1991k, Jam today, bigger jam tomorrow, *Economist*, July 6, p. 30.

Economist 1993a, Asia: Teaching old values, *Economist*, November 28, p. 29.

Economist 1993b, Slowly does it: developing countries should free their financial markets – but slowly, *Economist*, December 11, p. 82.

Economist 1994a, Workers of the world, compete, *Economist*, April 2, pp. 73–4.

Economist 1994b, Singapore: keeping secrets, *Economist*, April 9, p. 32.

Economist 1994c, Hong Pong, *Economist*, July 16, p. 26.

Edwards S 1988, Financial deregulation and sequential capital markets: the case of Korea, *World Development*, Vol. 16 No. 1, pp. 185–94.

Elek A 1992, Trade policy options for the Asia-Pacific region in the 1990s: the potential for open regionalism, *American Economic Review*, Vol. 82 No. 2, May, pp. 74–8.

Enke S 1974, Reducing fertility to accelerate development, *Economic Journal*, Vol. 84 No. 334, June, pp. 349–66.

Ensor P 1986, Supply side defiance, *Far Eastern Economic Review*, June 5, pp. 74–5.

Ensor P and Rowley A 1985, The performing twins on a greasy pole, *Far Eastern Economic Review*, September 26, pp. 100–1.

ESCAP 1991, Management of external sector policy, *Economic And Social Survey Of Asia And The Pacific*, p. 151.

Fairclough G 1993, Missing class: problems loom over failure to educate rural poor, *Far Eastern Economic Review*, February 4, pp. 25–6.

FEER 1989, Social indicators: Schooling and economic growth, *Far Eastern Economic Review*, August 3, p. 14.

FEER 1990a, Social indicators – Television sets and VCRs per 1,000 population, *Far Eastern Economic Review*, November 29, p. 14, and December 13, p. 14.

FEER 1990b, *Asia Yearbook 1990* (Hong Kong: Far Eastern Economic Review).

FEER 1990c, Social indicators – Educational attainment of female population in Hongkong, *Far Eastern Economic Review*, April 5, p. 12.

FEER 1990d, Business indicators – Increase in direct Japanese investment, 1986–88, *Far Eastern Economic Review*, June 21, p. 95.

FEER 1991a, Business indicators – Living standards: Taiwan soars, Australia and Philippines retreat, *Far Eastern Economic Review*, April 25, p. 63.

FEER 1991b, Business Indicators – Central governemnt budget deficits/ surpluses as a % of GDP, *Far Eastern Economic Review*, July 4, p. 51.

FEER 1991c, Business indicators – rebound: most Asia-Pacific nations expect faster GDP growth in 1992, *Far Eastern Economic Review*, May 2, p. 51.

FEER 1991d, Japan as No. 1: Singapore admires subtle blend of East and West, *Far Eastern Economic Review*, June 20, pp. 90–2.

FEER 1991e, Business indicators - Export volume growth in Asia: the rest overtake the NICs, *Far Eastern Economic Review*, August 22, p. 57.

FEER 1991f, Capital – a scarcer commodity, *Far Eastern Economic Review*, September 26, p. 49.

FEER 1991g, Business Indicators – Cumulative US direct investment in Hongkong, *Far Eastern Economic Review*, October 31, p. 75.

FEER 1991h, *Asia Yearbook 1991* (Hong Kong: Far Eastern Economic Review).

FEER 1992a, Business Indicators – Ten emerging economies ranked by competitiveness, *Far Eastern Economic Review*, January 30, p. 51.

FEER 1992b, Indicators, *Far Eastern Economic Review*, August 27, p. 65.

FEER 1992c, Lifestyles, *Far Eastern Economic Review*, July 30, p. 34.

FEER 1993a, Indicators, *Far Eastern Economic Review*, September 2, p. 67.

FEER 1993b, Money machines, *Far Eastern Economic Review*, August 25, p. 46.

Fanjzylber F 1981, Some reflections on Southeast Asian export industrialization, *Cepal Review*, No. 15, December, pp. 111–32.

Fei J, Ranis G and Kuo S W Y 1979, *Growth With Equity: The Taiwan Case* (New York: Oxford University Press).

Felix F 1972, *World Markets of Tomorrow* (New York: Harper Row).

Fong C O 1989, Malaysia: in pursuit of Newly Industrializing Economy status, *Asian Development Review*, Vol. 7 No. 21, pp. 68–87.

Forster-Carter A 1989, The myth of South Korea, *Far Eastern Economic Review*, August 3, pp. 46–7.

Frank A G 1969, *Latin America: Underdevelopment or Revolution?* (New York: Monthly Review Press).

Frank A G 1983, Global crisis and transformation, *Development And Change*, Vol. 14 No. 3, July, pp. 323–46.

Freeman K B 1976, The significance of McClelland's achievement variable in the aggregate production function, *Economic Development And Cultural Change*, Vol. 24 No. 4, July, pp. 815–24.

Friedland J 1989, Breaking the mould: Australia's BTR Nylex expands Asian operations, *Far Eastern Economic Review*, August 24, pp. 52–3.

Friedman M and Friedman R 1980, *Free to choose* (Harmondsworth: Penguin).

Fry M J 1991a, Domestic resource mobilisation in developing Asia: Four policy issues, *Asian Development Review*, Vol. 9 No. 1, pp. 15–39.

Fry M J 1991b, Mobilizing external resources in developing Asia: Structural adjustment and policy reforms, *Asian Development Review*, Vol. 9 No. 2, pp. 14–39.

Fujita N and James W E 1989, Export promotion and the 'heavy industrialization' of Korea, 1973–83, *The Developing Economies*, Vol. 27 No. 2, June, pp. 235–50.

Fujita N and James W E 1990, Export oriented growth of output and employment in Taiwan and Korea, 1973–74 – 1983–84, *Weltwirtschaftliches Archiv*, Vol. 126 No. 4, pp. 737–53.

Fukuyama F 1992, *The end of History and the Last Man* (Harmondsworth: Penguin).

Galbraith J K 1979, *The Nature of Mass Poverty* (Harmondsworth: Penguin).

Garnaut R 1989, *Australia And The Northeast Asian Ascendancy* (Canberra: AGPS).

Garnaut R and Drysdale P 1994, *Asia Pacific Regionalism: Readings in International Economic Relations* (Sydney: Harper Educational Publishers).

Gillis M, Perkins D H, Roemer M and Snodgrass D R 1987, *Economics Of Development* (New York: W W Norton).

Gittelsohn J 1990, Light on their feet: South Korea shoe firms enjoy sales surge, *Far Eastern Economic Review*, June 14, pp. 53–4.

Goad P G 1993, Singapore takes steps to boost investment and links in China, *Asian Wall Street Journal*, May 17, pp. 1, 12.

Goldstein C 1986, Taipei looks to recovery, *Far Eastern Economic Review*, June 5, pp. 74–5.

Goldstein C 1988a, Playing to lose, *Far Eastern Economic Review*, March 31, p. 57.

Goldstein C 1988b, Rags to riches – no more, *Far Eastern Economic Review*, November 17, p. 107.

Goldstein C 1988c, Government pushes Singapore into wafer fabrication, *Far Eastern Economic Review*, August 18, p. 85.

Goldstein C 1991, Brand of hope: Asian firms seek to produce own-name goods, *Far Eastern Economic Review*, October 3, pp. 52–3.

Goll S 1992, Model student: Hong Kong fashion group moves in style, *Far Eastern Economic Review*, August 27, pp. 62–3.

Grabowski R 1988, Taiwanese economic development: an alternative view, *Development And Change*, Vol. 19 No. 1, January, pp. 53–68.

Gregory P R and Stuart R C 1986, *Soviet Economic Structure And Performance* (New York: Harper and Row).

Griffin K B 1970, Foreign assistance: objectives and consequences, *Economic Development And Cultural Change*, Vol. 18 No. 1, April, pp. 313–27.

Griffin K B 1971, *Underdevelopment in Spanish America* (London: Allen and Unwin).

Griffin K B and Enos J L 1970, *Planning Development* (Reading, Mass: Addison-Wesley).

Griffith W H 1987, Can CARICOM countries replicate the Singapore experience? *Journal Of Development Studies*, Vol. 24 No. 1, October, pp. 60–82.

Hagen E E 1962, *On The Theory Of Social Change* (Homewood, Illinois: Dorsey Press).

Hagen E E 1986, *The Economics Of Development* (Homewood, Illinois: Irwin).

Hall P 1983, *Growth And Development* (Oxford: Martin Robertson).

Halliday F and McCormack 1973, *Japanese Imperialism Today* (Harmondsworth: Penguin Books).

Hamilton C 1987, Can the rest of Asia emulate the NICs?, *Third World Quarterly*, Vol. 9 No. 4, pp. 1225–56.

Handley P 1988a, Engineering trained workers: Thailand needs proper policies to produce a qualified workforce, *Far Eastern Economic Review*, September 29, pp. 96–7.

Handley P 1988b, Thailand hits the wall: Overbudened infrastructure threatens to curb rapid economic growth, *Far Eastern Economic Review*, September 29, pp. 94–5.

Handley P 1991, Thailand: some like it hot, *Far Eastern Economic Review*, April 18, p. 72.

Handley P 1992, AIDS at work, *Far Eastern Economic Review*, March 12, p. 48.

Handley P 1993, Stuck in traffic, *Far Eastern Economic Review*, April 8, p. 68.

Hanneman P 1992, Malaysia faces labour shortage as its economy continues to expand, *Australian Financial Review*, May 21, p. 10.

Harris S and Cotton J 1991, *The End Of The Cold War In Northeast Asia* (Melbourne: Longmans).

Harris N 1992, States, economic development and the Asian Pacific Rim, in R P Appelbaum and J Henderson (eds), *States and development in the Asian Pacific Rim* (Newbury Park, California: Sage Publications), pp. 71–84.

Hart D 1989, Adidas and others make tracks, *Asian Business*, Vol. 25 No. 2, February, p. 75.

Havrylyshyn O and Alikhani I 1982, Is there cause for export optimism? An inquiry into the existence of a second generation of successful exporters, *Weltwirtschaftliches Archiv*, Vol. 118 No. 4, pp. 651–63.

Henderson J and Appelbaum R P 1992, Situating the state in the East Asian development process, in R P Appelbaum and J Henderson (eds), *States and development in the Asian Pacific Rim* (Newbury Park, California: Sage Publications), pp. 1–26.

Hill H 1986, Has planning really helped Asia's NICs?, *Far Eastern Economic Review*, March 20.

Hill H 1991, The emperor's clothes can now be made in Indonesia, *Bulletin of Indonesian Economic Studies*, Vol. 27 No. 3, December, pp. 89–127.

Hill H and Suphalachalasai S 1992, The myth of export pessimism (even) under the MFA: evidence from Indonesia and Thailand, *Weltwirtschaftliches Archiv*, Vol. 128 No. 2, pp. 310–29.

Hirata A 1988, Promotion of manufactured exports in developing countries, *Developing Economies*, Vol. 26 No. 4, December, pp. 422–37.

Ho S P S 1987, Economics, economic bureaucracy, and Taiwan's economic development, *Pacific Affairs*, Vol. 60 No. 2, Summer, pp. 266–47.

Hoffman K 1985, Clothing, chips and competitive advantage: the impact of microelectronics on trade and production in the garment industry, *World Development*, Vol. 13 No. 3, pp. 371–92.

Holloway N 1985, Singapore: Now, birth de-control, *Far Eastern Economic Review*, September 18, pp. 42–3.

Holloway N 1986a, Big, biggest, busted: Singapore looks for a soft crash-landing, *Far Eastern Economic Review*, June 5, pp. 58–60.

Holloway N 1986b, Building on a glut, *Far Eastern Economic Review,* June 5, pp. 60–1.

Holloway N 1987, Singapore seeks to bridge the generation gap, *Far Eastern Economic Review,* July 16, pp. 60–1.

Holloway N 1988, Down in the dumps, *Far Eastern Economic Review,* June 23, p. 81.

Holloway N 1989a, Japan's price fixers, *Far Eastern Economic Review,* June 8, p. 101.

Holloway N 1989b, The numbers game: NICs expand investment in Southeast Asia, *Far Eastern Economic Review,* November 16, p. 71.

Holloway N 1990, Beating the blues, *Far Eastern Economic Review,* October 1990, p. 54.

Holloway N 1991a, Gangs of dragons, *Far Eastern Economic Review,* June 27, p. 58.

Holloway N 1991b, All eyes are on interest rates, *Far Eastern Economic Review,* May 23, pp. 40–1.

Holloway N 1991c, Automobiles: a bumpy road to new markets, *Far Eastern Economic Review,* May 30, p. 51.

Holloway N 1991d, The new NICs, *Far Eastern Economic Review,* February 28, p. 72.

Holloway N, Clifford M and Moore J 1989, Bitterness beneath the trade boom, *Far Eastern Economic Review,* June 8, pp. 55–6.

Holloway N, Rowley A, Islam S and Vatikiotis M 1991, An insurance policy: East Asian trade grouping at top of region's agenda, *Far Eastern Economic Review,* July 25, pp. 52–3.

Holloway N and Clifford M 1991, Creaking conduits: South Korean financial system proves resistant to calls for overhaul, *Far Eastern Economic Review,* June 13, pp. 64–6.

Hsia R 1978, Industrialization and income distribution in Hong Kong, *International Labour Review,* Vol. 117 No. 4, July-August, pp. 465–80.

Hughes H 1988, Too little, too late: Australia's future in the Pacific economy, *Australian Economic Papers,* Vol. 27 No. 51, December, pp. 187–95.

Hughes H 1989, Cathing up: the Asian Newly Industrializing Countries the 1990s, *Asian Development Review,* Vol. 7 No. 2, pp. 128–44.

Hughes Hallet A J, 1994, The impact of EC-92 on trade in developing countries, *World Bank Research Observer,* Vol. 9 No. 1, pp. 121–46.

Hultman C W 1986, G-5 exchange market intervention and commercial policy, *The Journal Of World Trade Law,* Vol. 20, pp. 287–93.

IMF 1993, *Direction of Trade Statistics Yearbook 1993* (New York: International Monetary Fund).

Islam I and Kirkpatrick C 1986, Export-led development, labour-market conditions and the distribution of income: the case of Singapore, *Cambridge Journal Of Economics*, Vol. 10 No. 2, June, pp. 113–27.

Islam I 1992, Political economy and East Asian economic development, *Asian-Pacific Economic Literature*, Vol. 6 No. 2, November, pp. 69–101.

Islam S 1988, A question of clout: the EC is angry that its trade gap with Japan continues to widen, *Far Eastern Economic Review*, February 4, p. 93.

Islam S 1990a, Benefits of doubt: Asian exports can expect fewer EC concessions, *Far Eastern Economic Review*, July 19, pp. 38–9.

Islam S 1990b, Blind man's bluff: farming deadlock raises Asian fears over trade blocks, *Far Eastern Economic Review*, December 20, p. 57.

Islam S 1991a, Electrified fence: European hi-tech firms prepare to repel Asia, *Far Eastern Economic Review*, May 2, p. 38.

Islam S 1991b, Double standards: Japanese cars made in EC to be counted as imports, *Far Eastern Economic Review*, August 8, pp. 54–5.

Islam S and Clifford M 1991, Seoul mates: EC-South Korea try to put ties on new footing, *Far Eastern Economic Review*, October 24, p. 67.

Jacoby N H 1966, *US Aid To Taiwan* (New York: Praeger).

Jaffe I 1988, The NICs climb up the industrial ladder: Challenge and opportunity for developed countries, *OECD Observer*, March/April, pp. 10–5.

Jain A K 1981, The effect of female education on fertility: a simple explanation, *Demography*, Vol. 18 No. 4, pp. 577–95.

James W E, Naya S and Meier G M 1989, *Asian Development: Economic Success And Policy Lessons* (Madison: University of Wisconsin Press).

Johnson C 1985, Political institutions and economic performance: the government-business relationship in Japan, South Korea and Taiwan, in R A Scalapino, S Sato and J Wanandi (eds), *Asian Economic Development – Present And Future* (Berkeley: University of California Press), pp. 63-89.

Johnston W B 1991, Global work force 2000: the new world labour market, *Harvard Business Review*, March–April, p. 125.

Johnstone B 1991, Look who's talking, *Far Eastern Economic Review*, April 25, p. 70.

Jones E, Frost L and White C 1993, *Coming Full Circle: an economic history of the Pacific Rim* (Melbourne: Oxford University Press).

Jun Yongwook and Simon D F 1992, The pattern of Korea's foreign direct investment: implications for the internalisation of China's economy, in R Garnaut and Liu Guoguang (ed), *Economic Reform and Internationalisation China and the Pacific region* (Sydney: Allen and Unwin).

Junne G 1987, Automation in the North: Consequences for developing countries' exports, in James A Caporoso (ed), A *Changing International Division Of Labour* (London: Lynne Rienner).

Kahn H 1979, *World Economic Development* (London: Croome Helm).

Kahnert F et al. 1969, *Economic Integration Among Developing Countries* (Paris: OECD Development Centre).

Kamaluddin S 1991, Malthusian nightmare: overpopulation and lack of land behind cyclone's toll, *Far Eastern Economic Review*, May 16, pp. 12–3.

Kanapathy V 1983, ASEAN and the Pacific Community: problems and prospects, *UMBC Economic Review*, Vol. 19 No. 2, pp. 38–60.

Kang T W 1989, *Is Korea the next Japan?* (London: Collier Macmillan).

Kaplinsky R 1984, The international context for industrialization in the coming decade, *Journal Of Developing Studies*, Vol. 1 No. 21, October, pp. 75–96.

Kaplinsky R 1991, Direct foreign investment in Third World manufacturing: is the future an extension of the past?, *IDS Bulletin*, Vol. 22 No. 2, April, pp. 29–35.

Kaye T and Wallace T 1993, Savings show Australia living beyond its means, *Australian Financial Review*, May 3, p. 3.

Kelley A C 1988, Economic consequences of rapid population change in the Third World, *Journal Of Economic Literature*, Vol. 26 No. 4, December, pp. 1685–728.

Kim L 1990, Korea: the acquisition of technology, in H Soesastro and M Pangestu (eds), *Technological Challenge In The Asia-Pacific Economy* (Sydney: Allen and Unwin).

Klein L and Ohkawa K 1968, *Economic Growth: The Japanese Experience Since The Meiji Era* (Homewood, Illinois: Richard D Irwin).

Koh A T 1987, Linkages and the international environment, in L B Krause et al., *The Singapore Economy Reconsidered* (Singapore: Institute of Southeast Asian Studies).

Kohama H and Urata S 1988, The impact of the recent Yen appreciation on the Japanese economy, *Developing Economies*, Vol. 26 No. 4, December, pp. 323–40.

Kojima K 1966, A Pacific Economic Community and Asian developing countries, *Hitotsubashi Journal Of Economics*, Vol. 7 No. 1, June.

Koo H 1984, The political economy of income distribution in Korea: the impact of the State's industrialization policies, *World Development*, Vol. 12 No. 10, October, pp. 1029–38.

Koo H and Kim E M 1992, The developmental state and capital accumulation in South Korea, in R P Appelbaum and J Henderson (eds), *States and development in the Asian Pacific Rim* (Newbury Park, California: Sage Publications), pp. 121–49.

Korporaal G 1990, Oz goes offshore: Australian firms emerge from behind their barricades, *Far Eastern Economic Review*, March 7, pp. 38–9.

Korporaal G 1991, Heading north, *Far Eastern Economic Review*, June 13, p. 68.

Kohsaka A 1987, Financial liberalization in Asian NICs: a comparative study of South Korea and Taiwan, *The Developing Economies*, Vol. 25 No. 4, pp. 325–46.

Krause L B 1987, *The Singapore Economy Reconsidered* (Singapore: Institute of Southeast Asian Studies).

Krause L B 1988, Hong Kong and Singapore: twins or kissing cousins?, *Economic Development And Cultural Change*, Vol. 36 No. 3, April, Supplement, pp. 45–66.

Krause L B 1989, Government as entrepreneur, in K S Sandhu and P Wheatley (eds), *Management Of Success: The Moulding Of Modern Singapore* (Singapore: Institute of Southeast Asian Studies), Chapter 20, pp. 436-54.

Krenin M E and Plummer M G 1992, Effects of economic integration in industrial countries on ASEAN and the Asian NIEs, *World Development*, Vol. 20 No. 9, September, pp. 1345–66.

Kreuger A O 1990, Asian trade and growth lessons, *American Economic Review*, Vol. 80 No. 2, May, pp. 108–12.

Krueger A O 1979, *The Developmental Role Of The Foreign Sector And Aid* (Cambridge, Mass: Harvard University Press).

Krugman P 1990, Technology and changing comparative advantage in the Asia-Pacific region, in H Soesastro and M Pangestu (eds), *Technological Challenge in the Asia-Pacific Economy* (Sydney: Allen and Unwin).

Krommenacker R J 1986, The impact of information technology on trade interdependence, *The Journal Of World Trade Law*, Vol. 20, pp. 381–400.

Kulkarni G 1985a, Hi-tech vision of a low-growth future, *Far Eastern Economic Review*, March 14, p. 68–71.

Kulkarni G 1985b, Building for a boom that did not come, *Far Eastern Economic Review*, March 14, p. 70–1.

Kulkarni G 1985c, Progress at a price, *Far Eastern Economic Review*, March 14, p. 70–1.

Kulkarni G 1985d, Sanitized culture leaves tourist beds empty, *Far Eastern Economic Review*, March 14, p. 70–1.

Kuznets S 1955, Economic growth and income inequality, *American Economic Review*, Vol. 45 No. 1, March, pp. 1–28.

Lal D 1988, Ideology and industrialization in India and East Asia, in H Hughes (ed), *Achieving Industrialization In East Asia* (Cambridge: Cambridge University Press).

Lall S 1991, Explaining industrial success in the developing world, in V N Balasubramanyam and S Lall (eds), *Current Issues In Development Economics* (London: Macmillan) pp. 118–55.

Landau D 1983, Government expenditure and economic growth: a cross-country study, *Southern Economic Journal*, Vol. 45, pp. 440–58.

Landau D 1990, Public choice and economic aid, *Economic Development And Cultural Change*, Vol. 38, pp. 559–75.

Lee J Rana P B and Iwasaki Y 1986, *Effects Of Foreign Capital Inflows On Developing Countries Of Asia* (Manila: Asian Development Bank), Economic Staff Paper No. 30.

Lee S A 1973, *Industrialization In Singapore* (Melbourne: Longman Cheshire).

Lee Tsao Yuen 1991, *Growth Triangle: The Johor-Singapore-Riau Experience* (Singapore: Institute of Policy Studies).

Leger J M 1994, The boom: how Asians started the 'Pacific Century' early, *Far Eastern Economic Review*, November 24, pp. 43–9.

Leipziger D M 1988, Industrial restructuring in Korea, *World Development*, Vol. 16 No. 1, pp. 121-36.

Leipziger D M and Thomas V 1994, Roots of East Asian success, *Finance and Development*, Vol. 31 No. 1, March, pp. 6–9.

Levine R and Renelt D 1992, A sensitivity test of cross-country growth regressions, *American Economic Review*, Vol. 82 No. 4, pp. 942–63.

Lewis W A 1954, Economic development with unlimited supplies of labour, *Manchester School Of Economic And Social Studies*, Vol. 22, pp. 139–91.

Lewis W A 1980, The slowing down of the engine of growth, *American Economic Review*, Vol. 70 No. 4, September, pp. 555–64.

Liang K S and Lee T H 1975, Taiwan, in Ichimura S (ed), *The Economic Development Of East And Southeast Asia* (Honolulu: University Press of Hawaii).

Liang N 1992, Beyond import-substitution and export promotion: a new typology of trade strategies, *Journal of Development Studies*, Vol. 28 No. 3, April, pp. 447–72.

Lim C Y 1989, From high growth rates to recession, in K. S. Sandhu and P. Wheatley (eds), *Management Of Success: The Moulding Of Modern Singapore* (Singapore: Institute of Southeast Asian Studies).

Lim L Y C 1983, Singapore's success: the myth of the free market economy, *Asian Survey*, Vol. 23 No. 6, June, pp. 752–64.

Lim L and Pang E F 1984, *Trade, Employment and Industrialization in Singapore* (Geneva: International Labour Organization).

Lim Y 1981, *Government Policy And Private Enterprise: Korean Experience In Industrialization* (Berkeley: University of California Press).

Lin T B 1985, Growth, equity and income distribution policies in Hong Kong, *Developing Countries*, Vol. 23 No. 4 December pp. 391–413.

Lin T B and Sung W S 1985, Changing comparative advantage in Hong Kong trade, *Southeast Asian Economic Review*, Vol. 6 No. 2 August pp. 95–111.

Linnemann H, van Dijck P and Verbruggen H 1987, *Export-Oriented Industrialization In Developing Countries* (Singapore: University of Singapore Press).

Little I M D 1979, An economic reconnaissance, in W Galenson (ed), *Economic growth and structural change in Taiwan* (New York: Cornell University Press).

Little I M D 1981, The experience and causes of rapid labour-intensive development in Korea, Taiwan Province, Hong Kong and Singapore; and possibilities of emulation, in E Lee (ed), *Export-Led Industrialization And Development* (Geneva: International Labour Office) p. 43.

Little I M D, Scitovsky T and Scott M 1970, *Industry And Trade In Some Developing Countries: A Comparative Study* (Paris: OECD).

Lorenz D 1989, Trade in manufactures, Newly Industrializing Economies (NIEs), and regional development in the world economy: a European view, *Developing Economies*, Vol. 27 No. 3, September, pp. 221–35.

Lubeck P M 1992, Malaysian industrialization, ethnic divisions and the NIC model: the limits of replication, in R P Appelbaum and J Henderson (eds), *States and development in the Asian Pacific Rim* (Newbury Park, California: Sage Publications), pp. 176–98.

Manning C and Pang E F 1990, Labour market trends and structures in ASEAN and the East Asian NIEs, *Asian Pacific Economic Literature*, Vol. 4 No. 2, September, pp. 59–81.

Mackie J A C 1993, Overseas Chinese entreprenuership, *Asian-Pacific Economic Literature*, Vol. 6 No. 1, May, pp. 41–64.

Macomber J D 1987, East Asia's lessons for Latin American resurgence, *The World Economy*, Vol. 10 No. 4, December, pp. 469–82.

Mayo M 1973, Attitudes toward Asia and the beginnings of Japanese empire, in J Livingson, J Moore and F Oldfather (eds), *The Japan Reader 1: Imperial Japan, 1800–1945* (Harmondsworth: Penguin Books), pp. 212–21.

Mazur A and Rosa E 1977, An empirical test of McClelland's 'Achieving Society' theory, *Social Forces*, Vol. 55 No. 3, March, pp. 769–74.

McClelland D C 1961, *The Achieving Society* (New Jersey: Van Nostrand).

McKinnon R I 1973, *Money and Capital in Economic Development* (Washington: The Brookings Institution).

Meier G 1989, *Leading Issues in Economic Development* (New York: Oxford University Press).

Ministry of Trade and Industry 1991, *Economic Survey Of Singapore* (Singapore: Ministry of Trade and Industry), August.

Mizoguchi T 1985, Economic development policy and income distribution: the experience of East and Southeast Asia, *Developing Countries*, Vol. 23 No. 4 December pp. 307–24.

Mondejar R 1991, Cross-border insurance, *Far Eastern Economic Review*, October 10, p. 70.

Moore J 1988a, Social unease and the price of development, *Far Eastern Economic Review*, September 15, pp. 52–4.

Moore J 1988b, Leaving under a cloud: Taiwan plastics group to build a giant plant in Texas, *Far Eastern Economic Review*, November 24, pp. 70–1.

Moore J 1990, Free but not easy, *Far Eastern Economic Review*, August 30, pp. 46–7.

Morisset J 1989, The impact of foreign capital inflows on domestic savings re-examined: the case of Argentina, *World Development*, Vol. 17 No. 11, November, pp. 1709–16.

Nakajo S 1980, Japanese direct investment in Asian Newly Industrializing Countries and intra-firm division of labour, *Developing Economies*, Vol. 18, pp. 463–83.

Nayyar D 1978, Transnational corporations and manufactured exports from poor countries, *Economic Journal*, Vol. 88 No. 349, pp. 59–84.

Nemetz P 1990, *The Pacific Rim: Investment, Development and Trade* (Vancouver: University of British Columbia Press).

Nolan P 1990, Assessing economic growth in the Asian NICs, *Journal of Contemporary Asia*, Vol. 20 No. 1, pp. 41–63.

Norman N 1975, *The Effective Rate Of Protection: An Exposure* (Canberra: Australian Industries Development Association).

Ohmae K 1982, *The Mind Of The Strategist* (Harmondsworth: Penguin Books).

Organization for Economic Co-operation and Development 1979, *The Impact Of The Newly Industrializing Countries On Production And Trade In Manufactures* (Paris: OECD).

Organization for Economic Co-opoeration and Development 1988, *The Newly Industrializing Countries: Challenge And Opportunity For OECD Countries* (Paris: OECD).

Oshima H T 1986a, The construction boom of the 1970s: the end of high growth in the NICs and ASEAN? *Developing Economies*, Vol. 24 No. 3, September, pp. 207–28.

Oshima H T 1986b, The transition from an agricultural to an industrial economy in East Asia, *Economic Development and Cultural Change*, Vol. 34 No. 4, July, pp. 783–809.

Oshima H T 1987, Savings and investment in Asian productivity growth, *Malaysian Journal of Economic Studies*, Vol. 26 No. 1, June, pp. 39–63.

Oshima H T 1988, Human resources in East Asia's secular growth, *Economic Development and Cultural Change*, Vol. 36 No. 3, April, Supplement, pp. S103–S122.

Paisley E 1991, On the China stage, *Far Eastern Economic Review*, October 23, pp. 60–1.

Paisley E 1992, Time for a new start: with cheap labour ended, a new costly high-tech base is needed, *Far Eastern Economic Review*, August 13, pp. 29–34.

Paisley E and Kiernan T 1994, Reforms boost capital flows, *Far Eastern Economic Review*, May 26, pp. 53–7.

Paauw D and Fei J 1973, *The Transition In Open Dual Economies* (New Haven: Yale University Press).

Page J 1994, The East Asian miracle: building a basis for growth, *Finance and Development*, Vol. 31 No. 1, March, pp. 2–5.

Page S 1990, *Trade Finance And Developing Countries* (London: Harvester Wheatsheaf).

Page S 1991, The role of trade in the new NICs, *Journal of Development Studies*, Vol. 27 No. 3, pp. 39–60.

Pan L 1988, Playing fast and loose with Confucian values, *Far Eastern Economic Review*, May 19, pp. 46–7.

Pan L 1991, *Sons Of The Yellow Emperor: The Story Of The Overseas Chinese* (London: Mandarin Paperbacks).

Panagariya A 1994, East Asia: a new trading bloc? *Finance and Development*, Vol. 31 No. 1, March, pp. 16–9.

Pang E F 1988, The distinctive features of two city-states' development: Hong Kong and Singapore, in P Berger and H H M Hsiao (eds), *In Search Of An East Asian Development Model* (New Brunswick: Transaction Publications).

Pang E F, Tan C H and Cheng S M 1989, The management of people, in K S Sandhu and P Wheatly (eds), *The Management Of Success: The Moulding Of Modern Singapore* (Singapore: Institute of Southeast Asian Studies).

Papanek G 1972, The effect of aid and other resource transfers on savings and growth in LDCs, *Economic Journal*, Vol. 82, September, pp. 863–74.

Papanek G 1973, Aid, foreign private investment, savings and growth in LDCs, *Journal Of Political Economy*, Vol. 81, pp. 120–31.

Papanek G 1988, The new Asian capitalism: an economic portrait, in P Berger and H H M Hsiao (eds), *In Search Of An East Asian Development Model* (New Brunswick: Transaction Publications).

Papanek G F and Kyn O 1986, The effect on income distribution of development, the growth rate and economic strategy, *Journal Of Development Economics*, Vol. 23, pp. 55-65.

Park S I 1988, Labour issues in Korea's future, *World Development*, Vol. 16 No. 1, pp. 97–119.

Park Y C 1990, Development lessons from Asia: the role of government in South Korea and Taiwan, *American Economic Review*, Vol. 80 No. 2, May (Papers and Proceedings), pp. 118–21.

Pazos F 1973, Regional integration of trade among less developed countries, *World Development*, Vol. 7.

Pennar K 1993a, Is democracy bad for growth? *International Business*, June 7, pp. 26–9.

Pennar K 1993b, Milton Friedman: still singing *Let It Be*, *International Business*, June 7, p. 29.

Pernia E M 1991, Aspects of urbanization and the environment in Southeast Asia, *Asian Development Review*, Vol. 9 No. 2, pp. 113–36.

Petri P A 1988, Korea's export niche: origins and prospects, *World Development*, Vol. 16 No. 1, pp. 47–63.

Porter M E 1990, *The Competitive Advantage Of Nations* (London: Macmillan).

Rabushka A 1988, *The New China: Comparative Economic Development in Mainland China, Taiwan and Hong Kong* (Boulder, Colorado: Westview Press).

Ram R 1986, Government size and economic growth: a new framework and some evidence from cross-section and time-series data, *American Economic Review*, Vol. 76 No. 1, pp. 191–203.

Ram R 1988, Economic development and income inequality: further evidence on the U-curve hypothesis, *World Development*, Vol. 16, No. 11, pp. 1371–6.

Rana P B and Dowling J M 1988, The impact of foreign capital on growth: evidence from Asian developing countries, *Developing Economies*, Vol. 25 No. 1, March, pp. 3–11.

Randolph S 1990, The Kuznets process in Malaysia, *Journal Of Developing Areas*, Vol. 25 No. 1, October, pp. 15–32.

Ranis G 1985a, Can the East Asian model of development be generalized? A comment, *World Development*, Vol. 13, April, pp. 91–104.

Ranis G 1985b, Employment, income distribution and growth in the East Asian context: a comparative analysis, in V Corbo, et al., *Export-Oriented Development Strategies* (Boulder: Westview Press).

Ranis G 1989, The role of institutions in transitional growth: the East Asian Newly Industrializing Countries, *World Development*, Vol. 17 No. 9, pp. 1443–53.

Rao V V B 1988, Income distribution in East Asian developing countries, *Asia-Pacific Economic Literature*, Vol. 2 No. 1, March, pp. 26–45.

Rao B 1990, Income distribution in Singapore: trends and issues, *The Singapore Economic Review*, Vol. 35 No. 1, pp. 143—60.

Rashid A 1989, No dogs, cats or girls, *Far Eastern Economic Review*, April 20, p. 40.

Reardon-Anderson J 1992, *Pollution, Politics and Foreign Investment in Taiwan: the Lukang Rebellion* (New York: M E Sharp).

Rees J 1989, First step taken: historic meeting gets regional economic forum started, *Far Eastern Economic Review*, November 16, pp. 10–1.

Reynolds L 1981, The spread of economic growth in the Third World, 1850–1980, *Journal Of Economic Literature*, Vol. 24 No. 3, pp. 941–80.

Riedel J 1988, Economic development in East Asia: doing what comes naturally? in H Hughes (ed), *Achieving Industrialization In East Asia* (Cambridge: Cambridge Univeristy Press), pp. 1–38.

Riedel J 1991, Intra-Asian trade and foreign direct investment, *Asian Development Review*, Vol. 9 No. 1, pp. 110–46.

Rieger H C 1989, Regional economic co-operation in the Asia-Pacific region, *Asian-Pacific Economic Literature*, Vol. 3 No. 2, September, pp. 5–33.

Roberts G 1985, *South Korea to 1990* (London: Economic Intelligence Unit), Special Report No. 225.

Robinson T W 1991, *Democracy And Development In East Asia: Taiwan, South Korea And The Philippines* (Washington: The American Enterprise Institute Press).

Rodan G 1989, *The Political Economy Of Singapore's Industrialization* (London: Macmillan).

Rowley A 1989a, The East is ready: reform in Eastern Europe offers opportunities and challenges to Asia, *Far Eastern Economic Review*, November 23, pp. 84–6.

Rowley A 1989b, Carving up world trade, *Far Eastern Economic Review*, June 15, p. 53.

Rowley A 1989c, Parisian model: OECD may set pattern for future APEC structure, *Far Eastern Economic Review*, November 16, pp. 12–3.

Rowley A 1990a, Spendthrifty Asia, *Far Eastern Economic Review*, May 31, p. 53.

Rowley A 1990b, Yen in doubt, sell: currency weakness underlies market crisis, *Far Eastern Economic Review*, April 5, p. 57.

Rowley A 1990c, NICs lose knack, *Far Eastern Economic Review*, July 5, p. 54.

Rowley A 1990d, Double jeopardy: EC considers new leverage over Asian exporters, *Far Eastern Economic Review*, November 22, p. 63.

Rowley A 1990e, NICs lose knack, *Far Eastern Economic Review*, July 5, p. 54.

Rowley A 1991a, Yen for a model, *Far Eastern Economic Review*, July 4, p. 46.

Rowley A 1991b, Toil and Trouble, *Far Eastern Economic Review*, March 28, p. 60.

Rowley A 1991c, Saviour savers? *Far Eastern Economic Review*, August 15, p. 46.

Rowley A 1991d, Odd man out, *Far Eastern Economic Review*, October 3, p. 57.

Rowley A 1991e, Boom to recession? *Far Eastern Economic Review*, October 17, p. 120.

Rowley A 1991f, Test for Miyazawa: economic slowdown poses first hurdle for new Japanese premier, *Far Eastern Economic Review*, November 7, pp. 48–50.

Ruffin R J 1993, The role of foreign investment in the Asian and Pacific region, *Asian Development Review*, Vol. 11 No. 1, pp. 1–23.

Saith A 1983, Development and distribution: a critique of the cross-country U-hypothesis, *Journal Of Development Economics*, Vol. 13 No. 3, December, pp. 367–82.

Salem E 1989a, Men or machines? Hong Kong manufacturers under pressure to automate production, *Far Eastern Economic Review*, April 27, pp. 62–3.

Salem E 1989b, Hostage to China, *Far Eastern Economic Review*, June 29, pp. 52–4.

Sandilands R J and Tan L H 1986, Comparative advantage in a re-export economy: the case of Singapore, *Singapore Economic Review*, Vol. 31 No. 2, October, pp. 34–56.

Sayle M 1987, Success turns sour: cracks run along Japan's post-war path to prosperity, *Far Eastern Economic Review*, April 30, pp. 44–51.

Sazanami Y 1990, Japanese trade in the Pacific Rim: the relationship between trade and investment, in P Nemetz (ed), *The Pacific Rim: Investment, Development And Trade* (Vancouver: University of British Columbia Press), pp. 68–87.

Scatz S P 1965, Achievement and economic growth: a critique, *Quarterly Journal Of Economics*, Vol. 79 No. 2, May, pp. 234–341.

Schlossstein S 1990, *Asia's New Little Dragons: The Dynamic Emergence Of Indonesia, Thailand And Malaysia* (Chicago: Contemporary Books).

Scitovsky T 1985, Economic development in Taiwan and South Korea, 1965–81, *Stanford Food Research Institute Studies*, Vol. 19, pp. 215–264.

Shinohara M 1983, More NICs in time, *Far Eastern Economic Review*, April 28, pp. 66–7.

Sicat G P 1983, The Newly Industrializing Countries and world markets, *Asian Development Review*, Vol. 1 No. 1, pp. 54–62.

Simon J L 1986, *Theory Of Population And Economic Growth* (Oxford: Basil Blackwell).

Simson S 1991, Asia's lessons for Australia, *Business Review Weekly*, April 26, pp. 22–5.

Singh R D 1985, State intervention, foreign economic aid, savings and growth in LDCs: some recent evidence, *Kyklos*, Vol. 38 Fasc. 2, pp. 216–32.

Singh R D 1988, The multinationals' economic penetration, growth, industrial output, and domestic savings in developing countries: another look, *Journal Of Development Studies*, Vol. 25 No. 1, October, pp. 55–82.

Sjahrir 1992, *Reflexsi Pembangunan Ekonomi Indonesia*, 1968-92 (Jakarta: PT Gramedia Pustaka Utama).

Smith C 1986a, Matsushita seeks Yen relief offshore, *Far Eastern Economic Review*, December 25, pp. 66–7.

Smith C 1986b, Two-way tradeoff: a strong Yen has both pluses and minuses for the NICs, *Far Eastern Economic Review*, March 6, pp. 58–61.

Smith C 1987a, Under the volcano: Japan fears fallout from US economic pressure, *Far Eastern Economic Review*, April 30, pp. 70–1.

Smith C 1987b, Mixed blessings: success of Japan's import policy creates problems, *Far Eastern Economic Review*, December 31, pp. 40–1.

Smith C 1988, Curse of the J-curve, *Far Eastern Economic Review*, February 4, pp. 88–9.

Smith C 1989a, The backroom boys: Japanese supportive, but wary of the limelight, *Far Eastern Economic Review*, November 16, pp. 11–2.

Smith C 1989b, Asian misses out on Japan's cash, *Far Eastern Economic Review*, June 8, pp. 59–60.

Smith C and do Rosario L 1990, Empire of the sun: Japanese investment creates foundations of regional trading bloc, *Far Eastern Economic Review*, May 3, pp. 46–8.

Snodgrass D R 1980, *Inequality And Economic Development In Malaysia* (Kuala Lumpur: Oxford University Press).

Snyder D 1990, Foreign aid and domestic savings: a spurious correlation?, *Economic Development And Cultural Change*, Vol. 39 No. 1, October, pp. 175–82.

Soligo R and Stern J J 1965, Tariff protection, import substitution and investment efficiency, *Pakistan Development Review*, Vol. 5, Summer.

Stavig G R 1976, The impact of population growth on the economy of countries, *Economic Development And Cultural Change*, Vol. 25 No. 2, July, pp. 735–50.

Stillitoe P 1985a, All manufacturing roads lead back to Tokyo, *Far Eastern Economic Review*, October 3, p. 71.

Stillitoe P 1985b, Seeking a new style, *Far Eastern Economic Review*, April 4.

Straits Times 1992a, Lam Soon Oil to relocate production to Malaysia, China, January 7, p. 38.

Straits Times 1992b, EC starts anti-dumping probe on S'pore scales, January 13, p. 40.

Straits Times 1992c, Hard-headed approach the best way to help Singapore progress, January 6, pp. 24–5.

Stutchbury M 1990, Questions about North East Asian ascendancy, *Australian Financial Review*, May 4, p. 75.

Sudo S 1991, Towards a Pacific Century, *Far Eastern Economic Review*, January 31, pp. 16–7.

Suh S M 1986, The macro and micro roads to economic success, *Far Eastern Economic Review*, June 26.

Sung Yun-Wing 1992, The economic integration of Hong Kong, Taiwan and South Korea with the mainland of China, in R Garnaut and Liu Guoguang (eds), *Economic Reform and Internationalisation: China and the Pacific region* (Sydney: Allen and Unwin).

Tai H C 1989, The Oriental alternative: a hypothesis on East Asian culture and economy, *Issues And Studies*, Vol. 25 No. 3, March, pp. 10–36.

Tai M C 1991, Peace and insecurity: Asian governments resist pressure to cut arms budgets, *Far Eastern Economic Review*, November 7, pp. 52–3.

Tambunlertchai S 1989, Economic prospects and external economic relations of Thailand, *Asian Development Review*, Vol. 7 No. 2, pp. 88–112.

Tasker R 1990, Back to basics: conference stresses pivotal role of primary schools, *Far Eastern Economic Review*, March 22, pp. 20–1.

Tasker R 1993, Rendered surplus: idled by machines, workers go on strike, *Far Eastern Economic Review*, July 22, p. 18.

Tasker R and Handley P 1993, Economic hit list: time for politically-focused Chuan to tackle the problems, *Far Eastern Economic Review*, August 5, pp. 38–44.

Taylor M 1991a, Inflating expectations, *Far Eastern Economic Review*, May 23, p. 66.

Taylor M 1991b, Boom with a queue: Hongkong has too much cash chasing too few assets, *Far Eastern Economic Review*, August 22, p. 48.

Taylor M 1991c, Wisdom deflated, *Far Eastern Economic Review*, September 12, p. 44.

Teikener A C 1980, Need achievement and international differences in income growth, 1950-60, *Economic Development And Cultural Change*, Vol. 28 No. 2, January, pp. 293–320.

Thee K W 1991, The surge of NIC investment in Indonesia, *Bulletin of Indonesian Economic Studies*, Vol. 27 No. 3, pp. 55–88.

Thirlwall A P 1978, *Growth And Development* (London: Macmillan).

Tiglao R 1990, Wheels within wheels, *Far Eastern Economic Review*, March 29, p. 71.

Tiglao R 1991, Tariff cuts mangled: Aquino yields to special interests, *Far Eastern Economic Review*, August 8, pp. 62–3.

Tjondronegoro S M P, Soejono I and Hardjono J 1991, Rural poverty in Indonesia: trends, issues and policies, *Asian Development Review*, Vol. 10 No. 1, pp. 67–90.

Todaro M P 1985, *Economic Development In The Third World* (New York: Longmans).

Tran V T 1988, Foreign capital and technology in the process of catching up by the developing countries: the experience of the synthetic fiber industry in the Republic of Korea, *Developing Economies*, Vol. 26 No. 4, pp. 386–402.

Tsuruoka D 1990, Pick a project: foreign investors are rushing in to pour money into Malaysian manufacturing, *Far Eastern Economic Review*, February 1, pp. 34–5.

Tsuruoka D and Vatikiotis M 1991a, Finding a focus: Anwar's task is to put flesh on Mahathir's economic plans, *Far Eastern Economic Review*, May 16, pp. 60–1.

Tsuruoka D and Vatikiotis M 1991b, Building on success: new development plan downplays ethnic targets, *Far Eastern Economic Review,* June 27, pp. 16–17.

UNDP 1991, *Human Development Report 1991* (New York: Oxford University Press).

Uppal J 1969, Work habits and disguised unemployment in under-developed countries: a theoretical analysis, *Oxford Economic Papers,* Vol. 21 No. 3, November, pp. 387–94.

Vatikiotis M 1990, Faltering first steps: little to show at APEC's first major meeting, *Far Eastern Economic Review,* August 9, pp. 9–10.

Vatikiotis M 1991a, Search for a hinterland: Singapore appeals to neighbours' self-interest, *Far Eastern Economic Review,* January 3, pp. 34–5.

Vatikiotis M 1991b, Back to the future: Medan business needs to look east, *Far Eastern Economic Review,* January 3, pp. 36–7.

Vatikiotis M 1992, Where has all the labour gone, *Far Eastern Economic Review,* April 16, pp. 46–7.

Vatikiotis M 1993, Cars out, planes in: Malaysia eyes new market in Asean, *Far Eastern Economic Review,* August 26, pp. 54.

Velasco E T 1990, The textile industry, in H Soesastro and M Pangestu (eds), *Technological Challenge In The Asia-Pacific Economy* (Sydney: Allen and Unwin).

Vittas M and Cho Y J 1994, The role of credit policies in Japan and Korea, *Finance and Development,* Vol. 31 No. 1, March, pp. 10–2.

Wade R 1988, The role of government in overcoming market failure: Taiwan, Republic of Korea and Japan, in H Hughes (ed), *Achieving Industrialization In East Asia* (Cambridge: Cambridge University Press).

Wade R 1990, *Governing The Market: Economic Theory And The Role Of Government In East Asian Industrialization* (New Jersey: Princeton University Press).

Waller A 1994a, Winds of change, *Far Eastern Economic Review,* April 28, pp. 64–6.

Waller 1994b, The lion's share, *Far Eastern Economic Review,* April 28, p. 66.

Waller 1994c, Stitched up: Asia's textile and clothing trade is set to boom, *Far Eastern Economic Review,* April 28, pp. 68–70.

Wallerstein I 1979, Dependence in an interdependent world: the limited possibilities of transformation within the capitalist world-economy, in I Wallerstein, *The Capitalist World Economy* (Cambridge: Cambridge University Press).

Wang Gangwu 1977, *China And The World Since 1949* (London: Macmillan), pp. 48–50.

Watanabe T 1980, An analsysis of economic interdependence among the Asian NICs, the ASEAN nations and Japan, *The Developing Economies*, Vol. 18, pp. 393–411.

Waters D 1990, 21st *Century Management: Keeping Ahead Of The Japanese And Chinese* (Singapore: Prentice-Hall).

Weber M 1958, *The Protestant Ethic And The Spirit Of Capitalism* (New York: Charles Scribner's Sons).

Weiskel T C 1993, UNCED and after: global issues, country problems and regional solutions in the Asia Pacific region, *Journal of Developing Areas*, Vol. 28 No. 1, October, pp. 13–20.

Weisskopf R 1976, Transversing the social pyramid: a comparative review of income distribution in Latin America, *Latin American Research Review*, Vol. 11 No. 2, pp. 71–112.

Weisskopf T 1972, The impact of foreign capital inflow on domestic savings in LDCs, *Journal Of International Economics*, Vol. 2 No. 1, February, pp. 25–38.

Weisskopf T 1974, *American Economic Interests in Foreign Countries* (Ann Arbor: University of Michigan), Centre for Research on Economic Development Dis. Paper No. 35.

Westfield M 1994, Australia in Asia, *Far Eastern Economic Review*, April 14, pp. 44–9.

Westphal L E, Rhee Y W and Pursell G 1979, Foreign influences on Korean industrial development, *Oxford Bulletin of Economics and Statistics*, Vol. 41, pp. 359–88.

Williams F 1989, One step ahead: world growth to slow, but East Asian will still set pace, *Far Eastern Economic Review*, September 14, p. 74.

Wilson D 1988, European attractions: East Asian manufacturers set up factories in Britain, *Far Eastern Economic Review*, August 25, pp. 60–1.

Wong Y C 1987, Women's work and the demand for children in Hong Kong, *Developing Economies*, Vol. 25 No. 2, June, pp. 188–99.

Woo J E 1990, *Race To The Swift: State And Finance In Korean Industrialization* (New York: Columbia University Press).

Woo J H 1991, Education and economic growth in Taiwan: a case of successful planning, *World Development*, Vol. 19 No. 8, August, pp. 1029–44.

World Bank 1981, *World Development Report 1981* (New York: Oxford University Press).

World Bank 1984, *World Development Report 1984* (New York: Oxford University Press).

World Bank 1986, *World Development Report 1986* (New York: Oxford University Press).

World Bank 1987, *World Development Report 1987* (New York: Oxford University Press).

World Bank 1988, *World Development Report 1988* (New York: Oxford University Press).

World Bank 1990, *World Tables* (Baltimore: Johns Hopkins University Press).

World Bank 1991, *World Development Report 1991* (New York: Oxford University Press).

World Bank 1993, *The East Asian Miracle: Economic Growth And Public Policy* (New York: Oxford University Press).

Woronoff J 1986, *Asia's 'Miracle' Economies* (New York: M E Sharpe).

Worthy F S 1991, You can't grow if you can't manage, *Fortune*, June 3, pp. 81–9.

Wright C L 1978, Income inequality and economic growth: examining the evidence, *Journal Of Developing Areas*, Vol. 13 No. 1, October, pp. 49–66.

Wu Y L 1983, Chinese entreprenuers in Southeast Asia, *American Economic Review*, Vol. 73 No. 2, May, pp. 112–7.

Wu Y L 1987, Models of development: a comparative study of economic growth in South Korea and Taiwan – a review, *Weltwirtschaftliches Archiv*, Vol. 123, pp. 377–80.

Yamazawa I, Hirata A and Yokota K 1991, Evolving patterns of comparative advantage in Pacific economies, in M Ariff (ed), *The Pacific Economy* (Sydney: Allen and Unwin).

Yamazawa I 1993, Trade policy issues in the Asian-Pacific region: the case of the textiles and clothing industry, *Asian-Pacific Economic Literature*, Vol. 7 No. 1, May, pp. 1–8.

Yanagihara T 1987, Pacific basin economic relations: Japan's new role? *The Developing Economies*, Vol. 27 No. 4, December, pp. 403–20.

Author Index

A

Alikhani   214, 215, 218, 219, 221, 246
Amsden   38, 43, 53, 67, 68, 69, 84, 99, 102, 106, 116, 122, 301
Anderson   297, 298
Appelbaum   43, 293
Athukorala   51, 95, 219, 220, 221

B

Balakrishnan   173, 200, 204, 206, 208, 223, 224
Balassa   2, 68, 94, 95, 126, 127, 166, 275, 301, 304, 205
Bello   210, 294, 297, 298
Bowring   75, 170, 176, 268

C

Castells   69, 110, 119
Cavanagh   130, 188, 218, 219
Chenery   27, 53
Clifford   40, 50, 149, 151, 152, 153, 173, 192, 198, 202, 203, 204, 205, 206, 244, 286, 289, 295
Cline   218
Cotton   129, 205, 293

F

Fosters   43
Fukuyama   125
H
Hagen   122
Hamilton   120, 216, 217, 229, 230
Handley   234, 235, 236, 238
Hanneman   231
Havvylyshyn   214, 215, 218, 219, 221, 246, 248, 305
Henderson   43, 293
Hill   44, 244
Hirata   148, 217, 236
Holloway   40, 81, 127, 152, 161, 177, 184, 185, 187, 189, 203, 204, 217, 223, 233, 273

I

Islam   3, 74, 110, 125, 161, 191, 192, 193, 257, 273

J

Johnson   43, 45

K

Kahn   123, 125, 274
Kelley
Kojima   272
Kranse   38, 106, 117, 175, 179
Krueger   38, 45, 117, 302, 304
Kuznets   72, 73, 74, 77, 78, 301

L

Lall   69, 102, 126, 176, 300
Lin   74, 99   Little   137
Lubeck   127, 231

M
McClelland   122, 125
Moore   204, 289, 297, 298

N

Nolan   43, 115, 117, 118, 125, 218

O

Ohkawa   19, 71, 111, 165, 166, 167, 171, 172, 173, 175, 176, 178, 180–182, 193, 200, 215
Oshima   115, 116, 118, 119, 122, 123, 126, 129, 176, 181

P

Page   100, 102, 103, 111, 219, 301, 307
Pang   43, 105, 293
Pernia   296

R

Rama   37
Randolph   73, 229
Ranis   45, 74, 218
Riedel   40, 43, 52, 97, 131, 213, 247, 284
Rosenfeld   210, 294, 297, 298

S

Schlossstein   213, 239
Scitorsky   61, 123

Shinshara   215, 216
Sicat   219
Sjahrir   242, 243
Stuart
Sung   99, 285, 287, 288

T

Tasker   236, 239
Todaro   2
Tong

V

Vatikiotis   204, 223, 224, 225, 230, 231, 244, 273

W

Whitlam   267

Subject Index

A

ability   45, 106, 111, 113, 219, 230, 231, 239, 307
access   9, 103, 187, 191, 192, 216, 292
acquisition   232
administration   46, 69, 116, 120, 133, 142, 190, 194, 222, 242, 243, 246
administrations   46, 121, 217, 305
adoption   45, 222, 304
advanced industrial countries (AICs)   1, 4, 20, 85, 96, 97, 237, 305
advantage   11, 46, 49, 50, 71, 100, 102, 103, 128, 129, 130, 131, 135, 142, 164, 188, 195, 196, 197, 198, 200, 201, 210, 213, 220, 228, 239, 254, 257, 265, 268, 270, 272, 275, 276, 280, 282, 302, 303, 307
adversaries   46, 75, 305
affluent   9, 292
aged   296
agencies   42, 219, 231, 232, 300, 305
agricultural   11, 17, 26, 54–58, 60, 61, 76, 115, 116, 209, 217, 222, 235, 236, 241, 243, 276, 284
agriculture   54–61, 65, 72, 80, 115, 116, 181, 224, 225, 232, 235, 241, 243, 297, 298, 299
AIDS   238
aircraft   244, 250, 254
Airlines   107
allocation   40, 44, 68, 242, 302, 303
Angola   240
anomaly   113
apparel   155, 220, 249, 250, 255
appliances   39, 96, 142, 226, 227, 229, 250, 252
appreciation of the Yen   157, 158, 160–162
arbitration   291
Argentina   2, 3, 306
ASEAN   158, 159, 200–202, 226, 237, 239, 269, 274, 276, 277, 278, 290
Asia   1, 3, 4–9, 11, 13, 14, 15, 40, 78, 82, 97, 117, 126, 128, 132, 142, 153, 154, 165, 167, 178, 180, 201–203, 208, 210, 211, 213, 217, 218, 222–224, 229, 231, 232, 238–240, 246, 247
Asian   3–9, 11–25, 37, 39–54, 58, 60, 61, 67–71, 74–78, 80–85, 93, 94, 96–100, 102–114, 117–132, 144, 146–149, 151–155, 158–160, 162, 164–169, 170,

171–174, 176, 178, 179, 184–194, 196–198, 200–211, 213, 214, 217, 219, 220, 222–225, 227, 229, 231–234, 237, 238–240, 243, 246, 247, 249, 255, 268, 291–294, 296, 299–308
assembly   96, 140, 141, 195, 196, 245
atmospheric   174, 175, 297, 298
attainment   81, 215, 224, 231, 241
Australia   8, 9, 15, 23, 108, 142, 208, 231, 248, 257, 259, 261–265, 267–278, 282, 283, 290, 299
Austria   296
authoritarian   120, 121, 123, 143, 229, 239, 245, 291, 303, 304, 305
authoritarianism   293
authority   70, 180, 235
autonomous   231, 232

B

Baht   233, 234, 238
balance, current account   161, 172, 193
balance of payments   61, 96, 109, 138, 166, 171, 203, 238, 251, 302, 303
balance of trade   165, 181, 250, 267, 308
Bangkok   235, 236, 238
banking   22, 101, 116, 141, 232, 242, 252
barrel   165, 171, 175, 176, 242
barriers   68, 71, 120, 138, 159, 165, 191, 203, 243, 256, 281, 282, 307
bases, military   66, 137
bid   160, 204, 205, 290, 298
boycotts   298
Brazil   3, 190, 206, 306
bribery   121, 230, 246
brothels   238
Brunei   269, 277
budget   22, 82, 83, 107, 161, 180, 302, 206
Bureau   258, 270, 271, 297
bureaucracy   230, 304
businessmen   10, 133, 184, 211, 232, 245, 273
Butterworth   228

C

Cameroon   233
Canada   83, 184, 187, 189, 191, 203, 204, 231, 252, 272, 273, 274, 275, 277, 278, 298
capital   11, 17, 21, 24, 26–31, 33–38, 40, 42–44, 49, 56, 57, 62, 64, 94, 96–98, 103, 105, 106, 109, 111, 148, 149, 151,

155, 158, 164, 178, 181, 182, 183, 195, 197, 205, 206, 207, 213, 223, 228, 229, 240, 244, 251, 256, 269, 292, 294, 301, 303, 306
capital inflow   17, 109, 303
cash   297
Catholic   122, 208
CBD   299
censorship   292
centres   17, 40, 118, 241
chaebol/s   13, 75, 103, 181, 182, 205, 212, 275, 284, 296, 300
chemical   181, 227, 299
chemicals   39, 146, 150, 152, 156, 158, 209, 250, 252, 254, 297
China   1, 6, 11, 16, 18, 19, 25, 40, 41, 59, 67, 75, 78, 97, 98, 107, 114, 117–119, 127, 128, 167, 183, 191, 199, 200, 203–205, 211, 247, 252, 258, 266, 267, 273, 276, 277, 278, 281, 283, 284, 285, 286, 287, 288, 292
Chinese   119, 121, 124, 125, 127, 128, 133, 135, 136, 230, 231, 232, 245, 274, 284, 285, 286
Christians   245
Chung   76, 296
circuits   146, 196, 209, 236, 237
cities   56, 104, 241, 297
citizens   292
civil service   110, 116, 133, 231, 232
classes   217
clothing   49, 95, 96, 98, 140, 141, 148, 155, 158, 160, 174, 175, 197, 209, 214, 215, 227, 236, 243, 244, 264, 264
COE   298, 299
Colombia   3, 214, 221
colonial   291, 300
colony   114, 115, 119, 120, 211
commerce   116, 122, 133, 137, 139, 153
commercialization point   58
commodity   150, 154, 159, 176, 220, 225, 226, 227, 236, 237, 249
communications   17, 115, 116, 129, 130, 133, 134, 239, 281, 304
Communism   16, 288
comparative advantage   11, 45, 49, 50, 71, 85, 94, 96, 99–103, 111, 142, 148, 164, 195, 196, 197, 200, 213, 220, 239, 265, 275, 276, 280, 302, 303, 307
comparative costs   94
competition   47, 135, 154, 156, 182, 209, 231, 253
complementarity   135, 144, 145, 146, 150, 152, 269, 275, 276, 278

composition   64, 218, 220, 243
condition   19, 48, 76, 100, 110, 154, 291, 293, 304, 307
conflicts   245, 246
Confucianism   121, 123–127
congestion   298, 299
conglomerates   245
constraints   231, 292, 304
construction   51, 141, 156, 176, 177, 179, 180, 199, 225, 243, 292
consumer   13, 22, 62, 67, 71, 98, 99, 144, 146, 150, 151, 152, 161, 162, 164, 173, 174, 197, 203, 205, 237, 268, 284, 288
controls   45, 61, 242, 301
conversion   126, 243, 288
copper   297
correction   100, 178, 294, 307
corruption   121, 211, 230, 231, 239, 246
coup d'état   12, 238
credit   44, 103, 108, 216, 217, 236, 301
crisis   19, 103, 107, 108, 165, 166, 171, 173, 175, 193, 210, 214, 237, 307
critique   73, 126, 219
crops   297
crude oil   165, 171, 172, 175, 242, 243
cultural factors   121, 123, 126, 128
cultural values   124, 125, 126, 127, 128
currency   39, 108, 161, 166, 173, 180, 192, 193, 211, 228
customs   242, 279
Cyprus   3, 214, 221

D

Daewoo   82, 203
debate   40, 44, 68, 280, 293
debt   25, 44, 181, 182, 216, 238, 252, 303
deficit/s   23, 151, 152, 161, 166, 171, 190, 238, 251, 255, 268, 303, 306
degrees   81, 83, 241
demonstrations   292
dentists   11
departure taxes   179
dependence   37, 38, 47, 60, 61, 149, 150, 155, 164, 172, 201, 202, 231, 249, 279
depreciation   301
deregulation   22, 239, 301
designs   197, 244
detention   292
deterioration   73, 172, 181, 185, 199, 299
devalue   161
developing   13–15, 99, 102, 105, 115, 144, 167, 191, 195, 197, 201, 202, 209, 210,

218, 220, 221, 230, 233, 248, 272, 274, 275, 283
development/s   14, 112, 128, 130, 132, 208, 216, 221, 222, 224, 229, 230, 232, 236, 238, 239, 241, 244, 247, 253, 257, 281, 282, 285
dictatorships   252, 292
dioxide   297, 298
disabled   296
disadvantaged   294, 296
discipline   304
disputes   291, 294
dissent   291, 293
distribution   4, 14, 64, 65, 72–79, 118, 141, 222, 229, 245, 294, 295
division of labour   144, 146–148, 154, 155, 156
doctors   10
domestic   11, 17, 18, 22, 23, 25, 26, 28–32, 37, 38, 46, 48, 61–66, 68, 71, 79, 82, 86, 101, 103, 107, 112, 135, 141, 156, 186, 201–204, 210, 216, 223, 231, 233, 235, 240
dominance   13, 135, 136, 182, 217, 228, 301, 303, 308
Draconian   292
dumping   192
duties   209, 235

E

earnings   22, 27, 33, 35, 36, 178, 225
economic hub   118
economic locations   117, 118
economies   1–4, 8, 11, 65, 67, 79, 96, 105, 120, 125, 127, 150, 152, 162, 165, 170, 172, 173, 184, 187, 189, 190, 195, 196, 210, 211, 221, 256, 268, 269, 272, 275, 282, 283, 290, 303
economists   25, 30, 33, 64, 65, 73, 93, 214
economy   7, 13, 19, 27, 28, 73, 93, 94, 99, 100, 101, 102, 109, 111, 113, 114, 117, 118, 122, 131, 133, 135, 137, 141, 142, 144, 150, 154, 156, 157, 164, 170, 171, 172, 180–186, 189, 199, 200, 204, 211, 214, 222, 223, 224, 225, 228, 229, 233, 234, 235, 236, 242, 243, 246, 247, 250, 262, 269, 274, 279, 282, 284, 289, 296, 296, 304, 307
educated   100, 116, 123, 134, 137, 143, 224, 292, 296, 306
education   81, 102, 106, 111, 115, 116, 122, 123, 133, 142, 198, 207, 216, 222, 224, 241, 282, 293, 306
educational   215, 224, 231, 234, 241, 247

Effective Rate of Protection (ERP)   64, 65, 86, 87, 88, 91, 267
efficiency   47, 156, 161, 282, 303, 305
efficient   23, 39, 40, 44, 46, 65, 68, 71, 109, 111, 115, 116, 120, 121, 133, 134, 137, 140, 153, 154, 161, 195, 196, 217, 222, 224, 230, 246, 304, 305
efficient administration   120
election   292
electrical   39, 50, 96, 142, 148, 152, 153, 170, 214, 215, 226, 227, 229, 249, 250, 252, 254, 255, 262, 263, 265, 288
electricity   175, 235, 241
electronic   13, 39, 96, 146, 150, 192, 196, 250, 259, 268, 288, 292
electronic products   39, 99, 150, 205, 237
electronics   13, 39, 98, 99, 129, 141, 146, 153, 158, 173, 174, 181, 192, 195, 197, 203, 205, 206, 220, 223, 237, 244, 252, 286, 288
elite   122, 231
empirical   15, 37, 74, 79, 106, 146, 213, 214, 219, 276
employed   51, 76, 141, 156, 193, 286, 300
employers   178
employment   3, 44, 51, 52, 58, 59, 61, 64, 65, 66, 71, 75, 77, 93, 103, 110, 140, 158, 170, 186, 198, 219, 224, 267, 281, 286, 293
engineering   83, 207, 235, 241
engineers   83, 207, 231, 306
engines   235
enrolment   52, 84, 224, 241, 306
enterprises   42, 43, 62, 68, 69, 70, 107, 110, 139, 232, 302, 304
entrepreneurs   122, 124, 125, 270, 286
entrepreneurship   122, 124, 125, 126
environment   41, 46, 69, 85, 109, 111, 120, 121, 123, 188, 216, 218, 219, 221, 246, 270, 297, 298, 299, 300, 304, 307
environmental   41, 79, 296, 297, 298, 299, 300
equality   76, 77
equipment   39, 98, 146, 148, 151, 175, 206, 215, 220, 227, 249, 250, 252, 255, 259, 262, 263, 264, 268
establishment   38, 40, 41, 68, 77, 113, 116, 132, 139, 187, 193, 205, 210, 217, 272, 273, 274, 279, 280, 290
ethnic   245
EU   15, 39, 39, 99, 149, 152, 157, 158, 160, 161, 162, 168, 170, 173, 182, 183, 184, 187, 188, 190, 191, 192, 194, 197, 201, 202, 203, 208, 209, 210, 226, 227, 237,

245, 248, 251, 254, 255–257, 266, 273, 274, 279, 281, 289, 290

European 8, 141, 191, 192, 202

examination 16, 33, 216

expansion 55, 61, 63, 66, 140, 181, 187, 194, 217, 218, 223, 233

expansionary 303

expatriate 10

expenditure 5, 23, 43, 107, 206, 238, 296, 305

expenditures 82, 83, 101, 118, 166, 176, 206, 216, 224, 296, 305

export 3, 5, 6–12, 15, 17, 26, 27, 28, 35, 37, 44, 46, 47, 48, 49, 50, 51, 54, 61, 66, 69, 80, 71, 96–98, 100, 102, 103–105, 106, 110, 111, 132, 139, 140, 142, 145, 146, 147, 149, 150–152, 156–158, 160–162, 164, 165, 168–170, 172, 175, 176, 182, 184, 185, 188, 191, 193, 198, 200, 201, 202, 207, 209, 210, 214, 216, 219, 220, 221, 223, 225, 226, 227, 236, 244, 249, 250, 254, 255, 259, 266, 268, 276, 285, 288, 290, 297, 302, 303, 304, 307

export-orientation 46, 245, 304, 307

export-oriented 3, 4, 5, 8–10, 11, 14, 15, 16, 100–105, 108, 125, 126, 144, 164, 165, 166, 183, 188, 193, 216, 219, 221, 222, 232, 236, 239, 247, 265, 294, 300, 301, 303, 307, 308

exports 3–6, 27–29, 44, 47–52, 54, 65, 68, 71, 84, 91, 94, 96–99, 103–105, 108, 109, 130, 140, 142, 144–151, 153, 157, 158, 160, 161, 163, 164, 166, 168, 170, 172, 173, 175, 176, 181, 182, 183, 184–186, 188, 190, 191, 193, 194, 196, 199, 201–203, 206, 209, 214–216, 219–223, 225–228, 236, 237, 239, 240, 242–246, 265, 268, 269, 273, 275, 276, 279, 284, 285, 287, 288, 290, 301, 302, 303, 304, 307

external shocks 71, 165, 302

F

fabrics 148, 154, 155, 243, 244

facilities 6, 11, 17, 79, 98, 116, 139, 158, 191, 198, 204, 210, 241, 257, 266, 281, 289

factories 165, 192, 203, 286, 297

factor/s 14, 21, 76, 93, 102, 110, 112, 114, 117, 118, 120, 121, 122, 123, 126, 128, 132, 137, 142, 143, 164, 170, 176, 179, 180, 185, 186, 192, 202, 252, 253, 256, 288, 289, 302, 304, 306

Far Eastern Economic Review 20, 59, 100,

106, 107, 108, 118, 151, 159, 167, 177, 188, 203, 247, 287

farmers 296

farming 58, 70, 115, 296

fees 33, 35, 81, 298

fertile 238

fertilizers 71, 244, 288, 297

fibre 154, 155, 156, 160, 267

finance/s 21, 22, 23, 25, 26, 29, 30, 31, 37, 38, 40, 44, 48, 51, 58, 70, 101, 103, 110, 116, 133, 134, 137, 141, 164, 168, 181, 182, 186, 188, 216, 219, 225, 232, 236, 252, 272, 303

financial 11, 13, 22, 23, 33, 39, 40–42, 44, 54, 55, 59, 62, 69, 75, 78, 81, 85, 101, 102, 108, 113, 116, 118, 129, 133, 139, 140, 142, 157, 161, 163, 182, 184, 189, 200, 205, 216, 219, 242, 243, 252, 253, 274, 281, 285, 285, 286, 294

financial markets 22, 186, 301

firms 13, 33, 35, 36, 38, 44, 47, 65, 68, 70, 71, 77, 103, 104, 105, 106, 107, 110, 112, 118, 121, 123, 125, 128, 133, 139, 140, 149, 153, 174, 178, 181–183, 185, 186, 197–199, 200, 205, 206, 208, 211, 256, 257, 272, 282, 285, 286, 287, 294, 297, 301, 302

first tier 93, 99

fish 242, 260, 261, 297

fluctuations 24, 65, 107, 183

foods 134, 237, 242

footwear 49, 50, 96, 140, 141, 169, 192, 227, 237, 240, 244, 249, 254, 264, 265, 288

foreign investment 11, 14, 25, 33, 34, 35–39, 96–98, 105, 106, 108, 109, 121, 129, 137, 139, 140, 144, 152, 153, 154, 155, 156, 158, 159, 161, 162, 198, 202, 203, 205, 218, 227, 228, 233, 234, 236, 240, 251, 252, 256, 257, 269, 270, 271, 272, 284, 286, 288, 289, 300, 303, 308

foreigners 11, 33, 34, 140, 270

formation 38, 98, 202, 240, 246, 280, 291

Formosa 115, 117, 298

foundations 114, 115, 133, 218

freedoms 291, 292, 293

fuels 276

fundamentalism 245

G

gang of four 1

Gas 104

GDP 2, 3, 4, 5, 10, 11, 19, 20–23, 25, 37, 38, 39, 40, 43, 47, 48, 58, 59, 60, 73, 118, 140, 141, 166, 167, 172, 176, 179, 181,

184–186, 187, 188–190, 199, 211, 217, 221, 223, 225, 233, 238, 240, 242, 243, 253, 284, 285, 303

geographical   118, 137, 139, 220, 248, 266, 278, 285, 287

geographical factors   71, 117

Germany   157, 170, 187, 204, 254, 284, 289, 296

Gini   72, 73, 74, 75, 245, 294

global   112, 139, 154, 219

GNP   8, 9, 10, 17, 18, 20, 101, 108, 134, 166, 170, 171, 182, 206, 233, 235, 239, 240, 274, 275, 303, 306

goals   42, 67, 75, 78, 110, 123, 130, 293, 305

Goh Chok Tong   292

goods   5, 6, 26, 47, 48, 51, 61, 62, 64, 67, 68, 71, 92, 94, 95, 96, 97, 98, 103, 106, 129, 130, 132, 133, 138, 139, 140, 142, 144, 146, 148, 149, 150, 151, 152, 153, 157, 158, 160, 161, 162, 164, 165, 179, 180, 181, 183, 197, 199, 206, 213, 214, 215, 218, 220, 222, 223, 225, 226, 227, 236, 237, 243, 245, 246, 249, 250, 254, 256, 257, 259, 260, 265, 268, 270, 275, 276, 284, 288, 289, 302, 308

government   5, 18, 22–24, 40, 41, 42, 43, 44, 45, 46, 55, 62, 66, 67, 68, 69, 70, 75, 82, 83, 85, 96, 101–104, 107–109, 110, 11, 112, 116, 119, 120, 123, 127, 138, 140, 141, 142, 151, 157, 161, 166, 178, 181, 182, 185, 191–193, 199, 200, 205, 207, 208, 211, 217, 222, 223, 225, 228–232, 235, 238, 239, 242, 243, 245, 246, 252, 267, 269, 273, 283, 292, 293, 294, 296, 297, 298, 299, 300, 302, 303, 304, 305, 307

governments   41, 42, 43, 46, 47, 68, 69, 70, 74, 75, 69, 82, 107, 110, 111, 113, 120, 121, 123, 128, 130, 217, 253, 273, 291, 292, 293, 296, 301, 302, 303, 304, 305

grade   246

graduates   83, 207, 234, 235

Greece   3, 19, 37

Greenhouse   298

Group of five   157

growth triangles   204

Gulf war   184, 221

H

hardworking   123

harmony   123, 230

health   11, 79, 80, 115, 133, 185

heating   298

heavy industry   13, 116, 125, 146, 181, 225, 244, 265, 296, 298, 299, 304, 307

hectare   224, 241, 296

heterogeneity   240

hinterland   17, 66, 119, 132, 137

historial   222, 269, 279, 285

historical factors   114, 126

HIV   238

Hong Kong   17, 18, 19, 20, 22, 24, 37–39, 40, 42, 43, 44, 47–50, 52, 54, 58, 59–61, 67–69, 70, 74, 75, 76, 78, 80, 82, 83–85, 96, 97, 99, 105–107, 114, 116–120, 123–125, 127, 129, 130, 141, 143, 148, 153, 154, 159, 160, 166, 167, 168, 172, 173, 175, 177, 178, 184–186, 189, 190, 193–195, 199–201, 204, 205, 207, 208–211, 228, 233, 234, 238, 240, 241, 243, 247, 249–252, 254–257, 259, 260, 262, 263, 265, 266, 267, 269, 270, 271, 272, 273, 274, 278, 281, 283–289, 291, 292, 294, 296, 298, 299

horizontal   28, 31, 35, 54, 56, 146, 147

hospital beds   11

households   142, 173, 224

housing   9, 42, 69, 107, 178, 179, 296

hub   117, 118

hypothesis   33, 72, 74, 77, 94, 95, 99, 100, 228

I

imbalances   231

implementation   46, 111, 126, 142, 229, 239, 291, 305, 307

import   11, 18, 26–30, 45, 47, 48, 50, 51, 52, 61–68, 71, 91, 92, 101, 106, 111, 117, 121, 138, 141, 145, 147, 148, 149, 151, 152, 155, 156, 158, 162, 165, 166, 172, 176, 181, 190, 192, 207, 212, 249, 254, 256, 266, 267

imported   19, 28, 62, 71, 85, 103, 104, 132, 164, 179, 208

importer   63, 99, 133, 155

imports   5, 26, 27, 28, 29, 30, 48, 50, 61–64, 66–68, 73, 82, 85–91, 101–103, 121, 138, 145, 147–150, 151, 153, 155, 157, 160, 161, 172, 188, 189, 190, 191, 192, 199, 206, 209, 249, 250, 254, 255, 258, 260, 261, 262–267, 268, 269, 275, 276, 280, 281, 285, 287, 288, 302, 308

improvement   73, 75, 78, 80, 81, 253, 293

incentive   72, 119, 304

incentives   55, 62, 68, 69, 81, 103, 139, 140, 178, 217, 243, 302, 304

incomes   2, 7, 8, 9, 22, 23, 24, 26, 61, 71, 76,
    84, 103, 141, 188, 198, 202, 224, 229,
    245–296
increases   9, 22, 27, 31, 43, 70, 101, 105, 178,
    182, 185, 197, 198, 199, 293
independence   120, 292
index   3, 146, 147, 148, 275, 276, 278, 292,
    298
India   3, 6, 107, 190, 191, 230, 234
indices   63, 142, 224
indigenous   133, 136, 231
individuals   246
Indonesia   3, 4, 19, 43, 50, 78, 83, 97, 134,
    136, 137, 154, 159, 179, 180, 200, 202,
    204, 205, 208, 213, 214, 217, 218, 233,
    234, 238, 239–247, 256, 257, 269, 275,
    277, 287
Indonesian   11, 18, 136, 241, 242, 243, 246
industrialists   125, 231
industrialization   3, 5, 13, 15, 16, 18, 39, 61,
    66, 67, 70, 93, 98, 101, 111, 102, 116,
    122, 125, 126, 127, 128, 130, 131, 138,
    142, 164, 165, 181, 183, 188, 217, 219,
    221, 222, 228, 229, 232, 236, 247, 275,
    294, 296, 300, 303, 307, 308
industrialized   2, 4, 60, 61, 189, 209, 227, 260,
    268, 298
industries   11, 44, 46, 51, 55, 65, 67, 68, 69,
    70, 71, 75, 78, 85, 88, 100, 102, 103,
    105, 112, 114, 151, 166, 175, 179, 181,
    182, 197, 199, 216, 231, 234, 239, 244,
    245, 247, 270, 288, 300, 301, 305
inefficiency   13, 231
inequality   4, 72, 73, 75, 76, 78, 79, 229,
    294
infection   238
inflation   24, 44, 85, 166, 182, 185, 187, 198,
    199, 201, 211, 222, 229, 238, 252, 253,
    302, 303
inflows   17, 21, 30, 31, 33, 37, 38, 218, 227,
    233
infrastructural   31, 241, 286
infrastructure   17, 21, 41, 69, 79, 85, 100, 104,
    111, 112, 114, 115, 116, 117, 133, 134,
    137, 139, 142, 176, 211, 216, 222, 223,
    224, 235, 239, 240, 241, 247, 304
innovation   202, 305
inputs   58, 62, 68, 71, 72, 86, 103, 104, 160,
    162, 164, 194, 197, 206, 221, 299, 301,
    306
instability   44, 238, 239
institutionalist   68
institutionalization   231

institutions   39, 40, 44, 69, 83, 127, 128, 189,
    216, 231, 232
integrated circuits   146, 209, 236, 237
integration   247, 278, 279, 280, 285
intelligence   104, 243, 244
interaction   68, 124
interests   110, 114, 117, 120, 230, 281, 283
intermediation   39
internal   18, 41, 112, 119, 133, 136, 137, 170,
    176, 185, 186, 191, 210, 216, 221, 256,
    285, 292, 301
internationally   112, 156, 206, 269, 301, 302
intervention   41, 44, 45, 46, 49, 69, 70, 85,
    110, 111, 142, 300, 305
intra-firm trade   153
intra-industry trade   150
invasion   119
invest   55, 191, 257, 297
investigation   192, 220
investment   5, 11, 13, 14, 17, 21–25, 26, 27,
    29, 30, 33, 34, 35, 36, 37, 38, 39, 43, 49,
    52, 56, 58, 68, 73, 77, 79, 84, 96, 97, 98,
    101, 102, 105, 106, 108, 109, 110, 113,
    118, 144, 152, 153, 154, 155, 156, 158,
    159, 161, 162, 166, 179, 181, 183, 191,
    196, 198, 201–203, 205, 211, 215, 216,
    218, 219, 222, 223, 224, 227, 228, 231,
    233, 234, 236, 240, 248, 251, 252, 254,
    256, 257, 269, 270, 271, 272, 282, 284,
    285, 286, 287, 288, 289, 290, 297, 300,
    303, 308
investor   228, 233, 269
investors   33, 109, 140, 224, 231, 271, 305
Iran   241, 245
iron and steel   169, 215, 259, 261
Islamic   245
islands   11, 204, 240, 245
ITPN   244

J

J curve   161
Japan   1, 4, 5, 6, 9, 10, 14, 15, 17, 19, 20, 21,
    37, 38, 39, 50, 60, 69, 78, 94, 96, 98, 99,
    114, 115, 117, 118, 119, 120, 125, 127,
    130, 142, 144, 145, 146, 147, 148, 149,
    150–152, 153–156, 158–163, 170, 175,
    188, 189–191, 193, 194, 197, 201, 202,
    209, 218, 226, 227, 233, 234, 237, 240,
    243, 245, 248, 251, 256, 258, 259,
    266–272, 274, 275–280, 285, 287, 290,
    297
Japanese   10, 13, 14, 17, 69, 76, 99, 106, 114,
    115–118, 125, 144, 145, 147–150,
    151–160, 161, 162, 185, 186, 187, 189,

192, 228, 233, 258, 261, 272, 273, 285, 290
Java   241, 245
jobs   51, 70, 76, 138, 170, 183, 246
Johor   204, 228
Jordan   214, 221

K

Kalimantan   241
knowledge-intensive   94, 207
Korea   2, 3, 4, 5, 6, 7, 8, 11–13, 17–20, 24, 25, 37, 38, 39, 40, 43, 47, 48–50, 53, 54, 59, 66, 67, 69, 70, 74, 75, 76, 77, 78, 80, 82, 83, 96, 97, 98, 99, 101–103, 105, 106–110, 113–115, 117–120, 121–125, 127, 146, 148, 149, 150, 152, 153, 154–156, 158, 160, 166–168, 172, 176, 178, 181, 182, 183, 184, 185, 189, 190, 191–193, 194, 198, 201, 202–207, 209, 210, 223, 226, 229, 234, 235, 237, 240, 243, 244, 249–256, 258, 260–266, 268, 269, 270, 272, 277, 280, 282, 288, 289, 291, 292, 294, 295, 296, 297, 298, 299, 300, 302, 303, 306
Korean   5, 7, 10, 11, 38, 44, 45, 69, 70, 83, 103, 104, 106, 116, 119, 151–153, 156, 160, 173, 178, 182, 192, 194, 201, 203, 205, 256, 288, 300, 303, 307
Kuala Lumpur   224, 228
Kuro   198

L

labour   6, 37, 41, 42, 44, 48, 49, 50, 51, 52–54, 55–58, 64, 65, 67, 68, 71, 72, 75, 76, 78, 79, 81, 84, 86, 94–96, 100, 104, 111, 112, 122, 123, 129, 130, 138, 139–141, 142, 144, 146–148, 155, 156. 158, 162, 164, 165, 178, 185, 194, 195, 196, 197, 198, 199, 200, 202, 204, 25, 205, 207, 208, 210, 213, 214, 215, 217, 218, 220, 222, 223, 224, 228, 229, 231, 234, 237, 239, 240, 243, 244, 246, 253, 257, 265, 267, 269, 282, 283, 285, 286, 288, 289, 293, 294, 301 302, 303
labour markets   11, 15, 97, 170, 178, 186, 198, 294
ladder   94, 95, 96, 97, 99, 100, 142, 202, 205, 206, 207, 213, 215, 228, 288
Lampung   241
Lanka   23, 73, 214, 221, 238
Laos   239
laws   105, 140, 292, 293

LDC   132, 133, 134, 142, 143, 246
LDCs   1, 20, 301, 304, 305, 306
leader   46, 98, 135, 136, 246
leadership   138, 231, 293
Lee Kuan Yew   292
Lesotho   240
less developed country   25, 27, 30, 34, 132, 134, 219, 232, 239
levels   18, 19, 37, 49, 64, 65, 73, 75, 81, 94, 108, 111, 125, 130, 182, 198, 202, 207, 216, 222, 225, 232, 234, 239, 247, 297, 281, 282, 289, 292, 293, 296, 297, 301, 302
liberal   292
licences   64, 212
life expectancy   78
link   81, 122, 123, 124, 125, 133
literacy   76, 82, 84, 224, 234, 241
livelihood   296
loans   25, 103, 105, 108, 139, 177, 287, 303
lobby   270, 298
loss   138, 158, 173, 199, 200, 231, 266
loyalty   123, 124
luck   128, 131

M

machinery   39, 49, 50, 97, 98, 106, 117, 149–151, 152, 153, 158, 181, 209, 212, 214, 215, 220, 227, 237, 249, 250, 254, 255, 259, 260, 262, 263, 264, 265, 276
macroeconomic   23, 24, 44, 85, 111, 302, 305, 306
macroeconomic stability   23, 24, 106, 109, 302
mainstream   14, 25, 31, 113, 142
mainstream view   25, 27, 41, 93, 100, 111, 112, 131, 142, 213, 215
maize   236
Malay   119, 230, 232
Malays   230, 231, 232
Malaysia   3, 18, 19, 43, 61, 66, 78, 97–99, 119, 136, 137, 138, 139, 154, 159, 179, 180, 200, 202, 204, 208, 213, 214, 216–233, 238–240, 243, 244, 245, 246, 256, 257, 269, 270 275, 277, 280, 287, 304
Malaysian   11, 224, 225, 229, 230, 231, 232, 273
Malta   3
management   23, 33, 35, 41, 42, 69, 85, 97, 105, 109, 111, 113, 123, 125, 139, 182, 207, 282, 302

managers 231
manning 293
manufacture 13, 32, 41, 45, 53, 58, 59, 78, 90–92, 96, 129, 152, 153, 155, 160, 164, 174, 183, 195, 196, 197, 213, 244, 245
manufactured 3 5, 6, 47, 48, 49, 50, 51, 54, 71, 84, 88–90, 92, 96, 103, 104, 105, 130, 132, 133, 135, 138, 140, 142, 144, 148, 151, 152, 153, 156, 157, 158, 160, 164, 165, 183, 195, 199, 206, 213, 214, 215, 216, 218, 220, 221, 222, 223, 225, 226, 227, 236, 237, 239, 240, 242, 243, 245, 246, 249, 253, 254, 256, 259, 260, 262, 265, 268, 270, 275, 276, 289, 302, 308
manufacturers 78, 88, 129, 154, 165, 174, 205, 206, 244, 250, 298
manufacturing sector 2, 11, 18, 38, 51, 52, 54, 60, 64, 84, 123, 134, 140, 153, 156, 170, 198–200, 222, 225, 235, 238, 251, 256, 286, 294
marginal 28, 30, 54, 56, 57, 282, 293
marine 297
market-oriented 67, 68, 69, 70, 85, 100, 102, 121, 126, 296, 298
markets 11, 13, 15, 16, 22, 23, 27, 40, 41, 44, 46, 67, 68, 69, 71, 79, 95, 97, 100, 102, 104, 106, 111, 112, 130, 134, 138, 142, 149, 160, 162, 165, 170, 173, 175, 181, 182, 185, 196, 188, 190, 192, 193, 195–198, 201–203, 215, 216, 218, 219, 222, 225, 226, 227, 248, 249, 250, 259, 260, 283, 287, 289, 290, 294, 301, 305, 307, 308
martial 294
massacre 190, 192
materials 17, 115, 117, 132, 135, 148, 245, 268, 275
Mauritania 240
measures 3, 31, 103, 161, 166, 201, 218, 255, 275, 299
meat 242, 260, 261
mechanism 41, 45, 98, 113, 242
media 292
medium 27, 31, 77, 133, 183, 205, 211, 292
merit 125, 296
metal 146, 148, 158, 214, 227, 252, 255, 264, 265
metals 181, 259, 260, 261, 297
metric 298
microprocessor 173, 219
microwave ovens 203
migrants 231
militant 110, 229, 270

military aid 18, 38, 71, 117
military dictatorships 110, 120, 252, 292
milk 242
milling 245
mineral 27, 95, 150, 214, 227, 276
mining 95, 225, 243, 272
minister 136, 186, 232, 273, 292
ministry 48, 53, 168, 186, 198, 225, 251
miniaturization 129
minority 135, 140, 245
model 25, 27, 28, 29, 54, 55, 60, 61, 67, 68, 69, 72, 116, 196, 230, 253, 281, 300
monetary 7, 70, 106, 109, 113, 142, 157, 163, 166, 169, 174, 180, 187, 219, 249, 253, 277, 303
monopoly 245
Morocco 8, 214
motor 145, 158, 196, 265, 298, 299
motor vehicles 6, 95, 98, 153, 157, 298, 299
motorcycles 297
MRT 45, 199
multinational companies 129, 197, 198
Muslims 245

N

native 115, 245
NEC 215, 220
neo-classical 67, 298
Nepal 234
nepotism 230
network/s 111, 124, 133, 154, 228, 234, 241
New Exporting Countries 97, 214
New Industrializing Economies 1
news 292
NIC 2, 3, 4, 132, 133, 141, 142, 143, 215, 221, 222, 231, 232, 238, 239, 247, 249, 257, 289, 290, 305
Nicaragua 232
NICs 1–5, 7, 8, 9, 11, 12, 13, 14–16, 17, 25–35, 37–39, 42–45, 47–53, 57–69, 71–79, 85–91, 93, 94, 96, 100, 102–114, 117–132, 133–137, 139–149, 151–155, 158, 160, 162–168, 170–174, 178, 179, 184–186, 187–190, 191–198, 200–207, 209–211, 213–222, 224, 227, 229–234, 237–249, 243, 246, 247, 248–262, 265–271, 274–280, 282–285, 287–290, 291–294, 296, 300–308
Nigeria 233
Nominal Rate of Protection (NRP) 64, 85–91

O

OELD 2, 20, 95, 101, 184, 186, 187, 201, 203, 206, 210, 219, 220, 228, 245, 281

offices   104, 129, 139, 151, 269, 296
offshore   129, 154, 158, 201, 203, 244, 298
oil   19, 71, 111, 165, 166, 167, 171, 172, 173, 175, 176, 178, 180, 182, 193, 200, 214, 223, 226, 229, 237, 242, 243, 259, 262, 265, 304, 307
OPEC   165, 171, 172, 175, 242
opportunities   33, 34, 52, 100, 112, 128, 129, 130, 131, 210, 213, 257, 272, 282, 288, 306
opposition   292
optimistic   214, 218, 221, 246
organizations   139, 296
origin   27, 62, 124, 191, 240, 254
outbreak   119, 130, 187, 230
outcome   14, 62, 93, 94, 100, 111, 122, 183, 240
outflow   33, 34, 36, 129, 161, 203, 231, 301
output   24, 27–29, 30, 31, 32, 35, 43, 53, 56, 57, 116, 140, 175, 186, 197, 219, 267, 284, 303, 306
outputs   301
overvalued   301
ownership   41, 42, 44, 69, 70, 103, 106, 270, 299
oyster   297

P

Pacific community   274–275
paddy   224
Pakistan   71, 84, 107, 118
palm   223, 226
parents   235
parliament   232
Park   12, 41, 67, 104, 181, 291
parliament   232
partner   108, 145, 147, 151, 227, 285, 289
partners   15, 46, 75, 82, 85, 87, 92, 123, 137, 144, 148, 155, 180, 194, 232, 248, 278, 281, 305, 208
patronage   231
pattern of trade   149, 162, 278
payments   61, 96, 109, 138, 165, 166, 171, 203, 238, 251, 302, 303
peak   64, 66, 105, 153, 175, 182, 201, 233, 235, 287
penalties   45, 304
Penang   131, 204, 228
per capita   2–4, 7–10, 12, 17–20, 22, 37, 72, 73, 85, 103, 134, 141, 142, 193, 202, 223, 224, 233, 239, 240, 284, 296, 298
permit   220
perspective   48, 219, 230
Peru   3, 214, 221

pessimistic   158, 193, 194, 210, 218, 219, 221
pesticides   297
petrochemicals   153, 181
petroleum   39, 130, 151, 164, 175, 223, 226, 227, 252, 259, 262, 263, 265
Philippines   3, 25, 63, 64, 97, 98, 107, 134, 179, 207, 208, 214, 217, 220, 221, 233, 269, 277, 281
photographic   220, 259
plantation   115, 132, 224
plants   65, 129, 165, 192, 203, 228, 298
plastic   154, 156, 199
Plaza Agreement   157, 161, 173
plywood   244
policies   14, 22, 44, 45, 61, 93, 100, 102, 105, 106, 109, 111–113, 120, 125, 126–128, 131, 142, 144, 166, 183, 187, 191, 193, 217, 219, 229, 231, 232, 239, 253, 283, 291, 298, 299, 300, 301, 303, 304, 305, 306, 307
political factors   118
politicians   211
politics   291
pollution   41, 297, 298, 299
polyester staple   155, 156
populated   124, 241
population paradox   79
populations   12, 74, 102, 241
ports   135, 235
Portugal   2, 3, 8, 19, 84, 142, 203
poverty   76, 79, 127, 224, 245, 295, 296
powers   114, 117, 119, 305
pressures   109, 165, 166, 178, 188, 194, 200, 203, 239, 305
prices   24, 27, 45, 58, 65, 68, 86–88, 91, 100, 101–104, 109, 111, 149, 156, 160, 161, 164, 165, 166, 171, 175, 176, 182, 183, 216, 225, 229, 301, 302, 305
primary   52, 54, 82, 94, 96, 220, 223, 224, 225, 237, 241, 306
privatization   239
privatizing   242
product   39, 42, 44, 50, 54, 55, 56, 57, 62, 63, 65, 67, 85, 86, 88, 94, 96, 98, 99, 102, 106, 112, 129, 135, 144–147, 154, 190, 192, 195–198, 220, 223, 225, 255, 275, 276
product range   160
productivity   25, 31, 35, 40, 47, 49, 52, 53, 54, 58, 59, 72, 79, 81, 96, 103, 105, 111, 130, 156, 158, 178, 182, 195, 197, 199, 200, 286, 294, 295, 304
profit   25, 33, 34, 35, 36, 57, 62, 103, 107, 158

profit margins 160, 162
profitability 107, 158, 182
programme 66, 107, 292
prohibition 209, 291, 292
projects 23, 31, 43, 108, 176, 199, 205, 211, 286, 287, 288, 297, 298
promotion 69, 104, 109, 140, 142, 166, 217, 236
prosperity 18, 110, 127, 290, 291, 292, 293, 295, 296, 299
protection 45, 64, 65, 67, 70, 85, 88, 120, 135, 181, 192, 210, 225, 245, 247, 267, 269, 272, 282, 297
protectionism 185, 188, 190, 192, 202, 203, 205, 210, 219, 248, 273, 280, 289
provinces 1, 84, 241, 247, 283, 284, 287
provision 9, 15, 22, 41, 68, 103, 110, 111, 190, 209, 280, 296
provisions 133, 209, 210
prudent 23, 85, 109, 113, 302
publications 292
purchase 103, 151, 206, 292, 298
purchasing 10, 299
puritan 179

R

racial 137, 230, 239
radical 14, 30, 33, 37, 93, 142
radical view 30, 37, 113, 131, 142
rail 11, 133, 299
rank 6
ranking 6, 82, 282, 292
ranks 4, 93, 136, 214, 215, 216, 217, 218, 232, 274
rates 4, 5, 8, 9, 19–24, 25, 27, 37, 40, 43, 48, 49, 52, 59, 64, 65, 70, 71, 76, 79, 80, 85, 89, 91, 96, 96, 97, 101, 103, 105, 106–110, 114, 141, 142, 161, 164, 165, 167, 168, 169, 170, 176, 178, 179, 188–190, 192, 194, 198, 199, 201–203, 209–212, 213, 215–219, 221–222, 224, 228, 229, 231, 233, 237, 238, 240, 241, 245, 258, 270, 272, 286, 301, 302, 303, 304, 306
ratio 3, 5, 28, 30, 31, 32, 35, 38, 39, 40, 43, 47, 52, 61, 72, 74, 75, 85, 101, 102, 108, 141, 145, 181, 192, 225, 238, 240, 245
rationale 25, 138, 146, 155, 156, 274, 295, 303
ratios 5, 17, 21, 22, 23, 25, 26, 38, 39, 40, 76, 83, 144, 155, 158, 182, 222, 223, 238, 240, 305
recession 15, 19, 23, 51, 71, 107, 159, 164, 166, 167, 170, 174, 176, 179, 180, 181, 184, 185, 186, 187, 188, 189, 190, 192, 210, 219, 223, 228, 229, 233, 238, 262, 294, 299, 307
recipient 105, 218, 228, 233
reductions 58, 64, 176, 180, 209, 210, 253, 280, 281
refineries 175
reform 76, 115, 211, 242
reforms 14, 69, 101, 102, 239, 240, 242, 244, 253
region 9, 25, 117, 118, 119, 133, 202, 208, 233, 246, 248, 257, 274, 275, 276, 278, 279, 281, 282, 285, 287, 289, 290
regional 15, 134, 154, 192, 193, 202, 208, 211, 245, 272, 273, 274, 278, 279, 280, 290
regional administrative centre 118
regions 154, 236
registration 298
regulation
regulations 46, 270
relations 229, 248, 282, 291, 294
relationship 15, 28, 37, 40, 46, 72, 73, 74, 123, 160, 162, 231, 232, 245, 271, 285, 287
relationships 123, 232, 284, 305
relative prices 45, 67, 100, 161, 301, 302, 305
reliance 44, 123, 302
replacement 62, 67, 181, 292
represent 300
repression 101, 294
resistance 65
resource 12, 68, 95, 148, 242, 244, 275, 303
resource endowments 275
resources 13, 29, 31, 44, 65, 66, 79, 82, 100, 102, 113, 118, 137, 301, 302, 305, 306, 307
restructuring 158, 161, 205, 210, 282
retirement 46, 178, 292
revalue 194
revenue 22, 62, 172, 225, 238
revenues 172, 238
revolution 129, 219
rice 10, 224, 236, 241, 242
rights 123, 245
risks 15, 70, 129, 164, 165, 306, 307
risks of export-orientation 307
rivers 297
roads 223, 235, 241, 299
role 5, 14, 25, 29, 39, 41–43, 44, 45, 46, 68, 69, 102, 104, 105, 110, 123, 152, 156,

232, 238, 246, 253, 280, 282, 283, 300, 304, 305
role of government 41, 45, 46, 68, 69, 109, 110, 112, 304, 305
rubber 50, 96, 132, 223, 224, 226, 227, 236
rule 115, 120, 134, 192, 291
rulers 232
rural 76, 224, 229, 241, 245, 295

S

salary 178, 237
Samsung 182, 203
satellite 129, 292
saving 19, 22, 67, 109, 240, 303
savings 3, 17, 21, 22, 23, 24–26, 27, 28, 30, 31, 32, 37, 38, 39, 52, 54, 65, 80, 101, 102, 215, 216, 219, 222, 223, 233, 240, 301, 303
scale 12, 13, 31, 44, 62, 65, 67, 75, 77, 79, 176, 181, 183, 195, 205, 256, 286, 288, 292, 298, 299, 300, 303
schemes 103, 217, 279
school enrolment 241
schooling 23, 234
scientists 83, 84, 306
secondary 52, 76, 82, 83, 84, 224, 234, 241, 247, 306
sectional 120, 230, 283
sector 11, 23, 38, 43, 46, 49, 51, 52, 54, 56, 57, 58–60, 64, 69, 70, 71, 75, 76, 83, 84, 97, 102, 103, 105, 108, 109, 115, 116, 123, 135, 140, 146, 153, 156, 170, 176, 177, 180, 182, 183, 198–200, 217, 222, 224, 225, 232, 235, 237, 238, 242, 251, 256, 286, 294, 297, 299, 304, 305
sectors 2, 11, 18, 40, 42, 51, 54, 58, 61, 70, 93, 105, 140, 158, 177, 181, 182, 209, 224, 243, 272, 296, 297, 307
security 41, 108, 396, 305
semi-conductor 173, 220, 226
servants 46, 110, 246
sewage 297
SGS 243
shellfish 297
shoes 6, 50, 197, 244, 289
shopping 179, 296
shortages 27, 51, 58, 59, 72, 75, 84, 141, 142, 178, 198, 199, 204, 205, 207, 224, 231, 234, 239, 241, 283, 293, 294, 298
shortfall 30, 235
Singapore 2–6, 8, 9, 10, 11, 17, 18–20, 22, 25, 37–40, 42, 43–47, 48–54, 59, 60, 61, 66, 70, 74, 75, 76, 78, 80, 81, 82, 83, 85,

96, 98, 102–108, 110, 111, 114, 116, 117, 118, 119, 120, 121, 123, 124, 125, 127–130, 132–143, 145, 146, 147, 148, 151, 153, 156, 159, 166, 167, 168, 170, 171, 172, 173–175, 177, 178, 179, 180, 181, 184, 185, 186, 189–191, 192–194, 200, 201, 204–208, 211, 217, 218, 224, 226, 227, 228, 229, 230, 233, 234, 237, 240, 241, 249–253, 255–260, 262, 263, 265–270, 277, 281, 282, 284, 287, 291–294, 296, 298, 299, 300, 304, 307
skill-intensive 50, 78, 84, 94, 202, 207
skilled 16, 67, 84, 94, 112, 197, 208, 231, 239, 257, 289, 300, 306
slowdown 172, 175, 177, 185, 186, 187, 189, 199, 240, 308
societies 125, 126, 293, 296
sociological 122
Southeast Asia 97, 128, 132, 136, 154, 180, 201, 203, 204, 218, 223, 229, 239, 269
specialization 94, 145, 155
specialization ratio 145, 146, 155
Sri Lanka 23, 73, 214, 221, 238
stability 23, 24, 106, 109, 121, 140, 222, 245, 289, 291, 292, 302, 303
stages theory 94, 220
stagnation 66, 219
standards 6, 7, 10, 60, 61, 72, 80, 85, 110, 134, 141, 142, 224, 282
staple 155, 156
statistics 33, 48, 53, 150, 163, 168, 169, 171, 227, 236, 237, 249, 258, 270, 271, 277, 295
status 1, 4, 15, 18, 40, 72, 93, 119, 122, 127, 219, 221, 223, 229, 231, 239, 246, 247
steel 13, 95, 98, 150, 158, 169, 181, 205, 215, 244, 259, 261
strategic 117, 181
strategy 13, 15, 16, 18, 61, 64, 65, 66, 67, 70, 71, 76, 82, 101, 112, 130, 138, 154, 164, 165, 201, 204, 205, 219, 222, 236, 257, 292, 300, 303, 304, 307, 308
streamlining 243
strikes 104, 171, 291
structural 3, 14, 183, 219, 222, 225, 231, 243
structure 3, 11, 14, 49, 54, 59, 94, 97, 112, 216, 225, 226, 236, 270
subsidies 44, 46, 179, 209, 305
subsidization 41, 44, 65, 302
subsistence 21, 54, 224, 235
substitution 18, 61, 63, 64, 65–67, 69, 75, 71, 117, 138, 155, 175, 196, 219, 220

success   5, 13, 41, 68, 71, 102, 110, 111–113, 121–128, 131, 165, 188, 192–194, 219, 232, 236, 291, 298, 300, 306
sugar   45, 182
Suharto   245, 246
sulphate   297
sulphur   297
Sumatra   204, 241, 245
suppression   245, 291
surplus   24, 51, 54, 55, 56, 58, 62, 107, 141, 151, 152, 157, 160, 161, 190, 193, 208, 250, 255, 267, 268, 302
surpluses   22, 71, 109, 157, 160, 165, 183, 193, 194, 203, 250, 255, 303, 307, 308
surveillance   243
survey   4, 9, 49, 97, 121, 126, 230, 246, 251
survival   119, 137, 292, 296
Sweden   73, 296
Swiss   242
synthetic fabrics   154, 155
synthetic fibres   155, 156, 160
synthetics   219

T

Taiwan   1–6, 8, 9, 11–17, 18, 19, 20, 22–24, 27, 37, 38, 39, 40, 43, 47, 48, 49, 50, 52, 53, 54, 59, 60, 61, 66, 67, 69, 70, 74, 75, 76, 78, 80, 82, 83, 96, 98, 101, 102, 104, 105, 106, 107, 108, 110, 114, 115, 116, 117, 118–120, 123–125, 127, 129, 130, 141, 148, 149, 151, 152, 153, 154, 156, 158, 166–169, 172, 174, 183, 184, 185, 192, 223, 228, 233, 234, 235, 237, 240, 243, 244, 247, 249–256, 258, 260–262, 264–271, 273, 277, 280, 282, 284, 287–289, 297–300, 306
Taiwanese   67, 83, 115, 116, 119, 121–123, 151, 152, 157, 173, 183, 184, 194, 201, 203, 206, 207, 208, 284, 287, 289, 297
targets   103, 110, 181, 182, 205, 301
tariff   18, 45, 62, 64, 65, 66–68, 71, 85–87, 89–91, 120, 181, 190, 192, 209, 210, 225, 243, 254, 269, 280, 281, 282, 307
tariffs   61, 62, 71, 86, 88, 100, 138, 151, 190, 209, 216, 242, 267, 268, 272, 279, 280, 281, 302
taxes   33, 103, 104, 116, 179
TCF   95, 237, 265–267
techniques   37, 58, 195, 294
technocrats   139, 245
technological ladder   94–97, 99, 100, 142, 202, 205, 206, 207, 213, 215, 228, 288
technology   13, 25, 47, 49, 50, 64, 71, 81, 84,

94, 96, 97, 99, 105, 106, 111, 116, 122, 129, 146, 153, 154, 155, 157, 158, 162, 164, 165, 178, 183, 195, 196, 197, 202, 205, 206, 207, 210, 213, 216, 220, 224, 234, 248, 253, 284, 288, 290, 297, 307
telephones   134, 223, 235, 241
tertiary   83, 224, 241, 247
textiles   49, 96, 97, 98, 140, 141, 147–150, 152, 153, 160, 167, 169, 174, 195, 197, 208, 209, 214, 215, 220, 226, 227, 236, 239, 240, 243, 255, 260–266, 281, 284, 288
Thai   159, 238
Thailand   3, 4, 19, 78, 97, 98, 99, 134, 154, 179, 180, 191, 200, 202, 204, 207, 213, 214, 216–221, 228, 232–239, 245, 246, 257, 269, 270, 275, 277, 281, 287, 304
theoretical   15, 37
thrift   122, 123
Tiananmen   189, 292
tier   4, 93, 99, 195, 213, 214, 215, 246, 304
timber   150, 226
time zones   118
Timor   245
tin   95, 132, 223, 226
titanium   298
trade frictions   157, 194, 279, 290
trading   5, 19, 48, 85, 100, 102, 104, 107, 108, 116, 129, 132, 133, 137, 142, 144, 145, 147, 148, 151, 165, 186, 187, 188, 189, 190, 192, 193, 194, 202, 208, 210, 211, 219, 227, 248, 272, 273, 274, 278, 279, 280, 281, 285, 288, 289, 290, 302, 304, 308
traffic   129, 235, 298
transformation   27, 58, 155, 222, 225, 300
transition   7, 46, 49, 68, 132, 142, 219, 221
transport   9, 17, 39, 43, 100, 111, 115, 116, 130, 148, 151, 175, 215, 226–228, 235, 249, 250, 252, 255, 262, 281, 304
transport costs   129, 135
travel   184, 235
trucks   235
Tunisia   3, 214
TV sets   78, 134, 142, 146, 147, 192, 196

U

umbrellas   305
UMNO   136, 230
undervalued   228
UNDP   292, 295, 298
unemployment   79, 81, 138, 141, 170, 171, 178, 185, 199, 224, 266

uniformity 302
unions 51, 104, 110, 229, 270, 291
universities 142, 241
unrest 18, 140, 185, 222, 229, 293
unskilled 94, 129, 199, 204, 208, 231
upvaluation of the Yen 157, 160, 161, 162, 181
urban 54, 56, 179, 224, 241, 245, 298, 299
Uruguay 2, 187, 192, 208, 214, 273, 279
USA 5, 15, 18, 20, 38, 39, 40, 50, 66, 96, 98, 99, 104, 117, 129, 130, 148, 149, 152, 156, 157, 158, 160, 161, 162, 168, 170, 172, 173, 175, 182, 184, 187–191, 193–195, 196, 197, 201–203, 209–211, 226, 231, 234, 237, 240, 245, 248–256, 266, 269–275, 277–280, 285, 289, 290, 298
utilities 107, 235, 272

V

value-added 38, 63, 64, 78, 86, 87, 88, 89, 90, 91, 92, 294
VAX 196, 197
vehicle 125, 153, 181
vehicles 6, 98, 157, 273, 263, 264, 265, 298, 299
ventures 155, 305
Vietnam 130, 239
violence 137, 230, 238
virtuous circle 216
visitors 179, 287
vulnerability 165, 307

W

wage freeze 182
wages 11, 37, 43, 49, 50, 51, 56, 58, 70, 71, 72, 75, 96, 97, 104, 105, 106, 109, 111, 130, 140, 164, 165, 178, 182, 185, 194, 197, 198, 199, 200–205, 213, 216, 218, 222, 224, 228, 234, 237, 238, 239, 243, 246, 252, 257, 265, 270, 286, 289, 293, 294, 295, 301, 302, 304, 307
warfare 221
waterways 297
wealth 46, 69, 70, 77, 111, 122, 295
welfare 43, 63, 107, 108, 296, 302, 305
wheelchairs 296
wood 227
work ethic 122, 123, 124, 125, 126, 127, 143
workers 43, 49, 123, 141, 156, 174, 183, 185, 198, 199, 204, 207, 208, 232, 286, 292, 293
workforce 122, 141, 143, 234
world trading system 208, 210

Y

yarns 147, 148, 214, 243, 244
yields 224, 241

Z

zealous 238
Zimbabwe 233
zones 6, 59, 104, 111, 118, 176, 217, 229, 285